KATHERINE ARENS

Department of Germanic Languages,
University of Texas at Austin

STRUCTURES OF KNOWING

Psychologies of the Nineteenth Century

KLUWER ACADEMIC PUBLISHERS

DORDRECHT / BOSTON / LONDON

Library of Congress Cataloging in Publication Data

Arens, Katherine, 1953–
    Structures of knowing : psychologies of the nineteenth century /
Katherine Arens.
        p.   cm. -- (Boston studies in the philosophy of science ; 113)
    Bibliography: p.
    Includes index.
    ISBN 0-7923-0009-2
    1. Psychology--History--19th century.   I. Title.   II. Series:
Boston studies in the philosophy of science ; v. 113.
BF38.A7 1988
150'.9'034--dc19   88-8432
                                                                     CIP

ISBN 0-7923-0009-2

Published by Kluwer Academic Publishers,
P.O. Box 17, 3300 AA Dordrecht, The Netherlands.

Kluwer Academic Publishers incorporates
the publishing programmes of
D. Reidel, Martinus Nijhoff, Dr W. Junk and MTP Press.

Sold and distributed in the U.S.A. and Canada
by Kluwer Academic Publishers,
101 Philip Drive, Norwell, MA 02061, U.S.A.

In all other countries, sold and distributed
by Kluwer Academic Publishers Group,
P.O. Box 322, 3300 AH Dordrecht, The Netherlands.

printed on acid free paper

CONTENTS

ACKNOWLEDGMENTS

Summer research grants provided me by the National Endowment for the Humanities (1982) and the University Research Institute of the University of Texas at Austin (1981 and 1984) greatly facilitated the work on this manuscript. I acknowledge this support with gratitude.

Special thanks are due to my friend and colleague, Professor Janet K. Swaffar, for her numerous discussions and incisive comments on these topics which made this volume much more than it would otherwise have been.

William R. Woodward of the University of New Hampshire deserves special mention for his careful page-by-page critique of the final manuscript, particularly for his suggestions on continuity, contextualization, and supporting references; he also provided me with numerous offprints. The work he did made my work much easier and considerably stronger; any faults remaining are mine alone. Mate··als were also generously provided to me by Josef Brozek of Lunigh University, Kurt Danziger of York University (Ontario, Canada), and Robert J. Richards of the University of Chicago. My thanks extend to them all for facilitating my work in this way. I also wish to thank my anonymous readers at *The Journal of the History of the Behavioral Sciences* for their thoughtful comments on an early version of part of the Mach chapter which appeared there.

The first draft of the manuscript was typed by Rachel J. Halverson; Denise Sechelski made major contributions to editing and proofreading. Many thanks to them, as well as to William H. Russell for moral support.

The following publishers and copyrightholders are acknowledged for their permissions of the material used: Excerpts from Sigmund Freud, "Project for a Scientific Psychology", included in *The Origins of Psychoanalysis: Letters to Wilhelm Fliess, Drafts, and Notes: 1887–1902* (© 1954; Basic Books); Excerpts from Edmund Husserl, *Phenomenological Psychology*, Trans. John Scanlon (© 1977/1962; Martinus Nijhoff); Excerpts from Immanuel Kant, *Anthropology from a Pragmatic Point of View*, Trans. Mary J. Gregor (© 1974; Martinus Nijhoff); Excerpts from Franz Brentano, *Psychology from an Empirical Standpoint*, ed. Oskar Kraus/Linda L. McAlister, Trans. A. C. Rancurello, D. B. Terrell, and L. L. McAlister (© 1973; Routledge & Kegan Paul); Excerpts from Sigmund Freud, *The Interpretation of Dreams* and "The Claims of Psycho-Analysis to Scientific Interest" (© 1953; Hogarth Press).

PART 1

THE METHODOLOGICAL QUESTION

CHAPTER 1

THE CASE FOR A REORIENTATION IN THE HISTORY OF PSYCHOLOGY

Psychology is a relatively new field whose antecedents as a systematic discipline are generally acknowledged to extend back to the nineteenth century. Despite this short history, the prominence of the field in the twentieth century has led to a considerable body of work on its origins. The development of the field has been traced in the ground-laying work of Edwin Boring and others, in 40 years of effort towards establishing a canon of teachers, schools, and publications of note.[1]

Histories usually restrict themselves to a collection of facts, organized into a representation of reality. They often stay in the realm of internal history, isolating one preset group of facts, such as a record of completed experiments. They rarely analyze the premises on which those experiments are built. The histories of psychology thus first provide documentation for the field and only later seek to identify its essence as a systematic science, a discrete discipline with an underlying paradigm, in the sense introduced by Thomas Kuhn -- that is, a distinct style of thought, set of problems, chosen data, procedures, and publicly recognized goals. Such paradigms are only beginning to be delineated by historians, and they tend to be formulated from the point of view of the twentieth century, sometimes overlooking the environment of the original discourse. The extensive documentation on the history of psychology which is accumulating thus often serves present purposes more than historical ones.

The studies in this volume will address the need to reconsider the history of psychology by attempting to derive a possible discourse paradigm for the emerging psychology of the nineteenth century in the German-speaking world. Such goals require a different approach to historical data than often has been used by histories of the field. The search for a paradigm for a discipline

3

involves more than a reordering of the who's, what's, and where's of historical fact. Rather, the present volume will seek a conceptual unity behind these real facts: a consistent pattern of investigation encompassing consistent choices in fields of data to be addressed by the field, acceptable investigatory procedures and avenues of proofs, and the goals and applicability of results assumed by the work in the field. Together, such information constitutes the closure of a science as a paradigm -- as a conceptual unity of investigation and style of scientific thought demarking one science from others.

However, delineation of a paradigm for psychology in the nineteenth century involves more than just uncovering overt historical facts. Its self-expression, its fashion of discourse, must be outlined, and so criteria other than those familiar from its institutional form in the twentieth century must often be sought. This second task of the paradigm historian does not require attention to parallel data, nor continuations of experimental set-ups between student and teacher. Rather, the discourse of a paradigm reveals communalities in the underlying assumptions in works which may be separated geographically, institutionally, temporally, and even in terms of disciplinary boundaries.[2] The discourse paradigm does not stress unanimity or equivalency of results. Instead, it reveals itself in communalities of acceptable data (such as observational or experimental), a shared sense of adequacy and validation for goals set and results achieved, as well as the scope of applicability for procedures and results which limit the field for the investigators involved. The uncovering of a discourse paradigm for a field thus implies an orientation towards the processes which constitute a field -- the style of formulation, conceptualization, and approach. This goes beyond both the more common orientation of histories towards the products of the scientists associated with it, as well as the lesser definition of a paradigm as a common set of problems.

Looking at psychology as a discourse paradigm answers a need that has been felt for many years. Setting the German-speaking world as a boundary will allow us not only to add to existing history of psychology, but also to elucidate the particular problem of psychology as a science. A redefinition of psychology in terms of a reconceptualization of its origins has been suggested by historians for over twenty years. Since the late 1960's, a call for historical retrenchment has been raised with increasing frequency. Its thrust has been varied, motivated by a need to define and legitimate a field. A few samples of solutions from the 1960's to the 1980's can suggest the dimensions of the problem to be faced.

In 1965, for example, the *Journal of the History of the Behavioral Sciences* came into being to encourage extensions of the work which Edwin G. Boring and others had initiated in assessing the current state of the field.[3] At the same time, the search for historical roots in terms of culture-bound problems was being conducted along similar lines in other sciences. The *Journal of the History of the Behavioral Sciences* was followed in 1968 by *The Journal of the History of Biology*, which hoped to assess biology historically and theoretically, as a set of culture-bound problems as well as an area of active research.

In the same period, two recognized leaders in the history of psychology and science, Robert I. Watson in 1967 and Josef Brozek in 1969, were concerned about the assumptions that should inform the future direction of the history of psychology. Brozek discussed the need for an expansion of historical typologies to reflect the character of the field of psychology; Watson differentiated between paradigms and prescriptions in an attempt to see how Thomas Kuhn's *The Structure of Scientific Revolutions* would apply to the social sciences. More recently, voices such as those of Mitchell G. Ash and Ulfried Geuter are trying to expand the bases on which histories of psychology are written.[4] Each position deserves mention in the introduction to a volume such as this: a book identifying the derivation of the paradigm which guides the development of psychology in the nineteenth century.

1.1 Brozek's Typologies

Brozek's "History of Psychology: Diversity of Approaches and Uses"[5] begins: "It is the central point of this presentation that we have (and should have) *histories*, not a history, of psychology reflecting the multiplicity of approaches and the variety of uses." With this statement, he stresses to historiographers of psychology that histories are written for different purposes, with different procedures and standards of evidence conditioned by these purposes. A history is only superficially a study of "facts and their interconnections," and often represents in addition a critique, interpretation, synthesis, analysis, or documentation. These additional didactic or investigative purposes may turn a chronology into something quite different, such as a science of science (a history of theory construction and concomitant developments of science), or a study of the developments of smaller problem areas of the larger field (Brozek, 116). In the case of the history of psychology, Brozek isolates four trends: "History of Psychology and the General History of Science," "Borderline Disciplines" (history of psychology as the developments in an array of other sciences), "General versus Regional (or National) Histories of Science," and "General History of Psychology versus the History of Special Fields of Psychology," supplemented perhaps with a fifth, more recent trend towards a quantified history (Brozek, 118-9).

These approaches to the history of psychology represent significant achievements in their own right, yet do not answer the question: what fundamental assumptions direct the course of the discipline? Brozek seeks to answer this question by suggesting the need for empirical assessment criteria:

> Of challenging questions, both broad and narrow, there is a plethora: What are the patterns, the time-course of scientific activity, productivity, and creativity under the present conditions -- not in the Renaissance, not in the first half of the nineteenth century [science in other eras]? What motivates the investigator when he is 20, 40, 60 years of age [biographical influences on science]? What are the ingredients of significant success and what are the causes (or, if you prefer, the concomitants) of stagnation and failure [fiscal and personnel problems]? What are the characteristics of the more effective and of the less effective teams of investigators [psycho-social group dynamics]? (Brozek, 119)

Brozek is suggesting that the scope of psychology may better be represented if factors such as the psychologies of the psychologists or institutional constraints on their productivity be included.

Yet this will leave the history of psychology produced in much the same state as those which presently exist because it remains essentially descriptive. Brozek's call is, however, for more than just descriptive historical expansions:

> We need, then, a new and a different "history of science" (or whatever label you wish to attach to this embryonic field of endeavor), a history oriented toward the present and toward the future. We need to look around and to add to "retrospective" studies some "circumspective" ones as well. But this is not good enough. In the history of science, just as in the epidemiology of coronary heart disease, we must set up "prospective" studies, focused on factors affecting the growth of scientific knowledge. (Brozek, 125)

Brozek's call for "circumspective" and "prospective" studies is tantamount to a call for a history of science that is more than descriptive: a historical science with an inherent causality which relates success/failure to environmental factors, to planning, or to decisions about productivity or validity of hypotheses. Brozek argues for a type of history largely absent in his contemporaries' treatments. In doing so, however, Brozek fails to suggest an epistemological basis for his new history -- he does not turn to the nature of the discipline and its potential underlying paradigm.

1.2 Watson: Prescription Versus Paradigm

Watson's article, "Psychology: A Prescriptive Science," addresses these issues, thereby providing a crucial second phase in revising the history of psychology.[6] Watson discusses the nature of psychology itself -- is it a science in the traditional sense, and how might its phases or transitions be organized. As Brozek also realized, such questioning is crucial, since the commonly accepted divisions of a field may have little to do with the historical nature of the discipline. That is, a history which looks at institutions from the point of view of their existence today may produce radically different pictures than one that follows contemporaneous projects or research strategies.

Watson's article assesses Thomas Kuhn's notion of paradigms with respect to psychology, as if the history of the science would describe transitions among paradigms of investigation. According to Kuhn, when the style of investigation in a science changes (as in the "Copernican Revolution"), the paradigm of investigation is said to have shifted. Yet since Kuhn's analyses apply to the "older, more mature sciences," the concept of a paradigm may not be applicable to a fledgling discipline such as psychology (Watson, 435).

To argue this, Watson emphasizes that a general consensus about what constitutes a field is a key feature of a scientific paradigm:[7]

> In one of its meanings a paradigm is a contentual model, universally accepted by practitioners of a science at a particular temporal period in its development. With this agreement among its practitioners, the paradigm defines the science in which it operates. (Watson, 435)

When this group of consenting scientists reaches a novel problem area, an anomaly which cannot be accommodated by the old paradigm and causes repeated problems, a new paradigm will created. This leads to an extended definition for a paradigm:

> In all of its meanings, a paradigm has a guidance function. It functions as an intellectual framework, it tells [scientists] what sort of entities with which their scientific universe is populated and how these entities behave, and informs its followers what questions may legitimately be asked about nature. (Watson, 436)

However, Watson points out that not all sciences are blessed with a period of general agreement among their practitioners. Watson considers the lack of a defining paradigm the critical difference between psychology and fields such as physics or biology (Watson, 436).

The type of history of science proposed by Kuhn, dealing with investigative paradigms alleviating at least some of these difficulties is thus not really appropriate to psychology:

> Either psychology's first paradigm had not been discovered or it has not yet been recognized for what it is. . . . The present task is to answer the question -- if psychology lacks a paradigm, what serves to take its place? (Watson, 436)

To ascertain whether or not a paradigm exists is the task of the present historiographer of the discipline. To this point, Watson feels that historiographers have not looked in appropriate places for the answer.

Watson, like Brozek, finds that, instead of investigative paradigms (a discrete style of investigation), psychology has tended to have themes, such as "empiricism-rationalism" or "functionalism-structuralism." As such, these themes represent *prescriptions*:

> The overall function of these themes is orientative or attitudinal; they tell us how the psychologist-scientist must or should behave. In short, they have a directive function. They help to direct the psychologist-scientist in the way he selects a problem, formulates it, and the way in which he carries it out. (Watson, 437)

These prescriptions do have the temporal dimension associated with a paradigm; yet they, too, represent an orientation, and not the activities of psychologists (Watson, 438). Prescriptions state an adherence to a fixed model, such as "the unconscious as formulated by Freud," without considering the ramifications of adopting such a model. As such, they represent habits of thought or tendencies in approach rather than paradigms, and they tend to be construed as "dominant and counterdominant prescriptions" in history (Watson, 439). Prescriptions represent the overt rhetoric of the field, not its closure as a research paradigm with tacitly acceptable procedures, data, and goals.

According to Watson, the prescription or theme approach to

history has many of the same weaknesses identified by Brozek, especially since it may ignore the frame of the practicing historian or scientist.   Consequently, such historians can frame the psychologist's tasks in terms of fragments of the paradigm, rather than the whole set of issues involved. For example, differentiating between philosophy and psychology without considering their possible shared context or paradigm can lead the historian to emphasize differences which may not originally have been perceived by scientists of the day. This implies a conflict between philosophy and psychology on the basis of their "contentual characters," the specific set of problems they address. Such an approach can result in no more than a prescription for a conflict, which, in turn, represents only one aspect of a comprehensive paradigm.

Watson's next example of such fragmentation in the history of psychology is the historian's "borrowing from other fields" with their "methodological guidance" (Watson, 440). When such borrowings, as fragments of a larger paradigm, form the basis of investigation, fields of data are prescribed for the historian without questioning their sufficiency vis-à-vis a conceptual unity of investigation -- schools, trends, or patterns of genesis (Watson, 441). Historians following these prescriptions operate on tacit assumptions, such as the fact that influential scientists hold institutional posts. Such an assumption will inevitably lead the investigator into problems: the work that Einstein did while employed by a patent office would be seen as an exception because he did not have the institutional confirmation that his contemporaries enjoyed. Watson thus acknowledges that neither schools nor issues will answer the prime need for the uncovering of a paradigm as a prerequisite for understanding the history of psychology. Prescriptions remain selection criteria below the level of paradigms:

> Prescriptive trends fall and rise again, combine, separate, and recombine, carry a broader or narrower scope of meaning, and enter into different alliances with other prescriptions, change from implicitness to explicitness and back again, and concern themselves with different psychological content and its related theories. (Watson,

442)

Not only the history of psychology, but the discipline itself "seems to lack a unifying paradigm" and "functions at the level of guidance by prescriptions," albeit prescriptions which include affinities and temperaments of the psychologists involved and various political movements in the trends which are followed (Watson, 443). In effect, Watson sees that a history of psychology is no more than a chronicle of ideological warfare, not a science with a paradigm in a historical period.

Brozek identified the essential weaknesses in extant histories of psychology; Watson specified these complaints by referring specifically to the paradigm as the missing element in these considerations.   Yet twenty years passed before the next substantive recommendation for a new history of psychology was made.

1.3 The Case for the Independent Science in the 1980's

As statements about the historiography of the discipline, the assessments of Brozek and Watson have essentially held sway into the 1980's with implications which are only now being more widely acknowledged.[8]

Recently, a series of newer voices has arisen to broaden the questions raised by earlier historians. Mitchell G. Ash's "The Self-Presentation of a Discipline: History of Psychology in the United States between Pedagogy and Scholarship" stresses the ideology inherent in writing history (Graham, 143). From the same volume on *Functions and Uses of Disciplinary Histories*, Ulfried Geuter's "The Uses of History for the Shaping of a Field" particularly stresses recent changes in the historiography of psychology as they emerge from recent social and political conflicts in Germany (Graham, 191). Bernard J. Baars begins his study of *The Cognitive Revolution in Psychology* with a preface about the need for revisionist history.[9] He confronts Boring (briefly, p. viii, and in detail about Wundt, p. 30 ff.), the scientific prescription which psychologists assumed about 100 years ago (p. 9), Kuhn and Popper's work on paradigms (p. 10 ff.), thematic histories (e.g., the "mind-body problem," p. 20), and Watson (on behaviorism as legitimizing the "conceptual space" of the discipline, p. 55). All concur that historiography itself must be a central concern today for those writing histories of psychology, and they suggest ways in which older histories still lack evaluations of the discipline.[10]

In 1982, a collection by Woodward and Ash, *The Problematic Science: Psychology in Nineteenth-Century Thought*, reframes the history of psychology in terms resembling those questioned by Watson and Brozek:[11]

> To our surprise and satisfaction, the responses to our rather vague prescription [their call for papers "on the history of psychology"] turned out to focus upon a single important issue: did psychology become autonomous, wither intellectually or socially, in the nineteenth century? The consistently negative answer provided by these chapters poses a challenge to the reigning assumption that psychology was in some sense "liberated" either from parent disciplines or from external social concerns during its formative period. (W & A, v)

Woodward and Ash improve somewhat on the positions of Brozek and Watson, accommodating many of the challenges raised by historians in the 1980's. Their assessments of the essays they include suggest additions to the field of prescriptions already active: social, historical, and intellectual contexts; a suggestion that the "professionalization thesis" ("the central assumption that all roads lead to the present state of the discipline, namely, as institutionally separate and intellectually autonomous," 13) is in error; and the warning that the emergence of the discipline of psychology must be considered a twentieth-century phenomenon, since in the nineteenth century, the discipline remained scattered throughout other disciplines, especially philosophy, physics, and biology (W & A, 14).

They conclude that the significance for the discipline of psychology is that the traditional institutional history is, indeed, inadequate to the "facts" of psychology as a discipline:

But the liberation of psychology [from its nineteenth-century interdisciplinary bondage], such as it was, was nowhere a simple matter of one part of philosophy, or of medicine, reaching a certain stage of development and then splitting off more-or-less inevitably and developing further on its own, supported by independent institutions. Instead, we are dealing here with complex processes of conceptual construction, reconstruction, and transformation, which took place in various historical settings. The successful institutionalization of some kinds of psychological thinking was only one of these processes; it did not end psychology's intellectual and social embeddedness, but only changed its structure. (W & A, 347-48)

Institutionalization or prescriptions will not suffice to exhaust the material of the discipline. Similarly, the twentieth-century situation of the discipline may not be used to determine the significant aspects of the nineteenth century retroactively.

Woodward and Ash, as some of the latest revisionists in the history of psychology, offer mainly negative recommendations towards the establishment of a paradigm for psychology in the nineteenth century -- a list of prescriptions which may clearly no longer be used, supplemented by an alternate offering of social and intellectual contexts. They conclude:

With or without a unifying paradigm, [psychology's] problematic social situation is no different in its essential features from that of physics. . . . struggling for orientation in an increasingly complicated world. (W & A, 364)

They thus reconcile themselves to a call for more open typologies for the history of psychology, including intellectual, social, and particularly institutional frames.

Mitchell G. Ash, in his "Self-Presentation of a Discipline: History of Psychology in the United States between Pedagogy and Scholarship," adds to the foreword and afterword of *The Problematic Science* by stressing the ideologies of institutions.

That is, a science (particularly a newer one like psychology) will attempt to legitimize itself. One of the easiest ways to do so is by adducing a "grand tradition" of which that science is a part -- that is, write a history of the field, explaining its great contributions. Such history-writing will automatically accompany the pedagogy of a field, because it serves to establish a canon against which the younger generation may orient itself. Such attention to the socialization of a discipline represents a distinct advance over prescriptive histories in the narrow sense and opens the way towards considerations of discourse paradigms.

Despite such advances, the latest proponents of the history of psychology have advanced only in scope and thoroughness through the recommendations made over 15 years ago by Brozek and Watson. While these historians concur with Brozek that new types of histories are needed -- particularly the social and cultural histories they are supplementing in their own historical work -- a paradigm for the discipline in the nineteenth century as outlined by Watson has not emerged, probably because recent work in the history of psychology still stresses individuals and themes instead of national cultural milieux. Rather than consider the discipline as a paradigm based on a common set of precepts shared by its major proponents of the nineteenth century, they focus largely on a shared institutional or intellectual frame which anticipates the situation of the twentieth century. Consequently, the issue of a discourse paradigm common to the influential work in nineteenth-century psychology is displaced onto the historically separate issue of institutionalization and the institutional development of the discipline. It is one thing to assert that the discipline did not achieve its institutional independence in the nineteenth century. It is quite another to claim that the institutional existence of the discipline will correlate with the existence of its paradigm. The present volume will contend that the paradigm was, in fact, present (at least in the German-speaking countries), despite its acknowledged institutional diffusion in the nineteenth century.

1.4 Documenting the Paradigm

The project for this volume is, then, to provide the outline of the emerging paradigm of psychology in the nineteenth century. To do so defines the "history" of science differently than suggested by Brozek, Woodward, Ash, or others, and pursues Watson's distinction between a prescription and a paradigm. But while Watson was uncertain as to whether or not psychology had a paradigm, this volume will take a different point of view: that a paradigm does underlie the prescriptions which characterize nineteenth-century psychology -- a specific body of conceptual problems and material which had to be considered. Yet because the discourse of the psychological paradigm in the nineteenth century has not heretofore been traced, the underlying paradigm of the discipline has not been uncovered by subsequent historians in the field. The purpose of this volume is thus to document and argue the case for the existence in nineteenth-century psychology of a paradigm which has been overlooked in the histories of psychology which presently exist. As such, it will look not for a unified body of research, but rather for a set of similar research and conceptual strategies that may have led to widely divergent ends.

Two criteria must be fulfilled prior to outlining the evolution of the paradigm of conceptual psychology. First, the traditional geographic, national, idea-, school-, or theme-oriented histories of nineteenth-century psychology will be sketched very briefly in terms of their data and the approaches they delimit or exclude. Following that historical-critical analysis, an alternate approach to evolving the paradigm underlying nineteenth-century conceptual psychology will be suggested.

The following sections of this introduction will provide the historical overview of nineteenth-century psychology in order to suggest weaknesses in traditional categories from the history of psychology. Such an analysis will begin to guide a revised history of nineteenth-century psychology. The first chapter of this book will then put forth a proposal for the reformulation of the history of a discipline. Finally, the individual chapters of the book will outline stages in the emergence of the paradigm itself. As an afterword, a concluding chapter will review the gains made by such a reconceptualization of the history of psychology: the tenets implied by the nineteenth-century paradigm and their reflexes in the twentieth century.

1.5 The Historical Canon: Eighteenth Century

Following the lead set by E.G. Boring, the typical history of psychology begins to look for the origins of the modern field of psychology at the end of the eighteenth century.[12] There it finds models of the mind, as well as speculations on philosophical, moral, or personal behavior, learning, and thought.[13] The search is traditionally conducted in terms of specific themes or types, with little attention paid to the contexts in which the individual discussions occur or to the intellectual strategies they involve.[14] If, however, the author wishes to make a case for a longer tradition for the field, he or she may well look back as far as the Greeks to uncover preliminary notions of central terms such as the "unconscious."[15]

Sources will be evaluated and contributions marked as "central" if the teachers or texts involved introduce terminology or experiments which will find resonance in later generations, regardless of how these generations will use or misuse them. The adoption of such terms is designated "important" when they recur. This is taken as a symptom of influence, often without an assessment of the degree to which the innate intellectual strategies represented by such coinages have also been assimilated.

When limiting the field of data to German, Austrian, and Swiss psychology as a test case for a new paradigm, the first generation of psychologists can arguably be reduced to Wolff and Leibnitz in the seventeenth and early eighteenth centuries, and to Kant, Herbart, and Lotze in the eighteenth and early nineteenth centuries. Such a designation is derived only through a cut-off of dates, not through any of the selection options already discussed.[16]

1) Gottfried Wilhelm Leibnitz (1646-1716) was more closely associated with problems of philosophy than with problems of cognition, since his most famous book, the *Monadology* (1714), outlines the structure of nature as it proceeds from the central point of genesis for all creation. Each element of this structure is a *monad* endowed with a degree of consciousness and self-motion as well as an ability to perceive the world. As such, the monad may be considered a first model for the mind as a reflection of the Divine Intellect, and as a conscious, reflexive, and apperceiving

individual. Leibnitz did not, however, concentrate on the mind of an individual but rather on the general phenomenon of mind as such.

2) Christian von Wolff (1679-1754) is more familiar in the context of the history of ideas as the popularizer of Leibnitz, yet in the history of psychology, he is remembered as the father of Faculty Psychology. Through two major texts on psychology, *Empirical Psychology* (1732) and *Rational Psychology* (1734), Wolff provided seminal discussions on the "faculties of the soul," the rational and appetitive capacities innate in every man, and the relation of these innate capacities to man's potential for development and enlightenment.[17]

3) According to most psychologists, Immanuel Kant (1724-1804) has a problematic role in the history of psychology. For most university professors at that time, the fields of their endeavors were not as tightly circumscribed as they are today. Kant, while in his life-long chair at the University of Königsberg, taught courses and published books not only on philosophy, but also on mathematics, ethics, anthropology, law, and other related fields. His major contribution to philosophy remains the *Critique of Pure Reason* (1781/87), in which he delineated a relationship between rationalism and empiricism in philosophy through a discussion of the apperception and cognitive capacities of the mind. For psychology, this philosophical model left two important guiding notions: *subjectivism*, deriving from the notion of the faculties that the processes of the mind and mental phenomena represent a reality not correlate to that of empirical reality; and *nativism* (a term used only in psychology, not in philosophy), which declared the intuitions of time and space to be *a priori* features of the mind, not learned experience. Less familiar because it is dismissed as primitive anthropology is Kant's own psychology, which will be discussed in this volume. His *Anthropology from a Pragmatic Viewpoint* (1798) represents an extension of the vocabulary and concept repertoire of faculty psychology into a cognitive or conceptual psychology -- a psychology of mental processing of empirical data. Often mentioned in conjunction with Kant is the psychologist J.F. Fries, who in 1820-21 wrote a systematization of Kant's work supported with biological facts.[18]

4) Johann Friedrich Herbart (1776-1841) is a figure better known in his age than in ours, where he has been relegated to the role of "father of scientific pedagogy" or "educational psychology." Interest in developmental pedagogy led to a Herbart renaissance in America at the turn of this century.[19] Herbart developed a learning hierarchy -- preparation, presentation, association, generalization, and application -- as the steps to effective teaching strategies on the basis of his theory of the mind. In his own century, however, he was known as a philosopher. In 1809, he was appointed to Kant's chair in Königsberg, and in 1833, to a professorial chair in philosophy at Göttingen. In this role, he developed his work on the mind-body interface which laid the groundwork for psychophysics and the study of physiological thresholds, and for studies of effects of habit and conceptual adaptation of organisms to their environments as primary affectors of thought patterns. Among his many students (the "Herbartians"), Wilhelm Drobisch was perhaps the most famous due to the wide circulation in Germany of his *Handbook of Psychology* (1842).

5) The third member of the elder generation of German psychologists, Rudolph Hermann Lotze (1817-1881), was almost an anachronism; his work belongs next to that of Kant and Herbart although he was a generation younger. Lotze was a doctor who succeeded to Herbart's chair of philosophy at Göttingen in 1844, and remained there until 1881. Here, he was the teacher of the major psychologists of the nineteenth century, among them Franz Brentano, Carl Stumpf, and G.E. Müller. His major contribution was a delineation of the notion of psychological space as it builds up out of sensations from sense perceptions. This work was particularly parallel to that of his friend Fechner in its reliance on a modified mind-body parallelism and a cultural perspective. This antithesis to the nativist concept of space perception led to the later concept of the isomorphism between psychological and empirical space perception. His work was varied and includes *Logik: Drei Bücher vom Denken, vom Untersuchen und vom Erkennen* (1843), *Metaphysik* (1841), and *Mikrokosmus* (various editions around 1848).[20]

From the point of view of a possible paradigm for nineteenth-century psychology, the first two names in this list can be disqualified because they share a much earlier historical position

than the latter three. They saw the mind in a framework of a
consubstantiation of Divine thought and Creation which does not
correspond to modern psychology. Thus any association of these
five names as intellectual contemporaries will lead to more contrasts
than communalities. Similarly, the attempt to broaden a
prescription into a paradigm for all five only yields a generality: it is
all "work on the function of the mind," without more substantive
similarities in procedures or goals such as those which will be
argued for Kant, Herbart, and Lotze. Such an association ignores
their very different philosophical environments and life projects.
One did indeed teach the other, but they do not use similar fields of
data or procedures. In fact, these thinkers present at least two
radically different pictures of the function and development of
mind, and they carried out their respective philosophical programs
under widely varying procedural constraints.

1.6 The Historical Canon: Nineteenth Century

Once the discussion of psychology reaches the nineteenth
century proper, most historical accounts of the discipline tend to
enumerate chains of influence according to either their "home
disciplines" before psychology emerged independent, or their
teacher-student chains, as Brozek had indicated. In so doing, a few
scholars are left on the outskirts as somehow not institutionally
legitimized because they never held university chairs. One example
is Franz Gall, the father of phrenology, whose books on the
subject, originally appearing between 1810 and 1819, led to
significant physiological studies such as Broca's localizations of
brain functions.[21]

Yet another fact complicates this distinction between fields of
endeavor and institutional existences: many of the psychologists or
protopsycholgists had inordinately long tenures as professors. The
institutional reality of the German university system prescribed that
there be only one full professor per department, one *Ordinarius*.
Other teacher-scholars of rank could, in extraordinary
circumstances, be appointed associate professors (an
außerordentlicher Professor), but most remained at the level of
lecturer (*Dozent*). In certain cases, scholars waited an extended

period of time for their promotions behind long-lived, if not always productive, senior members who were not removed by mandatory retirement. In other cases, a series of migrations on very short notice may be traced. These people took chairs as full professors at minor universities in order to establish that they were, indeed, of professorial caliber. Often, too, they remained in these minor positions only very brief periods, perhaps one year or less.

This one-professor-per-department rule is responsible for a student situation totally alien to twentieth-century higher education. The German professor in the mid- to late-nineteenth century was the autocrat of the department, the only connection to professional advancement and the unique tone-setter of his department.[22] To complete their degrees, students were forced to adopt the professor's style. If they could not do so, they often changed universities in order to find alternate styles. However, if the student could not move, he often was forced to adapt to retain professional viability. (This situation was still apparent even in Freud's university career, when the decision to join Brücke's neurological laboratory was not just accepting a post-doctoral research post for a year, but tantamount to cutting off a hospital career.)

The second problem in this system was one of needing to establish a distinct profile in order to be upwardly mobile in the restricted professional hierarchy. Specialties were stressed and claims as generalists kept quiet, because the professors were going to be hired and promoted on the basis of their personal and distinct areas of achievement. Again, Freud's career reflects this system's last stage of development: he bemoaned the fact that his general medical knowledge did not qualify him as a general practitioner, even though he was gaining fame as a neurologist.

Ironically, when the mid-nineteenth-century student could wait for an appointment to an academic chair and did not have the pressures of a family to support, he did accrue the general knowledge to support his specialty -- assistants tutored basic studies or survey courses. When, however, the universities expanded toward the end of the century, a generation of professors were appointed without an extended apprenticeship period (the case of Nietzsche in philology is perhaps the most famous example of this reverse in pressure). As a result, regardless of what discipline they supposedly taught, these scholars remained essentially "dissertation specialists," with no overview of the field in which their specialties were immersed.

Yet another pecularity of the German university in the nineteenth century was that a worthy individual sometimes was given a chair in a related field when it was obvious that his ideal chair would not come free for many years. Often, such an appointment would occur whether or not the individual knew the basics of the appointed field -- after all, the assistants were there. To further confuse the relations of departments and specialties, professors tended to talk to professors, and not to their departments, since institutionalized fields did not necessarily reflect the mental affinities of an individual scholar.[23] Moreover, the position to which many professors aspired was, of course, the senior chair at the university, which had the most prestige in the humanities -- a chair which, at many universities, was for historical reasons in philosophy.[24]

The tendency of modern historians, then, to separate psychologists from philosophers in the nineteenth century represents a contamination from modern institutional practices which does not in any way correspond to the situation in the nineteenth century. Thus, if one is going to use their institutional or job fields as their designations, the grouping of nineteenth-century psychologists is an arbitrary undertaking. Chairs in psychology simply did not exist in many universities, and professors aimed for the prestige of chairs in philosophy or the money of those in medicine instead. The procedure of sorting professors by chairs or themes is, nonetheless, the prevalent one in present-day historiography. This leads to a major, if arbitrary, division of the canonical figures in psychology into physiologists, experimental psychologists, act psychologists, and finally, near the end of the century, a differentiated group of specialists in learning and personality.[25]

1.6.1 Experimental Physiologists and Psychophysicists

The earliest of these groups are the physiologists who tied into the physics of perception, and whose rise contributed to the preeminence of German medical training through the First World War.[26]

1) Ernst Heinrich Weber (1795-1878) was first a professor of anatomy and then of physiology at Leipzig from 1818 virtually to his death. His major contribution from the point of view of later psychology was his work on physiological thresholds in perception, and his theory of "just noticeable differences" in sensations which pointed again to the work in physiological psychology by Fechner, Wundt, and others.

2) Gustav Theodor Fechner (1801-1887), the "father of psychophysics," was at Leipzig virtually his entire career, from student days on. He occupied the chair of physics there from 1834 to 1839, when he retired due to illness, yet his affiliations with the university community continued until his death. Fechner's generally acknowledged contribution is to mathematical psychology, due to his work in the physiology of sensations. Such work was, however, only part of a voluminous oeuvre, including his *Psychophysics* (1860), and works on Eastern thought. His influence, particularly from his experimental procedures, was felt by Weber in his physiological work, and later by Helmholtz and Mach; his work on cultural influences on the individual psyche paralleled Lotze's.

3) Johannes Müller (1801-1858) has the claim, along with Albrecht von Haller (today remembered largely as a poet), of being "father of experimental physiology." He occupied the first chair of physiology at the university of Berlin beginning in 1833, and was known throughout Europe for his textbook, *Handbuch der Physiologie des Menschen* (1833-40), which was to remain a standard for many years -- one of the first modern international classics. His experimental work included, in the mid-1820's, experimental measurements of the specific energies of nerves and of conductivity. His theories were later disproved, but not his experimental techniques. Among his students were Helmholtz, Brücke (Freud's teacher), du Bois-Reymond, and Ludwig -- all great experimentalists of the next generation.

4) Hermann von Helmholtz (1821-94) was known for his work on nerves, in some ways a continuation of work inherited from his teacher, Johannes Müller, yet he himself was trained as a

physicist and then a medical doctor. His academic career saw him initially as a professor of physiology, first at Bonn from 1856-58, then at Heidelberg from 1858-71; finally, he received the chair of physics at Berlin. This range of appointments reflects the diversity of his own research. His early work, in the 1850's, led him to measure the speed of nerve impulse conduction; later, he moved on to experiments in physiology and physics, on hearing and visual interference, and on color and tone sensations. His experimental results are acknowledged by psychologists, but the conceptual underpinnings are largely ignored since he is considered a physicist and physiologist. His work is seriously underrated in many circles today.

5) A lesser-known physiologist than Helmholtz, who is in a similar position among psychologists, was Ewald Hering (1834-1918). In 1878, he published one of the first scientific theories of color vision, in which the colors red, green, blue and yellow, together with black and white, were identified as the primary colors. He studied with E.H. Weber and Fechner, and was noted for opposing the empiricist theories of space perception put forth by Lotze, Helmholtz, and Wundt. Hering espoused a nativist theory of visual space perception, thus harkening back to a position more like that of Kant. His academic career was not as distinguished as that of certain of his contemporaries: he had a chair of physiology in Prague from 1870 to 1895, at which time he was called to a Leipzig chair in the same discipline.[27]

These early proponents of one branch of psychology are associated largely on the basis of student-teacher prescriptions which arbitrarily obscure more substantive issues which might constitute elements of a shared scientific paradigm. If, for example, their work was considered on the basis of today's differentiation between perceptual psychology and physiology, one would uncover very different research programs underlying their commonly-held assumptions about acquired versus inherited biological conditioning.

1.6.2 *Experimental Psychologists*

Differentiating between the foregoing group of experimental

physiologists and the following group of experimental psychologists is not always an easy proposition. Today's historiographers do so, however arbitrarily, in relying on their institutional positions. In such an undertaking, they are actually dividing these scholars on the basis of prominence in the modern discipline of psychology. The work and influence of the experimental psychologists was greater from the twentieth-century point of view than that of their predecessors in physiology or psychophysics, and so they formed the core of the next generation to be considered in the history of psychology. Today's historians of psychology thus choose their ancestors in terms of their visibility, and reject others on the basis of their institutional affiliations -- although both groups held chairs with the same titles.

1) Wilhelm Wundt (1833-1920), the father of experimental psychology, was perhaps the most visible figure in psychology before Freud in the latter part of the nineteenth century. He began by studying physiology under Johannes Müller in 1856, after which he was called to be first a lecturer and then an "extraordinary professor" of physiology in Heidelberg from 1856-1874. From 1874 to 1875, in what seems to be a career move, he assumed the title of Professor of Inductive Philosophy at Zürich, and from there, was called to the chair of philosophy at Leipzig. By 1879, he opened at Leipzig what was to become the world's preeminent psychological laboratory. His work in this field can be traced back as far as 1867, when he gave his first course in experimental psychology in Heidelberg. His written credentials in the field rested on his great textbook: *Principles of Physiological Psychology* (1873-74). By 1881, he co-founded the first psychology journal in Germany, the *Philosophische Studien.* His own work, the enormous numbers of students who proceeded through his school, and the work transmitted in this journal have identified Wundt's contributions with the beginnings of structuralism in psychology, the field which assumes that psychology is the science of immediate experience and that the structure of the mind's activities depend directly on the environment of the organism. Moreover, since prominent American psychologists, particularly Titchener, studied in this laboratory, Wundt's work is intimately connected with the first generation of psychologists in this country. To call Wundt an experimental

psychologist, however, does not give adequate credit to the theory of mind inherent in his work.

It seems that Wundt, like many of his contemporaries, wished to be associated not only with the emerging discipline of psychology, but also with philosophy -- as evidenced in the titles of his chairs and the journal he founded. In part, this may be due to the residual reputation of philosophy as the "queen of the sciences," or perhaps to the fact that philosophy chairs were the most established (and hence the most prestigious) in most universities at that time. Yet such a self-attribution may also indicate that Wundt felt himself more the theorist than he is normally given credit as being: a theorist on the nature of the acculturation inherent in learning.[28]

2) Ernst Mach (1838-1916) is considered today more a physicist than a psychologist. Yet to his contemporaries, he was known for his series of proofs of various psychological phenomena which were related to physiological restrictions on the organism, including preliminaries to what became field-and-ground experiments. From 1867 to 1895, he was professor of physics at Prague; only in 1895 was he called to the chair of "History and Theory of the Inductive Sciences" at Vienna. His books seem to have been more influential there than his person. Mach did not have contact with Brentano (whose personal life forced him to absent himself from his chair in April, 1895), and he held his chair there only until 1901, when he was disabled by a stroke. The thrust of his work was in the epistemology of the sciences: he differentiated among the data of experience as independent or dependent experience, explaining both psychology and physics as sciences of experience, yet as sciences whose results were conditioned by different points of view on their fundamentally similar data. In all cases, the experimental framework would be responsible for conditioning the areas of results which were to be achieved. His epistemology will be treated in greater detail below, although the tendency among historians of psychology is to dismiss it with only a brief mention. Although labeled mainly a philosopher by later generations, the outline of problems addressed in his *Psychology from an Empirical Standpoint* will be shown to be entirely commensurate with his contemporaries in calling attention to the cultural restrictions inherent in thought.

3) Carl Stumpf (1842-1936) is the third member of this middle generation of experimental psychologists and is known as the father of the psychology of music. He had studied with Lotze in Göttingen from 1867-68, and served there as a lecturer in philosophy from 1870-1873. At that time, he was called to replace Franz Brentano at Würzburg in the chair of philosophy, where he stayed until 1879. The rest of his academic career was peripatetic; he spent about five years each at Prague, Halle, and Munich, ending up in Berlin in 1894. Only in Munich did he finally have a laboratory, and there he completed the research for his *Tonpsychologie* (1883-1890), which criticized the work that had come out of Wundt's laboratories -- Stumpf espoused a nativist, rather than an experiential, point of view. At Berlin, Stumpf was promoted over Ebbinghaus, who left shortly thereafter, leaving Stumpf with a laboratory and one of the most prestigious chairs (that of philosophy) in Germany. He stayed in the position until 1921, and even served a term as Rector (president) of the university during his tenure.

Perhaps his greatest achievements were his students, Husserl and Wertheimer, who rose to prominence after the turn of the century. Their individual programs pushed experimental psychology in Stumpf's sense into a secondary position, yet still reflected their common background in his theoretical framework. Such a situation was not unusual, since there was little or no compulsory laboratory work in a course of study -- students went to lectures, or experimental lecture-demonstrations, without necessarily having to develop experimental technique themselves. Nonetheless, all three share an emphasis on Gestalt, experience, and phenonemology -- a focus on the link between mind and perception.

These three major figures from widely varying institutional and disciplinary perspectives are united under the narrow prescription of "major influence;" that is, they taught the next generation, either directly or through their writings. Such a prescription designates them as major figures without necessarily indicating what should be done with them, or how they made major contributions to the paradigm of the emerging discipline of psychology, referring to their purportedly major experiments as merely milestones in the emerging field. This relegates these three major figures to the ranks of interesting and influential fossils, making them part of a prescription of "major influence" without questioning if they did, indeed, share a greater paradigm which made their work especially significant for students and colleagues.[29]

The traditional affiliation of these three names as teachers highlights only certain affinities in their data. Histories based on this point of view stress effects of psycho-physical programming on human development, for example, and pay little attention to the larger philosophical or anthropological programs which brought fundamentally different scientists to similar experiments. In contrast to such an undertaking, this volume will demonstrate paradigmatic communalities between the work of Mach and Wundt: their common choices of data, respect for cultural milieu, and their status as theoreticians of the "inductive sciences," in other words, the titles of their chairs.

1.6.3 *Act Psychology*

Apart from the group of experimental psychologists in the latter part of the nineteenth century, the history of psychology has a bit more difficulty dealing with the so-called "act psychologists" of the period. This area of psychology explicitly merged with philosophy, because its premise was that the activity of the mind was crucial in constituting knowledge or world experience. As such, these theories emerged into psychology proper as precursors to James and "functional psychology," which also concentrated on the workings of the mind in perception.[30]

1) The father of act psychology was Franz Brentano (1838-1917), a secularized priest whose academic career in Austria was disturbed by conflicts with the Catholic Church. He began as lecturer in philosophy at Würzburg (1866-1873), until Lotze arranged for him to be awarded the chair of philosophy at Vienna (1874). In 1880, he was forced to resign (he wanted to marry, which was not tolerated there, because he was an ex-priest). After he married in a Protestant ceremony in Germany, he was able to return to Vienna immediately (still in 1880), but only as a lecturer. His list of prominent students was remarkable: Stumpf, Edmund Husserl, Christian von Ehrenfels, Freud (briefly), and Alexius

Meinong (1853-1920), founder of the so-called Graz School.[31] Brentano's most influential book on psychology (aside from extensive publications on the history of philosophy) was the 1874 Psychology from an Empirical Standpoint, which distinguished between the contents of consciousness and the acts of consciousness which construe them in the mind. Today, he is included in the psychological canon more as a teacher, and less on the basis of the conceptual strategies underlying his work, a connection which would tie him more closely to the central paradigm of his age.[32]

2) Edmund Husserl (1859-1938), Brentano's student (after having studied briefly with Stumpf), is known as the father of phenomenology, a philosophical discipline seen as evolving out of act psychology, yet distinct from it in the opinion of most histories of psychology. Whereas psychology attempts to explain experience, phenomenology is the science which attempts to describe it, thus logically preceding psychology in its focus on the preconditions for experience itself. This volume will attempt to pull Husserl's psychology into closer proximity to the psychological tradition from which it purportedly seceded.[33]

3) Christian von Ehrenfels (1859-1932) was another student of Brentano's, but one whose prominence lay mainly in being a precursor: in 1890, he explained the notion of the "gestalt quality" of thought -- the mind's tendency to strive towards wholes, even with information missing -- making him the forerunner to the work done at Würzburg and by those psychologists known as the Gestalt School. He studied with Brentano at Vienna, then with Meinong at Graz. Vienna called him back as a lecturer from 1889-1896, when he finally moved to Prague as an associate and then full professor of psychology.[34]

This group of thinkers, influenced by Brentano's Jesuitical thought, is somewhat discredited by today's psychology and considered appropriate only for the philosophers of mind, not for psychologists interested in behavior. Such a designation is a prescription constituting an institutional inclusion -- they taught philosophy, and so are given over to the philosophers, thereby neglecting the fact that many "psychologists" up through the mid-century also held academic chairs in philosophy because chairs in psychology did not exist. Even Ehrenfels' work is neglected, except in the context of Meinong's work on the philosophy of science. Yet their work betrayed great affinity with the emerging paradigm of psychology in the nineteenth century and served as a stimulus to the psychologists of the turn of the century.

1.6.4 *Experimental Psychologists: The Second Generation*

Apart from these "act psychologists," several other names were prominent as teachers and scholars of psychology in the latter part of the century. Many were influenced by the act psychologists, yet attempted to synthesize an experimental component into their individual work.

1) Oswald Külpe (1862-1915), the father of the Würzburg School, provided an experimental verification for Brentano's distinction between the contents and the activity of consciousness. He had studied with Wundt and G.E. Müller, then served as an associate professor at Leipzig in 1893. Starting in 1894, he assumed the professorship of philosophy at Würzburg, forming the nucleus of the most prominent anti-structuralist groups in psychology. They systematically investigated how thought and volition, task structure, mental set, and attitudes affect perception, and again provided evidence supporting the later Gestalt movement. Max Wertheimer, who received his Ph.D. at Würzburg in 1904, continued their work well into this century.

2) Max Wertheimer (1880-1943), after his training at Würzburg, became known as the true father of Gestalt psychology. From 1912 on, his work centered on experiments distinguishing the part-versus-whole aspect of perception.

3) In a somewhat different vein, Theodor Lipps (1851-1914), a third student of Brentano, achieved prominence with work concentrated on empathy (*Einfühlung*). He was a widely-known teacher, holding chairs at Bonn (1877-1890), Breslau (1890-1894), and Munich (1894 to his death in 1914).

These figures can be associated in their shared concern for personality and individuality, thus giving a striking degree of conformity in their choices of data, method, and goals, the basis for a paradigm. Yet the canon sets a prescription obscuring this consistency: Freud's work in personality is mythically granted status as the first in the area with credibility. This attribution reflects the prejudices of today's psychological establishment, which prides itself on its family tree of teachers and analysts who worked with either Freud himself or one of his students. Moreover, such a prescription excludes the significance of earlier generations. Despite the fact that these three figures are cited in virtually every academic psychology book of the latter part of the nineteenth century and the beginning of the twentieth century, Külpe, Wertheimer, and Lipps are mentioned only in passing in today's traditional history of psychology.

1.6.5 *Psychological Technicians*

Three other names which still occur in most histories of psychology are profiled as practical innovators rather than as major contributors to psychological theory.

1) Georg Elias Müller (1850-1934), after lecturing at Göttingen and Czernowitz from 1876-1881, was called to replace Lotze in the chair of philosophy at Göttingen -- a chair that had had only two occupants, Herbart and Lotze, in 40 years. He had studied under Drobisch, another student of Herbart's, at Leipzig, and is remembered for being "the first experimental psychologist . . . who was little more than an experimental psychologist."[35] Müller, however, did develop the memory drum and standardize the difficulty scale of nonsense syllables which are used in memory experiments. Here, he developed Ebbinghaus' work towards a more dynamic model, including the notion of an "anticipatory set" in approaching nonsense syllables.

2) Hermann Ebbinghaus (1850-1909), remembered for having Stumpf promoted over him in Berlin in 1894, gained prominence through his learning experiments. In 1885, he did the first experiments in serial learning and forgetting, later incorporating statistical methods and timed rates of presentation into these experiments. He also introduced various memory aids into tests, and developed a completion test which was the precursor to the analogy test used in present IQ testing. From 1880 to 1894, he was first lecturer, then associate professor in Berlin; he then

replaced Lipps in Breslau (1894-1905), and spent the remainder of his career in Halle. More importantly, he was responsible for founding the second journal in psychology in Germany. The *Zeitschrift für Psychologie und Physiologie der Sinnesorgane*, founded in 1890, documents more practical experiments and differentiates itself from the first journal's interest in philosophy and the theory of psychology.

3) Emil du Bois-Reymond succeeded Müller as professor of physiology in Berlin and is known mainly for his experiments on animal electricity using galvanometers. His name is encountered most frequently among the ranks of practicing experimentalists in the middle of the nineteenth century.

These three teachers, extremely visible in their own day, are today relegated to the ranks of developers of useful hardware for the psychological laboratory. Such a designation is a prescription which indicates the present historians' bias towards a theoretical rather than an experimental image of psychology in its emerging period. The paradigm which this volume will develop for the work in the period will better accommodate the span between experiment and theory which presently forces such work into the shadows without an independent assessment of its scope and quality. The revaluation of these figures must start with the fundamental question of their goals in developing their hardware, as well as suggesting their relationship within the scientific paradigm of their age. They were the dominant teachers of their generation, who influenced not only academicians, but also practicing therapists and physicians.

1.7 Implications

With some variation, this is the canon of psychologists in the nineteenth century according to a great number of the present historians of psychology.[36] Today's historians of the field have assumed the viewpoint of modern therapists or largely experimental psychologists without questioning if there was a unifying paradigm beneath their work. More serious from the point of view of this volume, they have overlooked a main undercurrent of the work in all camps: a cultural approach, the more or less hidden agenda questioning the acculturation of learning and conceptualization.

Recently, as already noted, more studies have arisen based on typologies of single authors, institutions, teacher-student relations, or intellectual prescriptions such as "worked on experimental hardware." These groupings document the "whats" of history without addressing other questions. Why were these innovators, in fact, innovators? On what basis was their work influential? If such questions are answered, one comes closer to the point of view of a paradigm.

The present volume, then, will re-examine figures from the canon outlined above with a fundamental difference in approach: their work will be considered in terms of common intellectual assumptions -- their common paradigm. To do so means that institutional, experimental, and biographical prescriptions, as well as those of influence, will be largely ignored in favor of direct appeals to a more substantive communality in their work, to the discourse they share. Here, the more prominent figures from the paradigm (Freud and Wundt particularly) will be analyzed in relation to thinkers whose work is either less familiar or has been deemed outside the realm of psychology proper. Often, as in the case of Husserl, a name does not apply because he "is a philosopher," not a psychologist. The configuration of psychologists which this volume offers justifies itself on the basis of their shared discourse. Their own articulations of the problems they addressed are often strikingly similar in terminology and formulation despite the discord in their stated purposes. The goal of this new juxtaposition is to see beyond institutional differences and prejudices represented by prescriptions, and to set forth the outlines of the intellectual paradigm which joined the work of these various sources together into a common conceptual endeavor. An approximation of the paradigm which prescriptive histories have tended to obscure and an outline of the discourse which is the key to this paradigm will be given here.

To uncover the paradigm which the psychologists of the nineteenth century shared to a greater or lesser degree provides a basis with which to answer the questions of influence and significance which have not been satisfactorily addressed by prescriptive histories of the discipline. The elucidation of this paradigm will suggest the strategies which motivated psychologists' choices in work, both in terms of which experiments they included or excluded, and in terms of what models of the mind and behavior would have been innately accepted or rejected because of the discourse environment in which the discipline was evolving.

As a prelude to the investigations of the individual authors, this volume will first outline a method which can supersede the prescriptions outlined above, in order to approach the paradigm for psychology in the nineteenth century. The project of the following chapter is to provide a new model for organizing the history of a science. This new model, which can fill the desiderata put forth by Brozek, Watson, Woodward, Ash, and Geuter above, involves the definition of a paradigm as expressive of the unity of scientific strategies and the discourse of an age, and a clarification of its advantages in correlating the historical data of a science with the strategies which distinguish it as a unique branch of investigation.

CHAPTER 2

COUNTERPROPOSITION: PSYCHOLOGY AS DISCOURSE

The brief outline of the accepted canon of psychology betrays the overriding weaknesses found in many modern histories of the discipline. Their continuities are provisory, and the assessments of influence incomplete or topical (as "x continued y's experiments"). These histories, in general, do not address the conceptual under-pinnings of psychologists' works, but rather tend to trace back twentieth-century terminology and experiments to their roots. Even when they turn to intellectual history, they often overlook that terminology favored by the twentieth century was often peripheral to the core thought patterns of the nineteenth century in which it originated.[1]

Clearly, then, any history of nineteenth-century psychology which purports to do something new must include more than even the socio-cultural aspects of the history of the discipline, as (most notably) Woodward and Ash had recommended. A history based on new principles must turn towards a new type of closure for the discipline -- a new definition of the historical milieu of a science. Such a definition of an epoch in science constitutes a paradigm for psychology. This is a closed definition of the field reflecting its self-identification in the nineteenth century, as well as pointing towards its development in the twentieth. Such a paradigm has not been uncovered because present historians of psychology still utilize typologies or prescriptions derived from the twentieth-century identity of the field.

The calls put out by historians of psychology which were surveyed in the "Introduction" may be answered through application of new tools from historiography that expand the notion of paradigm defined by Kuhn. In the postwar decades, historiography as a science has been in a position to offer an alternative model for the selection, organization, and interpretation of historical data. The present volume will turn to this body of work for its methodological model: to the work of the so-called "post-structuralists" -- primarily Michel Foucault and Jacques Derrida, but also (implicitly) Julia Kristeva and the *Annales historians*.[2] Such a choice recommends itself not only because of the alternate model for historiography which they have generated, but also because this movement has, in recent years, done some of the most significant work extending Freud. Their notions of history have, therefore, been tried on the field of psychology already and will presumably accommodate it as a science.

The model of history these scholars offer construes the unity of a historical period not on institutional grounds, nor on the basis of teachers and students, nor in surface communalities of interest or continuations of experiments. They agree that these are all variations which have shown themselves to be inadequate in some way in the formation of the psychological canon evolved above.

Instead, the post-structuralists expand the definition of a paradigm as a group of work representing a consistent set of data within one conceptual environment with its concomitant prohibitions and assumptions -- a content group, to use Watson's phrase. For post-structuralists, a paradigm is a *discourse*, a term drawn from linguistics to suggest a new approach to historical data.[3] A discourse encompasses not only what is overt or evident, such as the experiments done, parallel to specific sentences which occur in a language, but the myriad of covert rules and prohibitions which constitute the knowledge of a "native speaker" of a language -- the rules outside the rule book for ordering concepts, the materials which are acceptable, and the valid formulations for those who are "inside" the group.[4] Construing history as a dominant discourse for an age thus represents an advance over typologies, prescriptions, or Kuhn's paradigms. In this setting, history addresses not only a common set of data, but also a consistent set of strategies associating data in a pattern distinctive for a particular epoch.

2.1 The Post-Structuralist Example: Freud as Discourse

The post-structuralists themselves provide an example of the questions and strategies represented by the discourse of psychology.[5] Particularly in recent years, the French have devoted much discussion to the delineation of Freud's work as a discourse, especially Jacques Derrida's "Freud and the Scene of Writing,"[6] Paul Ricoeur's *Freud and Philosophy: An Essay on Interpretation*,[7] and the works of Jacques Lacan.[8] These texts, supplemented by Michel Foucault's *Archaeology of Knowledge*[9] delineate the parameters of a discourse of psychology.[10]

Derrida has focused on Freud's work as a metaphoric communication system, in his terminology, a "logocentric discourse" (a system based on provisory human logic which purports to convey meanings to its users):

> Our aim is limited: to locate in Freud's text several points of reference, and to isolate, on the threshold of a systematic examination, those elements of psychoanalysis which can only uneasily be contained within logocentric closure, as this closure limits not only the history of philosophy but also the orientation of the "human sciences," notably of a certain linguistics. (SW, 198-199)

The "elements of psychoanalysis" he seeks are its introduction of the irrational into the rational, its specific point of differentiation from other human sciences. Derrida is defining psychoanalysis in the terms used by linguistics, consisting of a morphology (a set of defined meaningful units, such as pieces of historical data), a syntax (an innate logic of relations), and a semantics (a relationship of meanings conveyed by the system). The discourse of Freud's psychoanalysis, and of the psychology which lies behind it, is characterized by a novel delineation of these units of meaning as the relationships which are the traces of the activity of the mind.[11] Derrida finds the unique discourse of Freud's psychology to be a language in three parts: a juxtaposition of psychic content (the traces of lived experience of the organism involved -- its semantic repertoire), the text produced by the psyche (the material reported in the process of psychoanalysis -- its individual utterances or "speech acts"), and the workings of the mind (the covert rules according to which data will be processed -- syntax).

Derrida's metaphor of a discourse of psychoanalysis requires careful discrimination. Like the facets of the full phenomenon of language, the three fields which constitute psychoanalysis's data are not possible to isolate; they occur in unison, and their purported isolation in analysis is only a representation:

> It is no accident that Freud, at the decisive moments of his itinerary, has recourse to metaphorical models which are borrowed not from spoken language or from verbal forms, nor even from phonetic writing, but from a script which is never subject to, never exterior and posterior to, the spoken word. . . . Psychical *content* will be *represented* by a text whose essence is irreducibly graphic. The *structure* of the psychical *apparatus* will be *represented* by a writing machine. . . . what must be the relationship between psyche, writing, and spacing for such a metaphoric transition to be possible, not only, nor primarily, within theoretical discourse, but within the history of psyche, text, and technology? (SW, 199)

Derrida presents psychoanalysis as parallel to discourse, consisting of a reported history as overt content, the personal construction of that report, plus a set of covert rules. His stress on covert rules that affect the dynamic equilibrium of the individual's mind distances this definition from that of Kuhn's paradigm.

Freud's writing machine, in which the individual is seen as a discourse machine, is a model for a system of thought, with overt and covert facets. Yet it has one further crucial function: a discourse paradigm not only *includes* facts of reality, it also *excludes* -- it declares certain facets of reality unsayable using its signs. Derrida calls this exclusionary action a "difference," that is, the act of deferring, differing, and differentiating at once.

By adding the term "difference" to his description of a discourse, Derrida summarizes another aspect of a paradigm. It includes a defined (if often unconscious) set of data and relations of this data, and "defers" or excludes others, differentiating them from the system. Derrida believes that Freud constructed the discourse of psychoanalysis in the inherent "difference" in every mind, based on a primary distinction between that data in the mind which stems from the outside world, and that which is internal. This mixture of internal and external data is a juxtaposition of frames within the mind which does not locate the work of the mind, because all such data is perceived data, appearing in consciousness. The psychoanalysis of *difference* describes a discourse that is an interaction between mind and world:

> This is why, under the heading of "the biological standpoint," a "difference in essence" (*Wesens-verschiedenheit*) between the neurones is "replaced by a difference in the environment to which they are destined" (*Schicksals-Milieuverschiedenheit*): these are pure differences, differences of situation, of connection, of localization, of structural relations more important than their supporting terms: and they are differences for which the relativity of outside and inside is always to be determined. (SW, 204)

Here, Derrida identifies the uniqueness of Freud's program in its description of the relational processes of mind.

In Derrida's view, the mental signs (the data for the analyses of dreams) are "a system of stratified writing" (SW, 206). The "inside" of the system of trace and memory serves as the basis for an individual's reality. Differentiating further, the id, ego, and superego represent the types or strata of traces which have been left in these mental pathways. The stratification, or levels of intensity, which characterize these traces innately classify them as unconscious, preconscious, or conscious, according to their perceived intensity. Freud has thus identified within his system the sources of the traces which register in the brain -- the volition of the organism, the individual consciousness, or the group --, as well as the levels of intensity at which they will register, as a gauge to their prominence within the energetics of the whole. That is, he includes data drawn from a cultural environment, a set of rules, and descriptions of the products of the psychic system as a language.

Yet Derrida finds that this focus on the internal workings of the mental system was also the inherent weakness of Freud's discourse. Because of the novelty of this model in a medical frame, Freud was not able to exploit the model he formed. Instead, he stressed the data contained within the mind in his writings, not necessarily the functioning of the system. His work thus stops at delimiting a taxonomy of the mind. In linguistic terms, Freud derived a morphology and semantics of the mind system without a commensurate syntax.[12] He was left, in the *Interpretation of Dreams*, with the observation that each dreamer creates his own syntax on the basis of limited personal intentions like "wish-fulfillment" and "displacement." Freud, therefore, did not delimit the more complete interactions of these morphemes as they would function in a complete syntax of the energies of the mind, or as they might appear, not only in the individual, but in the general human mind:

> But in its operations [those of the 'writing of the mind'], lexicon, and syntax a purely idiomatic residue is irreducible and is made to bear the burden of interpretation in the communication between unconsciousnesses. The dreamer invents his own grammar. . . . As much as it is a function of the generality and the rigidity of the code, this limitation is a function of an excessive preoccupation with [individual] *content*, and an insufficient concern for relations, locations, processes, and differences . . . (SW, 209)

Moreover, in his evaluation of the model of the mind as a language system, Freud does not deal with the virtual character of the "outside" of the system; he does not seek a translation between "reality" and "perceived reality": "The difference between signifier and signified is never radical" (SW, 209). Both the signifiers (particularly the images of dreams) and the signifieds (the data of the "outside" which have become the traces of the brain) are conditioned to function within the breached paths of the brain. Thus Derrida sees that Freud was working actively on the internal formal rules of mind, and not really on the interface between mind and world. The "differences" of Freud's system were, according to Derrida, not accounted for in his work. Yet the present volume will contend that these differences did underlie his work, since they constitute the paradigm for nineteenth-century psychology.

For Derrida, then, this is the limit of the discourse metaphor. Freud is caught between an *a priori* functioning of the mind due to the breaching of its energetic system and the individuation of each mind, between the individuation of the *contents* of a particular mind and their associated breached paths, and the *associations* or *relations* which constitute the energetics of each and every mental system. To clear up this problem, Derrida shows that Freud still needed to differentiate between text (the mental image) and function (mental processing):

> This is what the last chapter of the *Traumdeutung* explains. An entirely and conventionally topographical metaphor of the psychical apparatus is to be completed by invoking the existence of force and of two kinds of processes of excitation or modes of its discharge . . . The conscious text is thus not a transcription, because there is no text *present elsewhere* as an unconscious one to be transposed or transported. (SW, 211)

For Derrida, the discourse of psychoanalysis is an example of a linguistic discourse, a system of meanings designed for communication. The mind is imprinted with paths of meaning of different intensities; nonetheless, these paths develop with the freedom of a dream in an idiosyncratic syntax. Any provisory syntax or logic represented in the workings of an individual mind may be augmented or supplanted by other logics, other path-breakings within the finished system. Freud did not generalize this model to imply that a syntax of dreams would be parallel in all minds -- that is too Kantian and underplays the role of environmental programming. The discourse of the mind is only partly representable by the metaphor of writing. It is a new economic definition of speech, and a mode of representation outside that of the conventional signified/signifier assumed of language. For Derrida, Freud's work really served to indicate how much is concealed *behind* the overt workings of the mind, similar to the way in which the uses of language represents an enormous stock of covert knowledge of the speaker. The greatest achievement of post-structuralism may be the realization that the store of an individual's unconscious knowledge can exert an even greater pressure than conscious knowledge.

Derrida points out one further facet of the paradigm underlying Freud's work: it did not correspond to an extant description of a discipline as institutionalized in his age. He notes, "That which, in

Freud's discourse, opens itself to the theme of writing results in psychoanalysis being not simply psychology -- nor simply psychoanalysis" (SW, 228). The discourse of nineteenth-century psychology reflected in Freud's psychoanalysis focuses on the confirmation and constitution of systems based on a taxonomy of signifiers (as in the *Dreams*) and the syntax of energetic levels (missing in the *Dreams*, but present in the *Project* and the descriptions of repression in *Civilization and its Discontents*, for example).[13] The central texts in psychoanalysis represent, then, a taxonomy of signifiers with assumed cultural validity, and lack the underpinnings sketched in the *Project*.. He assumed a discourse paradigm rather than explaining the overriding energetic processing mechanisms or syntax which would acknowledge both the general construction of the human mind and the experience of the individual.   Consequently, when Freud sought to uncover the values and devaluations inherent in the system of the mind, he only applied his results to individual therapy.

Freud's stress on psychoanalysis occludes the importance of the idea of an energetic psychic trace or breached nerve path as a key to the paradigm of psychology, construed as a body of theory on the mind's function.[14] Freud paralleled the discourse of nineteenth-century psychology by assuming the idea of the trace in the model of the mind which he uncovered between the *Project* and the *Interpretation of Dreams*, but he did not expand the model explicitly in his work.[15] His discipline, psychoanalysis, did not make the discourse of psychology explicit; it remained hidden. Analysis concentrated on the products of the mental system as they affect patients, and the traces of experience as they influenced future behavior.[16] This psychoanalysis was, however, not the psychology which would render explicit the model of the interface between mind and world with which he was working.

How could Freud have raised the discourse of psychology to the level of a discipline and thus expanded his work beyond therapy? Derrida's work does not address this question, but he points the way to a more general definition of discourse as a science or discipline:[17]

> The concept of writing should define the field of a science.
> . . . The science of writing should therefore look for its
> object at the roots of scientificity. A science of the

> possibility of science? A science of science which would
> no longer have the form of logic but that of *grammatics*? A
> history of the possibility of history which would no longer
> be an archaeology, a philosophy of history or a history of
> philosophy [focusing not on conveyed meaning, but on the
> units of meaning]? (GR, 27-28)

Derrida supplements the traditional concept of a science with a
consideration of its milieu and conditions of representability within
the field. Such a field of investigation is not only the study of
writing as the act of producing a fixed text or a set of rules; it is also
language, the rules and text plus living usage, institutional
practices, and their inclusions and exclusions -- a field including
institutions (customary usage), trace (data), and energetics
(processing).

Derrida adds this definition of a paradigm to the desiderata
sketched by the historians of psychology above. Derrida's work
thus exemplifies the search for a history on the level of a paradigm,
as opposed to that of a typology or prescription. Yet his work on
Freud is not exhaustive of other aspects of paradigms, as outlined
in the work of Foucault. Unlike Foucault, Derrida underplays the
cultural context of the work as a stable intellectualized context.
Foucault stresses the importance of cultural identity for a paradigm
and of the social and institutional role it plays, as a variant of
Woodward and Ash's desiderata for the social history of
psychology.

Another French Freud scholar, Paul Ricoeur, stresses that the
location or nexus in which the discourse of psychoanalysis
functions is that of culture:

> This is how psychoanalysis belongs to modern culture. By
> interpreting culture it modifies it; by giving it an instrument
> of reflection it stamps it with a lasting mark. The
> fluctuation in Freud's writing between medical
> investigation and a theory of culture bears witness to the
> scope of the Freudian project. (FP, 4)

Although Ricoeur does not examine this in depth, his statement
echoes a primary goal in the uncovering of a discourse paradigm

for psychology in the nineteenth century. This discourse paradigm must account for the historical locus of a psychological discourse. The rules underlying this paradigm must express both an inside (a model of the procedures, rules and data it encompasses) and an outside (the cultural influences and disciplinary boundaries which exclude items from its purview). The paradigm sought must, at the same time, include an energetic or dynamic model of the mind (the crux of Freud's fundamental research which allowed the development of his psychoanalysis), as well as account for the effects of culture and environment on the mind's mechanisms.

The social approaches to discourse paradigms, suggested by Foucault and expanded by Bourdieu and other French social theorists, broaden the base of the "linguistic model" for a paradigm. As a discourse, a paradigm will accommodate not only cultural signs, but the pressures of cultural survival and adaptation (a biological metaphor) initiated by the community that uses it. In terms of a cultural community, a discourse paradigm necessarily synthesizes philological and biological approaches -- minds and bodies are not separate from the point of view of discourse analysis, a sociological approach to language stressing the dynamic equilibrium between the two poles.

Together, then, the work of various post-structuralists on Freud argues for the derivation of the paradigm for a science both in terms of its content-orientation, as Watson recommended, as well as in terms of the cultural pressures or "differences" which exert influence over its conceptual development. Where earlier historians deal in influences, themes or problems, institutions, and teachers, the post-structuralists will deal in *discourse*: the contents, rules for approach, and prohibitions (particularly cultural) which circumscribe a field. According to this model, psychology can be said to have emerged only when its paradigm has an overt discourse. That is, psychology is a paradigmatic science when a consistent set of conceptual procedures, vocabulary, and strategies have emerged, not merely when an institution emerges and proclaims an independent existence. Moreover, such a historiographical strategy often merges terminology or themes in an unfamiliar fashion. For example, "biological" approaches are traditionally distinguisted from "cultural" ones; in the paradigm of the nineteenth century, however, the two came to be merged.[18]

2.2 The Outline for the Paradigm

In contrast to the histories of psychology outlined above, the present volume will contend that psychology in the nineteenth century had indeed emerged as a paradigm, an identifiable intellectual strategy. To be sure, it still largely lacked the institutional validation that traditional historians seek in order to legitimize their unifications of epochs. Moreover, the distinct psychology outlined here was practiced by professionals in many fields, a situation which furthers obscures its commonality of terms.

The authors and thinkers presented dealt in individual ways with the problems constituting the basis of the discourse of psychology.[19] Immanuel Kant established the primary inclusion and exclusion rules of this discourse in establishing the categories of pure reason and applying them to anthropology. Johann Friedrich Herbart followed Kant, yet expanded the discipline toward an energetic model of the mind's function in his analysis of the innervations of the senses. Under the influence of Empiricists Richard Avenarius, Wilhelm Wundt, and Gustav Fechner (particularly the latter's *Psychophysics*), a conflict arose about the foundation of a science of culture -- a conflict fought within the emerging philology of the nineteenth century, as represented by Hermann Paul and Wilhelm Wundt.

Another perspective on the science of culture was outlined by Wilhelm Dilthey, as an investigation which brought him some distance from his more familiar work in the history of ideas. In addressing psychology, he questioned the premises of his work in culture and hoped to verify his generalizations about the spirit of an age. Ernst Mach discussed the existence of the purportedly pure sciences as artifacts of culture, and the necessity of including considerations of psychology in theoretical disciplines. The mechanisms of the mind will underlie all products of mankind, be they "pure science" or "cultural." Franz Brentano and his student Edmund Husserl discussed formalizations of the psychological discipline which differ in premises only a little from those sketched by Freud; the differences, however, delimit a psychology which remained theoretical, with no application to a therapeutic discipline and no involvement from the sphere of culture.

Finally, the psychoanalysis of Freud himself relates to cultural psychology as the capstone of the century's work on psychology. His discourse began as that of a psychology, yet ended in the related therapeutic discipline; the *Project* was abandoned for the *Interpretation of Dreams*, and psychoanalysis superceded the distinct discourse of nineteenth-century psychology.

The blueprint for the investigations gathered in the present volume is the delineation of a discourse paradigm which arose as an adjunct to a variety of fields in the nineteenth century, and which would, as the twentieth century began, emerge as a psychology concerned with the integration of man and culture -- a psychology lacking both institutional unity and full consciousness of its underlying paradigm. Michel Foucault's statement of the relation of discourse or discursive practice to disciplines characterizes the assumptions on which this work is based:[20]

> Discursive practices are characterized by the delimitation of a field of objects, the definition of a legitimate perspective for the agent of knowledge, and the fixing of norms for the elaboration of concepts and theories. Thus, each discursive practice implies a play of prescriptions that designate its exclusions and choices. (HST, 199)

> [The analyses of discursive practices] often serve to regroup a large number of individual works. . . . it is usually the case that a discursive practice assembles a number of disciplines or sciences or that it crosses a certain number among them and regroups many of their individual characteristics into a new and occasionally unexpected unity. (HST, 200)

Philosophers, philologists, and physiologists may participate in the discourse paradigm, no matter how different their professions and stated purposes.

Foucault conceives history as the history a particular set of discursive practices: "[History] belongs to that field in which the questions of the human being, consciousness, origin, and the subject emerge, intersect, mingle, and separate off" (AK, 16). In delineating a paradigm for a historical era, Foucault realizes he must attempt to account for the statements made within defined disciplines, then try "to define the dispersion of these objects, to grasp all the interstices that separate them, to measure the distances that reign between them -- in other words, to formulate their law of division" (AK, 33).

This position requires an analysis of data from the standpoint of an outsider to the system. Needed is not only an exposition of the premises of the science under consideration, but also the institutional and social existence of the scientist, the location of that science with respect to others, and the chosen field of data with its inclusionary and exclusionary limits and restrictions:

> Thus conceived, discourse is not the majestically unfolding manifestation of a thinking, knowing, speaking subject, but, on the contrary, a totality, in which the dispersion of the subject and his discontinuity with himself may be determined. It is a space of exteriority in which a network of distinct sites is deployed. . . . it must now be recognized that it is neither by recourse to a transcendental subject nor by recourse to a psychological activity that the regulation of its enunciations should be defined. (AK, 55)

Foucault's discourse is a broad definition of a paradigm. Such a discourse is not an ontic totality, but rather a dynamic system of possible meaning structures within a temporal unity, a system of signs in use as signifiers by a cultural unit at a particular time whose signification will depend on the dynamics of the system itself. With this emphasis on the concrete and historically particular, as well as the systematic and rule-based, Foucault points the way to the analysis of Freud that neither Derrida nor Ricoeur was able to accomplish.

Following these examples and definitions, the present volume will delineate a conceptual psychology as the precursor of modern psychology, with a unique nineteenth-century focus on the interrelation of mind and environment and on the scientific validation of its results. This term -- conceptual psychology -- is coined here to cover the discourse paradigm of psychology, not a particular discipline.[21]

As Watson indicated, the twentieth century does not necessarily acknowledge the existence of a developed general science of psychology before the turn of the century. For the nineteenth century, however, the present volume will contend that this discourse was integral in the minds of those in many disciplines who used its tenets. Thus, this conceptual psychology was practiced while lacking a distinctive presence and set of procedures compelling enough to warrant its break into an independent discipline. Only such a rupture would have yielded the type of institutional documentation that the typological and prescriptive historians seek. Instead, conceptual psychology remained a leitmotif within other disciplines, guiding their validation criteria while lacking an overt existence, perhaps because of its general acceptance.

Until Freud's clear break with the institution and his establishment of a new non-institutional role for the humanist-practitioner in psychoanalysis, conceptual psychology was diffused into other programs with institutional prescriptions which accommodated certain of its aspects. From the twentieth-century vantagepoint, it existed only as a discourse, not an institution. Since the institutional backing was limited, cultural psychology was in a situation which minimized its chances for historical recognition as a discipline with its own channels of transmission and standards for research. Its existence was too easily diffused into the social, cultural, and institutional prescriptions of twentieth-century historians of science.

Conceptual psychology remains a discourse hidden from those historians who require institutional closure, although it more than amply fulfills Foucault's definition of an established discursive practice: "a body of anonymous, historical rules, as determined at the time and space that have defined it in a given period, and for a given social, economic, geographical, or linguistic area, the conditions of operation of the enunciative function" (AK, 117). With the gradual withdrawal of Freud's students from the ranks of the medical profession, an opportunity for the emergence of an institutional identity for psychology as an independent discipline was emerging around the turn of the century. Even Freud, with his continued insistence that he was a neurologist or an analyst, continued the fiction that the results of psychology still could be confined within the set of problems addressed in other disciplines. Yet Freud's analysis emerged, perhaps to suppress conceptual psychology.

This situation, together with the limitations of conventional histories of psychology revealed briefly above, indicate that a more realistic picture of psychology is needed. While acknowledging the specifically non-institutional nature of conceptual psychology, the present set of studies will delineate stages in the development of a particular type of psychology as a discourse. Each chapter will pinpoint emerging regularities in assumptions and unarticulated subgoals of the disciplines in which the discourse of conceptual psychology gradually emerged.

The need for such a history is answered by a quick glance at the remaining question: why don't historians isolate psychology as a discipline -- strictly apart from physiology and philosophy-- until after Freud? A partial answer is provided by the case of Freud's psychoanalysis, which magnified that the institutional and personal constraints on the early representatives of this discourse again obscured its emergence -- not to its contemporaries, but to the minds of historians.

Freud's case is typical of many who were at odds with the system, since they needed audience, salary, and professional credibility. His correspondence with Wilhelm Fliess indicates that he was aware of the institutional implications of the work he was doing, although the work represented a non-institutional paradigm. Frank Sulloway summarizes these presumptions about Freud as follows:[22] "In a word, Freud feared mediocrity and others' anticipation of his ideas more than he feared error in science, and he fully accepted the risks inherent in this particular choice of values." Freud knew he was in a race between his contribution to conceptual psychology (his psychology) and his professional existence (psychoanalysis).

Freud did not win this race as a representative of conceptual psychology. His theories receded behind his development of more pragmatic and lucrative applications; psychoanalysis paid, psychology did not. Such an explanation tallies with Freud's own account of the publication of the *Studies on Hysteria* and *The Interpretation of Dreams*. Moreover, it accounts for Freud's break with Breuer, who was scientifically more cautious and less pragmatic than Freud -- Breuer retained his profession and rejected the paradigm of conceptual psychology. Freud, in contrast, realized that his institutional position precluded an overt stance vis-à-vis a nineteenth-century paradigm which was not yet considered outside the overt prescriptions of the university institutions. His break with Breuer represents a first attempt to reconcile the paradigm in which he worked with the institutional prescriptions afforded to him by the nineteenth century.

These biographical answers are not the only key to a broader paradigm. Freud himself acknowledged that his interests were not always as they were represented publicly. Biographical additions can prescribe only one additional facet for Freud's work and still do not reveal the greater paradigm in which he worked -- a paradigm of which he was seemingly aware.

Early in his career (1888), Freud lamented his specialized medical training and wished that he had been trained as a general practitioner who could make money and have freedom:

> The whole atmosphere of Vienna is little adapted to steeling one's will or to fostering that confidence in success which is the prerogative of you Berliners and without which a grown man cannot think of changing the whole basis of his livelihood. So I must stay as I am; but I have no illusions about how unsatisfactory a state of affairs it is. (29 August 1888; OPA, 57)

The role of psychologist-practicioner did not exist yet, so he tried analyst-practicioner instead.[23]   And just as Freud was loathe to even consider changing his field or engaging in further medical studies due to his financial situation, he feared the opinion of the public who were the basis of his practice and his livelihood. His personal research, therefore, had to be conducted circumspectly, out of the public eye:

> . . . a man like me cannot live without a hobby-horse, a consuming passion -- in Schiller's words a tyrant. I have found my tyrant, and in his service I know no limits. My tyrant is psychology; it has always been my distant, beckoning goal, and now, since I have hit on the neuroses,

> it has come so much the nearer, I am plagued with two ambitions: to see how the theory of mental functioning takes shape if quantitative considerations, a sort of economic of nerve-force, are introduced into it; and secondly, to extract from psycho-pathology what may be of benefit to normal psychology. (25 May 1895; OPA, 119-120)

Freud's psychology -- the thing he left behind -- did, indeed, resemble the paradigm of conceptual psychology.

The motto of the *Interpretation of Dreams*, "Flectere si nequeo superos Acheronta movebo," "If I cannot move heaven, then I will move hell," shows that Freud knew that only his psychoanalytic work would bring the acknowledgment he sought.[24] This, plus the priority of publishing, led him to write up partial results in popularized essays, all as part of his on-going search for metaphors to convey the essence of his theories and to render his conclusions clearly and simply, in order that they might be used.

Freud was trapped in self-perpetuating restrictions and had lost the time to work in his area of theory. As he grew older, he was pigeonholed by his contemporaries as a therapist, and his gambit for academic recognition from a position outside the academy was of limited success. His success, he wrote to Fliess on September 27, 1897, was moderate, if indeed at all ascertainable:

> I might be feeling very unhappy. The hope of eternal fame was so beautiful, and so was that of certain wealth, complete independence, travel, and removing the children from the sphere of the worries which spoiled my own youth. All that depended on whether hysteria succeeded or not. . . . There is something else I must add. In the general collapse only the psychology has retained its value. The dreams still stand secure, and my beginnings in metapsychology have gone up in my estimation. It is a pity one cannot live on dream-interpretation, for instance. (OPA, 217-18)

With this observation, Freud acknowledges that his allegiance was to a half-hidden paradigm of research shared with many contemporaries. His livelihood, however, was tied to the overt institutional prescriptions of his day. This dichotomy led him to brilliant writing which attempted to bridge the gap between his work and the audience which responded only to the programming in terms of institutional prescriptions, i.e., the discipline's therapeutic applications.[25]

Freud's statements confirm his consciousness of the discrimination between the discourse paradigm of psychology in which he worked, and the discipline of psychoanalysis which earned him his livelihood and secured for him, however belatedly, the professorship which would mean his financial security. Psychoanalysis was the popular end of his enterprise, the treatment which could be sold to the medical establishment and to the wealthy patrons of his day; the theoretical discourse of his "metapsychology" would never be formalized by Freud himself into the systematic discourse it represented, a paradigm addressing the mechanisms of cognition as they related to man's survival in culture.

In 1897, he again wrote Fliess, this time musing "whether I should use the term 'meta-psychology' for my psychology which leads behind consciousness" (OPA, 246). Such a statement locates quite accurately the discourse which Freud pursued privately -- a psychology dealing with the structure and function of the psyche, not a psychoanalysis which could appeal to established institutions and their public. Thus, as his position became somewhat more secure, he wrote Fliess that he could pay less attention to the public sphere (2 March 1899):

> I have given up my lectures this year in spite of numerous enrollments, and do not propose to resume them in the immediate future. I have the same fear of the uncritical adulation of the very young that I used to have for the hostility of their elders. (OPA, 280)

And in February 1901, he would give Fliess a lengthy tale about a set of lectures he was to have given to a club, canceled when the membership committee attempted to impose limits on his use of examples because of the "objectionable matter" he was to present (OPA, 329). Thus Freud's letters suggest a further reason for the non-emergence of psychology as a discipline: institutionally and professionally, the medical and therapeutic discourses which would have to subsume this new scientific discourse refused to do so, no matter how persuasively they were argued.

Freud's ambivalent research program was not unique. The studies in this volume will represent other thinkers whose work was perceived by their contemporary audiences and historians under similar restrictions; the great majority of the "psychologies" under discussion here are texts which are the oddities in a particular author's corpus, texts which formed the basis of lectures, or whose contents did not conform with the public image of their author's works as developed by later historiographers. Yet in their times, they were considered hallmarks of their fields, works which exerted great influence and which were oft-quoted by their contemporaries. They were influential and useful, the two indices which can witness a communality of paradigms for contributions in varying fields. Occasionally these texts are treated in great depth, but only as internal histories, in terms of the intellectual biography of an author or school.

The work which must be done in tracing the development of the "hidden discourse" of psychology's discourse in the nineteenth century is, therefore, twofold. First, the specific premises on which the formalization of psychology's paradigm is built must be outlined; second, individual contributions must be placed in their own tradition, a tradition often opposed to the more familiar contexts in which the author is placed. The developed psychology will, moreover, not be traced as a continuum through the century. The present treatment will focus on moments in which the psychological discourse was absorbed and utilized within other fields with more distinct institutional identities.

A few preliminary remarks must be emphasized. First, philosophy is the mother discipline of psychology, and so philosophers may be disproportionately represented. Yet their work is astoundingly parallel to that of Lotze, Fries, Trendelenburg, William James, Ribot, and Wilhelm Griesinger, all of whom could be represented here.[26] These names share the paradigm of conceptual psychology outlined, unlike historical proponents of reflex theory, hypnosis, phrenology, or evolutionary biology in the canonical sense. Second, the work in conceptual psychology ties more closely into the modern Marxist-influenced French analytic tradition than it does to the Anglo-American canon.[27]

Further: each individual investigation will be guided by several principles already introduced.

Each contribution to conceptual psychology will be explicated in terms of the modern definition of discourse proposed by Foucault and Derrida -- in terms of the location of data and authority which limit its functions and which uniquely determine the extent of its legitimacy as a potential discipline.

Each will be analyzed in the terms suggested, although not carried out, by Derrida in his work on Freud, which uncovers a system of culturally allowable meanings for the discourse which was presented as a psychology. Derrida outlined Freud's system of meanings and meaningfulness as an interplay between an energetic model (focusing on breaching of pathways [Bahnbrechung] in the brain and the traces or facilitations which are left behind) and a topographic model (focusing on depth of processing as a function of the organism's tendency to defer sensations). At the same time, he failed to consider Freud's own delineation of the data which enter into the processing of these model systems. Derrida ignores Foucault's critique of culture; that is, Derrida ignores the question of the pressure that world data exert on mental equilibria, a pressure outside of the intellectual system in the historical world.

Each will be seen as an attempt to create a conceptual psychology dealing in the relative meanings presented to the human organism in its cultural milieu and comprehensible to humans in other milieus.

Each parallels the distinction between psychoanalysis and psychology in Freud's work. Psychology is, in all cases, conceived as an adjunct discipline used to validate the explanations of the facts of culture which other disciplines purported to furnish -- just as the model of the mind furnished in Freud's Project supplied the theoretical substantiation for his therapeutic techniques in psychoanalysis.

Finally, each is commensurate with a paradigm for conceptual psychology which did not emerge as independent in the period in question, perhaps because of a general unwillingness to accept the implied message of total relativity of knowledge which did not become generally accepted until the twentieth century. Perhaps this psychology did not emerge as an independent discipline in its time because its premises seemed so common and self-evident that they were not seen as needing the special exclusionary status which a separate institutional identity would have given them.

The Freud case has been used here to exemplify the arguments for drawing paradigms on the basis of a discourse because the material is generally familiar. Yet if we uncover this discourse paradigm, we will find it is the paradigm that Freud left behind. (Mach is the last figure to preserve its synthesis.) This lost paradigm is a distinctive mixture of focus on psychic content, individual utterances, and the functions of the mind as they exist in a dynamic equilibrium of the individual caught between environment and individual history. Stating the paradigm this way will focus attention less on American histories of psychology, and more on the questions raised by Mitscherlich, Habermas, Adorno, and the Frankfurt School.[28] These share an emphasis on anthropology and sociology as additions to psychology and philosophy; they parallel studies of individual psyches with those of societal types, in a modern tradition of neo-Marxist thought leading up to the French.

The result of the adoption of these principles will be the delineation of a new context for the humanistic disciplines from the mid-nineteenth century through the twentieth century and the consistent push for an explanation of knowledge relating to cognition and to the data of the environment in which the knowledge is developed. Unlike the canonical histories sketched above, the paradigm of cultural psychology in the nineteenth century will be delineated on the basis of a shared repertoire of concepts and procedures, and will have to acknowledge, rather than decry, the affinity of psychology with philosophy, the theoretical mother discipline in the period. Only through such a break in the accepted patterns of canonization can the history of psychology transcend the ideological in-fighting which characterizes the twentieth century in its focus on prescriptions and on the establishment of the legitimacy of its genealogical tree, rather than on the basis of theoretical authority and communality. With this realization, a reconsideration of the relationships among the human sciences and their proliferation in the latter part of the nineteenth century can begin.

PART 2

THE PARADIGM OF CONCEPTUAL PSYCHOLOGY

CHAPTER 3

KANT AND HERBART:
THE INITIATION OF CONCEPTUAL PSYCHOLOGY

The "Copernican Revolution" which Kant identified as an equivalent to his work in *The Critique of Pure Reason* is commonly used as the starting point for modern philosophy. This text delineated a watershed between the study of philosophy as affiliated with theology or moral philosophy and a philosophy whose standards were to be likened to those of the emerging physical sciences. Before Kant's work, a majority of philosophical treatises addressed not only problems of knowledge and cognition, but also ontology, eschatology, and theism, without differentiating greatly between what today seem to be very different disciplines. Kant's *Critiques* changed the course of philosophy: he belied the existence of a general philosophy accommodating such different realms of investigation. Instead, he advocated a general set of philosophical procedures which could be applied to various objects, as he himself did in the *Critique of Practical Reason* and the *Critique of Judgment*.[1] Kant initiated a renewal in methodology for the human sciences that was to effect the entire nineteenth century.

Perhaps because of the enormity of his central contribution to the development of Western thought in the eighteenth and nineteenth centuries, other aspects of Kant's oeuvre are often slighted, even though they, too, reflect such central shifts in the conception of the disciplines to which they belong.[2] Traditionally, Kant is considered an Idealist, a member of the dominant paradigm for late eighteenth- and nineteenth-century German thought. In many ways, however, he is not, for his work in method can be applied both to the epistemological questions of Idealism and to more empirical sciences. Consequently, Kant's impact is broader than his original corpus of work -- or rather, he addresses a broad range of topics in more minor essays than are represented in his major works. A series of lectures, published under the title

Anthropology from a Pragmatic Point of View, is an example of
Kant's preliminary work on a discipline. Here, he applies his new
scientific method to the sciences of anthropology and psychology.[3]
This work, together with several texts on psychology by Kant's
student Johann Friedrich Herbart, demonstrates how Kant's
"Copernican Revolution" also affected the sciences of the mind, as
well as philosophy. How did these two scholars initiate the
development of a conceptual psychology? That is, what new
factors did they initiate into the discourse of psychology to
differentiate them from their predecessors?

First and foremost, Kant's model of mind from the *Critique of
Pure Reason* outlined reason, understanding, and judgment as
innate capacities of the mind. This definition was different from the
explanations of the various *Geistesvermögen* (capacities or
faculties of the mind) which had been the purview of the
seventeenth and eighteenth centuries, and so predicated a new view
of psychology. Where in earlier models the capacities of the mind
had been assumed to be specific to defined areas of human behavior
such as morality, appetition, or logic, Kant shifted this definition so
that the innate capacities of the mind were a set of *activities* applied
to the data with which humans come into contact. This shift
constitutes the first part of a new paradigm, a focus on mental
activity rather than physiological localization. In Kant's view,
morality and human appetites are genetic processes which develop
as the mind works on data through its understanding, reason, and
judgment, ultimately to evolve a world view appropriate to that
mind's position in the flow of history. Kant's new "capacities of
the mind," therefore, refer not to a finished knowledge in the
human mind, but rather to a capacity for the interaction between the
world and the mind in specific areas of private and social existence.

Here, Kant introduces a second key aspect leading to a new
paradigm: the question of mental context, that is, the environment
in which the mind is functioning. In this instance, each region of
data may correlate to a different aspect of a world view. Since the
mind and the world interact to encompass the data of experience,
new studies or sciences may develop outside traditional
philosophical or theological disciplines' formulations. Thus Kant
also considered the development of mankind and human knowledge
with respect to both environment and the psychology of the thinker.

Kant's new thinking human being is a "citizen of the world" (*Weltbürger*), subject to anthropological and psychological analyses with respect to his environment.[4]

The third shift towards a new paradigm for a conceptual psychology is Kant's acknowledgement of man as not only a mental and physiological being regulated by the plans of God or nature, but also as a social entity. Man as a social being would be responsive to the pressures of not only the environment, but also the social group, pressures which directly affect the course of man's development and condition recoverable differences between peoples of different ages and races. This anthropology and psychology of groups are part of the study of individual mind and its rational capacities in the narrower sense set by the *Critique of Pure Reason* or *Practical Reason*. This third innovation treats products of culture as influential in mind -- a radically new stance that will account for more than just the products of mind, because it assumes that these products will exert a reciprocal influence on further developments of mind.

The present discussion seeks to outline these shifts in the paradigm as systematically effected first by Kant in his *Anthropology*, and then by Herbart in a form more oriented to physiology.[5] Neither was able to completely free his work from the goals set by the generation of their predecessors with regard to group morality and the teleology of historical development. Both, however, aided in the delineation of the discourse of conceptual psychology under discussion here. Each also was instrumental in freeing the inherited philosophical vocabulary from the metaphysical assumptions which had to that point impeded the development of either an anthropology or a psychology which conceived of man as an historical being rather than only a cognitive one.

In making this association, we are moving beyond the stereotypical conception of Idealist psychology to look for a correspondence on the level of a paradigm. Kant said that one could not apply mathematics to the soul -- true enough. Yet in his work on psychology, Kant opened a new field where mathematics could be used by including biological and historical influences on mental activity. Particular biological influences are quantifiable (Herbart's work stressed these), and they will also play a part in the

development of a paradigm for psychology which accommodates
pragmatic, as well as theoretical, mind.[6]

3.1 The Position of Kant's Anthropology

The *Anthropology from a Pragmatic Point of View* was a set
of lectures delivered by Kant, first in the 1772-73 academic year,
and then repeatedly until 1795-96. These lectures, in a certain
sense, constituted Kant's own attempt at popularization.[7] They
were his demonstration of an *application* of the procedures
introduced in the *Critiques* to another science. They were originally
published in 1798, with a second edition in 1800, and seem to have
attracted attention in broad circles of intellectuals and authors, not
necessarily within the philosophical community. The poet Goethe
found them "charming," although too much to read in one dose
(one had to read it a bit at a time, since Kant was not optimistic
about human development), and further noted: "From this
perspective [the development of mankind], man always sees
himself in a pathological condition, and since, as the old man
[Kant] assures us, one cannot become reasonable before one's
sixtieth year, it is a bad joke to declare the rest of one's life
foolish."[8]

Goethe's comments echo the general reception of the piece -- a
work accepted as Kant's amusement. Schleiermacher considered it
a travesty, since it did not answer "how it would be possible to
reflect about the mind, if there is no freedom in this reflection, and
no proof of the truth in it is present" (a strict Idealist's criticism).[9]
Only Herbart, in 1833, gave the text perhaps a fairer review,
acknowledging it as a popularization, "in part as an introduction to
physiology and to psychology, insofar as these two meet in
anthropology."[10] Herbart, too, mentions that many of Kant's
assertions lack empirical proof from nature, but adds that
mathematical psychology (his own enterprise) could provide these
missing proofs.

That the work is a popularization, however, does not mean
that it is any less consistent as an example and application of
transcendental philosophy. Kant's application of transcendental
philosophy separated the facts of human existence, their influence

on human development, and the structure of the mind. The "pragmatic intent" with which Kant prefaces his work is none other than an empirical study exemplifying the utility of a transcendental approach to the human sciences. When this approach is applied to the realm of historical existence, two distinct sciences emerge: a physical anthropology of the type associated with the major ethnographic studies of the nineteenth century, and a conceptual psychology as a science of the mind accounting for the physiological change and development in history of the human organism. Kant's lectures leave both sciences as sketches subject to misconstrual, but they do introduce a synthesis of history and transcendental philosophy in the pragmatic realm.

The differentiation between transcendental philosophy, anthropology, and psychology is one of the direction of approach. Transcendental philosophy stresses mind; anthropology starts from the physical existence of man and looks for evidence of mind; psychology starts with the individual mind or soul, and tries to constitute the inner sense of a being, instead of formal consciousness. Moreover, as M.J. Gregor adds:

> [Kant] wants to distinguish pragmatic anthropology from both psychology, which traces mental phenomena to a principle other than the body (a "soul"), and physiology, which traces them to the brain. Pragmatic anthropology does not try to "explain" mental events and human behavior generally by tracing them to their sources in a principle or substance, whether corporeal or incorporeal. (KA, XIII-XIV)

This stresses the relationship of the three disciplines. Still, Kant's approaches to both anthropology and psychology tend to be dismissed as independent contributions to knowledge, since they are in the pragmatic sphere. In the worst formulation, Kant has provided a Machiavellian "how-to use other men" for your own purposes on the basis of knowledge of their motivations, or as an incomplete description of man's social relationships (KA, XIX, XXV).

For the purpose of uncovering a paradigm, we will explore Kant's *Anthropology* as a popularization with a coherent epistemological program representative of a new discourse -- a redefinition of the term "popularization," and its underlying attention to a redefinition of both anthropology and the psychology which grounds it. The structure of the text itself is instructive in seeing not only the positions which Kant had inherited as the structures of these disciplines, but also the direction in which this, his critique of the social sciences, would lead into the conceptual psychology of the nineteenth century.

3.2 The Program of the Anthropology

In a brief preface to the *Anthropology*, Kant defines the scope of his program for his readers; he wishes to acknowledge humans as "earthly beings." Still, he can pursue one of two options in acquiring that knowledge:

> A discussion of knowledge about man, systematically composed (anthropology), can adopt either a *physiological* or a *pragmatic* perspective. -- Physiological knowledge of man focuses on the discovery of that which *nature* makes of man; the pragmatic, on that which he as a freely acting being makes, or can and should make, of himself. . . . when he uses his observations about what has been found to hinder or stimulate memory in order to expand or apply it, and needs knowledge of man for this purpose, this would be a part of anthropology for *pragmatic* purposes; and that is precisely what concerns us here. (KA, 3)

This program, which is an attempt to delineate the parameters of a new science, is commensurate with those represented in the *Critiques*. In this case, however, Kant does not investigate the limits on thought, moral activity, or aesthetics, but the limits on man's development as regulated by his social intercourse. Eschewing the purely physiological restrictions on man's activity, Kant investigates the limits which man's own thoughts have on his development, as a product of choice, memory, and self-purported goal.

Kant terms such an investigation "pragmatic." This

investigation will focus on interpersonal functions within society. First, it will delineate the practical restrictions on the realization of the moral, ideational, and aesthetic goals, or clearness and distinctness criteria, proposed in the three *Critiques*. That is, an anthropological investigation outlines the interactions between mind and world that can prevent the group from realizing the abstract potentials of mind. History and custom, for example, can impede knowledge. Kant's *Anthropology* is a modern discipline that will *a priori* admit and circumscribe the boundaries of our ability to become "citizens of the world" (*Weltbürger*). A pragmatic anthropology in Kant's sense distinguishes the real from the theoretically possible.

The structure of Kant's book reflects the preface's two-fold aim with an "Anthropological Didactic" and an "Anthropological Characterization." These are two greatly unequal sections, with the first constituting Kant's delineation of the powers of the mind applied to man's existence in the world, and the second defining humans as individuals in anthropological terms, relating them to the races of the world. Kant's *Didactic* is the key to the new discourse of conceptual psychology -- it connects anthropological thought to epistemology. Here, Kant explains the cognitive capacity of man (*Erkenntnisvermögen*), as it relates to appetition, aversion, and volition (*Lust, Unlust,* and *Begehrungsvermögen*).

Kant's discussion of the fundamental activities of the mind is comparatively brief. He sketches the "ego" and its role in the primary derivation of concepts of our sense data, guided by volition and the appetition of the individual. For Kant, all knowledge is predicated on self-consciousness and a sense of the ego (*egoism*). This sense of self, however, conditions the individual's first knowledge, that derived from individual perceptions, which is not the general knowledge to which all thinking beings have access (KA, 10-11). Theoretically, all humans share the categories; pragmatically, all individuals base their knowledge on a sense of self.

The beginnings of utilitarian knowledge -- knowledge which extends beyond the purview of the individual -- come with the ability to take conscious control of the products of mental activity, the "representations" or "ideas" (*Vorstellungen*; KA, 13):

The attempt to become conscious of one's representations

> is either *paying attention to* (attentio) or the *turning away
> from* (abstratio) a representation of which I am conscious.
> . . . a real act of the cognitive capacity by which one idea
> of which we are conscious is held apart from its connection
> with other ideas in one consciousness. (KA, 13)

For Kant, then, knowledge is composed in three successive stages:
first, representation (an active presentation of sense data to
consciousness, associated in the *Critiques* with the activity of the
productive imagination); then, a conscious paying attention, with
volition attempting to take perceptions under conscious control; and
finally, an abstraction, a schematized idea which represents the
"condition of its ideas under [the mind's] control" (KA, 13).

Attention is the basis for all developments in thought, both in
the more limited realm of self-reflection, and for the larger
orientation of a thinking being within the data of experience (KA,
14). Through attention, knowledge becomes available to thought,
which is necessary because "the field of *obscure representations* is
the largest in man" (KA, 17). Before attention is paid to received
data, representations are only partially available to conscious
thought because they have not achieved the level of clearness and
distinctness which comes through abstraction:

> The consciousness of a representation which suffices to
> *distinguish* one object from another is *clearness*. But that
> through which the *composition* [Zusammensetzung] of
> representations becomes clear is called *distinctness*. Only
> the latter allows a sum of representations to become
> knowledge . . . an ordering of the manifold . . . (KA, 18)

These are the first terms crucial to the new paradigm: the questions
of composition and differentiation of representations, showing the
mind as a registration machine.

Here, then, is Kant's pragmatic definition of cognition
[Erkenntnis] as knowledge attained. It results from the mind's
movement towards an increasingly clear and distinct perception and
control of entering sense data. Kant realizes that this is an active
definition of knowledge as a result of the process of perception.
He conceives of this as a redefinition of the terminology of the

Critiques in terms of the schematizing activity of the mind:

> One sees readily that, if the capacity for *knowledge* in general is to be called *understanding* (in the most general sense of the term), understanding must include *the capacity to construe* given representations in order to produce *intuitions, the capacity to differentiate* what is common to several of them in order to produce *concepts*, and *the capacity to reflect* in order to produce *knowledge* of the object (attentio, abstratio, and reflexio). (KA, 19)

These new definitions represent a contribution to the paradigm, because they construe thought as fundamental activities of mind applied to data of the world, thereby introducing a potential social dimension into the model.

This model of the mind represents Kant's synthesis of the principles developed in the *Critiques of Pure Reason* with his announced pragmatic perspective. This "pragmatics" is relativizing, focusing on the relation of the sense data which are filtered through the body to the development of concepts according to the mechanisms of understanding and reason. The capacity to construe representations (*Auffassungsvermögen*), the capacity to differentiate properties (*Absonderungsvermögen*), and the capacity to reflect (*Überlegungsvermögen*) are the separate capacities of the mind summarized under the term "understanding." Together, these are descriptions of the basic schematizing activities of mind which differentiate the joinder between the sphere of sense knowledge and that of intellectual knowledge. This opens the possibility of the relativity of mental processing, which is the theme of the later part of the nineteenth century, and a crucial term in the discourse of conceptual psychology.

Moreover, this model for pragmatic schematization considers individual volition as it may affect the developments of either intuitions based on sense data or the intellectual knowledge (*Erkenntnis*) abstracted from it. "Attention" is also part of the schematizing process; it is a sense of focus given by the individual to the data he wishes to consider. A lack of attention creates problems of clearness and distinctness, problems which play such a crucial role in intellectual knowledge in the *Critique of Pure*

Reason. Attention is a second facet of pragmatic thought, for Kant has made knowledge of the world contingent upon the receptivity and focus of each individual's life world. Attention is a conscious volition to think according to a particular innate interest of the individual.

What is later called "experience" is for Kant "empirical knowledge" (KA, 21). This empirical knowledge must be entered into the individual's conscious processing before knowledge is evolved. This is done by means of attention, which attaches a concept or representation to the empirical data. The pragmatic thought resulting from this processing has two aspects:

> Because of this, consciousness is divided into *discursive* consciousness (which must come first since, as logical consciousness, it gives the rule) and *intuitive* consciousness. Discursive consciousness (pure apperception of our mental activity) is simple: *the "I" of reflection* contains no manifold and is always the same in every judgment, because it is merely the formal element of consciousness. *Inner experience,* on the other hand, contains the matter of consciousness and a manifold of empirical inner intuition, *the "I" of apprehension* (and so an empirical apperception). (KA, 22)

This is again a crucial differentiation between formal processing and the material which is processed, stressing the relativizing aspect of the new discourse as part of the data source.

Kant relates experience, the perceiving subject, and knowledge in a fully active triad. Here, he differs from his predecessors in acknowledging the virtual (*Schein*) as central to subject-object relationships and thought. Receptivity to sensations and the formation of inner intuitions are the first reflexes of conscious mind. This mind is "formal" and a locus of "discursive consciousness" -- that is, it is a point of origin and of inherent focus for the activities of the mind, the point of reference from which all concepts are formed. The "*I* of apprehension," in contrast, is the image of "myself" which forms itself in consciousness as the total experience of the body's contact with its surroundings. The "*I* of apprehension" is the concept of "me in the world" which reflects the historical accretions of the "me as reflection," the conceptualized experience of the physical presence to which the thinking ego is attached. One's "appearance" as a being in the world of sense is as much a part of the manifold of sensation as is any other sensual intuition which has not achieved the level of a concept through the process of differentiating or judgment. Experience then is not only the empirical knowledge of the objective world, but also a vehicle for the concept of the self as truth in the world. This split of the ego into two equal halves attaches mind to world in characteristic fashion for the new paradigm, thus stressing their reciprocity.[11]

Kant's statement is at odds with the concept of the relation of the self to the world familiar from systems such as Leibniz' *Monadology*, and thus are keys to the new discourse. There, and in other interpretations of the mind from the Enlightenment, the mind and its products have a privileged position vis-à-vis sense data. The typical eighteenth-century notion was that both mind and world originate from the same source in the Creation. Mind purportedly mirrors a greater part of the plan of Creation than does the material world. In contrast to this older position, Kant does not assume a complete mirroring between Creation, the mind and material. Instead, he sees that the mind and the material world exist in a continued interaction through which human knowledge may be increased by means of the senses. In consequence of this shift towards an interactive model, Kant vindicates the senses from charges of causing disorder, dominating over the understanding, or deceiving (KA, 24-25). In Kant's new model, the senses stand under the control of the understanding, while acting as the channel through which intuitions of the world may be built. In the older paradigm, the senses are negligible in the development of knowledge of the world, secondary to the rational mirroring of all the elements of Creation. For Kant, the senses serve as a horizon of experience for the activity of the understanding and as a source for undifferentiated intuitions out of which knowledge can be constituted. Moreover, this horizon of the senses remains subject to the clearness and distinctness criteria applied to knowledge, thus raising them to higher validity than in the older paradigm.

The senses continue to play a role in higher-order thought (that is, thought about matters in the realm of the understanding rather

than of sensible intuition). Kant presents in detail the different
horizons in which the senses operate, as horizons imposed onto
human capacity for cognition and knowledge. First and foremost,
the senses condition the dealings which understanding has with the
world. "Appearance" (*Schein*), illusions, and other images are
misuses of the power of the senses. With them, especially the false
morality of society, certain humans attempt to use sense data
against the power of the understanding. Despite this negative
capacity, imagination and the senses contribute in a meaningful way
to the workings of the understanding:

> The *sensibility* in the capacity for knowledge (the capacity
> for representations in intuition) contains two divisions: the
> *senses* and the *imagination*. (KA, 32)

Kant defines the imagination as the capacity to deal with time, and
as the way to associate present and past representations. Moreover,
this capacity reverses relationships between mind and world,
allowing the mind to generate representations.

The distinction between directions is also important in
distinguishing types of representations:

> The former is the capacity for intuition in the presence of
> the object, the latter, also when the object is not present. --
> The senses, in turn, are divided into the *outer* senses and
> *inner* senses (*sensus internus*). In outer sense, the human
> body is affected by physical things; in inner sense, by the
> mind. We should distinguish between *inner sense*, which
> is a mere capacity of perception (of empirical intuition),
> and the feeling of pleasure and displeasure -- that is, our
> susceptibility to be determined by certain representations,
> either to maintain or avoid the condition of this
> representation -- which could be called *interior sense*
> (sensus interior). A sense representation of which we are
> conscious as such is called *sensation*, especially when the
> act of sensing [Empfindung] simultaneously calls attention
> to the state of the subject. (KA, 32)

Sight, touch, and hearing are the "outer senses" which tend to provide more objective knowledge, knowledge of things outside us. The "inner senses" are taste and smell, which are more subjective in that their evidence is more difficult to separate from the organ in which they are located. Kant's third division, the "interior sense," is a mark of affect: the long-term effects which sense data has on our nervous system. This tripartite division anticipates the division made by Ernst Mach in his *Analysis of the Sensations*. For him, there are three frames of reference in which sense data is presented to our consciousness: A, B, C, . . . (the data of the outside world); K, L, M, . . . (the subset of the objects of the world which seems under our more intimate control, mainly our bodies); and α, β, γ, . . . (those sensations which do not correspond to immediately present objects, such as memories and sensations of pain, pleasure, and the like). This division is characteristic of the new paradigm; it constitutes a recognition that the knowledge tied to each of these spheres of data may be of a fundamentally different type, and unified only in the activity of cognition itself.

Kant modifies each of these definitions somewhat. Outer senses are those that identify objects as outside us (KA, 31). However, if they receive sensations above a certain threshold value, the receiving consciousness will also experience a correlate sensation within its organism. This correlate sensation is the mark of inner sense (what he later started calling interior sense):

> Inner sense is not pure apperception, a consciousness of what man *does*, for this belongs to the capacity for thinking; but rather of that which he undergoes, as far as he is affected by his own play of thoughts. Inner intuition lies at its base, and therefore also the relation of representations in time (as they are simultaneous or successive in it). (KA, 31)

This is Kant's definition of the ego of experience, built up out of representations over historical time.

The inner experience he speaks of is not "anthropological" (based on outside data), but rather psychological -- a region peculiar to itself. This description provides the final aspect of Kant's pragmatic breakdown of the transcendental unity of the manifold, an expansion on the *Critique of Pure Reason*. This inner sense is a kind of staging area related to inner intuition and reflection -- the ability to think about sensations, and constitute them into coherent inner experience and a world view. For Kant, these are the only conditions under which the interface between the mind and the world can be explained; they are the core of Kant's definition of the pragmatic realm. In this definition, Kant has explained the difference between mere organic registration of facts, and the ability to use these facts of the sensations in the mind with attention or reflection. This pragmatic anthropology thus defines the space for a new psychology, not teleological or Idealist, but one focusing on the individual.

After describing the registration and conscious processing of facts, Kant further differentiates the model. First, he correlates the characteristics of sensations with their likelihood of entering into active use by the mind. He defines various threshholds as pragmatic limits on their registration: "The sensations of the senses are increased in intensity by 1. contrast, 2. novelty, 3. change, 4. intensification" (KA, 40). That is, if a sensation contrasts with others around it, it will set itself off so the mind can more easily take note of its unique characteristics. Newness or novelty serves similarly to differentiate sensations as not habitual; change breaks monotony, and intensification increases tension (*Anspannung*), thus pointing towards a maximum on a scale which had to this point not revealed itself. These are further pragmatic critera added to Kant's interactive model of mind, and further terms in the new discourse of psychology.

Kant's second expansion of his interactive model differentiates between the productive imagination and the reproductive imagination. The capacity of the mind which Kant designates as "imagination" aids in the process of thought and reflection. It is a staging area accommodating time differences as part of the interface between inner sense and interior sense. Again reflecting the definitions found in the three *Critiques*, Kant associates the imagination with the ability to call up and maintain attention to a pool of data before understanding or judgment processes it into knowledge.

Reproductive imagination is added in the *Anthropology* as the ability "to bring back into the mind an empirical intuition previously undergone (exhibitio derivativa)" (KA, 44). This imagination is part of schematizing, because it is also "dichtend" (poeticizing or making dense) and "retrieving." In contrast, the productive imagination works before the sense experience of its objects. It is not, however, a creative imagination in the sense used in the poetics of Romanticism, for it cannot create classes of sense data which it has never encountered:

> . . . it is still not creative, but must get the *material* for its constructs from the senses. But these constructs, as we form memories of them, are not so universally communicable as concepts of understanding. (KA, 45)

This difference is crucial for the new paradigm of psychology, for it adds a complete diachronic dimension to the model. Such a dimension is not present in older paradigms -- any reference to innate ideas makes knowledge essentially synchronic.

Kant uses this model of psychological interaction in the *Anthropology* to constitute a program not normally associated with the more modern concept of "anthropology" as the science of man.[12] Kant's version is not devoted to physical geography or physiology, but rather synthesizes his research in epistemology with a view of man in the world. As he develops this model in the lectures, Kant often draws his examples from the realm of everyday experience, human habits, or behavioral patterns. Yet all were discussed in terms of representation, knowledge, and active versus passive cognition or imagination. This is the advent of the new paradigm, stressing mental contents, context, and activity.

Kant needed to develop an encompassing model for human thought patterns in the world. He did so in order to develop an anthropology accounting for human behavior in terms commensurate with the abstract or pure thought patterns which were the subject of the three *Critiques*. The *Anthropology* parallels the stricter programs of the *Critiques* while at the same time deferring them. In anthropology, he discusses the capacities of the mind associated with everyday behavior as parallel to understanding, reason and judgment. Still, the new anthropology and psychology he outlines deny the possibility of reducing human behavior to the theoretical clarity of abstract knowledge in his longer works. This is no longer Idealism in the strict sense.

Proceeding through his analysis of human behavior in systematic fashion, however, Kant moves beyond the preconditions for human knowledge or cognition, to turn to the products of the human mind -- to the fields which the mind produces. In traditional, pre-Kantian terms, each field of knowledge is attributable to a "capacity" or faculty of the mind (*Erkenntnisvermögen*). However, Kant reanalyzes these capacities from the pragmatic viewpoint he has already laid down.

3.3 The Mind's "Capacities" and Their Relation to Knowledge

Traditional definitions of the capacities of the mind such as imagination and appetition tended to analyze them in terms of the goals and types of knowledge they produced, or their field-specific analyses. In shifting to a new paradigm, Kant provides an alternate path to their understanding: an analysis of each capacity in terms of the precise fashion of mental processing which is associated with it. His new analysis describes the associations of sense data and the activities of mind which actually generate the knowledge formerly attributed to the capacities.

The imagination is the topic which leads Kant to discuss as his first capacity the *Dichtungsvermögen* (a "capacity for poetry," or -- in a nomenclature more parallel to the alternate definition of "dichten" as "to make fast or solid" -- "a capacity for invention"). He begins to describe how minds produce:

> There are three different kinds of the sensible capacity for invention: the constructing capacity of intuition in space (imaginatio plastica), the associative capacity of intuition in time (imaginatio associans), and that of affinity due to the common origin of representations from each other (affinitas). (KA, 50)

Each of these variants represents a different activity for making concrete representations. The constructing capacity relates to the gift of the artist, who creates figures; association is the capacity which evokes "traces of impressions as representations sympathetic to one another" in the brain, and so relates past to present (KA, 52). Affinity orients the imagination on the basis of similarity, as in the sense of chemical "elective affinities." The latter capacity identifies representations as likely to fit together. It posits combinations of representations which will exhibit new properties (KA, 52-53). Thus Kant does not differentiate the three types of imagination on the basis of the fundamental activity (association in the broader sense, an active comparison within the structure of the mind). Instead, he looks to their goals and products, their directions and materials with which they work (concrete characteristics, characteristics in the broadest sense, or complementary characteristics). These three capacities have restricted realms of activity. As Kant concludes: "Imagination is thus not as creative as one would pretend" (KA, 52).

At this point, Kant "deconstructs" each of the commonly named capacities of the mind, with the goal of seeing the activities and material with which they function. The term "deconstruct," drawn from Derrida, is appropriate here, for Kant explores what activities of mind each concept includes or defers, trying to find out what really is included in the coinages.

He anticipates the structuralists in dealing with paired capacities of the mind, the first of which are memory and foresight:

> The capacity to deliberately bring the past to mind is the capacity of remembering (*Erinnerungsvermögen*), and the capacity to represent something as future is the capacity of foresight. To the extent that they are sensible, both are based on the association of representations as past and future states of the subject with the present one; and while they are not themselves perceptions, they serve to connect perceptions *in time* -- that which is no more to be connected to that which is to come, through that which is present. (KA, 56-57)

Both memory and foresight are thus projections of representations in time. They compare the material of the sensations as it has been stored in the mind, and as it will affect future thought as expectations. However, there is an important difference between them. Memory (*Gedächtnis*) is the sum of what is remembered.

This is different than the reproductive imagination discussed earlier, because the reproductive imagination is concerned with representations on the level of the intuition, and thus of mental processing. In contrast, memory serves the higher capacities of the mind associated with ego and history. Kant explains, "To *hold* something in memory, to easily *reflect* upon it, and to *retain* it for a long time: these are the formal perfections of memory" (KA, 57).

Because it relates to experience rather than mental processing, the memory is under greater control and influence of the volition, and serves as, for example, "ingenious memory" or "judicious memory" -- a memory applied to the purposes of life. Foresight is equally under conscious control as "predictability" in the scientific sense. Foresight projects causal relationships among sensations into other situations. Moreover, foresight is often accompanied by an emotion because the concepts which it extends may be dark or obscure. The difficulties in processing obscure concepts can be interpreted as emotional reactions to the problems involved. This analysis of foresight does not only account for temporal projection; it also is developed in terms of the data addressed, again upholding the new paradigm, including mental processing, the data of experience, and a real-world interface. This is another pragmatic explanation, stressing a block to cognitive processing mostly overlooked in the *Critiques*. Kant will go on to differentiate "predict/vorhersagen," "prophecy/weissagen," and "divine/wahrsagen" according to the sources of their data: respectively, experience, "counternatural" circumstances, and the gods.

In adding memory and foresight to the capacities of the mind in his model, Kant has bridged the gap between lower- and higher-order thought in a way not done in the eighteenth century, but essential for the paradigm of the nineteenth century. He describes interactions of sensations as data of the mind, beginning at the level of concrete intuition, and moving through volitional manipulation of data, accompanied by subjective emotion when the mind is affected by illogical spots in the data it processes. In earlier philosophy, these were construed as separate capacities, yet from Kant's point of view, they do not introduce any new mental activities. They are differentiates only with respect to the source of data involved in each association -- they represent a question of scope, not of quality.

Perhaps the greatest break with the old paradigm is implied here. Kant implies that the *capacities* are not innate as such. Instead, each capacity is a concept for a set of innate mental activities, related to the individual's interaction with the environment and individual volition. Moreover, in this redefinition of the capacities, Kant recognizes the pragmatic limits of human control over the mental processes in his definition of the emotions, which is why he can discuss "mental disorders." He seeks to discover what actual defect or insufficiency in processing sensations they represent -- insufficiencies in terms of directional errors or misassociations of the data involved.[13] Using this processing model, Kant can also discuss those capacities of the mind not associated with conscious volition, such as dreams (KA, 63). Such involuntary movements of the imagination are probably necessary for the mind, but since they are involuntary, Kant does not discuss them further.

Very important for the nineteenth century is Kant's explication of another capacity of the volition, the capacity to designate (*Bezeichnungsvermögen, facultas signatrix*) or to use signs:

> The capacity to construe the present and connect the representation of the previously known with the past is the capacity to designate. -- The activity of mind which effects this connection is *designation* (signatio), which is also called *signalling*, the greatest degree of which is called *distinguishing* [Auszeichnung]. (KA, 64)

Kant uses this definition to preface a discussion of the nature of sign systems, symbols, figures, and characters. However, he is in fact also initiating one of the most powerful aspects of the new paradigm: a general discussion of *analogy* and *partial analogy* as they relate to the attention paid the data under consideration by the mind. This introduces a schematizing criterion that accounts for differences between lower- and higher-order thought.

In a typical redefinition of cognition accounting for the data input, Kant distinguishes between natural and artificial signs and portents (signs of miracles). These discussions are conducted in the terms of his day (referring to Swedenborg) and anticipate the

more developed discussions of sign systems to be found in the
work of Wilhelm vom Humboldt and Fichte:

> All language is the designation of thoughts, and, in turn,
> the finest means of designating thoughts is through
> language, this greatest of means by which one understands
> himself and others. Thinking is *speaking* with one's self .
> . . and consequently also internal *hearing* (by means of the
> reproductive imagination). (KA, 65)

This is a general theory of signs as they adhere in memory and
define an ego as history. Language is the best-developed
designation system; still, all signs (even including medals and other
distinctions [*Auszeichnungen*]) serve the purpose of
communication, both within the group and for self-improvement.
The capacity to designate, therefore, establishes the interface
between the cognition of the individual mind and that of the group
and opens up an avenue for the group's improvement. Through
language and other signs, the human mind responds to and
processes the sensible facts of the environment. More importantly,
through signs, the mind takes control of this environment in the
designations and concepts; they actively mark data for the
volition.[14]

Treating mental signs as means to communicate will become
typical of the new paradigm for nineteenth-century psychology.
Here, Kant initiates a discussion that will be completed by Mach
and Freud. The individual and the group will exert pressure on
each other in their interactions by means of signs drawn from their
shared environment. If their communication is to succeed, these
signs must be referentially valid (that is, they must conform to the
perceived experience of the group), not necessarily ontologically
valid. With this, the group establishes its norm for meaning --
terms like "well" or "ill" only have relative meaning within the
community of speakers, and rarely a discrete ontic reference.

Kant introduces sign systems into psychology as crucial to the
interaction between the individual and the group. In addition, he
also adds individuality by integrating volition into the model of the
mind. Adding volition as a mental process redefines the capacities
of the mind discussed in the three *Critiques*: understanding, reason,

and judgment. In the *Anthropology*, the popularized version of his work, Kant differentiates succinctly among the three capacities as an "anthropological comparison":

> 1) Understanding: "the capacity for cognition of rules (through concepts)";
> 2) Reason: "the capacity for deriving the particular from the general, and for representing it according to principles as necessary";
> 3) Judgment: "the capacity to discover the particular, insofar as it is an instance of the rules." (KA, 69-71).

These define processing strategies as the essence of inner sense. Kant distinguishes higher-order capacities of thought on the basis of the directionality of mental activity: particular to general, general to particular, and specification of the particular. These definitions are drawn from the perspective of mind alone, not as an anthropology of mind in the world, without reference to the data which will fill these capacities.

When these higher-order capacities of mind are projected into the world, he outlines a characterology of mankind on the basis of mental function, or of behaviors manifest in the social world. The *Critiques*, in which Kant discussed representations in general, are a model of the cognitive capacities of the mind. In the *Anthropology*, Kant turns to individual representations, and finally to externalized *systems of representations*, to social systems, behaviors, and character roles such as sagacity and genius pertaining to the appearance of the individual in the world. Kant is thus implying a synthesis of transcendental idealism, anthropology, and psychology, a combination which signals a paradigm shift away from eighteenth-century norms. Still, Kant does not manage to achieve the new discourse completely, even as he is redefining old terms on new principles.

Even the three capacities of the mind as defined in the three *Critiques* are linked with volition, and so can be shifted into the realm of personal psychology and cultural influence. They deal with the conscious setting of directions of investigation about the data of the sensations:

> Because in the last instance, the whole use of the cognitive

capacity for its own advancement, even in theoretical knowledge, requires reason, which gives the rule, according to which it alone can be furthered: thus one can summarize the claim which reason makes on this capacity in three questions, posed according to the three faculties: "What do I *want*? (asks the understanding); What does it *depend on*? (asks judgment); What are its *results*? (asks reason)." (KA, 95)

These three questions correspond to interest and attention consciously directed towards the data of sensibility, and tie individuality into Transcendental Idealism.

Kant has not, however, realized the full implications of the area he has opened. The volition manifest in these directions must, in the sense of the Enlightenment, be held under a moral governor. In the *Anthropology*, Kant's "maxims for thinkers" still echo his "What is Enlightenment?": "1) think for yourself;" 2) in communicating with people, posit yourself in the position of the other; 3) always think consistently with yourself (KA, 96-97). These are models for three types of thinking: setting negative or positive limits, or being consequent and following through (respectively, also freedom from constraint, liberal thinking, and consistency). Allowing for such general patterns of thought brings a deconstruction of prevailing eighteenth-century morality, since it stresses the intent of communication instead of norms.

The shift into new perspectives and the glimpse of the new paradigm fall away after the end of Book I of the lectures. This redefinition of the faculties of the mind concludes Kant's description of cognition. In Book II of the *Anthropology*, "The Feelings of Pleasure and Displeasure," and Book III, "On the Appetitive Capacity," Kant begins a series of analyses of the human cognitive capacities as they manifest themselves in man's activity in the world. Desire, boredom, interest, taste, and appetite all are presented in the terms already delineated. The emotions and appetites are conditioned as activities of the mind in an interface of previous experience with present sensible data and with the capacity for attention innate in the organism. As such, each affect constitutes a judgment on a set of representations pointing to the education and experience of that individual.

A hint of Kant's break with the Enlightenment remains. An affect or passion also has the chance of being blocked:

> An inclination that the subject's reason can subdue only with difficulty or not at all is *passion*. In contrast, an *affect* is a feeling of pleasure or displeasure in the present state that does not allow the subject to give rise to *reflection* (the reasonable representation of whether one should give himself up to it or refuse it). (KA, 119)

Affects thus make the individual unable to follow his principles and can cause the soul to be blocked. They do not stem expressly from the body, but rather hinder the normal functioning of the perceptual apparatus at the level of appetites, propensities, and instincts -- subjective motivations derived originally from the senses, but then adhering to the cognitive capacity of man. "Affects causes a momentary rupture in freedom and in self-control," and can stem from either natural or cultural conditioning of thought patterns (KA, 134). Again, this is a pragmatism not addressed in the *Critiques*, and is a break with strict Idealism.

Since affects act as deterrents to knowledge or human cognition, Kant discusses in great detail the particulars about various types of passions or affects. He proceeds from his theory to exemplification in the "Anthropological Characterization: On How to Discern Man's Inner Self from His Exterior," a discussion divided into characters of people, sexes, nations and species (KA, 283-285). This constitutes Kant's reinterpretation of the traditional four temperaments (sanguine, melancholic, choleric and phlegmatic) as a bridge into a new paradigm. He does not stop at an outline of types but ties temperaments to life histories. Kant's goal is to explain these life histories as they parallel mental development and as they affect individuals as citizens of the world. In redefining the temperaments, he takes an older, essentially ahistorical model, and grafts in historicity through personal psychology and experience.

3.4 From Kant to Herbart

What has Kant achieved in his synthesis of an anthropological model with a model of the mind appropriate to a conceptual psychology?

First, he has redefined the "capacities of the mind" in a scientific fashion -- in terms of a limited number of broadly applicable premises: intuition (registration of sense data), the associative activities of the mind, and the historical dimension of world experience referred to in each. This is not a mathematical science, but a systematic application of principles.[15]

Second, Kant has reformulated the sense of the question as to human abilities and positions in the world as a "Weltbürger," adding history to the eighteenth-century paradigm as suggested by Herder and others. Neither the mind nor the world has absolute primacy in determining the course of history for either an individual or any group. Instead, an interaction between these poles conditions both historical development and the psychological and physiological reactions which the individuals enjoy. "Anthropology" is not the study of the physical existence of mankind, but rather a "pragmatics" for Kant, focusing on the factors which limit both the intellectual and the historical existence of men. This consideration alters other disciplines in its course, incorporating both the individual and the world into their frameworks. In so doing, Kant has altered the frame of acceptable procedures for his paradigm, rejecting the blanket application of moral and ethical principles characteristic of the older paradigm. After Kant, sciences must be defined in terms of mental activity, personal history (ego, memory), and environmental interface (including culture as well as nature).

In consequence of these two breaks with the narrower tradition of the Enlightenment, Kant has initiated a fundamental shift in the paradigm of the social sciences, and has laid the groundwork of redefined terms which allowed psychology to emerge as a science commensurate with the epistemology represented in the *Critiques*. Instead of relying on a description of man's fixed intellectual and emotive capacities, Kant has moved a model of the mind into the center of the field which was to become conceptual psychology, a science of mind and culture. Kant saw that man's knowledge was no longer a question of clearness and distinctness about the knowledge inherent in the mind or available in the world around us. With his new awareness of social intercourse and history, Kant posited that knowledge was a question of the development of the mind through its own activity in the world; his categories assume that the constitution of the world is in some sense commensurate with cognition. Yet the psychology developed in the *Anthropology* points to a more flexible or pragmatic picture of the cognitive apparatus behind the categories. Mind includes also an apparatus for volition, association, and attention (working with data, by choice or by force), functioning with the categories of understanding in a much broader panoply in the mind.

Kant's psychology points the way to a new paradigm for psychology, focusing both on the activities of the mind and on the data which is to be processed. This will be a psychology of the interactions between mind and world, and of the development of the individual in response to reason, history, and environment. Kant opened the paradigm, but because he redefined old terms, he did not initiate its discourse; the radical nature of his innovation may not have been perceived, particularly since its most radical formulation is found in the *Anthropology*, merely a "popular" text. The terminology of affects and capacities which was available to Kant did not allow him to completely reformulate a comprehensive model of mind, world, and human individuality.

Kant goes part of the way towards a new discourse when he applies the premises of the new paradigm in a series of pragmatic studies. In his protracted discussions of particulars such as "madness" and "delusion," he goes to great lengths to achieve clarity about precise definitions of terms in common usage according to his new model. Kant's redefinitions provide a taxonomy of the regions in which the mind interacts with the world, thereby completely establishing a paradigm which defers the question of the world's ontology -- a paradigm with mind in a world without the *Ding an sich*. The world is given as data, society is to be built within it to a given end; the development of mind is directed towards the realization of that end through the body. As a consequence, character type and personality, as they differ due to sex, nationality, or race, become Kant's new pragmatic concerns. He must discuss them as processes, not as givens, as earlier anthropologists tended to do. Even the body is a product of mankind's development: it is made by consciousness, as are the social and political organizations which are familiar to the readers of Kant's other works. He even argues for nationalism and racial stereotypes on the basis of his interactive model of development.

Kant opened a new set of procedures for psychology, but he was unable to surrender an absolute priority of the mind in his psychology and anthropology -- he lapses into the logocentrism of his teachers. Yet his application of transcendental philosophy to individual mind in the world allowed the emergence of a scientific psychology. He separated knowledge from the structure of the mind and from the constitution of the world (albeit not cleanly due to the teleological world view which he possessed).[16]

Many implications were drawn from this new program, and Johann Friedrich Herbart took up one of the projects left after the *Anthropology*: the analysis of the mind's powers in processing the data of the world. He applied mathematics not to the soul itself, but to the senses, the windows of the soul, in order to better define attention, association, and other of Kant's terms. Herbart's physiological-mathematical approach required ten years and two large volumes to delineate: the *Lehrbuch der Psychologie* (*Textbook on Psychology*, 1816/1834), and the *Psychologie als Wissenschaft* (*Psychology as Science*, 1824).[17] This mathematical approach helped to round out the discourse of the new paradigm.

3.5 Herbart: Psychology as Science

In the Preface and Introduction to the *Lehrbuch*, Herbart goes to great pains to establish psychology as a science, though as "neither the deepest nor the highest in the totality of philosophy, but . . . the first of the three parts of applied metaphysics." This "applied metaphysics" pulls his project in line with Kant's, and away from the charges of metaphysics to which it is normally subject.[18] Herbart feels that the history of this discipline has only considered the superficial aspects of the science to this point, and not its theoretical foundation. He even admits that Germany has seen a tradition of empirical psychology, focusing on the external signs and systems of human life, such as the historical appearances of language and institutions. From his point of view, however, such an empirical or external approach has been contaminated with a metaphysics not proper to a science. Such an assumption would, for example, give the impression that a mental system exists apart from the activity of human cognition:

> The greatest damage, though, occurs when at last one adds to the unscientifically derived concepts of *what occurs in us* an assumption which is totally distainable for metaphysical reasons: that of *our capacities* [Vermögen]. Through such, psychology changes itself completely into *mythology.* (L, 302)

As a consequence of this realization, Herbart assumes a position parallel to Kant's: he does not dispute the terminology currently in use, particularly not that of empirical psychology. Instead, hedevelops a new foundation for them, a common ground of procedures for their definition. In this, he is definitely not a metaphysician.

The terms which Herbart targets as needing the greatest redefinition are "representation," "sensation," and "appetition" (*Vorstellung, Fühlen, Begehren*). His procedures follow Kant's: the definitions of these "capacities" must balance the evidence of both the outer and inner senses. Herbart borrows these terms virtually uncritically from Kant, since he uses Kant's definitions of reason, understanding, and judgment, not entirely rejecting what he terms "the old hypothesis of the capacities of the soul" (L, 306). Yet only Herbart systematically realized to what degree inner and outer empirical evidence must be split from the activity of the mind itself (perhaps under the pressure of Fichte's differentiation of the "Tathandlung," the originary psychic act on which all consciousness is predicated):

> All spiritual life, namely, which we observe in ourselves and in others, reveals itself as an occurrence in *time*; as a constant *alteration*; as a *manifold of contingencies of differing types in one*; finally, as a consciousness of the *"I"* and *"Not-I"* . . . (L, 305)

Therefore, to accommodate this differentiation between the activity of the mind and the evidence produced by that activity, Herbart divides his work into two major parts: "Psychological Evidence, Ordered According to the Hypothesis of the Capacities," and "Explanation of Psychological Evidence, Derived from the Hypothesis of the Representations as Energies [*Kräften*]" (L, 306-307). Again, this evidence criterion distances him from metaphysics, since it is clearly empirical.

The first of these two sections summarizes the degree to which Herbart's work depended on Kant's, reviewing traditional usages of sensibility, imagination, memory, understanding, reason, judgment, the affects, appetition, and the passions. Yet in the midst of these expositions falls an assertion which distances him greatly from the formal position Kant had assumed: he believes that none of the capacities may be considered in isolation, for they each exert pressure on each other in a cause-and-effect relationship of spiritual life or activity and the representations which they produce -- even so-called "pure reason," self-consciousness and the pure apperception which constitutes inner sense (L, 312-3). Since all the capacities exist simultaneously, they must be treated by psychology in a different light than before:

> Under this premise, psychology should therefore present in the order of its teachings *not* a progression from sensibility, but rather two series of observations parallel at their origin, for which reason and sensibility constitute the starting points; the convergence of both, however, would be the uppermost region and goal, in its manifold modifications. Empirical psychology can oppose nothing to this requirement. (L, 313)

Herbart used this modification of Kant as the fundament for his scientific psychology and for his particular expansion of the paradigm of conceptual psychology.

Herbart saw that a taxonomy and description of the capacities of the soul may work for many classes of empirical investigations (such as Kant's many detailed explications in the *Anthropology*). However, a taxonomy will not suffice to describe the dynamics of thought in the mind's function. Herbart, unlike Kant, does not stop with a taxonomy of the faculties on redefined premises. Rather, he wished to describe the dynamic tension which arises in the mind due to the interactions of data and representations. Herbart thus uses the first of his two major divisions to redefine Kant's definitions of the capacities in terms of a dynamic model. In the *Anthropology*, Kant began to formulate an *interaction* between mind and world, but he did not expand it to describe the *adaptation* of mind to the world

3.6 The Dynamic Model of the Capacities

Herbart begins his reclassification with a statement about the production of representations by the mind:

> That which belongs to the capacity for representation may be classified as follows:
> A) Production
>   a) of experience
>   aa) according to the material
>   bb) according to form
>   b) of concepts which go beyond experience
> B) Reproduction.
> We will proceed through the capacity for representation according to this outline, and, in this, take into account the traditional differentiation of the assumed capacities of the soul. (L, 321)

Herbart follows Kant in dividing the productive and reproductive imaginations but extends their descriptions. He still follows Kant's methods, since he does so in terms of their origin in a region of data or experience.

Data enters through the outer senses into the inner senses, where they are classified as "series-forms" (*Reihenformen*). These are associations of data under the forms of sensibility (time and space) identified by Kant.[19] Such series-forms are preliminary organizational groups of received data, organized in terms either of their "characteristic secondary determinations" or their similarity (L, 324). After the mind sorts data into series-forms, it processes them into "logical forms," at which point conceptual work commences, following on the heels of the perceptual work done in constituting the series-forms. Only at this point can judgments, intellectual intuition, and finally, transcendental or abstract concepts like "thing," "substance," and "mutability" be formed. For formal thought, reproductions must be added to the pool of data -- that is, an accommodation to the temporal dimension of the data involved.

In articulating this primacy of data, Herbart begins to redefine the capacity for feeling or sensibility. The most developed stages of sensibility are the affects and passions; the former have both psychological and physiological dimensions, and the latter, only a psychological one. According to Herbart's model, the appetitive capacity develops next out of sensations -- first, instincts; then, reason (determinations of means and purpose); and finally, reflection (*Besonnenheit*, the ability to project ahead). Beyond these, as still higher order activities of mind, Herbart posits freedom of will and moral sense. These activities use the most of human receptive capacity in producing representations.

However, Herbart does not stop with the delineation of characteristic capacities of mind; he moves beyond a taxonomy in the second of his major sections: "Explanation of Psychological Evidence, Derived from the Hypothesis of the Representations as Energies."[20] Here, the distinctiveness of Herbart's position vis-à-vis Kant and his distinctive contribution to the emerging paradigm of psychology come forth.

Herbart's first amplification questions the relationship between soul and life force -- a metaphysical question. For his solution, Herbart defines representations as energies (*Kräfte*) in terms which anticipate Freud's notions of traces in the neurones explicated in the *Project for a Scientific Psychology*.[21] He begins: "Representations become energies in their resistance to each other. This happens when several opposing ones converge" (L, 369). He thus builds on his earlier descriptions. Representations have formed by the translation of data in the sensibility into the logical capacities. Once they enter the cognitive structure of the mind, they make themselves felt by asserting their position within the mass of representations comprising the memory, experience and logical knowledge of an individual. Moreover, the influence which they exert on each other may be either facilitive or inhibitive. Entering representations may either aid the conceptual processing of further data, or cause a "degree of obscuring" (L, 370). This expands a mind model even further towards the pragmatic, since the reproduction of such traces or representations is not a question only of memory or will. It also depends on the quality and quantity of representations associated with the desired reproduction.

Herbart's innovation thus construes representations not as points of information, as Kant tended to do, but as a dynamic system which must find various internal equilibria according to the conditions of its functioning. Note that he speaks expressly of "The Equilibrium and Movements of Representations" (L, 371). A mass of representations settles into an equilibrium under dynamic tension, subject to shift, built of inhibitions and the interrelations of inhibiting energies of representations. Because of such dynamic tension, a threshold of consciousness exists as an energy level below which a new stimulus cannot penetrate the system of representations in its equilibrium. If a new representation enters the system, old ones may be suppressed. In another case, the threshold energy or duration of a representation can increase -- more intense energy may be required for such a representation to be accessible to consciousness or for other similar ones to set it in motion (L, 372).

Similarly, a representation may follow a habituated transfer of energy as a "relief" for the mind -- a transfer which does not act against extant representations. In the opposite case, if a new representation exerts pressure on a great number of the extant ones, the whole "laws of movement of the spirit" will change; the patterns of representation which are typical paths of information processing within a mind will alter (L, 373). Such statements are only possible with an interactive system model of the mind. Herbart is describing the mind as a dynamic system filled with data, a situation where all input and all functions of the mind exert influence or pressure on each other. This is once again crucial to the new paradigm; it is a strong move towards the individuality of thought, since standard mental processing must work with individual life experience.

Why does the mind function as a system? The soul, states Herbart, functions as a united whole for the purpose of "self-preservation" (L, 374). For the mind's organism to survive in the world, its representations must be bound together and

available to its activity, concentrated into "an act."[22] The
representations associate with each other in two ways:

> [F]irst, they join into complexes, insofar as they converge
> without inhibition (those not opposed to each other, like
> tone and color); second, opposing ones amalgamate in
> converging, insofar as they are affected neither by random
> foreign inhibitions nor by inevitable mutual inhibitions.
> Complexes *can be complete*; amalgamations are in their
> very nature *incomplete*. (L, 374)

This is also a move towards relativity, since Herbart is adding a
depth-of-processing criterion for concepts, arguing that certain
concepts are more durable or valid than others.

Complexes represent many associated characteristics and are
designated by words. In contrast, amalgamations do not enjoy the
degree of clearness and distinctness which complexes have: their
contents are often unanalyzed, and are stored in the mind together,
awaiting future resolutions. Complexes and amalgamations are the
products of the systemic interactions of sense data in the mind.
However, at the same time, they condition the inhibitions and
facilitations which the mind will experience in its future activity.
This goes further than Kant's version of the interactive model
stressing the pragmatics of the interactions of the mind and
environment.

Herbart easily integrates traditional definitions of the mind's
capacities into this model of the mind's fundamental functions. As
energies enter into the mind, the activity which they engender in the
mass of representations often leaves residues of energy. These
residues will associate themselves with representations or
amalgamations in the mind, and will be reproduced as feelings or
appetites. They are not individual representations, but rather
intensity markers attached to other representations (L, 382).
Moreover, as representations enter the mind marked with greater or
lesser intensities, they will enter the system of representations
marked with an automatic superordination or subordination within
the mass. Herbart follows faculty psychology in calling these
"appetitive capacities," yet for him they are not representations, but
relations between representations: "degrees of inhibition, breaching

[a term anticipating Freud's usage for the entry of new stimuli into the mind], and facilitation" (L, 385). With this expansion, Herbart has tied the affects and passions to a relationship between physiological pressure and psychological pressure within the system of the mind -- again, as processes, in a more convincing account than Kant's.[23]

Herbart redefines several other terms associated with the capacities of the mind. For example, he derives the concepts "time" and "space" from the series-forms in which sensible data is first organized within the mind. They thus represent innate orderings (L, 386). Understanding and its associated concepts are parallel representations:

> Already at the start of logic one can say that all our representations are concepts *with respect to that which is represented through them. Accordingly, concepts as such exist only in our abstraction.* They are in reality as little a particular type of representation as the understanding is a discrete capacity, outside of and next to the imagination, memory, and the like. (L, 392)

Herbart speaks of names or words as abstracted or schematized concepts. They serve as designations of complexes or amalgamations built in experience, "from which nothing can split out" (L, 393). Concepts are therefore determinate and further unanalyzable (*unbestimmbar*; L, 394). This ties concepts not into metaphysics, but into life in the world, since they are data units processed by the mind.

In contrast to such univalent sensible data, judgments are compound in nature, specifying a subject and a predicate which may be individually determined (*bestimmbar*) through analysis. The mind uses this process of determination (judgment) to identify new objects:

> Each word in the language is suited to be the subject of a judgment, due to its vacillation among several meanings. A sign which has been attached to designated objects several times, each with their shifting secondary determinations, bears with it the total impression of these meanings. This

> occurs due to the predicates which are often transformed
> into adjectives in developed languages, or which are
> disguised as other connecting parts of speech, in order that
> only the most important among the correctives appear as
> the predicate in the expression. (L, 395)

Judgment is thus not a formal operation but is tied closely to the
energy of representation, and thus to this world -- another facet of
the new paradigm.

This definition of language, concepts, and judgments is
commensurate with Herbart's model of the mental system.
Energies register in mind as determinations about or properties of
objects; they tend to attain a fixed association with the concepts to
which they are tied. Yet the names or concepts themselves remain at
the level of abstractions or schematizations, subject to shifts in the
conceptual patterns within the mind. The whole mass of
representations associated with particular words leaves behind
"impressions" which can affect or slant even the clearest
abstractions or individual representations.

This description of concept and judgment formation anticipates
the more detailed discussions provided by Ernst Mach in his
Analysis of the Sensations, and reflect the innate modernity of
Herbart's approach to the systemics of the mind and sensible data.
Although the *Lehrbuch* would be in part superseded by the later
Psychologie als Wissenschaft (*Psychology as Science*), Herbart did
not significantly expand in the later book the basic model of the
mind as an equilibrium of energies, his key contribution to the new
paradigm. In the second text, Herbart stresses mathematical
psychology, in order to get an idea of the perceptual boundaries
posited in his model of mental equilibrium.

3.7 The Mathematics of Psychology

The program of *Psychology as Science* is proclaimed in a much
clearer tone than in the earlier works:

> The intent of this work is to introduce a psychology which
> would resemble research in the natural sciences, insofar as

it presupposes a completely regular connection of appearances overall, and traces it in a consideration of facts, through cautious conclusions, through daring, tested, corrected hypotheses, finally (wherever possible) through measuring magnitudes and through calculations. (PaW, 185)

The explicit considerations of the magnitudes of the energies is the chief addition of the *Psychology as Science* to Herbart's original model. His impetus for this project came from an amalgamation of Kant's project with that of the Empiricists in light of Fichte's work -- said Herbart, "[Fichte] wished to discover the act of production in addition to the products of the human spirit" (PaW, 180). This confirms Herbart's advance on Kant's *Anthropology*, for he wishes to account for incoming data, processing strategies, and products of the mind.

A shift in terminology accompanies this new goal. In the earlier *Lehrbuch*, Herbart confined his discussions mainly to questions of representation and energies in the mind's capacities. Here, he addresses the desiderata of the scientific method while critiquing the psychologies inherited from Descartes, Locke, and Leibniz. His data, goal, and procedures fill the initial pages of the introduction to the volume:

> *Therefore we reckon among the facts of consciousness all real representing,* and . . . also the reflective products of our representing activity . . . (PaW, 193)

> Given, then, that the store of psychological facts be assembled, which type of regularities may be found in them in general, or at least surmised? That is the first question of speculative psychology. (PaW, 193)

> The whole of psychology can be nothing else than the supplementing of inwardly perceived facts, the tracing of the connections of that which can be perceived by means of that which perception does not reach, according to general laws. (PaW, 201-202)

This is neither metaphysics, introspection, nor an application of mathematics directly to the soul. Herbart is looking principally at the products of consciousness to uncover the laws of their formation.

Mathematics is integral to psychology as a supplement to the "clearness and distinctness criterion" imposed on inner reflection and the objects and activities of the human mind. Herbart's method will be to derive the mathematics of the changes in the dynamic equilibrium of the mind as expression of the changing quantity of psychological energy available, and to outline the rules for psychic energy in dynamic equilibrium. The mind's function will only be uncovered in its products, not by direct introspection (an allowable hypothesis with respect to the series-forms which sense data form in the mind, since much data will become summarized without remaining explicitly accessible to the mind). This supplementing activity constitutes a reach beyond empiricism, and towards a systems analysis of both the mind (as had been derived in the *Lehrbuch*) and the world view which emerges as the product of its activity. In the *Lehrbuch*, Herbart's model of the mind accommodated chiefly a reformulation of the concept of the mind's "capacities" with respect to representations and the energies of sensations. In contrast, the *Psychology* expands this model into a systematics of representation and of individual experience.

3.8 Psychology and the Ego

Before he evolves an acceptable theory for science, Herbart realizes that his model can only be meaningful as a frame of reference. That is, his mind model conceives a system of representations as originating from a determinate locus of the mental activity of representation. Fichte's reflections about the "I" and "Not-I" from the *Wissenschaftslehre* constitute the basic source for Herbart's assumptions about the possible constitution of this perceiving locus. His conclusions are, however, commensurate with the systems model of dynamic equilibrium already outlined, moving a philosophy of mind towards a more pragmatic psychology:

> What we represent to ourselves must in a certain manner
> transpose us out of the representing of ourselves. . . . The
> manifold representations must sublate [suspend, *aufheben*]
> each other, if "I-ness" [*Ichheit*] is to be possible. (PaW,
> 251)

The center of this suspension, the point at which our representations find their center of reference, will be considered the ego. His ego will, however, be posited in different terms than those used by Kant. It is a system in dynamic equilibrium with the environment and a focus for remembered representations, not a set of mental capacities or categories with an innate priority.

In construing the ego as the focus for the mind's representations, Herbart distances himself from Kant, who had tended to slight the individual's contribution to perception in favor of ideal perceptions and their limits (the transcendental unity of apperception). Kant discussed the representation system of the outside world as a function of the individual mind and the categories processing the data of sensations. Because of his shift, Herbart works from a triad: ego, change or process, and object. Through a comparison of the states of these three poles, Herbart constructs the hypotheses of reason or logic in an iterative process reminiscent of differential and integral calculus (PaW, 264ff.). This process or operation of comparison uncovers changes of the properties of these poles. As a result, concepts such as "causality" merely attribute modifications or changes to a substance, that is, a change in its accidents: ". . . every element of appearance must be considered as an indicator of a modification of an entity through another" (PaW, 269). Herbart works with the data of consciousness as tied into both mind and world -- he thus represents a teleo-mechanical approach.[24]

Herbart first identifies correspondences between the system's states on the basis of qualitative or quantitative modifications in the system's properties. After that, Herbart supplies the formal mathematics of the situation. Still, objects are identified only as "the represented," and stored as representations according to their their properties, and so Herbart is not falling prey to the metaphysical assumption of "things in themselves." He works with the constellations of represented objects and derives his formulae in terms of the energies of stimuli and the magnitudes and directions of their changes, not the absolute constitutions of objects. The first part of Herbart's mathematical derivation formulates the "Statics of the Mind: Sum and Ratio of Inhibitions in the Case of Total Contrasts" (the most extreme case of a dynamic equilibrium). Once contrast values are states, he proceeds to the second major section, "Principles of a Mechanics of the Mind (*Geist*)." These are the full methods of natural science, but they are no more a metaphysics than science itself. These are rules for observed data, perceived change, and its degree and magnitude. In drawing them, Herbart modifies the paradigm he inherited in distinguishing between the sources of data and mental processing.

The "Statics of the Mind/Spirit" explains the mind's systems of representation in dynamic equilibrium, that is, ready to change but not necessitated to do so, since the mind is in a stable state. In this situation, the mind is an ennervated system, charged with a determinate quantity of energy, or "inhibition":

> The *sum* of inhibition is the quantum of representing which, taking together those representations working in contrast, must be inhibited. (PaW, 282)

Herbart's goal here is to develop the equations through which the sum of inhibiting energy in any stable mental state may be determined. The formula for mental equilibria must also account for a threshold value for that quantum of energy which would be able to disequilibrate the stable state present -- a threshhold of perception. As Herbart indicated above, sensations which tend to be more closely associated within the system will be termed "complexes" (the equivalent of a viable concept); those which are more loosely associated are only "amalgamations." Complexes contribute to the energy of the system in equilibrium, while amalgamations may have to be broken down and analyzed before their energy is calculated. Complexes are "representations of various continua [which] can totally bind themselves together, so that they constitute a single energy and enter the calculation as such" (PaW, 308).

This is only a first step in the new model. The "statics," as a description of a stable state, constitute Herbart's description of a being himself in a stable state -- not learning or interacting with the environment. As Herbart himself cautions:

> If an equilibrium is already present, then it can be disturbed only by the addition of new energies. But since we speak of representations, an observation suggests itself: it is not permitted in considering them to assume equilibrium as their initial condition. Rather, they are originally all quite uninhibited; in this natural condition, they form a sum of inhibition (at the [energy] level where only a number of them present are opposed). This [sum of energy] must decrease, and thus a movement of representation is also present. In the course of our studies, we must first determine the equilibrium; in reality, movement precedes the equilibrium. (PaW, 338)

The mind is in a dynamic equilibrium which can be affected by either new or "re-awakened" impressions, and which is affected proportional to the "speed" or intensity (*Geschwindigkeit*) of the received impressions (PaW, 354ff.). That is, old stimuli help with the processing of the new. Herbart's "Mechanics of the Spirit" anticipates the description of neurological path-breaching which Freud used in the *Project for a Scientific Psychology*. Breached paths (paths used to process stimuli) serve to establish the stability of the equilibration of representations, which is perpetuated as new stimuli enter. Herbart agrees with Freud that "[t]he receptivity for certain perceptions renews itself, when earlier representations of similar types are driven to the static threshold" (PaW, 409). This fully amalgamates a biological perspective into the cultural interaction described by Kant. The new paradigm in which this model stands will also join biological or physiological perspectives to those drawn from Empiricism and Idealism.

What is the advantage of this model of the mind in dynamic equilibrium over that of the capacities of the mind in Kant's work? The chief advantage is in flexibility of world views: Kant still believed in the perfectibility of man's world, and so he did not pursue the question of imperfections in processing which his model opened. In contrast, Herbart differentiates between the world's development and the inner vision of the world which is human lived experience. Herbart must disagree that the categories are "empty vessels" into which human experience is poured, and whose contents can be infinitely refined (PaW, 430). Instead, he consistently maintains a different set of *a priori* terms: substance, reality, and energy (force). He notes, "Kant recognized that, in consideration of the true meaning of the categories, everything depends on the question: How is our experience constituted?" (PaW, 431). Still, Herbart must also stress that human experience is variable and growing.

Kant tended to work only with the concepts of substance, accidence, and things. Herbart felt that this was not sufficient -- the relations formulated are based on concepts in a continual state of flux. Instead, the systems model of the mind is more correct. It upholds a differentiation between inner and outer worlds to great advantage in completely dislodging categories in favor of mental dynamics:

> If this movement [of representations] has determinate laws, then even the categories can be products of thinking, and, to be sure, [they can be] unfinished products of a process of thinking to be continued further. (PaW, 432)

He completes the model which will stand at the base of the new paradigm when he includes mind, data from world, and representations.

More importantly, constituents of this thinking process are themselves constituted on the series which appear in consciousness. Herbart's mind model is potentially infinitely adaptable to the environment. Its processes of association and differentiation can build up to more patterns of processing than Kant's categories:

> They, the objects themselves, are considered to be the source of "appearing." The central point, at which the rays of appearing unify and cross, lay the ground of the *ego*, which still requires the *inner world* for its development. This ego, while moving around in the "outside world" or the "not-I," not only takes into itself and completes series, but also itself sends out some series from itself, while

intending to send out series through which it can confront the series impinging on it. In this way, one cannot say whether the ego appears more passively or actively, because each takes place to almost the same degree. (PaW, 425)

Thus, an interaction between mind and world constitutes the ego in a much more fundamental sense than in Kant's model.

It is precisely this growing "inner world" which will constitute the remainder of Herbart's discussions: world views are conditioned by the egos of a group, and their development is subject to the condition of mental equilibrium, together with their mathematical expressions. The long second volume of the *Psychology as Science* presents the analytics of the world's appearances -- an exposition to complement the synthetic portrait of the systems of the mind drawn in the first volume. Like the anthropological examples in Kant's second part, the subjects which Herbart addresses are many and varied: appearances, world history, statesmanship, and education (particularly the development of Kant's citizens of the world). These examples and applications of Herbart's principles constitute an analytic approach rather than a synthesis. They start with the institutions of the world, and then trace the effects which they have on the individuals subject to them. He exemplifies the development of the ego and mental processing subject to the world -- not how the mind produces, as Kant tried to explain. Such analyses also tie Herbart's work in psychology to his more familiar educational psychology, since he sees the power of institutions to mold thought patterns. His program is thus the reverse of Kant's, since he does not want to mold the world, only people.

While stressing the individual, Herbart does not give up history. Because the mind is in equilibrium, there are representations, collectively called feelings or appetition, of which we are not necessarily conscious. Yet like the conceptual structure of the mind, such feelings are historical, derived from the individual's life history and the community. "Feelings for life, aesthetic feelings, feelings of desire and revulsion" come in part from individual experience, but also are due to the norms of the society, which create inhibitions within the mind (PaW, II, 62).

More importantly, inhibitions from either source may exert equal pressure on conceptualization.

Conversely, conscious control over inhibitions and over the direction of conceptualization in general is also possible and termed "attention" (*Aufmerksamkeit*): "the capacity to produce an increase in representing," or the willful act of paying attention (PaW, II, 141; 148). The ego as a reference point is also subject to a cultural history, and so the kind of attention paid is indicative of the values of the culture in which the individual is immersed:

> *Science speaks of the soul* as the basis of the represented world and of one's own self. *In science, that which knows is the soul.* Hence, knowing and the known are one -- the soul in the system of its self-preservations. Thus I know about myself not through in-born knowledge, but through knowledge acquired forever. (PaW, II, 191)

With this stress on acquired knowledge, Herbart has evolved a very modern picture of the ego in the historical world -- an ego which is only a point of reference and recollection, a system adapting to the sensations which impinge on its energetic equilibrium.

This has consequences not only for thought, but for all science. An ego's self-preservation is jeapordized when the complexes within the mental equilibrium start to constitute not only a world view, but also a world, which is "brought on" by the psychological mechanism (PaW, II, 229). Since the mind is programmed by culture and the world, the trappings of pure logic -- syllogisms, antinomies, theories, and the like -- create metaphysics as schematized projections of physical experience and personal history. Moreover, even the individual's personality is a product of the complexes from the ego, adapted through the individual will. Personality is therefore an expression of delusions or positive conceptions about the world willed by the individual. The individual's world view is a mental equilibrium selected by the will on the basis of previous experience and affects.

3.9 Conclusion

Herbart himself assessed the need to develop a psychology on scientific principles which can accommodate both the transcendental unity of humans and their individuality. Up to his time, psychology had been a vehicle to stunt the progress of other discussions -- it dealt with normative mental behavior. The older psychology had even tainted other disciplines. Logic had been contaminated, since psychology seemed to provide an explanation of the mind's function, when in fact only a certain class of regularities had been addressed (PaW, II, 329). Similarly, psychology gave morality false predications about that which man could and should do. Metaphysics received a false notion of experience; pedagogy, an erroneous picture of the capacities of the soul working separately, allowing a one-sided view of education to evolve; and politics and history, an image of reason belonging to the individual, instead of relying on group experience or history. Most importantly, psychology itself had a self-image problem, fearing that it was not a natural science because of the "purported non-law-governance of the capacities of the soul, which seem to work in terms of desire and moods" (PaW, II, 323).

These disciplines can all receive crucial correctives if psychology is reformulated along the lines initiated by Kant's critique of the human mind and expanded by Herbart. Rethinking what was purported to be eternal lay at the heart of Kant's "Copernican Revolution," but Herbart felt that his addenda to the *Critiques* was essential in order to bring the concepts of ego/individual, education, knowledge, and world view into line. With Herbart's picture of the inner education of humans, one can explain "the concept of true character according to its psychological conditions" (PaW, 334). Moreover, splitting out what properly is the external and what is the internal purview of psychology, philosophy, history, and political science will give them all more clarity.

Herbart's message thus resembles Kant's, stressing a continuous reconsideration of the bases for the sciences, since the human sciences must be accompanied by psychology:

But we may not forget that the development of the sciences follows the path of a psychological mechanism. The effect of one science on another by no means depends only on whether principles and axioms for one are expressly drawn from the other. Rather there is a secret, an unwilling influence of the considerations which one feels compelled to assume in science. Many are so accustomed to the capacities of the soul, that these abominations [Undinge] still act as real forces [Kräfte], although in themselves they have no reality, because they exert a strong mastery in such heads as prejudices and opinions. Many people cannot think other than by relying on them. They can so little think otherwise, than they could cease accompanying their thinking with silent words in their mother tongue. Here it would help nothing to protest against the impermissible mixture; the false connections of thoughts would still work on in all their force. (PaW, II, 335-36)

Thus, even the assumption of fixed capacities of the soul (or even the categories themselves) can be a deterrent to the development of science, a deterrent imposed by a false psychology, and also propagated in 1820's Germany through the influence of so-called transcendental philosophy when it removes psychology from empirical proof.[25] ("The German philosophizing public . . . [is] washed in the misfortune of having come far away from the truth in the last decennia; about as far away proportionately as it found a greater taste for brash fantasies and disaccustomed itself from methodical thinking" [PaW, II, 337].)

Seen from this perspective, in what ways can the work of Kant and Herbart be seen as the initiation of a new paradigm for psychology?

First: both men aimed at dismantling the idea of the fixed capacities of the mind. Kant had attacked the notion first in the material of the three *Critiques*: intuition, understanding, reason, and judgment were demonstrated to be interactive, and to apply to different areas of human experience (perception, conceptualization, constructive speculation, and taste or evaluation). In the *Anthropology*, however, Kant applies these differentiations to what had earlier been considered passions or pure subjectivity. Thus he discusses concepts not only as they produce the understanding, but also as they are conditioned by the experiential capacities and environment of the individual. Herbart, freed to a greater degree than Kant was from the need to assume the primacy of the logical capacities over the subjective or emotive, was able to focus this dismantling of the faculties around the specifics of the energetics of the mind.[26]

Second: both the *Anthropology* and Herbart's *Psychology* reframe the concept of mind which they had inherited. Knowledge was no longer a question of coming to clearness and distinctness about the capacities of the mind, nor of the appropriate use of their content. The knowledge available to the mind in this nascent conceptual psychology developed according to experience and the environment or historical-cultural inheritance in which a particular individual finds himself. This opens two possibilities for the relativity of knowledge. It can be either culturally or individually relative, since minds function differently as a consequence of their development.

Third and most importantly: with the acknowledgment that conceptualization may have a relative dimension, a new vista has been opened for the development of science. The question of the ontology of knowledge or of epistemology becomes one of *validity*: in what system and in what environment a particular piece of knowledge is formed will be relevant questions in the study of the formation of systematic disciplines. Kant and Herbart inserted this question into the new paradigm, but only their successors, particularly Mach and Lotze, attempted to answer it.

Because of these innovations, the texts under consideration here constitute the beginnings of a new field, a new paradigm, and a new discourse: conceptual psychology. Kant and Herbart deconstructed philosophy or logical psychology in order to recase it into a psychology based on experience, history, and individual mental processing strategies. The effect of this work was to reconstruct the premises of many disciplines, so that they focused on *validity* instead of correctness -- these disiplines were now forced to account for all three aspects of knowledge (proximate and cultural sources, as well as individual mind). Moreover, these disciplines were also held accountable for strict empirical standards, usually the introduction of mathematics, which changed their methods. In essence, the work initiated by Kant and Herbart forced a combination of aspects of both Idealism and Empiricism that started a new paradigm for science. The medical discourse of the mid-nineteenth century provides an example of the new comprehensive discourse which scholars had to assume. Wilhelm Griesinger, in his *Mental Pathology and Therapeutics*, had to explain mental diseases as they related to heredity, environment, and individual mind, as well as consider ways to reprogram poorly functioning minds, so that they would begin to process environmental data in healthy patterns. As a student of both Idealism and Empiricism, Griesinger fully acquiesced to the criteria imposed on him by the new paradigm and its discourse.

Kant and Herbart initiated the model of the mind that enabled the new paradigm for psychological research to emerge. However, neither was able to complete the work begun and develop a coherent picture of higher-order thought and the way it develops the equilibrium of the mind's system. They had initated the new paradigm, but a concomitant discourse had not fully evolved, and so the new work remained somewhat obscured by older terminology. Nonetheless, the necessity for this new paradigm for the human sciences had been established: tying knowledge to the relativity of human experience requires that the program of each individual humanistic discipline be formulated commensurate to the findings of this new psychology. The work of Kant and Herbart, therefore, did establish the key concepts which later conceptual psychologists would develop: analogy and association, continua and psychic equilibrium, energy and inhibition.

CHAPTER 4

EMPIRICISM AND CONCEPTUAL PSYCHOLOGY:
PSYCHOPHYSICS AND PHILOLOGY

Within fifty years of the time that Kant and Herbart opened the way to a conceptual psychology dealing with the workings of the mind, its historicity, and its contents, several attempts were made to incorporate these advances into the foundations of humanistic disciplines.

In two cases, the attempt was made to employ the constructive method which Herbart's work had suggested to explain the historical genesis and development of products of the human spirit. The most familiar of these disciplines is psychophysics, particularly as represented in the works of Theodor Fechner[1] and, in a more philosophical form, in those of Richard Avenarius.[2] The second area was the psychology of peoples (*Völkerpsychologie*) as delimited by Wilhelm Wundt and echoed by the philosophical arguments of the Neogrammarian philologists, especially Hermann Paul.[3] Each sought to outline what they considered a complete human science: the former, a science of experience extending from physical experience to the development of a world view; the latter, a science of language, myth and custom as expressions of the world view and experience of a people or language group.

These four are linked by a common heritage. On the one hand, they rely on Kant and Herbart for their scientific account of the contents, as opposed to the forms, of thought. On the other, they reach back to the Empiricism of Hume and Locke, which is predicated on a model of the human mind associating learning with blanket experience of the environment. Wundt, Fechner, Avenarius, and Paul also believe in empiricism, but in a restricted way. They do not believe that empirical learning necessarily reflects the order in which experiences are presented to consciousness, since there are differences in individual consciousnesses. Thus, their position constitutes a compromise between the mind model of Kant and Herbart (which predicates learning on categorical processing subsequent to apperception) and the situation of Locke and Hume. Locke and Hume had conceived of the individual as a product of environmental and cultural conditioning. In contrast, Herbart and Kant interpreted both individual and group behaviors as products of mental processing, which subjects environmental stimuli to otherwise unmeasureable internal psychological operations. In an attempt to synthesize these poles, Avenarius, Fechner, Paul, and Wundt set out to ascertain whether or not the mental operations of the group would correspond to those of the individual. Their method was to examine the artifacts of culture which joined environmental stimuli to exert pressure on individual consciousness; their goal was to find the patterning rules in the objects produced by mind. The individual differences in the positions of Fechner, Avenarius, Wundt and Paul arise in their respective assessments of the degree of interaction between individual and group consciousness and the environment, and in their statements of the extent to which history and culture will enter into the environmental stimuli affecting human thought.

Traditionally, attempts to explain world views in terms of experience and the habituation of mind have not been considered an individual psychology. Usually, it has been associated with Empiricism, as a continuation of the work begun by Hume and Locke under the auspices of epistemology. Yet the psychophysics and philology under discussion here are divided from Empiricism in the strictest sense. They agree in fully acknowledging the relativity of mental habituation and use a method of construction to develop a hierarchy from the simplest to the most complex products of the mind. Yet, they are also trying to account for feedback effects between individual minds and inherited patterns of knowledge. That is, they stress not only how the group develops from the individual, but also the influence of the group on these individuals. The positions of Fechner, Avenarius, and Wundt contrast sufficiently to that of Hermann Paul's *Principles of the History of Language* to show how such divergent positions expand the paradigm formed by Kant and Herbart into a discourse -- the discourse of the conceptual psychology which will emerge most clearly in the later work of Ernst Mach and Freud.[4]

In order to delineate the positions inherent in psychophysics and the psychology of peoples, Fechner's *Psychophysics,* Avenarius' *Critique of Pure Experience,* Wundt's *Outline of Psychology* and *The Psychology of Peoples,* and Paul's *Principles of the History of Language* will be treated as a coherent whole in method, as attempts to apply the model of mental development outlined by Kant and Herbart in the cultural sphere.[5]

4.1 Fechner and Psychophysics

Gustav Theodor Fechner's *Elements of Psychophysics* was a book of considerable influence in its day -- it remained in print from 1859 to a third edition in 1907 and beyond. However, it is now largely dropped from consideration, perhaps because of its monolithic prose and dense formulations.[6] Yet, it was to Fechner that many of his contemporaries looked for his definition of "psychophysical parallelism" -- the concept of the parallel nature of the processes of the mind and those of nature, the classical formulations of a scientific empiricism.[7] Fechner was not confined to a pure Empiricism, however, which would concentrate on the mind as a product of the activity of the body. His program received a different formulation -- a definition of psychophysics:

> As an exact doctrine, psychophysics (as physics) has to be based on experience and on mathematical connections of facts of experience, which requires measurement of that offered by experience; and, to the degree which it does not yet stand available, this measurement must be sought. After the measurement is then given in terms of physical quantities, the first and primary task of this book will be the determination of measurements in terms of mental quantities, where it has been lacked heretofore; the second, the exploration of the applications and effects which are attached to them. (ElP, vii)

It is the second task of the book which sets Fechner's project apart from strict empiricism, and which brings him into the scope of conceptual psychology. Unlike positivists, who stress scientific observation, Fechner concentrates not only on mind, but on the cultural group.

Fechner acknowledges his debt to his predecessors in this project, but he also wishes to retain a distance, particularly in the issue of mathematics. He identifies Herbart as his source for the mathematical formulations of psychophysical relations, while still acknowledging contradictions in Herbart's positions:

> Yet in fact the following essays are founded on basic views which differ so fundamentally from his, that it hardly requires an emphasis on their differences, and it would be vain and inappropriate to attempt confrontation of the two, particularly since such a confrontation could not take place without an argument about fundamental philosophical problems, which is to be avoided here at any price. (ElP, xii)

Some of this is overstated, and it sounds like he is tryng to assert the scientific positivism for which he is known. Taking this statement from the point of view of the paradigm, however, allows a different interpretation, since we can consider him not as the first positivist, but as a psychophysicist. Fechner's innovation for the paradigm is that he does not follow Herbart in believing in the data of appearance. For Fechner, there is not only one set of such data, but rather many, corresponding to various perspectives imposed on this data by the cultural interests of the group -- each vested interest yields a different set of the data of appearance. Because of this skepticism, Fechner is minimizing the importance of individual mind, stressing instead the focus imposed on individuals by the group.

This difference in philosophy gives psychophysics a different starting point than Kant or Herbart had. Fechner believes that science must first determine the relationship of the spirit to the world. This was not a question for Herbart, who implicitly relied on Kant's division between the world of experience and the world of things in themselves. Fechner feels that this is an unwarranted assumption -- the point of view for a scientific observer is not necessarily that of an individual. In consequence, he explicitly requires a differentiation between an inner and an outer point of view in the determination of the data of science. An inner point of view encompasses the world of the spirit, which is a unity; the outer point of view is that of the world of appearances, which appears in multiple formulations according to an observer's various perspectives (ElP, 5). Another fact questions Herbart's assumption of an individual observer: not only may the observer's point of view vary, but also the conditions of the observer as facts are contemplated. Fechner's observers are thus much less reliable and much more important than Herbart's. He has tied science not to the individual observer, but to a choice of standpoint within the community of observers:

> The difference in an appearance does not depend only on the variance in stance, but also on the variance of those who assume it. . . . The natural sciences assume consequently an outer stance in contemplation of objects; the science of the spirit, an inner. Views of life are based on the alternation of the stances, natural philosophy on the identity of that which appears doubled on this doubled stance . . . (ElP, 5-6)

Thus, where the observed data was crucial for Herbart, Fechner asserts the relativity of the observer as the frame for any observations.

Fechner believes that the only way to circumvent reality is to base a science on "elementary facts" (ElP, 7). His psychophysics is such a science, based on only one metaphysical assumption: the existence of a perceiving consciousness which is integral unto itself. Positivism does, to be sure, rely on this assumption, but Fechner indicates greater remifications:

> We consider as part of the region of the soul (the spiritual or mental) that which is conceivable through inner perception or which can be abstracted out of it; to that of the corporeal (the body, physical, or material), that which is conceivable through outer perception or which can be abstracted from it. With this we designate only the regions of the world of appearances with whose relations psychophysics should busy itself. This presupposes that

one knows how to relate inner and outer perception (in the sense of normal usage of language) to the activities through which existence itself comes to appearance. (EIP, 8)

This assertion ties Fechner's program into conceptual psychology, for he stresses empirical data in relation to the relativity of the observer's stance and to the activity of the individual mind. But, like Herbart, Fechner still confines his assumptions to the *working* of the mind and not to its absolute constitution, "without leading back to the essence of body and soul behind the world of appearances in the sense of metaphysics" (EIP, 8). Fechner's psychophysics is more than positivism, and so must confine itself to "what belongs together in the world of bodies and of spirit, quantitatively and qualitatively" and to the laws which express these relations (EIP, 9).

Fechner is well aware that he is proposing a compound discipline:

> Related already in name to psychology and to physics, psychophysics has on the one side to base itself on psychology, and promises on the other to provide this study with mathematical supports. From physics, outer psychophysics borrows its aids and methods; inner psychophysics relies rather on physiology and anatomy (namely of the nervous system) and presupposes a certain familarity with them. (EIP, 11)

For this science, Fechner follows the new paradigm and chooses the concepts of stimulus, potential and vital energy, and equilibrium of the body as an organic system -- an energetic system conceived in terms of biological energy. He traces stimuli such as perception of weight, smell, and taste, their magnitudes, and the changes they call forth in bodies (EIP, 21). These stimuli, in affecting the activities of our bodies, transmit energies between the individual (vital energy) and the environment (potential energy):

> Only that all parts of the world do not complete their alternation between rising and falling, vital and potential energy like the parts of a string; rather, the most varied

parts of the world can find themselves in this respect in quite varied relationships; also, they only contribute to fulfilling the law in solidarity, so that what one body loses in vital energy in communication with the others does not accrue to it in potential energy, and vice versa, what it receives is not won at the cost of its potential energy; only for the *whole* system does the constant sum of both energies apply. (ElP, 33)

Fechner's data are part of a world set, for only a subset enters individual mind -- a formulation much different than Herbart's.

The interrelations between the body and the environment are expressible in terms of a continuum of energy and only the sum of energy of the system, not the energy inherent in any part of this interrelated system, may be ascertained.

The avenue of investigation for the empirical science of psychophysics lies in the determinations of changes in the energy levels of the system, the procedures and results with a goal conditioned by the broader program of conceptual psychology. This change of energy can be studied: boundary values, dependencies on change in circumstance, mean values, or constant values maintained through changes, all of which are discerned with a criterion of distinctness (ElP, 53). He specifies the "sensitivity" of an organism as it corresponds to the receptivity of a body in stable state with its environment. There is a threshold level for the stimulus energy to penetrate the system, and the boundary values of this threshhold can be determined through three scientific methods: the method of least-perceivable difference, that of true and false instances, and that of mean error in the energy or force level affecting the system (ElP, 70). Fechner's definition of the sensitive threshold echoes Herbart's:

> . . . each stimulus or difference in stimulus must have reached a certain finite size before it even begins to be noticeable, that is, before it produces a sensation which can affect our consciousness noticeably . . . [a point] we will call the threshold for short. (ElP, 237)

The great portion of Fechner's work expands this experimental

psychophysics and determines threshold and dependency values for
the human body. His expositions laid the basis for the experimental
psychology which the universities in Germany would adopt as their
own through the latter nineteenth century, and which would be
reflected in the work of William James in England. James' work
used a method not unlike that of Hermann Paul and many of the
academic psychologists in Germany of the period.

Yet this is not Fechner's only contribution -- he is more than a
positivist. The full model which grounds these investigations is
only stated by Fechner towards the end of the second volume of his
study. He asserts a position which gives the mind a much more
significant role as a dynamic system, expanding Herbart's model
again:

> Sensations, representations, have, to be sure, ceased to
> exist as real in the state of the unconscious, to the degree
> that one grasps them abstractly, from their fundament; but
> something continues in us -- psychophysical activity, of
> which they are a function and on which the possibility of
> the reemergence of the sensation depends . . . (ElP, II,
> 433)

This psychophysical activity grows, not just thoughts,
sensations, and memory; thus "the schemata which accompany
abstract thought, which we for brevity unite under the name
representations, . . . appearances of the sensual memory,
hallucination, and illusions join under the general concept of
modifications, special determinations of total consciousness . . ."
(ElP, II, 458). This is not only an energetic model of the mind,
since it stresses the organism's capacity to schematize both the
present and its past experience.

But Fechner is perhaps too enamoured of the link between
consciousness and energy as a life force, for he projects the
individual consciousness into a group consciousness, whose
energies also echo a contact of the organism with the environment.
Here he seriously diverges from Herbart in his idea of the
community of thinkers, each of whom is one frequency within the
energy frequency of the universe and who exerts pressure on
others. Fechner, the psychophysicist, converges with Fechner, the

mystic:

> Our main frequencies [Wellen], on which our primary
> consciousness depends, propagate frequencies on which
> our particular phenomena of consciousness depend. But
> cannot our main frequencies in their turn be considered as
> overtones of a greater main frequency? They are really so
> physically, why not also psychophysically? Because the
> total activity of the earthly system can be represented under
> the schema of a great frequency wave, to which the activity
> systems of individual organic creations belong only as
> small overtones; and the activity systems of the individual
> heavenly bodies are again only overtones of the general
> system of the total motion of Nature. The hierarchy which
> continues within us also continues beyond us. . . .
>
> The consequence of this model leads to the concept of
> an omnipresent conscious God in Nature, in which all
> spirits live, act, and are (as He in them), with individual
> spiritual medial stages (inherent in the heavenly bodies)
> between Him and us, which created spirits carry united
> within them in similar fashion as they themselves are
> carried within the godly Spirit; and as the created spirits
> again carry their sensual spheres and these their particular
> sensations in them. (ElP, II, 533-4)

This quotation points up the reason why his psychophysics cannot
be considered pure Empiricism, and why only his experimental
outline, and not the outline of his theory, was adopted by the
Empiricists among his contemporaries.

He delineated culture and Nature as group consciousness, in
the sense of a pantheism at odds with the strict empiricist or
positivist view of the world. Moreover, since Fechner has shifted
the point of validation for conceptualization away from the
individual into a random point in the field of data, the model as
outlined lacks any real space for the individual consciousness.
Fechner allows for individuals only as discontinuities in the greater
scheme of energy producing mind: ". . . insofar as a
distinguishable number [of psychical resultants] is present in the
unity of a more general consciousness, the continuity of a more
general consciousness does not preclude the discontinuity of

particular phenomena" (ElP, II, 519). Thus, although he began from principles which strongly resembled those of Kant and Herbart, and proceeded in an exemplary determination of empiricist experimental techniques, Fechner's work did not account for the historicity and the relativity to a particular time and place which would have brought him into closer line with the desiderata of a conceptual psychology.

Fechner belongs to the emerging paradigm of conceptual psychology, because he integrated mathematics into an interactive model of the mind that gave Empiricism its due in a way that Herbart's had not. Because of this greater stress on Empiricism, Fechner was able to highlight the fundamental triad of the model for conceptual psychology: mental processes, environment, and cultural inheritance. He did aid in deconstructing the primacy of the personal observer that Herbart stressed, yet he still shunted the importance of the data of the environment in his maintainance of a point of observation -- he had not completely realized the ramifications of this shift. It would remain for another "empiricist," Richard Avenarius, to attempt to account for the environmental factors (especially cultural ones) whose importance was not consistently acknowledged by Fechner.

4.2 Richard Avenarius and "Pure Experience"

The *Critique of Pure Experience* (two volumes, originally 1888) is perhaps a unique contribution and dead end in the attempts to realize the initiatives of conceptual psychology into a systematic discipline.[8] While eschewing experimentation or the delineation of experimental limitations, Avenarius draws up a principle science of experience, a set of postulates to be used when exploring the relationships between mind and body and knowledge. Insofar as his focus is the data of experience, the *Critique* may be considered empiricist. Yet from the empiricist point of view, Avenarius pays far too much attention to the whole of cognition which evolves in the mind after the sensations of experience have been received. Such settings are culturally relativized in Avenarius' mind. Similarly, his reliance on the *data* of experience will not allow consideration of the *Critique* as an early representative of phenomenology. In this text, historicity is acknowledged, and "pure" experience constitutes not the pure forms of intuition, nor those forms of thought revealing themselves after Husserl's phenomenological reduction. Avenarius is important in the paradigm of conceptual psychology, because he contributed the best statement of relative mind -- mind influenced by lived experience. His model did much to break the model for psychology out of its old discourse, and so was much-cited around the turn of the twentieth century. However, his own discourse did not prove productive to the scientific community. His model of the mind was couched in irreproducible terminology, which allowed its unique nature to emerge, but then rendered it unusable. At what point, then, does Avenarius' work diverge from the procedures set by Kant, Herbart, or Fechner?

Avenarius' most obvious contribution is the form and intent of his work, focused on the data of experience in a philosphical formulation. As his initial methodological dicta stress:

> It is perhaps not without purpose to preface this immediately with two assumptions which I (for the moment and without laying emphasis on the designation) would like to call *empiriocritical axioms*: the first, the axiom of *cognitive contents*, the second, the axiom of *cognitive forms*. (KrE, xx-xxi)

He follows Fechner in stressing the contents of consciousness where Kant and Herbart stressed the form, but he is not a strict empiricist, for he stresses that experience is "something constituted" (KrE, 4).

In differentiating the forms and contents of experience, Avenarius has made a choice not yet made by his predecessors. He has abandoned the assumption of a fixed pattern of conceptualization (Kant), or even a culture-specific priority of thought patterns (Herbart). Instead, the *Critique* makes thought-patterns the resultant of a stasis achieved by the mind in the face of lived experience. He will not stress the genesis of systems of thought in the mind, as Fechner did, nor a similar solution that Wundt assumes in his *Psychology of Peoples*. Avenarius gives as much weight to conceptual conditioning as he does to the elements of the experience which condition them:

> That means, though, that our critique of pure experience
> will have to be formulated first and thoroughly in the spirit
> of a *theory of experience*; that does not exclude, but rather
> requires, that it must be maintained at the same time in the
> sense of a *general theory of cognition* and that it is not
> completely removed from the meaning of a *general theory
> of human norms*. (KrE, 8-9)

These norms are not transcendental but evolve in the historical
experience of the group, to be passed on to the next generation.

Avenarius upholds his assessments of the relation of mind and
experience in determining the variables or energy values maintained
within a system of the mind. He systematically correlates the
mind's stable state with an entering perturbation or sensation, and
the final state for the thought patterns, either for the individual or
the group. He addresses the stasis of the system in terms of states
and "multiponibles," the multuplets of dependent variables in the
environment which together condition the system of the mind, the
"conditions of usage" and the "initial constitution of the changed
system" (KrE, 30). Aside from his stress on environment,
Avenarius conceives of mind systems within the group of
individuals, not necessarily as if that group had developed as a
consequence of individual desires.

Avenarius' particular innovation is that his model applies to the
individual as a representative of the group, and not to the group as a
sum of equally valid individuals. He considers the individual a
token of the historical type of the group's experience, and not as a
determinant of the group's conceptualization: "the conditions for
positive systemic development of individuals, generations, peoples,
and humanity itself are posited as extending through time and space
for each system" (KrE, 181). Thus, individuals will tend strongly
to resemble the group:

> If the limitedness and avoidability of the positing of
> historically developed individual multiponibles should be
> lessened, so too must their constitution be brought near to
> that of an independent, complete constant. (KrE, 189)

That is, individuals will tend to remain constant and not have the ability to affect the group significantly.

At any point in time, the cognition and world concept of a group is largely conditioned by habit and by the survival values of individuals in their respective environments. In this case, conditions on cognition are prior to its contents -- that is, whether or not a particular group of familiar facts is sure, real, or familiar. The conditions on entering facts as groups affect the thoughts and survival of the group:

> The general character of fidentiality [familiarity] is further specialized in three directions in statements, or it allows itself to be divided into three specialized characters. To be sure, fidentiality is distinguishable on the one hand as "being" ("that which is"), or "reality," on the second as "certainty," on the third as "familiarity" [*Bekanntheit*, accustomedness].
>
> I term the first value *existential*, the second, *secural*, the third, *notal*. (KrE, II, 33)

As the entering data are "fidential," they will condition the group as "functions of the environment" and as a constancy perceived in this environment (KrE, II, 47-48). Often repeated patterns in the environment will tend to set in and be considered reality.

Avenarius thus attempts to bracket the question of the primacy of either environment or mind by keeping the focus on their interactions. The exigencies of survival and the conservation of energy maintain the stability of the relationship between the environment and a group, and thus tend to set up stable and continuing patterns of mind. For the individual, this environmentally conditioned survival value with its three modalities becomes reified into a personal world concept. Its building blocks are the concept references and memory which is possible to an organism as a result of individual habituation on the basis of the group pattern. To these concepts, the individual attaches a personal survival value commensurate with that of the group, deriving a self-concept from the group:

> We therefore derive . . . a series of modifications for

> which an E-Value [survival value, *Erhaltung*] can be
> posited, and which we therefore from our standpoint
> designate as *posited forms*.
>   This is the series: object [*Sache*], reproduction
> [*Nachbild*], thought, afterthought. (KrE, II, 79)

Each of these concepts then becomes involved in "vital-series":
associations of experience which serve this survival.

With this image of the way in which all thought is dependent
on experience and survival in a mutually determining relationship,
Avenarius has highlighted the relativity of cognition and human
world-views. More than any of his predecessors, he acknowledges
that the communality of cognition and experience associated with
groups is not a function of the constitution of the outside world and
its knowability, nor of the absolute uniformity of the constitution of
the minds involved. Rather, vital-series, or associations from the
environment, are results only of the fact that human minds interact
with the environment for their own survival in terms of the values
set by the group, "whether the dependent values were designated as
'experience' by individuals or not" (KrE, II, 342).[9]

The human mind tends to seek a stable energetic state and to
complete a world concept from the point of view of relative
self-interest. This mind does not question the adequacy of the
concept to any purported reality, even if certain data involved has
had a pragmatic reality attributed to it:

> Each increase of the series of historical "world concepts"
> which does not at the same time continue the critical series
> does not approximate the historical evolution of "world
> concepts" to a possibly most tenable "general concept."
> (KrE, II, 383)

In this, he redefines Hegel, asserting that relative world views do
not eventually add up to a picture of reality.

Here, Avenarius develops an explicit relationship between the
limitations of cognition and those of experience in a fashion that
was not exploited by any of his predecessors. This is Avenarius'
distinct version of the paradigm, a contribution which would only
be echoed again in the work of Ernst Mach. In part obscured by

his diction, Avenarius realizes that all conceptualization is personal within the limits of conditioned and transmitted knowledge, and within culture, history, and geography:

> 1) First, "cognition" would be *exclusively* an "experience."
> 2) Then, "cognition" would be only *partially* an "experience," but, to be sure, an elucidated "experience," the other part would be "non-experience."
> 3) Finally,"cognition" would again be an *exclusivity*, but now also an exclusively *elucidated* "experience." (KrE, II, 409)

Avenarius pointed the way in which conceptual psychology would have to move if it were to become valuable explaining the phenomena of human existence as historically relative. Yet Avenarius himself reached no further than the decisive statement quoted above: that the mind of each individual was a closed and stable energy system whose development was contingent to and commensurate with that of the group, but which itself remained confined to the purviews of the individual. In evolving a systematic variant of the positions opened by Kant and Herbart, Avenarius accommodated the environment while delimiting the scope and purview of the conceptualizations of the individual.

Yet because he chose to restrict his project to first principles, Avenarius' work remained a torso largely ignored by future generations of theorists. He was important as a documentation for the new paradigm, because he tried to forge a discourse -- a distinctive set of terms that his predecessors had lacked. His hard-headed insistence on coining new terms did avoid the contagion of the old by the philosophical environment in which he was working. However, the arcane diction which arose from these terminological distinctions was not usable. The advance he represented thus remained unfollowed; although it found a distant echo in the analysis of a branch of the sciences, it was still an oddity in the paradigm of conceptual psychology.

Fechner centered the innovation of the paradigm by dividing science and the personal observer. In contrast, Avenarius exerted only oblique pressure on the development of psychology of a discipline. Thus Fechner's work found much resonance in a greater disciple, Wundt, who chose to make the group and its conceptualizations not only the producer, but also the product of the environment, and so extended the constructive analysis established by Fechner. The work of Wilhelm Wundt represented the major trend in academic psychology which aided to obscure the systemic analysis proposed by Avenarius.

4.3 Wundt: Group Psychology and the Environment

The work of Wilhelm Wundt distinguishes itself as one of the major influences on the development of academic psychology in the nineteenth century, and one which extended itself beyond the narrower range of the discipline of psychology into the realms of philology and anthropology.[10] This influence, however, did not maintain itself into this century -- he remains for the twentieth century a much-studied and little-perceived figure.[11] Yet in recognizing not only his physiological work, but also his work in the cultural sciences (following the lead of Arthur L. Blumenthal, above all), we have an important documentation for the new paradigm. Wundt tried to forge the discourse for the new paradigm of conceptual psychology that his predecessors had lacked.[12]

Adjusting his image by adding his cultural work is a recent corrective, since Wundt has been stressed in America as an Introspectionist due to the influence of one of his students, Titchener. Still, in the original corpus of work, Wundt clearly attempted to synthesize two points of view, taking from both Idealism and Empiricism.[13]

Wundt's work began from the principles of conceptual psychology as initiated by Herbart. Perhaps under the influence of Fechner, it diverged from this program by insisting on the primacy of environment in the programming of the psyche of the individual. Two texts allow a delineation of his position vis-à-vis conceptual psychology: the short *Grundriß der Psychologie* (*Outline of Psychology*, a school text) and the major *Völkerpsychologie* (*Psychology of Peoples*). The first of these outlines Wundt's model of the individual psyche; the latter, the interrelations of individuals and the group in which they are immersed.[14]

Wundt begins the *Grundriß* with his concept of psychology as a science -- what psychology is not:

> Two designations of the concept of psychology are dominant in the history of this science. According to one, psychology is the "science of the soul": psychical processes are considered as appearances from which one can work back to the essence of a metaphysical spiritual substance lying at their base. According to the second, psychical processes belong to a special type of experience which are immediately to be distinguished because its objects are given to "self observation" or (as one terms this in contrast to perception through the outer senses) to the "inner" sense.
>
> Neither of these concept designations suffices for today's position of the science. (GrP, 1)

This refutes both idealism and phenomenology, since there is neither transcendental mind nor introspection in the narrow sense.

In order to correct this deficiency, Wundt, like his predecessors, first turns his attention to the proper classification of the data of the science in which he is involved:

> The result of this is that the expressions outer and inner experience refer not to different objects, but to *different perspectives* which we employ in conceptualization and scientific processing of experience unified in itself. These perspectives also directly indicate that each experience divides immediately into *two factors*: into a *content*, which is given to us, and into our *conceptualization* of this content. We designate the first of these factors as the *objects of experience*, the second as the *experiencing subject*. (GrP, 3)

Wundt's psychology is, indeed, a science of experience, but it must deal neither with the pure forms nor with the contents of experience, but rather with the "immediate content of all experience" -- the triad of concerns at the base of conceptual psychology (GrP, 6).

This decision has been reached by Wundt in a conscious confrontation with the work of his predecessors. The English psychologists studied representations, and not the regularities or "natural laws" underlying them (GrP, 12). Herbart, although focusing on the laws governing representations, erred in making these laws primary to the experience he was purporting to explain. In making a "mechanics of representation," too much stress was laid on acts rather than positivism:

> Herbart attempted to derive the essence of representing itself, as well as the laws of its course from metaphysical presuppositions about the soul and its relation to other simple substances bound to it in the body. (GrP, 13)

Wundt thus wished to follow Fechner and investigate the processes associated with human experience, but in relation to experience (its contents), and not as fixed processes in themselves.

Wundt's work tries to account for the differentiation between inner and outer worlds, and the experience and conditioning that will result within individual mind:

> 1) Inner or psychological experience is not one special field of experience next to others, but it is *immediate experience* itself.
>
> 2) This immediate experience is not a fixed content, but a *constellation of processes*; it does not consist of objects, but of *processes*, namely the *generally applicable human experiences* and their rule-governed interactions.
>
> 3) Each of these processes has on the one hand an objective content, and is on the other a *subjective process*, and it thus includes in itself the general conditions on all cognition as well as on all practical activity of man. (GrP, 17)

He is taking a dynamic view of the mind in a process-stasis of experience as the fundamental data of psychology.

Wundt, then, has defined the data of psychology; now, he also describes the processes of his psychology as a science:

It is exclusively *processes*, not lasting objects, that

constitute the content of psychology. In order to investigate the commencement and the course of these processes, their constitution out of various components and the interactions of these components exactly, we must above all initiate this commencement willfully and vary the conditions on its according to our purposes, which here, as everywhere, can only happen by way of experiment. (GrP, 26)

He stresses processes, the interactions of these processes, and the contents of the mind. Thereafter, he tries to derive the laws for these states, echoing Avenarius' program (GrP, 31).

Wundt's science, however, has a goal reminiscent of Herbart's -- the explanation of "psychic constructs" (instead of "capacities") in terms of the components of experience which go into them:

Under 'psychic construct' we understand each composite component of our immediate experience, which through determinate characteristics sets itself off from the rest of the contents of experience in such a way that it is conceived as a relatively independent unit and, where practical needs require, is designated with a particular name. (GrP, 107)

These mental constructs are ordered hierarchically into classes and genera, and are representations such as affects and acts of will. This affinity of Wundt's work with that of Herbart continues throughout the entire work, in his definitions of consciousness,[15] attention, apperception,[16] associations and other "relational processes,"[17] amalgamations, assimilations and constructs, temporal series, and causality.[18] Each of these mental constructs is defined as a set of elements in a specific relation of processes.

Yet the explanations of the complex phenomena of consciousness were not the only goals of Wundt's work; he had to a degree adopted the model of the mind as a set of functions in dynamic equilibrium with the experiences of its environment. As such, he was forced to accommodate this equilibrium by a series of three "general principles of psychic occurrences . . . psychic resultants, relations and contrasts" (GrP, 398). First, the equilibrium of the mind will be a whole system which will manifest properties greater than those of the elements which formed that experience (a synthetic principle);[19] second, we may determine the relations of experience which constitute representations (an analytic principle);[20] and third, consciousness has both objective and subjective elements the latter relating to the processes of will as a sense of alternatives or opposites available.[21]

Prosesses of the mind create a holistic set of relations between mind and world:

> . . . the spiritual world is a mirror of the corporeal, the corporeal an objective realization of the spiritual world. . . . there is only *one* experience in and of itself, which, though, as soon as it becomes the content of a scientific analysis, allows in certain of its constituents a *double* form of scientific observation: one *mediate*, which investigates the objects of our representing in their objective relations to each other, and one *immediate*, which investigates them in their observable constitution in the midst of all other contents of experience of the knowing subject. (GrP, 395)

Human experience is thus subject to a double path of scientific investigation which traces the "spiritual growth" of an individual with respect to the environment. This is not only introspection or subjectively reported experience, but a model of the objectively observable products of human consciousness.

This is where Wundt's work will set itself apart from the later goals of phenomenology (see next chapter): the observability of the data must be found in the outside world, available to any observer, not only to the reporting subject. No matter how unprovable the constituency of the mind with respect to the world may be, the products of the mind, the world view of a people, and its products are undeniable artifacts of the activity of the mind. Wundt's science deals with these appearances according to the principles which control any development of the minds in question. These principles, three in number, construe minds as totalities responding to the pressures of history and environment and tie the mind's processes to the historical development of the group. First, a "law of spiritual growth" presupposes that minds are continuous (GrP, 404). Second, a "law of the heterogeneity of purposes" exists, "a law which rules the changes in the relations of single partial contents of mental constructs, originating in consequence of successive creative syntheses" (GrP, 404). This law accounts for the shifting relations among the contents of mental constructs as they enter into different states. Third, there is a "law of development in opposites":

> [F]eelings and drives which are at first of small intensity gradually get stronger through the contrast with overbearing feelings of opposing quality during a specific time, in order to overcome the motives dominating up to this point and then themselves win dominance over a shorter or longer period of time. (GrP, 405)

Thus, a system changes only after it builds up to a certain threshhold value. Here, Wundt has moved beyond the work of Fechner and Avenarius, for he does not seek to determine the principles governing thought, but rather to characterize the resultant thought patterns in terms of a restricted number of rules.

This focus on resultant thought systems explicitly turns the basic program of the *Völkerpsychologie* toward history and the environment, and away from the fundamental workings of the mind which the texts in psychology had espoused:

> It could appear as if psychology could be best served if the person who approached the problem of the psychology of peoples would combine the characteristics of the philologist and the historian with those of the psychologist. (V,v)

In this, he is joining individual psychology to group psychology by considering "a multiplicity of individuals," and not, like Avenarius, a number of types.

> For this reason, [psychology] requires a supplemental investigation which we assign to the psychology of peoples. According to this, the project for this partial area of psychology is the investigation of *those psychical processes which lie at the basis of the general development*

of human communities and of the origin of communal
spiritual products of general value. (V, 1)

The new supplementary discipline which Wundt suggests, the
"psychology of peoples," must strictly avoid being confused with
existing disciplines, "because it does not yet exist in a generally
recognized form" (V, 4).[22]
     Wundt's new psychology must account for various frames in
which the individual finds himself: family, culture, and cultural
inheritance. It is, however, not a social psychology in the narrow
sense:

> [T]his designation would again meet with
> misunderstandings on account of the meaning which has
> already been assigned to "sociology." Even in higher
> stages of culture, the people [as a group] is in any case the
> most important of the circles of life out of which the
> products of shared spiritual life originate. (V, 1-2)

This study does not work only on the group from a top-down
perspective, but also from the perspective of the individual's
relation to it.
     From this point of view, there are "psychological regularities of
communal life," but not national psychologies in the sense of
Kant's *Anthropology*. Instead, Wundt stresses the synergistic
effects between the group and the individuals in the products of
culture:

> Thus a concrete form of language can be of interest to it,
> because here there are expressed certain general human
> laws of language development in characteristic fashion.
> But this interest ceases as soon as such a form is used as a
> characteristic for a one-time connection of various peoples
> -- a point where, in contrast, the evidence wins its chief
> value for the historian. (V, 3)

This is not the psychology of a people, but rather the principles of
mind that will tend to appear in the individuals of a particular
group.

Wundt believes that the individual's consciousness is constructed out of the multifarious experiences to which it is subjected. Yet on the level of the psychology of peoples, Wundt retains only the assumption of the psyche as an equilibrium subject to the influences of environment and culture in the abstract. This psychology of peoples operates on the level of conceptual patterns underlying group history, not on overt cultural transmissions. He will, for example, not only trace which myths arrived in which countries and by what means they were adapted, but will also come closer to the procedures advocated by Lévi-Strauss in "The Structural Study of Myth" from *Structural Anthropology*.

The "soul" of a people relates to the environment as a set of mental processes originating in the norms of a community, like individuals sharing a set of cultural programming:

> The soul of a people in the empirical sense does not consist of a pure sum of individual units of consciousness whose circles intersect over a part of their extent. Rather, out of their connections there results peculiar psychical and psychophysical processes which could not originate within an individual consciousness, or at least not in the developed form it assumes as a consequence of the interactions of individuals. Thus, the soul of the people is a product of individual souls of which it consists; these are no less products of the souls of the people in which they participate. . . . [because of] complicated connections and relations of facts, concepts undergo necessary modifications according to the field of their application. (V, 9-10)

In this model, individuals retain their individuality as cognitive beings, yet will act variously according to the pressures of environment and the group in which they are immersed. The existence of the community does not, therefore, preclude the individual, but rather tends to guarantee a "continuity of psychic developments despite the repeated demise of their individual bearers" (V, 11). The region of data for the psychology of peoples is, therefore, the field of "general developments of the soul of the people belonging to human existence determined by natural history"

(V, 11). This leaves more space in the model for individual variances than in Avenarius' version.

In an adaptation of the vocabulary we have already seen in Avenarius and Fechner, Wundt attributes the creation of psychic values for present existence to the equilibrium of a people's soul. In contrast, philosophy will be the science dealing with future ideals, and ethnography will treat primitive cultures (V, 17-18). These mental values of the field of psychology will also not necessarily reflect the interests of the historians, who focus on one-sided individualism rather than the overriding interests of the group (V, 19). The values which Wundt discusses are those of the group, of the community, and of the interactive patterns of its minds:

> The psychology of peoples bases itself on the assumption that the community creates independent spiritual values which are rooted in the spiritual properties of the individual, but which themselves are of a specific type and which again add their specific contents to the individual soul's life. It would be impossible if the community did not continually produce new values, the psychological knowledge of which not being adequately met by the aids of individual psychology. (V, 19)

Nonetheless, the individual still is the medium for innovation in this group, since he introduces them into group transactions.

Wundt's main project in the *Völkerpsychologie* is to trace and interpret the facts of this communal life as representatives of the soul of the people and its "spiritual environment." This acknowledgement constitutes the major advance of Wundt's position over that of the other empiricists discussed thus far: the individual may indeed be conditioned as a thinking being by the environment, but through the medium of culture, the group of individuals changes the constituency of that environment and creates pressures for thought and interaction on itself.[23] This will necessarily cause psychology to look at individuals in ways attributed to other areas of study:

> Even general psychology cannot entirely ignore the fact that the consciousness of the individual stands under the

influence of its spiritual environment. Traditional representations, language and those forms of thought contained in it, and finally the deep-reaching effects of upbringing and education are preconditions for every subjective experience. In many respects, therefore, the contents of individual psychology can only be made available to our full understanding from the perspective of the psychology of peoples. (V, 25)

This is a full statement of the relativity of the mind -- its processing is innate on the level of comparison and discrimitation of elements, but its capacities develop relative to historical experience and inheritance.

Tracing individual development is a project not exhausted at the level of the origin of language and world view. Wundt stresses the relativity of higher-order thought as well, in a description of the complex products of thought which his predecessors had largely ignored:

And the latter applies everywhere that such constructs occur in sufficiently complete developing forms, as products of the consciousness of peoples -- such as many products of the activity of fantasy, or where the individual consciousness works with finished traditional forms originating in spiritual interactions, as in logical thought bound in its specific forms to language. (V, 30)

Pressures of communication and inheritance will be crucial in individual thought as well.

The first volume of the *Völkerpsychologie* deals with language as the primary of the products of communal spirit. Language is a phenomenon perhaps more encompassing than the other which may be investigated, but it ties into both history and the social net of speakers:

In *language* the *world of representation* of man is reflected. In the change of word meanings, the laws of change for representations are expressed, as they take place under the influence of changing conditions for association and

> apperception. In the organic construct of language, in the
> building of word forms and in the syntactic joining of parts
> of speech the regularity is revealed that rules the
> connections of representations under the specific
> conditions of nature and culture of the language
> community. *Myth* gives the representations laid down in
> language its content . . . *custom*, finally, encompasses all
> the communal *directions of will*, which have won rule over
> the deviances of individual habits . . . (V, 37-38)

Language is not (as Avenarius hinted) something that takes over the
individual; but it is the mental product most closely binding the
group and the individual:

> Language does not create itself, but rather is created by a
> speaking human. It is a *function*, or rather a constellation
> of functions, onto which the human who produces it
> transfers his own organizing power. (V, II, 459)

Despite these progressive definitions anticipating linguistic
terminology of the later twentieth century, however, Wundt's
expositions about the nature of language do not progress
appreciably beyond those of Fechner. He correlates facets of the
environment as experiential phenomena which emerge into
language. However, Wundt rarely considers the reverse case: the
effects which language will have on thought as correlated with the
environment. He discusses the facets of linguistic expression as
they express facets of the environment, and not in terms of the
interaction between the individual and the environment which they
condition. In this, Wundt has added mental products, the group,
and the individual to the model of his predecessors, but still not
gone as far as the new paradigm allows. Wundt still implies that
the speaking individual uses language as it is imposed upon him or
her from the standpoint of the environment, be it natural or cultural.
Moreover, he indicates that individuals may alter the system, but he
does not present how to accomplish that change.

Wundt's achievement is his elucidation of the importance of
cultural data as a product of the interaction of the individual, the
group, and the environment, in terms of the complex interactions

which extend in all directions around all poles of this situation. The expositions which Wundt provided do not, however, live up to the promise of his psychological theory, since they dwell at the level of physiology and primary language phenomena. Hermann Paul, one of his contemporaries who is also his interlocutor in philological matters, will be left to describe the interaction over historical time between the speaking individual and the products of culture which affect thought. Wundt takes Fechner's model and, stressing that psychology is a cultural discipline, establishes the discourse that Avenarius could not. Still, Wundt remained at the basic levels of thought -- he did not really correlate social functions to individuals. Wundt used the paradigm to establish a discourse, but he did not go far enough in accounting for feedback between the individual and culture -- that is the work of Hermann Paul and the Neogrammarians.

4.4 Hermann Paul and Language as Communication

Hermann Paul's *Prinzipien der Sprachgeschichte* (*Principles of the History of Language*) remains a valuable reference for philologists, because it is the most comprehensive example of the Neogrammarian movement. The so-called "Junggrammatiker" initiated a new science of language for nineteenth-century Germany that remains the pattern for modern philology today. Yet this text offers more for the present context: a consistent application of the principles of conceptual psychology to the question of language history, and an analysis of the interactions between mind and environment within one framework in the cultural sphere.[24]

Paul identifies his intellectual heritage in the foreword which he appended to the second edition of his text. Paul acknowledges his debt to Herbart's methodology, while also explicitly denouncing Wundt's tendency to slight the individual in favor of the group, and relying instead on typical experience as the norm for his analyses. He refuses, however, to debate Wundt in detail regarding their fundamental differences in principles:

> [A]nalogy, to which I have granted such great significance for the activity of speaking and the development of

language (in accordance with all of today's investigators into language), plays almost no role for Wundt . . . But a deeper and broader cleft divides us which cannot be bridged over in any fashion, a consequence of our respective stances with respect to the psychology of peoples.

Wundt establishes the psychology of peoples (just as the title of his great work demonstrates) next to individual psychology, and, to be sure in all seriousness, in a sense which I combatted in the introduction of my book. He believes he may do so as soon as a transcendental subject is not added to the life of the soul. The changes in language take place according to him through changes in the spirit of peoples, not in the individual souls. The problem which stands for me in the center of the investigation (the question of how interactions among individuals take place) is no problem at all for Wundt. He therefore always treats language only from the viewpoint of the speaker, not of the hearer. It is my conviction that no full understanding of the development of language can be won on this path. (PS, v-vi)

This is a clear statement of the premises of conceptual psychology: Paul relies on the interplay between the group and the individual.

In his criticism of Wundt, Paul also acknowledges that what he is doing in terms of a science of language does not in itself constitute a psychology -- psychology can aid the study of language, but the reverse is not necessarily true, a differentiation which Wundt does not feel compelled to make in stressing the processing of data (PS, vi). The psychology on which Paul's analyses of language rests is the exact science of the mind, a science of principles about the general nature of the mind's workings:

> Language is, like every product of human culture, an object of historical consideration, but just as for each branch of the human sciences, so, too, must the history of language be accompanied by a *science which deals with the general conditions of life of the object developing in*

*history, and which investigates the factors regularly
present in all change according to their nature and efficacy.*
(PS, 1)

The methodology of the psychology accompanying this science
must accommodate both the
equilibrium of the individual mind as well as the historical
conditioning to which that mind is subject. It must also clearly
isolate the various interactions of the mind, for
"[i]solating must precede summarizing, because as long as one
works with inarticulated complexes, one has not penetrated into a
scientific processing of the material" (PS, 2-3). Moreover, the
analyses include historical considerations of logic patterns as well,
since they, too, vary over time.

Such a methodological starting point recognized the two major
desiderata of conceptual psychology as begun by Herbart: the
historicity of thinking, and the individualization of thought with
respect to experience within the confines of the available forms of
representations. The science accommodating these principles will
be, for Paul, the quintessential science of culture, as opposed to the
historical natural sciences:

> The mental element is the most significant factor in all
> movements of culture, around which all else revolves, and
> psychology is, therefore, the most noble basis for all
> science of culture conceived in a higher sense. The mental
> is, therefore, not the sole factor; there is no culture on a
> purely mental base . . . In fact, there is only one pure
> human science: psychology as a science of laws. As we
> enter the field of historical development, we have to deal
> not only with mental energies, but with *physical* ones.
> (PS, 6)

Paul thus has a clear sense of the cultural sciences, history, and
psychology, dealing with "the general conditions under which
mental and physical factors, following their idiosyncratic laws,
succeed in interacting for a common purpose" (PS, 7).

Paul must therefore accommodate his version of conceptual
psychology together with his study of language, for language is a

product of culture, and a tool for the individual.[25] He upholds the following developmental sequence of the individual within the environment, resembling that encountered in the works of Fechner, Avenarius, and Wundt. His is the clearest formulation of the mind model of conceptual psychology as the ground for all science:

> First, in [the individual] mental constructs, complexes of representations are produced, which he would not have reached -- or only very much more slowly -- without their pre-formulations by others. Second, he learns to execute certain purposeful movements with the various parts of his body, which eventually serve to move foreign bodies, tools . . . Third, through the aid of the human bodies, objects of nature adapted or shifted from the location of their origin for any purpose (which become tools or capital for trade) are transmitted from one individual to another, from the older generation to the younger, and a common participation of various individuals in the adaptations or shifting of these objects takes place. Fourth, the individuals exert physical pressure on each other which can either be to the advantage or disadvantage of progress, but which cannot be split off from the essence of culture. (PS, 8)

The differentiation between Paul's project and those of his predecessors, however, lies in the fourth point cited -- in the realization that any assumed genesis for a particular product of culture (such as language) must necessarily reside at the level of theory. The development of the individual or of mental processes does not take place only in the face of pressures from the environment, as was the tacit assumption particularly for Wundt, but also under the pressures of social intercourse among the individuals who share in the culture concerned. Neither the individuals nor the group can be classified in terms of a univalent typical soul; they must be distinguished only in terms of available interactions:

> Psychology never deals with the concrete form of a single human soul, but rather only with the general essence of

> spiritual processes. . . . That would be hypostatization of a series of abstractions, and the covering up of the true essence of the processes. (PS, 10-11)

Thus, his psychology does not look for the individual at all, for the capacities are not real entities; they represent only familiar sets of processes.

The study of the mind in culture, therefore, requires the scientist to carefully differentiate the realms of the physical from those of the mental, in order that the products of culture are not hypostatized as evidence for the univalent constitution of the psyche. Such an assumption would unnecessarily obscure the historical randomness of cultural products, as well as the conditions of need and economy which limit their transmission. There are not two psychologies, as Wundt thought, but only a single individual one: "all purely mental interactions take place only within the individual soul" (PS, 12).

But there is history -- the influence of the group -- in the model:

> The second part [of individual psychology] is no longer a science of principles, but rather of history. It is easy to see that these complicated constructs could only have originated in the life of the individual among a series of other individuals in society. And in order to penetrate more deeply into the secret of their origin, one must try to make visible the various stages through which they gradually progressed in earlier individuals. . . . Everything, however, through which the effect of one individual on another is made possible, is not mental. (PS, 12-13)

Paul is not looking for a synergy in mental processing, it is not a model for group mind. He looks instead for a psychological pattern that conforms to typical mental activity:

> In order to call forth a connection of representations in another soul corresponding to that originating in itself, the soul can do nothing else than produce a physical product by means of motor nerves which then, in turn, calls forth the corresponding representations in the soul of other

individuals, again by means of the stimulation of sensitive nerves, and associates them correspondingly. (PS, 14)

This is less metaphysical in tone than Wundt, Fechner, and Avenarius, because it allows for the group to work on the products of culture. These products have their own lives and are available to influence other minds.

Paul bases his analyses on limitations on interaction which condition the relationship of the individual to the group. These restrictions concern personal experience (and personal inability to conceptualize that which has not yet been experienced) and the fact that concepts, once formed, can block the formation of other, potentially more useful concepts -- all restrictions, then, explored initially by Herbart, and in greater detail by Mach, contemporaneous to Paul:

> What enables these physical products to serve as the means for transmitting representations to another individual is either an *inner, direct connection* to the representations (one should think, for example, of a cry of pain, a gesture of rage), or a *connection mediated through the association of ideas* . . . Through this type of communication, no content of representation can be created anew in the soul. The content about which we are concerned must rather already be present there, and called forth through physiological stimulations. . . . *The content of representation itself is uncommunicable. Everything which we believe we know about those of another individual rests only on conclusions about our own.* . . . The greater the correspondence, the easier the understanding. (PS, 14-15)

Again, this cannot be interpreted as metaphysics, because a shared environment is the grounds for communication -- parallel patterning of individuals allows common signs to evoke echoes between sender and receiver.

This model is crucial for Paul's model of synchronic communication, but he also accounts for the diachronic facets of communication. Learning and inherited patterns help communication as well, because they train individuals in similar patterns. The valid connections of data which language refers to will seem valid to others sharing the same environment, and they will easily be communicated:

> This transformation [of indirect associations into direct ones] is completed within the individual soul; the result gained is, however, transmitted to other souls -- naturally by means of physical mediation in the way described. The advantage lies in the fact that the massed representations do not again need to make the same detour to reach each other as they made in the first soul. . . . Through such a savings in work and time . . . that which is saved can be used to create a further connection, for which the first individual no longer had time. (PS, 15)

The model has another facet, explaining why knowledge tends to age or go out of date, as a function of the contacts between mind and environments:

> While the beginning and end points of a series of representations are transmitted in direct connection, the medial members which originally aided in creating this connection must be lost for the greatest part for the following generation. That is, in many cases, a healing unburdening of useless ballast to create the room necessary for higher development. (PS, 16)

The interactions between the individuals and the group will, at best, remain limiting factors, flowing in both directions and limiting individual growth and perception of the environment.

Because of the interaction between culture and mind, the assumption that the group is in control of these restrictions is psychologically invalid from Paul's point of view:

> Here we are dealing with an interaction of all physical and mental factors with which man enters into relation. Even the most serious attempts will not succeed in completely clarifying the role which each individual of these factors plays. . . . Never do a number of individuals create

something together with unified energies and division of roles. (PS, 17-18)

Language is in an interesting position as a product of culture. It acts as a barometer of the concerns and experiences:

[L]inguistic constructs are generally created without conscious intent. The intent of communication is present, to be sure (except in the earliest phases), but not the intent of establishing something lasting, and the individual does not become conscious of his creative activity. In this regard, the formation of language differentiates itself explicitly from all artistic production. (PS, 18)

This is the reason that language cannot aid psychology -- language in general is too typified, although individual statements might help individual psychology. However, the randomness inherent in language is controlled by the requirements of communication. This assertion explains Paul's difference from Wundt -- one can use language with the proper constraints on its type. Paul fully recognized the relativity of conceptualization and of the concomitant limitations of environment and individuality in a way to provide a description not of the genesis of the products of culture, as did Fechner and Wundt, but rather the principles guiding its development -- a crucial turn away from metaphysics.

Paul is not stressing the absolute individuality of the members of a group, but rather he is acknowledging the statistical veracity of any results reached. The rules of psychology will apply to most individuals at any determinate point in history, but not necessarily to all:

It would be appropriate to demonstrate here to what degree the lack of intent of linguistic processes facilitates our perceiving their essence. The first consequence is again that they must be relatively simple . . . but also, that individual idiosyncrasy cannot make itself strongly felt. The most simple mental processes are the same for all individuals, their peculiarities rest only on combinations of different types of these simple processes. *The great regularity* of all linguistic processes in the most diverse individuals is the most essential basis for an exact scientific recognition of them. (PS, 19)

This is the key to the uniqueness of Paul's version of conceptual psychology: simple mental processes are shared by all members of a speech community, while more developed ones are idiosyncratic to the individual. This distinction between lower- and higher-order thought is crucial to the new paradigm, and it goes beyond the terminology introduced by Wundt.

Because the individual is framed within the group and within the historical environment, a science of language must be not only a science of principles, but also an historical science of culture. This is the reason for Paul's title, *Principles of the History of Language* -- a science of culture must be a historical study:

> The only thing remaining from a non-historical investigation would be general reflections about individual applications of language, about the behavior of the individual in the face of general language usage, in which is included the acquisition of language. However, it is exactly these reflections which are bound up most closely to the investigation of historical development which will be demonstrated in what follows. (PS, 21-22)

The true study of language encompasses both history and psychology and studies language as the products of the mind in history.

Next, Paul delineates the field of data for the study of language conducted on cultural terms as the representations of thought which become reified for the group as language. The researcher must heed one warning in studying these data: the conscious report of the individuals involved do not necessarily exhaust the relations of the data to the psyches involved:

> Only a part of these effective energies enters into appearance. The processes effective in the history of language are not only speaking and hearing; neither [are] the representations stimulated in these processes nor the

> language constructs going through consciousness in silent thought [evident]. . . . *quite a number of mental processes are accomplished without clear consciousness, and that everything that has ever been in consciousness remains in the unconscious as an effective moment.* (PS, 25)

This cannot be called introspection, for the individual is not necessarily the credible observer of him- or herself.

Moreover, both the unconscious and the conscious representations will be subject to the limitations of individual experience by the user. The attitude of the observer may be affected by environmental stimuli:

> Representations are entered into consciousness in groups and therefore remain as groups in the unconscious. . . . And not only individual words, but also larger series of sounds and whole sentences associate themselves immediately with the thought content which was placed in them. These groups, given at least originally by the outside world, organize themselves in the soul of each individual to much richer and more complicated connections which are completed only in the smallest degree consciously, and which have then further unconscious effects, in the greatest part never achieving even clear consciousness, and which are still nonetheless effective. (PS, 26)

These series echo Herbart's series-forms, but they attribute to both individuals and to the group a chance to be products, but not victims, of the environment.

More importantly, the conscious and unconscious documentation of the mind is found not in language, but in language use as it interfaces with the environment. For Paul, the essence of language use was the expression of the representations available to an individual, in terms of the "organism of representations" or complete equilibrated mental representations present in the mind according to individual experience. The "mental organism" manifests itself in the formation of such representations, as well as in facets of its products, such as grammatical categories, but its essence is never fully revealed in such manifest products of its activity. No individual mind is ever like the whole. They are related as a type and a special example, not only as a restricted or reduced variant as Fechner had assumed. Each mind is itself "an organism in constant change in the individual":

> All these associations can come to be without clear consciousness and prove themselves affective, and they are absolutely not to be confused with the categories which are abstracted in a grammatical reflection, even if they normally correspond to these. (PS, 27)

A grammar may reflect aspects of the mind but not exhaust them, because individuals vary:

> . . . the organism of the groups of representations relating to language develops in each individual in idiosyncratic fashion, and also achieves an idiosyncratic form in each. Even if it should be composed in various individuals out of exactly the same elements, these elements will still be introduced in different order, in different groupings, with different intensity, into the soul with greater or lesser frequency, and will, therefore, form their mutual power relationships and thus their groupings differently, even if we do not account for the difference in the general and specific capacities of the individual at all. (PS, 27-28)

His statement indicates that language use as conditioned by the environment has basic patterns in it, but that the weighting of these patterns is individual. A percentage prediction may be made about which patterns will occur, but this is not a unique, valid description of the minds of an age.

As already noted, the constitution of the mental organism is conditioned by the historical environment in which the individual finds himself ("The mental organisms described are the real bearers of historical development. That which is actually said has no development at all" [PS, 28]). Moreover, the minds serve as the reservoir of individual experience which must necessarily affect and the transmitted cultural properties through which it acts. As in the case of concrete utterances in language, each individual product of the mental organism's activity carries in itself no essential documentation of historical change. Again, however, the set of products which that organism produces may provide such documentation, discriminating between chance irregularities and newly won language habits. Moreover, any changes which occur cannot be considered the product of logical thought alone because of the reservoir of unconscious associations out of which the mental organism is composed, albeit on the basis of environment and culture:

> Grammar and logic do, therefore, not correspond, because the expansion and application of language does not proceed through strictly logical thought but through the natural, unschooled notions as masses of representations, which follow more or less logical laws not according to talent and education. . . . Whoever considers grammatical forms only always in isolation, without their relation to the individual activity of the soul, will never come to an understanding of language development. (PS, 36)

Both grammar and logic are predicated on the structures of mind shared by the individual, but each science develops a different set of mental processes according to the goals of these studies vis-à-vis the environment.

Thus, the data for Paul's science is constituted with an awareness of the more modern distinction between *langue* and *parole*: the relationship between the individual utterances of language and the language capability of a community of speakers, which is itself conditioned by historical development and environment, cultural as well as natural. Paul's mind model accommodates the possibility of language variants and allows for individual differences. The norm of experience of an historical era is differentiated by the individual in the activities of the unconscious and systemic aspects of the "mental organism" or equilibrated state of mind constituting the language-user's ego. With this model, Paul explains minor historical phenomena of language development in terms commensurate with the requirements of psychology. The group enforces regularity ("The unconsciousness of elements does not preclude an exact *control*" [PS, 53]). It guarantees a continuity of communications, while it also provides a clear base of expected usage which the individual may employ as a base for idiosyncratic explorations. A word in usage is tied up with expected representations and references for the community of users, but it is not exhausted by these expectations:

> Through the efficacy of groups, each individual is given the possibility and the occasion in generous quantity to reach beyond the norm already given in language. (PS, 114)

Dialects are one example of these options for expansion. Within the relationships of the individual to the conditioned group and the conditioning environment, dialect shifts constitute a "growing of individual differences out beyond a certain degree" (PS, 38). Like dialects, individual word meanings may also shift with respect to the group's expectations: they may specialize, become restricted to a portion of the contents of representation to which they originally referred, concentrate on spatial, temporal, or causal implications of the basic concept, or to extend through analogy of material or form (PS, 87, 91, 97, 106).

From the side of data, Paul's science has one other warning about its goals. It must not concentrate solely on the artifacts of culture but on *systems* of artifacts -- and therefore, in the sphere of language, on syntax of usage rather than on etymology or comparative grammars.[26] This means that language construed as usage has both covert and overt data. For example, the sentence is constructed from the point of view of the speaker, representing an individual mental organism of his experience:

> . . . the sentence is the linguistic expression or symbol for the fact that the connection of several representations or groups of representations took place in the soul of the speaker, and also the means to produce that same connection of same representations in the soul of the hearer. (PS, 121)

Even if the position of the speaking subject is not explicitly marked in the sentence, the representations formed are nonetheless reflective of an individual stance: "The psychological subject is just as little expressed in the sentence 'it is burning' as in the sentence 'fire'" (PS, 131). Such unmarked factors are encountered at other places in syntactic analysis, such as in the differentiation between statements and commands, as well as other optative expressions (PS, 133).

Paul's fundamental goal in the analysis of the forms of language, therefore, closely parallels Herbart's in the analysis of the forms of mental representation and stresses the conditions which shift representations. Like Herbart, Paul will consistently retain a differentiation between the forms and contents of thought, between relations and contents of representations as referring to different facets of world experience, or "the differentiation between the significance of a general connection in itself and that of the connection to a specific word" (PS, 151). Despite the habituation to which the groups subject the individual (stressed by Fechner and Avenarius), Paul concurs with Herbart in upholding the essential economy of the mental systems involved. In the economy of an individual mind, unused forms tend to deteriorate and be replaced with those of higher referential value for the individual. Individual language will be variable, while the system as a whole tends to "eliminate all useless irregularities" (PS, 227). As language develops, a multiplicity of words do also, but "it is little capable of preserving itself at length. *Language disdains luxury*" (PS, 251). Still, an individual cannot be totally idiosyncratic in language use because of the group:

> On the whole, though, a certain economic trait runs through the activity of speaking. Everywhere means of expression must be developed which contain only exactly enough as required for comprehensibility for a hearer. (PS, 313)

Where Fechner and Avenarius recognized the relation of the products of the psyche to the imprinting given them (including intensity and habituation), Paul will stress the inertia of representations to a greater degree. Individual minds generate differences:

> Each grammatical category is generated on the basis of a psychological one. The former is at first nothing but the emergence of the latter as an outer appearance. As soon as the efficacy of the psychological category is recognized in the means of expression of language, it becomes a grammatical one. (PS, 263)

Nonetheless, the inventions of individuals are subject to validation by the group " . . . by two other moments in the facilitating and inhibiting of compromise: the greater or lesser *firmness of connection of etymological groups* and the greater or lesser *intensity with which the single forms are imprinted into memory*" (PS, 205). When the intensity is not the same for all representations, or when an innovation is not founded on principles shared by the group, an innovation will fade -- as coined words often do.[27] Moreover, if a group perception shifts, word or grammatical categories can shift totally in "an occasion for an entrance into another group" (PS, 233).

Paul sees that the forms of language and culture reflect a selection of the psychological functions available at any point in history, not just an exhaustive account of their inventory. Their preservation is conceived also in terms of their pragmatic utility or function, which aids in retaining them. If the grammatical function retains a utility in expressing the relations within the mental organism of the speaker, it will be retained; if not, it will be shifted. Thus, the "usage" or established norm of a language is never actually present as given in the grammar books, since variant conditions of environment, history, or social pressure will all affect that norm:

> . . . the common language is not actually codified. It generally remains a usage conditioning the norm. It cannot, though, be the usage of the collective. For this is far removed from being unified. . . . the usage of a determinate, more narrow circle serves. (PS, 405)

Paul has, therefore, integrated a model of the functional adult mind as conditioned by culture and environment into his explications of language and of the methodology appropriate to a science of language. He does so to accommodate historicity, the feedback effects of culture and education, and the desiderata of mental stability or inertia as a conservation of individual energy. His proclaimed reliance on Herbart is consistently upheld in such a fashion as to have led his school of language and linguistic sociology to create broader effects than did Fechner, Avenarius, or Wundt.

While Fechner and Avenarius are largely forgotten, except as historical curiosities, and Wundt adopted as a physiologist, away from his cultural studies, Paul has opened up abroader field, a critique of the cultural sciences about a century ahead of itself. His work outlines for language the question of language repressing thought (which Derrida will assume under the notion of "difference"), and the issue of culture or cultural communication as a conditioning norm (Foucault's theme, if you substitute the notion of "signs of culture" for linguistic signs).

4.5 Conclusion

In what fundamental respects does Paul's work differ from that of Fechner, Avenarius, and Wundt, as part of conceptual psychology and the groundwork for a new approach to the humanities?

First, Paul and his co-workers initiated a "school" of linguists whose work was to be maintained well into the twentieth century. Fechner and Avenarius are not of present interest except in a historical context, and Wundt's students (who collected a proportionate number of academic chairs compared to Neogrammarians) constituted an academic psychology which was superseded almost completely by physiology, and thus withdrawn from the human sciences.[28]

The fundamental distinction between these camps is their respective definitions of empiricism. For Fechner, Avenarius, and Wundt, "empiricism" in their respective sciences of culture required that they describe the genesis of the products of culture, leading to a developmental series accommodating the simplest to the most complex of products. Yet to do so confuses how individuals learn to use cultural tools with how the group learns. In effect, this posits an exact parallelism between ontogeny and phylogeny. Paul realized that such an exact parallelism may be "true" or empirically verifiable statistically.   Such parallelism may typify the development of a representative individual, but an individual history would differ from the posited norm for the group.

Paul, therefore, did not study the historical genesis of language or consciousness, as did Fechner and Wundt.   Instead, he studies the use and the history of the products of consciousness as these products document regularities in mental development. He studies the principles for history, as his title indicates.   Fechner, Avenarius, and Wundt, in contrast, stress rules predicated on a causal genesis of an archetypical culture, and thus underplay the individual.

The empiricism of Avenarius, Wundt and Fechner (particularly as encompassed under the rubric "psychophysics") also tended to analyze cultural artifacts as products of environmental pressures on individuals and the groups they form. Avenarius, moreover, recognized that cultural pressures will also affect the development of the group. Yet only Paul realized the opposite of this emphasis: products of culture may infringe on each other. In particular, he describes how cultural conditioning will happen through language, so that certain linguistic phenomena will always tend to yield to others, in predictable (but not compulsory) variation.   The empiricists thus conceived of the individual psyche in equilibrium with the environment; Paul added the crucial realization that habituation does more in the mental life of the individual than enable survival. For Paul, the products of culture allow progress of the group spurred by individuals, as well as individuation within the language and conceptual norm, within which an individual functioned. At the same time, the products of culture could impede this progress, or at least randomize it because of historical necessity and pure chance in individual experience. The empiricists were left to speak of survival values; Paul could move on to principles of analogy and economy which express the freedom normally associated with an individual mind. Paul's work moves beyond a science of primitive culture to a true historical science of culture.

This fundamental differentiation in approach to the sciences of culture sets varying limitations for further research within the two group's respective programs. Once a developmental series is posited by the empiricists for unfolding a language or other cultural phenomenon, for example, the project is essentially done, except when new data enters. Although the individual psyche is accommodated, the "soul of a people" is largely determinate as a set of reactions typical for the dynamic equilibrium in which the individuals of that culture stand to their environment. Paul's model differs, since he posits a constant iteration between the data and the mental activities which guided the evaluation and assessment of data. Wundt's students set up laboratories in physiological psychology, studying psychological reaction times and reactions tied to physical stimuli.[29] In contrast, Paul's group drew up not only dialect geography maps and grammars of the Germanic languages, but also laid the principles for a science of language that was to eventually yield productive distinctions such as de Saussure's langue/parole and deep structure/surface structure (since Paul himself realized that language representations for concepts do not necessarily correspond to the experiential data which formed them).[30]

The empiricists (Fechner, Wundt, and Avenarius) thus became gradually confined to the relation of the body and the environment, while the Neogrammarians (following Paul) were in the position to expand the program of conceptual psychology and use the products of culture as keys to the "mental organism" or system of minds as feedback loops to the conditions of environment in which they developed. This shift is perhaps a symptom of the discourse paradigm. Fechner and Wundt were the most cited at the turn of the century, but from the point of view of the paradigm, Paul's work was ultimately more productive. Paul opened up an entire new field, turning linguistics from a taxonomic discipline into a cultural anthropology. He could do so because his discourse deferred, following Derrida's logic, the worst lingering problem facing the empiricists: for Paul, the mind lost its primacy once and for all. Only Paul accounts commensurately for mental processing, the products of the mind, and the context of both environmental and cultural inheritance. Moreover, in so doing, he treats more than first-order thought, and more than just the rudimentary capacities of the soul.

This latter program will be the key for both Ernst Mach and

Freud, as well as for the Neogrammarians, and will surface again in the work of Dilthey and other proponents of *Geistesgeschichte*, the history of ideas as presented in the next chapter. Wundt forged the new discourse successfully where Fechner and Avenarius could not, but only Paul opened the way to a new cultural science, instead of just another area of natural science. As such, Paul gave the paradigm of conceptual psychology its first discipline -- its first example of a finished discourse.

The next four chapters of this volume will trace four more disciplines that were developed, accompanied, or spurred on by the paradigm of conceptual psychology. The terms derived from empiricism and idealism that were synthesized by Paul and others will recur in the deliberations of a philosopher-historian (Dilthey), two phenomenologist-psychologists (Brentano and Husserl), a physicist (Mach), and a psychoanalyst (Freud). These four disciplines are all different, but they share a reliance on the discourse of conceptual psychology.

PART 3

CASE STUDIES

CHAPTER 5

DILTHEY AND DESCRIPTIVE PSYCHOLOGY

In the early part of the nineteenth century in Germany, the prevailing image of psychology was that of a therapeutic discipline concerned with the spiritual care (*Seelensorge*) of individuals.[1] As we have seen in the case of the Empiricists, however, a new question was raised with increasing frequency in the course of the century: the role of psychology as a discipline to guide and support the development of the natural sciences and the humanities. Such a suggestion was taken up with respect to the theory of knowledge and education by Herbart and Avenarius, to the question of language acquisition and change by Wilhelm von Humboldt and the Neogrammarians, and to the pure sciences by Helmholtz and Mach.[2]

These attempts at developing systematic sciences out of older fields incorporated not only the standards for evidence and reproducibility which are the chief criteria for the modern physical sciences, but also principles which described the elements of human consciousness and the processes of the mind which affected perception and, hence, all knowledge of a discipline. As the work on the new paradigm included above indicated, the inclusion of a psychological perspective (the paradigm for conceptual psychology) in such discussions of the sciences forced a concomitant shift in the nature of scientific theory-building. In the wake of Kant's "Copernican Revolution," scientific theories and explanatory models were conceived as simulcra of the functional dependencies of the data of the real world.[3] Such models were not validated in terms of "things in themselves," but in terms of their utility and plausibility in explaining and even predicting data -- their theoretical adequacy.

The texts discussed above showed the way to a new science of culture, evolving the basic model for conceptual psychology. August Boeckh's *Enzyklopädie der philologischen Wissenschaften* represents perhaps the first complete attempt to reformulate a humanistic discipline in light of the scientific criteria of verifiability, validity, and recreatability drawn from the natural sciences, and the notions of psychological adequacy drawn from conceptual psychology.[4]   With the field of classical philology as a model, Boeckh describes the methods for uncovering cultural meaning out of raw data as the concatenation of several disciplines. First, data of a field must be gathered and organized in a "hermeneutics."[5] Thereafter, this data must be interpreted according to its implications and the assumptions on which its organization is predicated in a "critique."[6] The results achieved are assumed to be indicative of the psyche of a culture, representative of its fashion of conceptualizing reality, in the sense evoked by Paul. Boeckh implicitly assumes that the "spirit of an age" will be recreatable for another age if the controls of data and allowable paths of interpretation are upheld. In this assumption, however, Boeckh follows Paul and anchors the shifts in world views between cultures and historical epochs in the data available. World views, like language, are determined by geographical and temporal shifts in conditions. Little credence is given to the suggestion that the patterns of conceptualization themselves may be historically relative, and not only the data available. Boeckh's work, consequently, remained only at the threshold for the development of true "sciences" of culture, no matter how progressive its differentiation between "critique" and "hermeneutics" remains even in today's light.[7]

The work of Hermann Paul and the Neogrammarian philologists filled the gap still left by work such as Boeckh's. Paul's *Principien der Sprachgeschichte* and Wundt's *Völkerpsychologie*, for example, both provide not only descriptions of acceptable data and analytic modes for the philological disciplines, but also the explicit attention to psychology treated only peripherally in earlier texts. The human sciences they developed stand as models for historical linguistics today, and provide catalogues of the mechanisms of the human mind which affect the development of language and other cultural artifacts. These texts were, however, focused around one class of data (linguistic or semiotic), and the psychologies they present did not consequently attempt to retain validity as a criterion for more than the particular branch of the human sciences under consideration. Moreover, Paul and Wundt attended only cursorily to the systematics of the human sciences, the "hermeneutics" and "critique" added by Boeckh.

Wilhelm Dilthey, at the end of the nineteenth century, extended the progress made by earlier scholars in the establishment of the human sciences as truly scientific disciplines, as "Geisteswissenschaften." The large part of his work was devoted to the systematics of the history ideas: a delineation of allowable data and interpretive procedures in discussions of historical epochs and their determining spirit or ideas.[8] In an 1894 essay, however, Dilthey highlights the role of psychology as an integral part of his human sciences, and as a scientific discipline in its own right. "Ideas toward a Descriptive and Discriminating Psychology" summarizes the desiderata of a psychology which could serve as the helpmate for both the natural and human sciences, and as a guarantee for valid avenues of investigation in terms of the constitution of the human psyche ("Seele" in his terminology).[9]

The core of this essay describes a psychology which deals with the conditions on the unity of human consciousness, and the changes and adaptations which such a consciousness undergoes through history under the pressure of processing conceptual data. In this explication, Dilthey uncovers perhaps the central tension in his age's concept of science and of the adequacy of scientific description: the need for new definitions of the closure and application of theories and experimental results. While seemingly unconcerned with the solutions to these questions provided by contemporaries such as Ernst Mach, Dilthey in this essay is proposing a fundamental redefinition of the sciences, that will be accomplished on the basis of a redefinition of the unity of human consciousness.

5.1 Dilthey's Psychology: Goal of the Discipline

The primary distinction Dilthey makes is that between an explanatory (*erklärende*) and a descriptive (*beschreibende*) psychology as the two forms which the discipline can assume.

An explanatory psychology is tied to traditional notions of

scientific causality and is related to empiricism and associationism (IP, 140).[10] The explanatory mode of this psychology, Dilthey feels, is bound up in apodictics. It develops what are assumed to be necessary truths about a posited form of human consciousness through a systematic hypothesis-building mechanism (IP, 144). Explanatory psychology believes that it is possible to explain the various capacities of consciousness on the basis of a comparatively limited set of mental elements. The modes of perception in consciousness, then, are explained as various syntheses of these elements and their interactions -- the procedure followed by Mill and Spencer, according to Dilthey (IP, 159-60).

The tacit assumption in an explanatory psychology is that hypothesis-formation will continually expand, reflecting an ever-increasing store of knowledge of our perceptions. The psyche or consciousness in this model grows in perception and knowledge. This growth is teleological and leans towards a fuller correspondence of perceptions with the objects of nature. Dilthey feels, however, that this assumption constitutes an unallowable and illicit reduction of the total facts of human consciousness and a lapse into metaphysics, into the realm of totally unprovable hypotheses (IP, 144). This error probably started with Kant, who applied the method of formal hypothesis-building to the powers of thought (IP, 149). In separating the forms of thought from its contents, Kant defined the categories of perception as constructs assembled out of perceived data by the innate structures of the mind.

Dilthey identifies a central fact overlooked in explanatory psychology: consciousness is, indeed, the subject of any psychological investigation, yet that same consciousness will condition the innate forms or modes of that investigation (IP, 143). Since this situation cannot be circumvented, Dilthey suggests that a new method of investigation be initiated if a valid psychology with provable tenets is to be developed -- that is, a hermeneutic approach. Instead of constructing the modes of consciousness out of posited elements and their arrangements or syntheses, the primary focus for the development of psychology should be in the facts themselves, not in hypothetical premises such as the natural sciences often use (IP, 143). For a valid psychology, we should not follow Kant:

We explain nature, we understand the life of the soul. . . .
This conditions a very great differentiation in methods with
which we study the soul, history, and society and those
which yield knowledge of nature. For the question under
consideration here, the given differentiation results [in a
situation] where hypotheses will by no means play the
same role in psychology as they play in the natural
sciences. In the latter, all dependencies are determined in
the formation of hypotheses, in psychology the
dependencies are originary and constant as experience: life
is given everywhere only as dependencies. Psychology
does not need, therefore, fundamental concepts developed
as deductions . . . (IP, 144)

For Dilthey, then, the development of psychology must take place
in light of the facts of experience, with the "lived world" as a
totality to be analyzed as a set of dependencies within the given
field of data. Only with such a hermeneutic approach, beginning
with the whole and analyzing out the dependencies which condition
it, can the human sciences avoid falling prey to the apodictic errors
of the natural sciences.

For Dilthey, the psychology which is required as an
accompanying validation by the human sciences cannot be
empirical. It is not tied to an independent objective constitution of
nature as corresponding to "things in themselves." Instead,
psychology deals with the appearances of reality as a continuum of
inner life:

Mental facts form the most important constituent [of the
human sciences]; they cannot be elucidated without a
psychic analysis. They contain dependencies in
themselves, because the life of the soul is a set of
dependencies. Thus the understanding of these inner
dependencies in us conditions at all points its knowledge. .
. . consistency and regularity exist in the life of the soul,
and make possible a similar ordering for the many units
[sub-regions] of life. (IP, 147-48)

Since "spiritual dependencies form the basis of the process of cognition," the totality of the psychic mechanism will condition not only the human sciences which arise from its activity, but also the psychology which is to act as validation for those sciences (IP, 151).

An explanatory psychology is inappropriate, because it is a natural science; yet the human sciences still need a psychology in order to systematize the disciplines of culture. For this reason, Dilthey delineates a "descriptive and discriminating psychology," in which the totality of lived experience -- the data of our perception -- is analyzed to reveal the psychological continuum on which such experience is predicated. The goal of this psychology is to specify the regularities in this mental continuum as the constant "forms of inner activity" which are the "content reality" (*inhaltliche Wirklichkeit*) of the psyche (IP, 153). Thus, the proper subject of such a psychological investigation is the fully developed adult *Kulturmensch*, or civilized human being -- an adult whose identity has been thoroughly conditioned by the thought and reactive patterns of his environment (IP, 157).

Dilthey's descriptive psychology does not, then, use the construction method of explanatory psychology and the natural sciences, but rather a heuristic, analytic method beginning from the totality of the inner life of the adult. From this continuum of given elements, the mind begins to distill lasting connections and raise them to the level of consciousness:

> But such connections are constantly becoming conscious to us. In the immeasurable variability of the contents of consciousness, the same connections return again and again, and thus their form gradually emerges with clarity. (IP, 171)

When associations of elements constantly emerge into consciousness, they achieve a semblance of permanence, and then become central to the functions of the mind. With familiarity, abstractions and generalizations are made on the basis of these observations, which then become subject to "elementary logical operations" such as summation or differentiation (IP, 171). The fundamental processes of mind, though, remain a raising to consciousness of perceived data: "the intellectualization of inner perception" (IP, 172). All understanding, all differentiation of more or less important elements, and all surety about the constitution of reality depends on this mechanism.

Such raising to consciousness of inner perception is only the first criterion for psychological research for Dilthey (IP, 172). The second ties in with the first: ". . . [psychological research] should grow out of experience itself, and must always keep its roots here, if it is to grow healthy and tall" (IP, 173). From these two fundamental principles, the avenue of development for Dilthey's descriptive psychology is clear:

> In psychology the *connections* of functions in experience is given *inside*. All discrete knowledge in psychology is only a *discrimination* of these connections . . . *psychological thought articulates and distinguishes beginning at the given connections and moving outward*. (IP, 173-174)

This process is clearly derived from hermeneutics: beginning at whole experience as presented to consciousness, and evolving, with the help of a clearness and distinctness criterion, towards a discrimination of the connections, dependencies, elements, and classes of elements which constitute these experiences. At no point can such work on a psychological discipline begin as do the natural sciences, using a set of hypotheses to analyze a chosen field of data. Any such hypotheses applicable as descriptions of the spiritual continuum of the psyche must be the *result* of the procedure directed at an analysis of its connecting structures (*Strukturzusammenhang*; IP, 176). Moreover, the concepts associated with these hypotheses must also be derived from experience; they should not be considered "transcendental antinomies," or again psychology will have been misled out of the realm of experience and into the realm of speculation (IP, 175).

Dilthey's descriptive psychology thus emerges as a discipline concerned with experienced reality as a continuum, and with the analyses of this given totality as such analyses raise the connections and categories of elements of experience into the consciousness of a perceiving being. His description of the desiderata of psychology as a discipline correspond to Boeckh's "Analytics" and "Hermeneutics" with one major differentiation, lying not in the procedures of the discipline, but rather in its preconditions: all analysis proceeds on the ground of lived experience by an analyzing consciousness -- on the basis of the constitution of the mind itself, and subject to its inherent limitations. Thus Dilthey must turn to an explicit discussion of the properties of the psyche as they affect lived experience. In this statement, he moves away from pure hermeneutics, and into the realm of conceptual psychology.

5.2 The Constitution of the Psyche

For Dilthey, the psyche has two roles: first, as a continuum in and of itself; and second, as a locus around which other structures are formed -- *Strukturzusammenhänge*, or "structural continua" (IP, 176). Each of these structures represents an analysis of a part of experience which has been abstracted and independently formulated as a heuristic aid for the consciousness in interacting and interfacing with further elements of experience.

Each structure continuum is subject to development, when the experience of the individual warrants it: "If a purposefulness and a system of values did not exist in the structure of the soul to drive it forward toward a particular tendency, then the path of life would not be development" (IP, 176). Each structure tends towards a stable state, corresponding to the life conditions in which the organism finds itself. In this way, the consciousness adapts to the necessities of its environment, more flexibly than is posited in transcendental idealism, and more consciously than Schopenhauer's "will."[11] Once a particular state of conscious has been evolved in the psyche and a continuum of experience has been stabilized, then the structures of consciousness are subject to progressive differentiation, in an adaptation guided by the attention or foregrounding of data for that organism (IP, 177).

Dilthey's idea of structure continua as the constituent mechanisms of consciousness reflects a useful assumption: that the potential capacity of the mind is at all times greater than its actualized part as represented in the structure continua. Since interest and foregrounding constantly modify the cognitive structures of an organism, the progressive differentiation of these structures will be affected by both biological interests and stimuli by the environment. In all cases, though, these structures are hypothetical constructs formed on the basis of observed data (IP, 179-180). Nonetheless, these structures and the continuum of consciousness which support them must be acknowledged in any description of the psyche.

Dilthey defines a structure as a combination of "the central power of our drives and feelings, their connection to external stimuli and, on the other hand, to our acts of will" (IP, 178). All these factors affect our states of consciousness, the reproduction of mental representations, and the influence of acquired concept groups on the conscious processes of our mind. The structures represented in a mental continuum do not, therefore, represent a fixed number of basic processes of intelligence, but rather represent those facets of intelligence called into play in a certain context or environment. Each structure thus represents a system of intellectual activity, with a distinct direction of interest and degree of liveliness. Therefore, Dilthey's descriptive psychology, dealing with these structures in the psyche, will be integrally interested in the more stable of them as reflections of permanent aspects of the psychic life which produced them -- not as a causal explanation of how structures arise, but rather as a description of typical modes of perception. The chief difficulty arising in this discipline is evident: in the realm of drives and feelings particularly, it is difficult for the investigator to distinguish psychic states clearly, and to systematically correlate the differentiations among states.

In the case of an act of will, to use Dilthey's example, the mental structure corresponding to it will be differentiated in terms of "setting of purpose, motive, . . . goal and means, choice and preference" (IP, 188). Yet this differentiation of the motive, purpose, and means represented by an act of will also defines the entire class of reactions yielded by the mental continuum of the individual under consideration. While modulated by the quantity of data of experience which the individual psyche can contain, consistencies of volition and of the motives or goals chosen will point to consistencies in the constitution of all psyches (IP, 190). For Dilthey, in consequence, it is an allowable generalization to consider culture and its forms as a product of group will conditioned by the constitution of the group psyche. Also, an analysis of the institutions and forms of such a culture must account for all significant differentiations in volitional activities among individuals.

The objection which may arise from this generalization -- that a lack of freedom is posited when a group psyche is acknowledged -- can immediately be countered, since the goal of an analysis of the group will be only the "objective regularities" which function as dominants in the group psyche, and will never have more than descriptive value (IP, 192). A descriptive psychology will never aspire to the predictive value of hypotheses but will choose to remain at the level of descriptions of the free systems. A very limited notion of causality is, to be sure, implicit in connecting "appearances" and "realities" even in Dilthey's limited version. Kant's assumption of the correspondence between the forms of reality and those of thought was, however, completely erroneous: the data of reality, not necessarily their forms, are perceived (IP, 194). To follow Kant's assumption is to severely reduce reality, much as the unsatisfactory explanatory psychology does.

5.3 The Development of the Psyche and Descriptive Psychology

The observations on the basis of which Dilthey outlined his descriptive psychology were simple. First, we are able to differentiate inner states of consciousness; second, consciousness itself, together with the will, necessarily affects these observations, because the thoughts we know are held in memory in the form in which they are retained, and thus subject to the psyche (IP, 197-98). Under these conditions, Dilthey feels a need to introduce an explicit criterion for validating any results achieved in a psychological analysis. He finds this criterion in his data, in the "objective products of psychic life," such as language, myth, literature, and art (IP, 199-200). In accounting for the regularities revealed in these cultural patterns, Dilthey feels that generally recognizable regularities of consciousness will be uncoverable for any analysis. Thus, the interest of Dilthey's descriptive psychology intersects with *Geistesgeschichte*, the history of ideas, in attempting to delimit the lived world which conditions the experience of a particular culture.[12] *Geistesgeschichte*, however, focuses on the large-scale patterns evolving from consciousness, whereas a descriptive psychology aims to describe or delimit typical associations and sets of associations (structures) as they underlie such a culture.

The relationship between the psyche and a culture are explicable for Dilthey through structures. A "structure" is a particular "articulation of inner states," a totality of consciousness which is a "condition encapsulated in time" with a distinguishable beginning, middle, and end (IP, 200). Therefore, such a structure is a miniature correlate of the relationship between that individual consciousness and the objective world, and an example of the typical relationship found between any individual and that particular environmental continuum. The mental structure appears to be permanent, yielding a pervasive sense of identity or self for that individual. Yet in actuality, only its unity is permanent, as a defined nexus of experience: all else in that structure is process; it is the interaction of a unity or totality with an environment in a series of processes continuous in time.

Within a consciousness, one may distinguish the components of a representation, outer and inner representations of pain and pleasure, and representations localized with respect to will or volition with differentiations into clear and distinct sensations (IP, 201). "Will" and "feelings" are, moreover, only two sides of the same process of the psyche, conditioned on its structure. The latter are representations formed in receptive behavior, while the former is a representing process which conditions a relation between the contents of the representation and the psychic structure (IP, 204). The "will" conditions representations by specifying an intention, an image (*Bild*), and a future reality to be realized. In all cases, however, the structure of the psyche will limit or direct the extent of the representation.

As the individual psyche develops habits and intentions from biological or environmental standpoints become determined and facilitated, acts of will achieve a degree of idealization. In this case, a determinate set of stimuli is habitually related to a reaction or numerous reactions, and the whole reactive sequence becomes abstracted as a unit by the psyche, as a distinct representation. Such abstractions, then, integrate these abstractions into its structures: "Both [stimuli and reactions] are bound into the connections of life, from this point of view their value for life becomes for the first time totally comprehensible: one has not to comprehend it" (IP, 204).

Dilthey stresses that there is automatically an evaluative dimension in perception and representation, a dimension corresponding at its most rudimentary levels to the biological exigencies of the perceiving organism. "Value" (*Wert*) corresponds to an intersection of will with a positively perceived set of stimuli. When a series of values, a series of successive perceptions, is adduced over historical time, the effect is to give the organism a sense life: "[T]he transitions from one state into another, the effects which lead from one to another, all fall into our inner experience. The connections of structures become experience" (IP, 206). These transitions between states conditioned by value constitutes the essence of human life and history for us, a memory of experience in which we can identify the purposes and motives which guide each human life. Again, this identification is aided by the consistency and totality of experience which constitutes the basis of consciousness.

Dilthey formulates this continuum of consciousness in order to refute partially Darwin's position on the evolution of species (IP, 207). The unity of the psyche in the individual does, indeed, correspond to a teleology in nature, enabling the organism to fulfill its drives through representation and memory. Yet such a model is not objectively verifiable, nor generalizable to the *raison d'etre* of a species: a teleology directed toward protection of the individual will not automatically guarantee the protection or improvement of the species -- this is not Darwin's teleology. Instead, Dilthey considers this a reflection of nature's trend towards economy in its constructions (IP, 209). Moreover, the organization of society represents a continuation or extension of this individual preservation into the sphere of group activity. Dilthey delimits both these notions with an accompanying warning:

> . . . each concept of purposefulness and teleology expresses only that which is encompassed and experienced in this connection of life. Purposefulness is absolutely not an objective concept of nature, but rather designates only the type of life connections experienced as drives, pleasure and pain in an animal or human entity. Seen from within,

the biological life unit tries to use the conditions of its milieu to satisfy its feelings for pleasure and its drives. (IP, 210)

The needs of the species may tend statistically towards one goal, but this tendency is predicated largely by the environment, not by any teleology as simple as "survival" which is a biological concept only.

Society itself functions as a regulator of man's drives beyond the exigencies of nature. All such world systems represent further differentiations or developments into more extended milieus of the biological systems which condition the perceptions of the individual. This does not correspond to a transcendental preconditioning of thought patterns as was suggested by Kant, but rather to a set of conceptual regularities which will be conditioned by the biological and environmental requirements of a group of individuals:

This inner mental continuum is conditioned by the situation of the life unit in its milieu. The life unit stands in a reciprocal relationship to the outside world; the particular nature of this reciprocity can only be conceived in very general terms, which here should only reflect the fact that, in the final instance, it only really is explicated with respect to human experiences and described with reference to them, as the adaptation between the psychophysical unit and the conditions in which it lives. (IP, 212)

Both life and conceptualization thus represent for Dilthey not a defined, objectively verifiable purpose, but rather a purposefulness (Zweckmäßigkeit) with respect to the interface between a life unit and its environment.

Dilthey's model of the psyche and its development is clearly predicated on the adult in a social world. The mental structures possessed by such adults are characterized, as outlined above, by "unity, stability and purposefulness" (IP, 214). Because of the immersion of these psyches in real and changing environments, however, their structures are subject to change, to "expansion" and "creation" (IP, 217). Three sources affect change: adaptation and habituation of its purposefulness; the values attributed to the life process as applied to the richness of experience presented to the mental structure; and the increasing articulation and differentiation of the structure as conditioned by the interest and attention paid to the data available (complexity and stability in the group). The organism and mental structures subject to these pressures do, indeed, develop to enhance survival, yet they lack any distinct goal except that of a differentiated movement towards a "broader, richer unfolding of life values" (IP, 219). This, then, is the core of the historicity of the life of the mental structures: life tends to form stable wholes out of the experience presented to it, with an appropriate foregrounding of a distinct set of life values. Because such stable structures are possible, "each epoch of life has its value," and thus presents a distinct set of connections and psychic regularities for a psychological analysis and description (IP, 220).

Such an acknowledgement of the historicity of consciousness constitutes Dilthey's particular application of conceptual psychology. His descriptive psychology, as a human science, must deal with and describe "milieu, structure continuum, life values, articulation, and the acquired psychic structures" (IP, 221). Any purported "developments" of the human psyche remain in the realm of descriptions as reconstructions of the regularities underlying observed facts and artifacts of culture without any necessary correspondence to ontic reality (IP, 224). Moreover, the human organism, the milieu, and the structures of the psyche are conceived as linked developmental series (echoing Herbart's series-forms), whose equal products are language, logic, and the culture of particular epochs. The scope of the descriptive psychology outlined by Dilthey must then account for the stabilities presented by the body, psyche, and milieu in analyzing the regularities of mental constructs inherent in the products of culture as such products are upheld by both individuals and the group (IP, 226).

Dilthey feels that such a descriptive psychology is possible as a science, because one individual's psyche is a fitting representative of the group and can present the material for analysis which will reveal the regularities of the general culture -- not the transcendental regularities from phenomenology, but a real, typical, historical mind. The most immediate goal of this science is, in consequence, the analysis and description of the components of individuality, for an individual is only quantitatively different from the group in terms of the amount of experiential data represented in a mental structure. The idiosyncrasies attributed to the individual reflect a degree of interaction with its milieu, and, to a lesser degree, the influence by factors such as sex and race that is represented in the structures and products of a group of individuals in a similar environment (IP, 235 ff.). "One becomes formed in development," states Dilthey, summarizing that the process of individuation of an organism takes place on the basis of a common humanity and culture interfaced with a distinct milieu and tempered by the adaptation and biological preservation of the organism.

5.4 Conclusions

Dilthey's "descriptive psychology" provides a description of the constitution of the psyche in terms of its structures and its life world. As such, it represents an application and expansion of an analysis of individual mental life into the realm of a true cultural science, parallel to Paul's concept of philology, as well as the concept of psychology as an adjunct to the sciences of the day. In an essay written in 1895/6, "Contributions to the Study of Individuality," Dilthey discusses a second application. He asserts that such investigations are initiated by the psychologists and linguists of his day, and that they parallel the methodology of his own "descriptive psychology."[13] Such a parallel indicates Dilthey's success in outlining the major criteria for a true "human science" as both scientific and adequate to the products of culture. He has identified a conceptual psychology as an adjunct to the human sciences in the terms developed here.

Dilthey's first achievement and expansion beyond Paul is specifying products of culture as the data appropriate to such investigations. In a much more thorough fashion than philologists such as Boeckh and Paul, Dilthey stressed that this data is evaluated not only in terms of manifest content, but also in terms of its underlying patterns. In so doing, Dilthey identifies the products of culture -- its arts, institutions, and philosophies -- as reflections of the structure and data-structuring activities of the human mind and of humankind when their structural regularities are extended. Therefore, this data is granted a history, yet only a limited teleology aimed at aiding the group in survival. The histories of such data must be tied to the stable structures of the group psyche in a historical epoch, and they must be described as continuous and reactive to the environment without being necessarily goal-oriented in its development -- a move beyond phenomenology.

The delineation of the interface between environmental factors and the regularities in the structure of the psyche is Dilthey's second achievement in his "descriptive psychology" -- an advance beyond pure hermeneutics in his inclusion of a feedback loop between mind and culture. He, perhaps more than any other thinker of his age, realized that "perceived data" has a form in which it presents itself to humans as a "life world," a developed abstraction summarizing large numbers of the beneficial and potentially hazardous data of the environment. These "life worlds" -- which differ for each historical epoch -- do not necessarily correspond with an ontic reality, placing Dilthey in agreement with contemporaries such as Ernst Mach (and disagreement with pure phenomenology). Life-worlds represent a synthesis between that perceived data to which particular interest or attention is granted, the inherited stable structures of the psyche which direct this perception, and a sensitivity to newly arising exigencies or interests presenting problems for the perceptions of a culture to solve. Dilthey has thus delineated a criteria for the data of culture to shift through time: not only the conceptual life of a particular culture can be studied, but the real environment may also be considered if any analysis of this data is to psychologically valid.

Dilthey's third advance in his "descriptive psychology" is his outline of an analysis procedure which accommodates both the individual human psyche and the group. This procedure complies with the primary dicta of hermeneutics in working from the whole through an analysis of the parts while respecting the interconnections of the system, thus allowing for higher-order thought. His procedure, governed by a plausibility criterion in generalizing the activities of the individual to those of the group, is aimed at a large field of data. It has as a goal the uncovering of structural regularities in the patterns of this data. Such regularities are *not* to be found on the surface level of the data itself -- not in the espoused philosophies of an age, nor in the proclaimed purposes of an institution or work of art. The regularities which are to be uncovered are themselves *procedural* ones, corresponding to associated chains of reflexes which represent habituated patterns of an organism dealing with a specified region of data. "Structures" are therefore not ideational in themselves, but rather are the mechanisms which provide the ground for ideas to form in a particular environment and for the survival purposes of a distinct culture -- the patterning of the mind.

Dilthey's mode of analysis, then, will focus on the development of the associations and correlations of data which went into the formation of a particular product of culture as responses to a particular environment. Moreover, single analyses will not suffice: any structure uncovered in such a procedure constitutes only a partial analysis, conducted for a specific and more restricted purpose than is reflected in the whole life world of an age. "Structures" underlie all products of culture. Nonetheless, the overt patterns on which these products are constituted, as proclaimed by those who form them, neglect the large unconscious tradition and adaptation which is also subsumed into the mental structure of a people: biological needs, inherited survival patterns, the adaptation of older cultural products to new situations without an overt break. The goal of Dilthey's analyses remains, then, a delineation and description of many structures, each representing a varying purpose in the survival of the individual or the people. Each such structure is one of the regularities in dealing with data which will be found in a given environment. He cannot exhaust the potentials of the mind, but he can suggest its tendencies.

How does Dilthey's "descriptive psychology" constitute a program different from that of *Geistesgeschichte* as a discipline, different from the cultural hermeneutics of a philologist like Boeckh, and different from a cultural psychology like Paul's?

First and foremost, Dilthey's psychology identifies the "life world" of an age in terms of biological and societal survival, not as ideological survival. That is, there is not a representative idea for an age, as is posited in texts such as Jakob Burckhardt's *Civilization of the Renaissance in Italy*.[14] What characterizes an age is a common fashion of dealing with the data of the environment. This shift may seem slight, but it is centrally determining. Using the "idea of an age" to analyze the products of culture, such as art, easily leads to scientific reductionism in which the scientist uses the pre-analyzed components of that idea as the telos toward which all available data is to be analyzed. Dilthey's procedures explicitly contradict such a method, which cannot adequately describe the interrelations of data and the psyche, nor the structures of the psyche as they influence the patterns of culture.

The acceptance of a mental pluralism, balancing many structures of the psyche between the individual and the group, is the second major differentiation between the programs of *Geistesgeschichte* and that of a descriptive psychology. For *Geistesgeschichte*, there is often a single mind-set for individuals assumed to be the product of the spirit of the age. For descriptive psychology, the milieu in which an individual psyche finds itself -- its relative richness or poverty, its survival requirements, and the like -- will influence the weighting, prominence, or significance in data processing of the structures innate in it. There are, in consequence, few, if any, blanket modes of information processing that can be assumed by the descriptive psychologist. At best, there are structures typical of an age, to be arranged in a hierarchy of prominence only in the cases of well-defined groups or individual lives. No absolute hierarchy is possible, because that would again be a case of reductionism of the data by the interpreter. Thus, descriptive psychology is inherently pluralistic, where *Geistesgeschichte* tends towards univocal descriptions.

In this, the third major differentiation between descriptive psychology and *Geistesgeschichte* emerges: the varied treatments of the interface between the individual and the environment. Because it refuses to posit a unified idea acting as the focus for the products of a particular culture, descriptive psychology will automatically attempt to incorporate more varied data in its analyses, and try to use a greater range of categories of associations suggested by such data. *Geistesgeschichte* tends to reduce a field of data to a univalent system of categories, all pointing towards "the" idea of an age. Descriptive psychology will unfold the field of data into its multiple facets and will describe their nexes and conditioning mechanisms. Dilthey's psychology will then much more successfully distinguish between the data systems inherent in the culture of an age and the interpretations of such systems (both from the point of view of an inhabitant of that age and from that of a later interpreter, following the dicta of hermeneutics). Only descriptive psychology is able to extend the purview of Boeckh's science of culture in providing not only descriptions of the data and interrelations of categories of data (an "analytics" and "hermeneutics"), but also a description of the habituated, stable mental structures which tended to result from a specific tradition and environment -- a psychology of probable types of individuals and activities of that age, closer to that which Paul predicated for language.

In consequence of these differentiations between their programs and the more prevailing versions of the sciences of cultures, the "Ideas toward a Descriptive and Discriminating Psychology" and the later "Contributions to the Study of the Individual" may be seen as Dilthey's acknowledgement of a need to expand the base of the tradition in which he was working. Such an expansion would accommodate history and the psychology of this day, particularly the question of the relativity of knowledge to the environment, the purpose for which it was formulated, and the point of view of the observer who constitutes it (as formulated particularly by Ernst Mach).

These two essays by Dilthey seem to have achieved little visibility and little impact in their own right, perhaps because they attempted to stem the trends of the major excesses of the *Geistesgeschichte* scholars. They represent Dilthey's attempt to integrate considerations of the power and influence of the individual psyche into descriptions or general characterizations of an age, and his attempt to integrate the desiderata of the new, scientific psychology of culture of his age into the scientific methods for handling data which *Geistesgeschichte* in its early forms represented. As such, these essays represent not "aberrations" in the tradition of intellectual history represented by Dilthey's name today, but a late development in the history of the cultural sciences often overlooked by Dilthey's colleagues and students.

Dilthey's work is also an additional document for the emergence of conceptual psychology before the turn of the twentieth century. His particular contribution echoes this tradition in stressing the context, products, and processes of the mind in historical context. However, they defer the question of teleology to a greater degree than any of his contemporaries.

CHAPTER 6

PHENOMENOLOGY AND CONCEPTUAL PSYCHOLOGY

The tenets of conceptual psychology already elucidated in the work of Kant, Herbart, and Hermann Paul diverge from strict empiricism (such as Fechner's and Wundt's), and from a human science like Dilthey's. Phenomenology, the science of the phenomena within the mind, also had to differentiate itself from this psychology, despite similarities in their procedures.

The affinity between these sciences and conceptual psychology is the relationship they posit between the mind and the world. The empiricists had made the mind contingent on the world in order to fix a genetic sequence for consciousness and for the more complex products of soul. The initiators of phenomenology, Franz Brentano and Edmund Husserl, reversed this sequence.

But just as Dilthey suggested descriptive analysis as an essential supplement for *Geistesgeschichte*, Brentano outlined a phenomenological psychology (termed "empirical") to accompany phenomenology -- a more complex analysis of mind in the world.[1] The focus of phenomenology, too, was the phenomena of mind in themselves: the presentations or representations evoked within the formed consciousness of human beings.[2] With this focus, neither Husserl nor Brentano stressed either the genesis of consciousness or the historicity of thought -- they dealt with the workings of the mind. In consequence, their attention turned more narrowly to the relationships among phenomena of mind, or the processes in mind which facilitate and sponsor phenomena's existence. That is, they stressed the ontology of mind and mental processes rather than an epistemology conditioned by historical relativity. They would find truth in consistency rather than utility. Where Herbart and Paul had spoken of typical processes of mind in historical context, Brentano and Husserl will focus on mental acts and the knowledge and truth inherent in them, removed from the empirical world. Thus, Husserl presents an analysis of "internal time consciousness" (perceived time as it relates to truth or knowledge) and Brentano, similar analyses of time and space.[3]

These differentiations must be explored in greater detail in order to elucidate the points of communality and differentiation between a conceptual psychology and a phenomenological one, and then to trace their relationships. Two texts will be taken as representative of phenomenology as opposed to psychology: Brentano's *Psychology from an Empirical Standpoint*, and his student Husserl's *Phenomenological Psychology*.[4] To highlight the distinctness of these positions vis-à-vis conceptual psychology, emphasis will be placed on their definition of the material, methodology and goals for the science which they propound, and on the scope and emphases of their analyses of mental phenomena.[5]

6.1 Brentano's Psychology

Brentano's unfinished *Psychology from an Empirical Standpoint* betrays an uneasiness about his model of the relationship of mental acts to the empirical world -- a problem between what is transcendental and empirical in the human sciences. The forewords attached to the 1874 edition and to the later 1911 edition show his growing defensiveness:

> The title which I have given this work characterizes both its object and its method. My psychological standpoint is empirical; experience alone is my teacher. . . . The first book discusses psychology as a science, the second considers mental phenomena in general. (PES, xv)

> One of the most important innovations is that I am no longer of the opinion that mental relation can have something other than a thing (*Reales*) as its object. In order to justify this new point of view, I had to explore entirely new questions; for example, I had to go into the investigation of the modes of presentation. (PES, xx)

These two preliminary statements of program indicate Brentano's starting point -- that the presentations of the mind are elements of the empirical world, not transcendental in the truest sense. He believes that the presentations or representations present in the mind are the product of real empirical experience, and so the response of the organism to its environment is the basis for higher-order thought.

His beginnings are familiar from our previous expositions, but Brentano automatically moves into what is associated with phenomenology. He remains content to assume the ontological validity of that experience, as opposed to its relativity or contingency on a historical or geographical framework. He does not explore historical depth. Instead, he focuses on the "modes of presentation" of that experienced data to the perceiving consciousness, the way that the neutral core of experienced data will be construed by the mind. This is a major departure from the positions of conceptual psychology, because he starts from empirical premises, but then discards them in an attempt to move behind appearances to the common core of experience available to all perceiving consciousnesses. Brentano is not alone in this position. His contemporary, Ernst Mach, will agree that most perceiving consciousnesses will, indeed, identify such a core in mental data. Mach, however, considers this purported reality to relate to the common conditioning and experience of the observers, and not to the data itself, as Brentano seems to do.

Brentano feels that his goal of moving behind experiences results from a historical consideration of his discipline's position. Brentano had originally dealt with "the most general characteristics of beings endowed with vegetative as well as sensory or intellectual faculties" (PES, 4). Later, it proceeded to usurp the province of the physiologist by relating all mental phenomena through the activity of the body. Finally, psychology added introspection to become "the science which studies the properties and laws of the soul, which we discover within ourselves directly by means of inner perception" (PES, 5). Thus, Brentano explicitly accounts for and rejects his predecessors, especially Fechner and Wundt, when they used the phenomena of mind to explore the mental being of mankind, and especially when they tied physical thresholds to mental phenomena of perception and constructed the phenomena of percpetions out of sensations defined operationally by these thresholds (PES, 6-7). While sharing starting assumptions with empiricism, Brentano wishes to develop a psychology which restricted itself to being a science of "mental phenomena," not physical phenomena or the science of bodies (PES, 9).

Yet even within the field of mental phenomena, Brentano makes a further specification of the data for this science. He differentiates between the objects of external perception and those of internal perception -- that is, those which seem to adhere to the outside world, primarily as affects, and those which seem to originate within the observer. While the former may lead to contradictions when the observer seeks to analyze their relations, the latter are presented to the mind as intact and truthful (PES, 19). It is the purview of the natural sciences to discern the truth of extenal perception: "Defining psychology as the science of mental phenomena in order to make natural science and mental science resemble each other in this respect, then, has no reasonable justification" (PES, 10).

Brentano's psychology thus treats internal perception by stating that "[t]he laws of the coexistence and succession of mental phenomena remain the object of investigation even for those who deny to psychology any knowledge of the soul" (PES, 12). Brentano seeks laws of mental phenomena, whether one calls the bearer of these phenomena a soul or not. However, should the soul exist as a useful analytic concept, it will not be a substance; it will have a different nature (PES, 16). "The phenomena of inner perception . . . are true in themselves. As they appear to be, so they are in reality . . . this constitutes a great advantage of psychology over the natural sciences" (PES, 19-20). Thus, the mental phenomena which are the data for Brentano's science constitute a truth criteria limited to internal perception -- the truth of the individual is found in abstract conceptualization. For Husserl, these criteria will become identified with eidetic truth, the truth of the pure forms of apperception.

Brentano has here divided psychology from other sciences. His nascent phenomenology will deal with the primary stratum of thought, leaving history for psychology (a phenomenological psycholgogy of a somewhat different emphasis than conceptual psychology). Still, all three disciplines derive from similar premises. He is merely trying to put an eidetic science before a cultural one, while not totally regaining Kant's transcendental model of the mental *a priori* -- he still wants to explain the world.

Brentano's psychology, the science of mental phenomena or inner perception, will also be a touchstone for the development of science, as was the conceptual psychology of his contemporaries: "psychology has the task of becoming the scientific basis for a theory of education, both of the individual and of society. . . . And so psychology appears to be the fundamental condition of human progress in precisely those things which, above all, constitute human dignity" (PES, 21). This "dignity" is to be found in the realm of the human sciences and in culture as truth in the appearances of the human world, and in the values which they condition.

Above all, this psychology is a touchstone for human truth in Brentano's eyes, and not only a systematic discipline. It prescribes that which is ultimately human through all historical change:

> We have advanced four reasons which appear to be sufficient to show the outstanding importance of the science of psychology: the inner truth of the phenomena it studies; the sublimity of these phenomena; the special relationship they have to us; and finally, the practical importance of the laws which govern it. To these we must add the special and incomparable interest which psychology possesses insofar as it instructs us about immortality and thus becomes, in another sense, the science of the future. (PES, 25)

Brentano's psychology thus distinguishes itself in his insistence on the ontic truth of the phenomena which he addresses. Where his contemporaries insisted on the utility and the economy of mental processes (mental processes' ease of use as epistemological constructs), Brentano's focus remains on the truth of mental processes (their ontological basis), on their essence as images in the mind which combine.

Brentano assumed the relationship of the data which yield these phenomena in the conceptualizing being. He thus describes psychology as a science which was to precede the sciences of culture, and which was to stand alongside the natural sciences, albeit in a privileged position of truth. In explicating these phenomena, therefore, Brentano will look for their modalities of appearance, and not for their survival value for the organism which bears them. He will search for their truth as opposed to their utility. He relies on the world interface without explicating it as his contemporaries under discussion here did.

6.2 Laws of Mental Phenomena

Brentano's discipline tries to explain the mind's "successively more and more complex phenomena" (PES, 28). It uses as its data the presentations of inner perception. Nonetheless, this is strictly differentiated from introspection in that it relates instead to the inner stasis of mind as "internal perception" or an inner ability to conceptualize:

> One of the characteristics of inner perception is that it can never become inner observation. We can observe objects which, as they say, are perceived externally. In observation, we direct our full attention to a phenomenon in order to apprehend it accurately. But with objects of inner perception this is absolutely impossible. . . . It is a universally valid psychological law that we can never focus our *attention* upon the object of inner perception. . . . It is only while our attention is turned toward a different object that we are able to perceive, incidentally, the mental processes which are directed toward that object. Thus, the observation of physical phenomena in external perception, while offering us a basis for knowledge of nature, can at the same time become a means of attaining knowledge of the mind. (PES, 29-30)

He thus follows the starting premises of conceptual psychology in finding processes at the basis of mind -- processes and data, instead of objects in mind.

For Brentano, this psychology cannot explain the passions as inner fact. They are not "real" in the same sense as objects, because they are presented in memory when they are subject to analysis. In memory, there are real data -- observed external objects transformed into objects of consciousness -- which can, in turn, reveal the patterning influence of that consciousness as applied to mental data. Brentano says that the processes through which this transfer happens can only be uncovered obliquely, through an examination of their influence on the data which it processes. This is acknowledgedly an extension of Kant's position; it includes Brentano's assertion that such memories are to considered *intentional* objects of consciousness, not only data: "For we can, by various means, arouse certain mental phenomena in ourselves intentionally, in order to find out whether this or that other phenomenon occurs as a result. We can then contemplate the result of the experiment calmly and attentively in our memory" (PES, 35).

The affect of an experience can be examined neutrally in a contemplative state with unskewed attention. Therefore, in a science of mind, this "testimony of memory" must be the basis not only for Brentano's new psychology, but for all other sciences, concentrating on the truths of inner perception (PES, 36). This science is restricted, since we have but "an indirect knowledge of the mental phenomena of others" (PES, 38). We may only assume similarities between the workings of our mind and others. Brentano's psychology must, therefore, account for the behaviors of others as empirical data:

> What we have said is sufficient to show from which areas the psychologist gains the experiences upon which he bases his investigation of mental laws. We found *inner perception* to be his primary source, but it has the disadvantage that it can never become observation. To inner perception we added the contemplation of our previous mental experiences in *memory*, and in this case it is possible to focus attention on them and, so to speak, observe them. The field of experience which up to this point is limited to our own mental phenomena was then extended, in the *expressions* of mental life of other persons (such as biographies or protocols) allow us to gain some knowledge of mental phenomena which we do not experience directly. . . . Inner perception, therefore,

> constitutes the ultimate and indispensable precondition of the other two sources of knowledge, . . . the very foundation upon which the science of psychology is erected. (PES, 43)

Inner perception is the registration of the data to be processed; the processing mechanisms themselves are revealed in their products, very much as in the model of conceptual psychology.

In effect, then, Brentano has reversed the sequence of knowledge emerging into the psyche accepted by transcendental philosophy. He does not stress the primacy of apperception as Kant did. Instead, he focuses on the neutral examination of the apperceptive experience.[6] Kant saw that knowledge began at the level of apperception and was raised to a level of clearness and distinctness. Brentano thinks apperception is unobservable, and so waits until such knowledge has reached a level of clarity where its products can be examined as mental phenomena.

Hence, the psychologist must work with perceived data, and so "establish the natural order as well as the number of fundamental classes of mental phenomena" (PES, 45). This taxonomy may lead to conclusions about mental processes but not account for them genetically, since "mental life never reverts from a later stage to an earlier stage" (PES, 46). Brentano's psychologist can never recreate a pure original experience -- he can never, for example, relive an experience the way a five-year-old would, even if the experience were preserved in memory. Brentano offers this alternative through the data of consciousness or "sensations:"

> The investigation of the primary mental elements is mainly concerned with sensations, since sensations are undoubtedly a source of other mental phenomena, and more than a few scientists assert that sensations alone are the source of all phenomena [a position Brentano denies] . . . The highest and most general laws of the succession of mental phenomena, whether these laws are valid for all phenomena or only for those of one fundamental class, are to be established directly by the general laws of induction [and not as a consequence of physiological laws]. (PES, 46-47)

That is, one can work from the products of consciousness to figure out what generated them. Moreover, this investigation would also allow for the existence of an unconscious (PES, 57). In this model, all of the laws of the mind do not need to be conscious to manifest themselves in mental products. The laws which may be discerned about the mental phenomena in question "can only be empirical laws subject to inadequacies and imperfections," as rule-governed mental acts applied to memory (PES, 63).

The laws derived by empirical observation of mental phenomena are, therefore, strictly differentiated from those drawn up by Kant, Fechner, Wundt, or Herbart, although Brentano explicitly cites them as sources (PES, 65-67). They erred in stressing physical experiments (assuming a series: apperception - perception - utility of knowledge) or in denying the model's predictive value for the complex areas of thought (particularly Herbart's error, in Brentano's judgment). Instead, Brentano's psychological laws "will be rich in examples which furnish an excellent illustration of deductive method in the empirical field, and of the three stages which the logicians have distinguished in it: induction of general laws, deductions of special laws, and verification of these laws by means of empirical fact" (PES, 71). This sequence is, moreover, reversible, since induction may also follow deduction, as in the case of the "historical method" introduced by Comte (PES, 72).

Still, this is not pure conceptual psychology. Because this model is not developmental or mutable through history, the laws which Brentano attributes to psychology are actually closer to metaphysics, since they give to the realm of internal perception a guarantee of consistency and permanency (PES, 72). They stand fast against the changes in personal experience or historical circumstance which the philologist-psychologists in the preceding chapter acknowledged. The laws for Brentano's "phenomenal psychology" (or empirical psychology) are derived using the criteria of formal logic. They will apply to a human psyche with not only a trans-subjective component, but also a transhistorical one -- Brentano's way of overcoming history. This removes the remainder of his work from the realm of conceptual psychology, and out of the range of the empiricism which he construes very differently from his contemporaries. He begins at the premises for a cultural science, but then shifts onto his own track towards a more transcendental psychology.

6.3 Brentano's Classifications of Mental Phenomena

After ascertaining the types of law on which his science of psychology is founded, Brentano turns back to the classification of mental phenomena, to determine which data-blocks his psychological laws must account for. "All the data of our consciousness are divided into two great classes -- the class of physical and the class of mental phenomena," begins Brentano's second book of the *Psychology* (PES, 78). The fundamental differentiation within the field of data is thus specified (a classification comparable to that used by Wittgenstein about language -- as ostensible and verbal definitions).[7] He begins to distinguish sources of data:

> Every idea or presentation which we acquire either through sense perception or imagination is an example of a mental phenomenon. By presentation I do not mean that which is presented, but rather the act of presentation. Thus, hearing a sound, . . . as well as similar states of imagination are examples of what I mean by this term. I also mean by it the thinking of a general concept, provided such a thing actually does occur. Furthermore, every judgment, every recollection, every expectation, every inference, every conviction or opinion, every doubt, is a mental phenomenon. . . . Examples of physical phenomena, on the other hand, are a color, a figure, a landscape which I see, a chord which I hear, warmth, cold, odor which I sense; as well as similar images which appear in the imagination. (PES, 78-80)

Brentano's fundamental differentiation within the field of data for psychology is perspective. To differentiate between the experience of the phenomenon of color and the color itself means to split off the two entangled facets of a single experience.[8] Psychology will necessarily concern itself with the former, by studying how the mind intentionally dwells on the presentation as inner perception.

First, all perception is directed at perceiving; it is an act that intends to do something in its processes: "We may, therefore, consider the intentional in-existence of an object to be a general characteristic of mental phenomena which distinguishes this class of phenomena from the class of physical phenomena" (PES, 91). Moreover, this inner perception guided by the intentionality of the observer will be immediately evident, a presentation requiring no analysis. Brentano has thus reduced psychology's field of data from mental phenomena to intentional objects only -- to those presentations which are acts of consciousness, however much such presentations may be influenced by the unconscious structure of the mind:

> It is not correct, therefore, to say that the assumption that there exists a physical phenomenon outside the mind which is just as real as those which we find intentionally in us, implies a contradiction. It is only that, when we compare one with the other, we discover conflicts which clearly show that no real existence corresponds to the intentional existence in this case. And even if this applies only to the realm of our own experience, we will nevertheless make no mistake if in general we deny to physical phenomena any existence other than intentional existence. (PES, 93-94)

Intentionality causes all phenomena to be processed. However, no matter how goal-directed the processes of the mind are, we still can only see the unconscious obliquely in the products of consciousness.

The consequence of Brentano's assertions is that any physical phenomena which the perceiving consciousness does not intend to acknowledge will not be registered by the mind as meaningful structures -- a conclusion consistent with Brentano's phenomenological approach. The primacy of intentionality in this system harkens back to his earlier distinction between external and internal perception, since only the objects of external perception may be subject to logical contradictions from their position as appearances or presentations. Brentano is not stating that these objects do not, in fact, exist, because he maintains that the source of all such presentations is in empirical experience. Instead, he stresses that the qualities which an individual may attach to such presentations are individually contingent. They are not the objects themselves, but the objects' intentional structure:

> Further we found that the *intentional in-existence*, the reference to something as an object, is a distinguishing characteristic of all mental phenomena. No physical phenomenon exhibits anything similar. We went on to define mental phenomena as the *exclusive object of inner perception*; they alone, therefore, are perceived with immediate evidence. Indeed, in the strict sense of the word, they alone are perceived. On this basis we proceeded to define them as the only phenomena which possess *actual existence* in addition to intentional existence. . . . [and] *always* appear to us as a *unity*, while physical phenomena, which we perceive at the same time, do not all appear in the same way as parts of one single phenomenon. (PES, 97-98)

In fact, he is arguing for *typical* mind in a way commensurate with conceptual psychology, stressing that the mind as a whole is in dynamic equilibrium, immersed in a less coherent world.

For Brentano, the contiguity or focus of mental phenomena justifies their assumed ontological status, in opposition to the randomness of external perceptions -- the boundary between I and world. What for Kant had been processing strategies (the categories) which systematize external perception are in Brentano's psychology the unexamined preconditions for external perception, a system of processes. Brentano thus ignores the interactive potential between external data and inner perception which was assumed by conceptual psychology. He is, therefore, explicitly bracketing any consideration of the causal mechanisms through which such data may enter the mind. His focus remains on the essences of the data once perceived, and so he closes off the cultural dimension tacit in his model.

This distinction places Brentano's psychology in a different category than those of his contemporaries, either as empirical or conceptual psychology. Others discussed here had granted credence to the existence of apperceived sensations as energies functioning in the stasis or unity of consciousness (exerting pressure on the stable energetic constellation of the mind, even if not themselves at the level of consciousness, and thus able to emerge at a future time). However, Brentano excludes such data from the evidence from which the pure laws of psychology are to be derived -- he is not looking for an outside source of mental inertia.

Because of this restriction, Brentano equates "mental phenomena" with "mental acts" (PES, 102). In consequence, his model of the mind will be less subject to historical or environmental pressures than that used by his contemporaries: the fundaments of conceptualization, similar to the rules of logic, will be only little (if at all) subject to historical relativity and ultimate structuring by the environment in which the mind is immersed. For Brentano, presentations are conscious, and the psychology which deals with them cannot account for or describe the unconscious, except as it appears in mental products. Since he slights environmental stimuli as subconscious sources for conscious perception, the questions of energetic intensity which had been so prominent in psychological discussions since Herbart (and through to Freud) disappear from Brentano's work. Particularly, he denies the model of mental programming that Fechner and Avenarius had propounded.[9] He rejects the primacy of the world, while acknowledging it as a data source:

> If correct, this conclusion not only refutes any possible attempt to prove the existence of unconscious presentations on the basis of the functional relation [between mind and world] under discussion, but, as we have already indicated above, it can be regarded as a proof that there really are no unconscious presentations in our sense of the term. . . . Analogy could lead us to suppose that in the case of other conscious mental activities there is also a functional relation between their own intensity and the intensity of the accompanying consciousness which refers to them, indeed, the same relation of simple equality which we have demonstrated in the case of conscious presentation . . .

> experience teaches us that a weak opinion can be
> accompanied by a presentation which is just as strong as, if
> not stronger than, that which accompanies complete
> conviction. (PES, 136-137)

He thus divorces "intensity" from survival, and moves back to the
randomness of the individual mind act.

Logical categories such as causality, contrast, or chronology
will emerge only very late in Brentano's system. He will consider
the data of mental presentations only with respect to modality: the
varying means through which such data is presented to the mind,
regardless of strength or other intentional colorings.

The first of these modalities is cognition itself. Brentano
equates this presentation of data to mind with a process of
judgment, a connecting of objects with attributes or of concepts
with each other (PES, 141). Cognition is thinking in logical forms,
as opposed to apperception or the act of presentation:

> In accord with our previous remarks, as a judgment, this
> cognition has two intensities: first, an intensity in the sense
> in which we say that presentations have an intensity;
> second, a kind of strength which is characteristic of
> judgment, i.e. the degree of conviction with which the
> judgment is made. If one or the other fell to zero, there
> would be no judgment. . . . Every mental act, therefore, is
> accompanied by a twofold inner consciousness, by a
> presentation which refers to it and a judgment which refers
> to it, the so-called inner perception, which is an immediate,
> evident cognition of the act. (PES, 142-43)

So cognition breaks down into two mental acts which determine its
emergence.

Beyond presentation and judgment, Brentano finds a third act
or modality of activity in a mental act:

> Experience shows that there exists in us not only a
> presentation and a judgment, but frequently a third kind of
> consciousness of the mental act, namely a feeling which
> refers to this act, pleasure or displeasure which we feel

toward this act. (PES, 143)

With this description of the affect accompanying the mental act,
Brentano has provided a model for thought processes in which
consciousness is broadly construed. It denies the existence of
organic reflex (a pragmatic application) which had accommodated
or accounted for pleasure and displeasure in his contemporaries'
models. Systems like Wundt's and Dilthey's identified the organic
reflex as a formative interaction between the perceiving
consciousness and the world environment (and thereby anchoring
their respective psychologies in historical and geographical frames).
In contrast, Brentano locates the perceptive act in pure form outside
such contingencies. As he summarizes:

> Every mental act is conscious; it includes within it a
> consciousness of itself. Therefore, every mental act, no
> matter how simple, has a double object, a primary and a
> secondary object. The simplest act, for example the act of
> hearing, has as its primary object the sound, and for its
> secondary object, itself, the mental phenomenon in which
> the sound is heard. Consciousness of this secondary
> object is threefold: it involves a presentation of it, a
> cognition of it and a feeling toward it. . . . Original
> differences in aptitudes, difference in acquired
> dispositions, differences in connection with other
> phenomena serve here, along with the intensity and quality
> of the primary object and diversity of references to it, to
> make this area one of the most varied and diversified fields
> of investigation. (PES, 153-154)

The "intensity" of which Brentano speaks, however, is not
comparable to the energetic levels encountered earlier, as in the
work of Herbart. Instead, it is a restatement of the traditional
clearness and distinctness criterion of classical philosophy.

Perception is, for Brentano, not cognitive processing in which
the mind seeks an equilibrium. Instead, he retreats somewhat from
a full dynamic model of mind to a taxonomy of energy levels in the
registration of various levels of consciousness as wholes. Nature
and nurture, the environment and the physical being of the

cognitive being, have been reduced from keys to apperception to the level of filters or mufflers on the clearness and distinctness of the feeling accompanying thought. Moreover, these feelings are not products of the increasing complexity of the cognitive apparatus, they are volitional, not tied to processing difficulties as they particularly were for Herbart. For this reason, Brentano slights the detailed discussion of the feelings as modes of cognition -- a discussion promised for a third volume of the *Psychology* never completed, and only partially recoverable from notes and drafts on the subject later.[10]

Brentano contents himself with a breakdown of the primary modalities of the mental act, and with the assurance that consciousness itself is a unity. However, the unity of consciousness is not interactive; it is constituted out of a plurality of parts (PES, 163-167). A plurality of goals characterize it, which will consequently condition the sub-classes of the modalities of mental acts. The intentionality of the mind structures reality:

> But my three classes are not the same as those which are usually proposed [because their pragmatic implications have been bracketed]. In the absence of more appropriate expressions, we designate the first by the term "presentation," the second by the term "judgment," and the third by the terms "emotion," "interest," or "love." (PES, 198)

Again, he splits apperception, logic, and emotions.

The unity of consciousness which Brentano describes consists, therefore, also of an acceptance or rejection of a presentation (as a judgment), and an indicator of interest or love (i.e. of interest-worthiness) of that presentation. Each judgment does, indeed, presuppose a presentation. However, their relationship is not one of dependence or priority, but rather of a twofold consciousness of one mental perception (PES, 201). With this basic model, Brentano feels that there can be no considerations of judgments such as good and evil, for those enter into the mental presentation as attached to love/hate or interest -- all different terms for (phenomenologically) the same thing (PES, 223). Moreover, love/hate designations are part of the unity of consciousness, representing the individuality of consciousness rather than its communality. When one reaches the realm of individuality, these presentations then "are subject to *special laws of succession and development*, which above all, constitute the main psychological foundation of ethics" (PES, 224). Thus Brentano finds studies such as ethics in a realm outside that of love/hate distinctions. To him, ethics is a cognitive discipline, based on judging, while the latter is confined to the realm of personal experience and its accompanying affect.[11]

Brentano has thus shifted the realm of individuality to a secondary position in the model, where it conditions the interest paid to a phenomenon -- a result already encountered by Fechner and Wundt. However, he shows a fundamental unwillingness to place such interest at the *foundation* of the development of higher-order thought, as his contemporaries had done. For Brentano, presentation and judgment, not affect, are the basis of higher-order thought and of the more complex appearances of mind. As he summarizes:

> Firstly, inner experience showed us that there is never any sharp boundary between feeling and will. We found that all mental phenomena which are not presentations or judgments are all alike in the way in which they refer to their content, and they can all be called phenomena of love and hate in an equivocal sense. Secondly, although it was impossible to cite any distinction between presentation and judgment at all when it was denied that there was a difference in the kind of reference, we have seen that quite the opposite is true in the area of love and hate. Here each particular class can be defined in terms of the special phenomena on which it is based, with the aid of the contrast between love and hate and their differences in intensity.
>
> And finally, thirdly, we have seen that no variation in circumstances, which usually occurs when there is a difference in the kind of consciousness, is to be found in feeling and will.
>
> So we may consider the unity of our third class to have been demonstrated. (PES, 255-56)

Judgment, love, and hate are all "relatively late phenomena of the will," all moved out of primary conceptualization because they are secondary to presentations and judgment (PES, 268). Therefore, emotions or affect will not substantively affect higher-order thought -- a much different stance than those of his contemporaries, who believed in the relativity of conceptualization.

Because of this reordering, Brentano will define further operations of mind in terms of pure logic, or of presentation and judgment (very much like Mach, who, however, still includes cultural conditioning). "Mental reference" (thinking about an object) contains a mental presentation of an object, and an oblique reference or analogy to something purported to exist -- something "quasi-relational/Relativliches," or relative to consciousness (PES, 271-72). This reference to an object is not the same as mental activity in itself, but it is rather part of external perception (PES, 275). Moreover:

> Not everything which is apprehended is apprehended explicitly and distinctly. Many things are apprehended only implicitly and confusedly. . . . Sensible space is alternatively full and empty in one place and in another, but the individual full and empty places are not clearly differentiated. If this is true of physical phenomena, something analogous is true of the mental activity which refers to it. (PES, 277)

This statement reveals the limits to the model of psychology which Brentano is proposing. It is more accurately a description of the limitations to the clearness and distinctness of conceptualization, and not a statement of the verifiability and economy of the ordinary and shaded functioning of the mind.

Despite the existence of unclear places in mental activity, judgments are still provably in a qualitative mode of mental activity, based on a temporal ground (PES, 280). Through an analysis prior to judgment, the obscurity of the presentation can be clarified: "a clarification of the presentation can come about through an analysis of its object both *in recto* [directly, as an object] and *in obliquo* [as a secondary phenomena, as mirrored in inner perception]" (PES, 282). In this, Brentano reduces the scope of knowing to the act of examining empirical data and analyzing the mind's own perceptual mode. The data themselves, the external stimuli *in isolatio*, do not inform either modality except as triggers. The objects of thought in the pure sense are data, yet their only function is to enable presentations to occur. They do not affect the fundamental equilibrium of the mind. To be sure, presentation and judgment will always accompany each other as part of a mental act, although an intensity may be absent in the case of logically clear concepts such as the number "three" (PES, 286). Judgments deal with truth and falsehood, while will is another name for the intensity of love or hate associated with a presentation -- its affects, related to intentionality (PES, 289).

However, since judgments are not conditioned by the environment or by the objects of thought in themselves, Brentano locates truth criterion within human perceptual capacities as well as in the ability to focus on pure experience, and not as a correlate to the structure of the real world. Even in the case of fiction, this disjuncture between judgment and affective presentations will occur, for the mental act is dealing with its own contents as they may or may not correspond with the objects which constitute the fiction (PES, 293). The objects of thought are not what is thought, for those are presentations (*Gedachtes*), but part of external perception (PES, 320). If they don't have a status in reality, they nonetheless represent functions in the mind.

The expressions *modus rectus* and *modi obliqui* thus reflect two ways to consider mental objects. The *modus rectus* considers an intentional object of consciousness directly, according to presentation, judgment, and intention. The *oblique modes* of consideration are relational, higher-order, or many-faceted, encompassing "mental, causal, and comparative references to an object" and expressions of contingencies and the like, and are thus more historical in nature (PES, 324). Oblique considerations move from mind to world; they lead to the sense of reality in the individual, to the primary and secondary continua which structure reality, such as relative time, continuity, spatial relations, and coincidence (PES, 330). These are higher-order, oblique, and more individual considerations, expressed in the locutions of language as products of mental activity (PES, 367).[12]

Brentano established limits for his psychology only in this

delineation of modes to consider mental presentations, based on a phenomenological picture of mind. He did not pursue interest in mental acts, an understandable omission, given his preoccupation with mental presentation and judgment. Brentano's model is therefore removed from the individual interference of interest. Its psychology does not pursue the physiological evidence stressed by Wundt and Fechner to enter into a determination of the relation of mental intensity to the stability of the mental constellation of processes. Again, he begins to build up to a consideration of culture, but ends up polarizing individuality and the trans-subjectivity of the group.[13]

6.4 From Brentano to Husserl

In 1895, Brentano again located his psychology vis-à-vis that of his contemporaries:

> My school distinguishes between psychognosy and genetic psychology (on the basis of a remote analogy with geognosy and geology). The task of the former is to exhibit all of the basic mental phenomena. All other mental phenomena are derived from the combination of these ultimate psychological elements, just as all words are built up out of letters. . . . Genetic psychology, on the other hand, is concerned with the laws according to which these phenomena come into being and pass away. Because the conditions of their occurrence are largely physiological, owing to the undeniable dependence of mental functions upon events in the nervous system, we see how investigations in genetic psychology are necessarily connected with physiological investigations. (PES, 369)

With such statements, Brentano acknowledges that, despite similar premises, his descriptive psychology is at odds with conceptual psychology. It brackets the conditions under which intuitions, presentations, and judgments are affected by the environment and the history of the perceiving organism, and relates them to their genesis in the strictest sense.

Brentano's student Husserl adopted and developed this distinction in conjunction with Brentano's focus on the intentionality of knowledge and its basis in cognition. Their shared conviction that a descriptive psychology must be based on ontological premises elicits Brentano's defense of his theoretical model. He wants a descriptive psychology on empirical principles, but not psychologism:

> In order to defend myself against such a weighty accusation, I must first of all ask what is really meant by it, for the dreadful name comes up again and again, even when very different things are meant. When, during a friendly encounter, I sought an explanation from Husserl, and then, as the opportunity arose, from others who use the newly introduced term, I was told that it means a theory according to which beings other than men could have insights which are precisely the opposite of our own.
>
> Understood in this sense, I am not only now not an advocate of psychologism, but I have always very firmly rejected and opposed such absurd subjectivism. . . . [which] does away with the unity of truth for all . . . (PES, 306)

This "unity" of truth, the premise that perceptual systems are similarly inherent to all human consciousnesses, is the assumption which grounds both Brentano's and Husserl's work on psychology.

The product of Husserl's work on psychology in the narrowest sense was presented in a series of university lectures given as "phenomenological psychology" in 1925, and in 1926/27 and 1928, as "intentional psychology," a title which allies his approach closely to Brentano's. John Scanlon, translator of the English edition of the *Phenomenological Psychology*, summarizes the position of this work with respect to psychology: "this work can be considered a distinctly phenomenological contribution to philosophical psychology or philosophy of mind. The point is that it is neither transcendental philosophy nor empirical psychology, nor even a discussion of the program for empirical psychology" (PhP, xi). Like Brentano, Husserl leaves behind history and culture.

Husserl used not only Brentano, but also Dilthey's work on descriptive psychology as an explicit starting point. In so doing, he tries to create both a science of the mind and a scientific method to be applied to mind:

> The new psychology [that of Dilthey's contemporaries] was reproached for being actually blind to the unique essential species of psychic life, blind to all essential forms specific to mentality as an intentionally active subjectivity, constituting mental formations and also cultural community. Therefore, it was said to be quite incapable of accomplishing what so-called exact and explanatory science had to do everywhere; for, all explanation is knowledge derived from essential concepts and guided by essential necessities based on them. (PhP, 3)

However, Dilthey saw that empiricism could not ultimately yield a science of mind (PhP, 4). As a comparison with the preceding chapter will make clear, Husserl's account of Dilthey focuses on a single aspect of his program rather than on the multi-faceted cultural model which Dilthey sought to evolve.[14]

Husserl affirms Dilthey's rejection of experimental psychology as a corroboration of his own search for a science of the mind, which will be brought about through intentionality and made possible because of "internal knowledge" (PhP, 5). Yet Husserl ignored that Dilthey had added a criterion for historical adequacy, including the experience of the thinking being and the life-world in which they are immersed. Husserl, following Brentano, will seek to move behind this:

> [Dilthey] has not yet seen that there is such a thing as a generic essential description on the basis of intuition, but not of an intuition of essence, as he has also not yet seen that the relationship to objects of consciousness, which comprises the radical essence of psychic life, is the proper and infinitely fruitful theme of systematic analyses of the psyche, and indeed as analyses of essence. (PhP, 8-9)

Therefore, Husserl, like Brentano, will finally dismiss the realm of historical or environmental influence, so that his program moves away from Dilthey's definition of the sciences of the life-world. In this, Husserl admits that he searches for a "typology of psychic life," and the *a priori* structure of experience (PhP, 11). This is "a psychology which provides necessities"; it will describe the constitution of the life-world as a necessary consequence of the mental typology of the individual, albeit without losing the individual by reducing his activity to the level of scientific causality (PhP, 13). How, then, does Husserl account for individuality in his psychological program?

6.5 Husserl and Phenomenological Psychology

Husserl ties into his psychology the greater thrust of his phenomenological program:

> In 1900-01, my *Logical Investigations* appeared as the result of ten-year-long efforts for a clarification of the pure idea of logic by a return to the bestowing of sense or the performance of cognition which occurs in the nexus of lived experiences of logical thinking. More accurately speaking, the single investigations of the second volume involved a turning of intuition back toward the logical lived experiences which take place in us whenever we think, but which we do not see just then, which we do not have in our noticing view whenever we carry out thought activity in a naturally original matter. (PhP, 14)

This is a description commensurate to that used by Brentano to describe the methodological foundation of psychology, a turning toward the individual mental acts through which knowledge comes into being. For both, the content of such mental acts are objects taken as logical forms, "in the most universal logical sense . . . concerning which statements can be made sensefully and in truth" (PhP, 15). Husserl thus believes in a psychology of eidetic (i.e. abstract logical) cognition and knowledge, not in the relativist psychologism of his contemporaries which Brentano, too, had denounced.

In part, the definition of the program of his psychology is identical with phenomenology:

> ... the attempt to go back radically and consistently from the respective categories of objectivities and ask about the modes of consciousness determinately belonging to them about the subjective acts, act-structures, foundations of lived experience, in which objectivities of such a character become objects of consciousness, and above all, become evidently self-given. (PhP, 19-20)

This is the general description of the science dealing with mental presentations, despite the subject area of the content of such presentations, or (in Husserl's terminology) phenomena. In narrowing this presentation to that of psychology, the focus will concentrate on the "internal experience of the subject by whose intentionality the mental act comes to pass" (PhP, 21). It is to supplement empirical psychology philosophically, as a critique of reason and ethics:

> One must first become acquainted with cognitive life itself, valuing and willing life itself in internal experience, and derive clear concepts from it in order to be able to gain a theory of knowledge, a theory of value and a theory of will. In other words, the task is to gain a clear understanding from within, of how "truth" arises as a product of "rational" knowing, how ethical goodness arises as a subjective product in ethically right willing. (PhP, 21-22)

Husserl's psychology moves to the intentionality of life ("willing and valuing") to see how mind construes and influences all fields.

With this assertion, Husserl specifies the scope of his psychology: a description of the operational modes of consciousness as hermetic phenomena, a self-enclosed and self-informing system underlying logic, ethics, and aesthetics. This represents an enterprise based on Brentano's, who did not complete it:

> [Brentano] never saw and took up the great task of going back from the basic categories of objects as possible objects of consciousness . . . and inquiring about the entire multiplicity of possible modes of consciousness by which such objectivities come to consciousness for us, and in principle can come to consciousness, in order to clarify . . . the teleological function of these modes of consciousness for the synthetic producing of truth by reason. (PhP, 25-26)

More so than Brentano, then, Husserl makes consciousness the determinant of the ultimate form of world experience and removes consciousness from the influences of environment or history. He has gone back to Kant's systems of mind, but not to categories or processes before logic.

Husserl considers this a guarantee of the "trans-subjective validity" which his science seeks (PhP, 29). His phenomenological psychology is not to be confused with the older science of capacities already rejected by Kant, which derives its definitions of the function of the mind from bundles of mental acts. Husserl will, to be sure, base his work on these capacities, but he will do so under the light of intentionality -- of the intentional focus on these acts of mind rather than on their contents or products (PhP, 28). This distinction precludes consideration of real-world impact of an act of mind. Moreover, the trans-subjective validity he seeks will serve to make empirically validatable sciences out of what had seemed random products of human activity, such as ethics and aesthetics.

In terms of the distinction between phenomenology and psychology in the narrower sense, "a phenomenological method essentially similar can also ground a naturally objective *a priori* psychology" (PhP, 32). This is possible as long as the investigator's focus remains on the objects of intentional consciousness, and not on the issue of trans-subjectivity in the transcendental (the truths which extend beyond all minds):

> Let us survey the basic characteristics of the new psychology under the mottoes: Apriority, Eidetic, Intuition or Pure Description, Intentionality; and let us mention also

the characteristic of abiding by the natural dogmatic attitude instead of the specifically philosophical, that is transcendental, attitude. (PhP, 33)

That is, Husserl's psychology will deal with the universal necessities of mind. It will not concentrate on the description of phenomena, but rather on their essences. It explicates the possible phenomenal worlds which result in a teleology originating within the individual consciousness, as opposed to a cultural-historical group consciousness. As such, it shows how the natural world phenomena derive from "the natural dogmatic attitude" about the way in which the world is constituted (and not with the way the world is constituted *per se*). Husserl's psychology will dovetail with a complete science of knowledge or of cognition, one which includes the pragmatic elements not accounted for in Husserl's system of phenomenology:

> Psychology has to do with mental facts, with men and animals, insofar as they are mental beings and abodes of mental, psychic happening: as universal psychology, with what holds in common everywhere, as psychological anthropology and animal psychology, with the human realm and the animal realm in their respective limits. (PhP, 39)

Husserl's psychology, in contradistinction to the empirically based conceptual psychology variants of Fechner and Wundt, will deal with the organism's world of experience, or its naive "concretization" (pseudo-concrete self-conception) of world experience (PhP, 40). Husserl states, "It is taken for granted that we are remaining in the natural attitude, and that means nothing else but that we accept experiential 'being' just as it gives itself, that is, as concretely existing" (PhP, 41). Such an assertion would seem to account for an energetic or dynamic interactive relationship between the experiencing consciousness and the source of the experience. However, because of Husserl's belief in the existence of an *a priori* truth, the concretization of the world which constitutes the data of experience will not be completely individual or idiosyncratic: "Amid all its subjective forms, changing in subjective living and working, this first sense of experiential world has evidently a certain universal structure and, as will soon be shown, not a contingently factual, but an *a priori* necessary structure" (PhP, 42). Since these underlying universal structures antedate individual historical or geographical variances for Husserl, they are ontological, not subject to the relativity of individual experience in perception.

In analyzing the concretization of necessary experience andthe general forms they assume, we explicitly are to ignore whether it is affected by previous experience, for we are aiming at uncovering the necessary in all perception, not the individualities of particular life histories (PhP, 43). This is possible because even within the individual, the world-experience tends to amalgamate into a single type of experience despite the individual data which is received into it. Individual experience tends to concretize on standard patterns, to form an experiential world which Husserl describes as a "unity of concordant total actuality" (PhP, 44). This does not happen because universals exist, or because one has an overview of all world data presented to consciousness. The universality stems from mind: "the world is not given merely by simple experience, but by a thinking which is combined with it" (PhP, 45). Husserl's famous example is a house: an observer can only see it from one side, but its existence (the other unseen walls) is always fleshed out by the thinker. Any change in perspective on that object does not lead that observer to think that a new object has emerged in place of the old, but rather that the object is presented from a new perspective (PhP, 45). Each appearance of the house is merely a new horizon in experiencing, an "*a priori* necessary structure" (PhP, 42).

Inherent in this world experience are universally generic notions of time and space, no matter what individual shadings these concepts become subjected to (PhP, 48). Each individual experience is part of the "experiential concept of the world" available to a "scientific performance" trying to uncover the necessary or generic character of the world (PhP, 51):

> Thus, also, what interests us here: the all-embracing *a priori*, that of this experiential world, since it is what is apodictically universal and necessary to any experiential

world at all, thus to a world which, as experiences, should
be able to be merely imagined. (PhP, 53)

This apodictic necessity is the *eidos* (the essence) of the experience,
which will remain the same no matter what the perspective or
shading on the experience to the individual (PhP, 55). The *eidos*
will survive free variation of the experience, or variations and
alterations such as change of position or color of objects:

> What counts is that all the optional single cases come in the
> sequence of their appearance to *overlapping coincidence*
> and thereby pass into a *synthetic unity* in which they all
> appear as variations of one another; and then, in further
> consequence, as optional sequences of single instances in
> which the same universal *eidos* is singularized. (PhP, 58)

This *eidos* is the ultimate data for Husserl's psychology, the "pure
conceptual essence" of experience which will be subject to different
modalities of appearance in consciousness (PhP, 59). Husserl's
phenomenological psychology will deal with these universals as
they become singularized in each individual mental act of
presentation.

In uncovering the *eidos*, the observer must intentionally set up
a variational sequence. Series of *eide* of similar type (as the series
of colors) will then be able to be ordered as genera, while staying
within the process: "the only demand is that the variation -- no
matter how -- moves on, as long as it is a variation at all; thus, it is
at all times combined in a synthesis of pervasively unitary
coincidence with a pervasively universal moment. That is the way,
therefore, toward the constitution of highest essential universalities
as highest genera which, particularly if they are concrete genera, are
called regions" (PhP, 61-62). The goal of collecting and
assembling these variations into series establishes phenomenal
universals:

> Thus, we cannot only vary experiential things, that is, final
> substrates for possible experiencing and higher actions,
> and thus gain concepts of things as essential universalities;
> but we also "experience" sets which we have collected by

our own activity, real states of affairs, internal and external relations, the seeing of which requires relating activities, etc. In this way we also gain pure and universal ideas of collections, of relations, and of all sorts of states of affairs, insofar as starting with the seeing activities in which they become given, we form multiplicities of variation precisely for all such objectivities and single out intuitively what is essentially universal and necessary. (PhP, 62)

So, fundamental classification systems (universals resembling Kant's categories) are pre-established fundamental structures in the mind. Our capacity to rotate the phenomenon of a house in mind is a universal experience of dimensionality applied to three-dimensional objects. Similarly, the mental act of differentiating color intensities reflects for Husserl an apodictic sequencing phenomenon -- a phenomenon which Mach will insist is generated by the necessities of organic survival, and is not innate.

This is, then, Husserl's general method of determining the data and classes of perception which constitute mental acts. In searching for ever more complicated eidetic examples or genera, "more complicated seeing, involving active comparative overlapping and agreement" will be required (PhP, 64). Therefore, more and more complicated activities of the intentional mind will be revealed in the constitution of these classifications of *eide*. And after the series of data have been established, the scientist can proceed to a "descriptive inner psychology," turn away from the data itself, and move toward the activity of mind which uncovered them (PhP, 65). This is "the method of ideation" searching out essential or eidetic universalities at the basis of cognition (PhP, 66).

The divergence of this system from the tradition of conceptual psychology lies in its failure to consider non-universal influences from an individual cultural-historical épistemè. Ultimately, Husserl posits a complete structure of the world emerging from perception alone. "[N]ecessary structural forms" constitute the universal "style" of the world as perception (PhP, 67). They predicate the universal necessities imposed on any data as appearance. Ultimately bracketing input from the senses while acknowledging that the mind needs data to function, Husserl's phenomenological psychology focuses on the analysis of the relations of objects of mind to mental acts. He stresses that the world is a product of mental acts involved in forming a purportedly natural concept of the world assumed to be shared by all perceivers. Despite the seeming similarity of this position with Kant's theory of categories, however, a fundamental difference remains that shows that the dynamic model of conceptual psychology is not totally lost. Kant's categories are processing mechanisms acting as filters for experience of the world, while Husserl's mental acts constitute a reality in themselves. The ontology of the objects of mind in itself is ignored, in favor of the perceptual mode of the perceiving consciousness: the stimuli or objects of perception do not interact with mind; they are subject to it. "In this sense the world is experienced just as well as a single thing, a single qualitative moment or member of the thing, a process of movement, a causal occurrence, a connection" (PhP, 72).

The pressure of conceptual psychology on the phenomenological model is clearest with respect to the individual. Individuality is, for Husserl as for Brentano, minimized in the face of phenomenological psychology's eidetic goals. Each individual performs an individual "passive synthesis" in order to develop a world view (as opposed to the conscious, intentional one of the scientist). Yet one cannot examine absolute mind -- data must be gotten through the individual. The *eide* themselves cannot be integrated into this synthesis before they have been activated as part of experience (PhP, 75). Thus, the scientist's first task in examining this world view is to distinguish between "self-sufficient or concrete reality" and "non-self-sufficient reality." His goal is to distinguish what is only an intuitive (i.e., unconsidered and personal) unity, from what is unitary (what has an *eidos*, and is not only an amalgam of characteristics [PhP, 76]). Then, causal determinations may be made so that the given field is reduced to a field of perceived data which may be designated "reality"; so, data becomes objects through activities of the mind:

> When several things are given together, they are not, therefore, one thing simply as the unity of a sensuous configuration. They are combined to make up one thing only if they bring about a whole which is an identical

> substrate of causal properties, which has a stable style, recognizable by disclosing experience, of behaving causally in the respective conditions of its existence. (PhP, 77)

The scientist goes beyond the individual, sorting out the categories inherent in individual mind.

Each sensuous configuration is thus individuated, but individuality is not left behind. Again, mind is approached through the world-based individual mind. The causal determinations uncovered move toward the *eidos*, but they will only reflect the substrate of the thinking mind:

> If accordingly we make a survey of the entire world of pure and simple experience, then it is clear that [the world] is articulated throughout into single real things, which can then be further united in real complexes of things, as things of a higher order. Every such reality in the specific sense is a causal unity related causally to its real environment and a substrate of stable causal properties in this play of changing causal transformations, therefore stably preserving its causal *habitus* (habituated value for the observer). (PhP, 78)

Husserl's reality is thus subject to a psychophysical analysis, separating those objects attributed with existences as objects from psychological experiencing subjects (PhP, 80-82). The appearance of a house will tie into a causal nexus of other phenomena -- doors, in order that one can enter; windows, for light; and other secondary or higher-order explanatory ties of this one phenomenon into a greater perceived reality. The links between the sets come from mind, because others may exist in a "real" world.

6.6 The Subject and the Experiential World

With the above determinations, Husserl closes off the discussion of the experiential data available to a psychology commensurate with phenomenology. Yet by his own definition, the clarification of the field of data (and of the phenomenological reduction through which it can emerge as eidetic intuition) will only partially accommodate his psychology. The problem arises because it is to deal with the life-world of the mental being, as Dilthey, too, had indicated. Husserl will accommodate the facets of the lived experience into the field of data for his science, but at the same time, he will search to eliminate subjectivity from the realm of experience -- to reach behind individuation in the individual's eidetic concept of the real world.

The ultimate goal of the science which he seeks encompasses a number of questions:

> In the direction of the other layer, that of the psyche, corresponding descriptive problems would ensue: questions concerning the fundamental descriptive characteristics of everything psychic; concerning its elementary types; concerning the connecting forms of unity; concerning what makes necessary the unity of *one* psyche purely as psyche; and how, further, several psyches can gain unity by a purely psychic relationship and connection in spite of all concrete separation, and how in this way mental association among human beings and animals, personal unity of a higher order, becomes possible. (PhP, 83)

His initial problem is the division which Brentano had already specified. An object of the life-world has two facets as a mental object: "The sense is not found next to the matter which expresses it" -- the intentional existence of the object is differentiated from its content (PhP, 84). Moreover, one aspect of this intentional sense will be cultural, corresponding to the education and experience of the individual involved (PhP, 85). An object's other aspects are a history, endowed with "a reality which includes a mental sense," and personal experience of the object, "an original realization in personal life" (PhP, 86; 87). Thus for Husserl, an object has a sense in itself -- a cultural sense, a historical one, and a mental one for personal experience (PhP, 88).

However, after introducing this distinction, Husserl reassumes his original eidetic hierarchy. He insists that these various senses must be stripped away from the essence of objects, in direct opposition to the interest in the individuation of thought expressed by his contemporaries. He verifies this difference:

> Though the experiential world may be furnished almost everywhere and ever so abundantly with cultural sense, and though it is continually being so furnished as a result of the culture-creating performance or bestowal of sense which we human beings have accomplished individually and in narrower or broader communities -- nothing prevents us from abstracting from these predicates of the experiential world, these subject-related irreal characters of such things, and directing our regard toward the universe of pure material realities which are united with them. . . . Once we have thus attained the pure world of things, we can manifestly go one step further back abstractively. For, if we abstract from the psychic characteristics of the animal realities, thus, if the originally mental is also disregarded, then only pure matter is left over everywhere, as that which is absolutely mindless. (PhP, 90)

If one splits out these aspects, the scientist can provide a pure view of the causality of the *physis*, of the experiential life-world. This enables the psychologist to separate the effects of the mental acts from those attached to the *eide* themselves (PhP, 91).

In effect, then, Husserl attempts to remove from the purview of psychology the cultural influences which he has acknowledged (PhP, 92). And, moreover, he wishes to assert that "there is an objective, conclusively true world, *the* true world" to guarantee the truth transcending experience (PhP, 95). This allows the psychologist to use the results of the natural scientist to systematically exclude the purportedly objective realm and focus on the subjective sciences of culture, unimpeded by the individuality of subjectivity: "The scientists of the mind, taking the word quite literally, make precisely the subjective their theme. That everything subjective which makes its appearance in various shapes belongs together is clear; but how it belongs together and how it can determine sciences, that is not yet clear by any means" (PhP, 99). Thus, the mental elements which constitute the person, and which form the traditional domain of the psychologist, are those which exist as life *outside of the cognitive realm as defined by the eidetic reduction of phenomenology*. And as such, Husserl's psychology in the narrow sense is the science of the personal, to be backed up by the results of phenomenology in the "purely cognitive" realm.

Since cognition is not adjunct to psychology in the sense of individual perceptual functions, Husserl begins to outline a psychology of subjectivity -- a "hierarchy of layers" to be peeled back from the *eide*, and to be differentiated out from the truth of cognition (PhP, 99). The truth of cognition is in transcendental schemata, not in personal history. The focal point at the center of experience, the "I," will seem to partially depend on the locality of the body with its sensuous apparatus (PhP, 100). As in the model of conceptual psychology, Husserl sees the ego as a nexus of energy:

> *Animation* designates the way in which mind acquires a locality in the spatial world, its spatialization as it were, and together with its corporeal support, acquires *reality*. (PhP, 101)

This location corresponds to the location of the organism in the world.

> An animal, a human being, has its stable causal style in the multiplicity of its changes, not only as to its sheer physical body but, as we said, psychophysically and psychically -- in the last respect, e.g., the psychic total character, individuality in the mental sense. (PhP, 103)

Consciousness is not, in Husserl's view, individual, because the locality of consciousness is a center to the stability of the world view of the organism, and only secondarily, "in the mental sense," the source of the psychic perspective and the cultural sense granted to perception.

Since Husserl strips away such cultural sense with phenomenology, his psychology must accommodate both the mental and the physical realms in terms of correlate operations. Husserl will do so by finding *typical* mental acts underneath the individual ego:

> Plainly the embodiment of psychic being in the spatial
> world -- in accordance with its structural division into
> single things which maintain a real unity amid all changes
> of states -- presupposes that parallel ordered complexes of
> states and lapses of states of the physically corporeal things
> on one side, and of the corresponding psychic on the
> other, are connected with one another by inductive
> causality, by coordination. Therefore, the psyches
> considered purely on their own must include an inductively
> effective typicality. Whatever psychic states appear
> together in any psyche and whatever proceeds in it
> universally in succession, must have a typical regularity
> which grounds a style of expectation, therefore a belonging
> together for inductive expectation. (PhP, 105)

This is the physical expression of the psyche -- the mental acts
manifest as appearances will be tied in some predictable way to the
mental realm itself; it will be tied to eidetic reality.
      For Husserl, then, the "I" is not primarily a locus of organic
individuation which evolves into consciousness, but rather a "unity
of the psychic," a "stream-unity" or continuum of mental states:

> However, the psyche is not just streaming life, but a life in
> which, inevitably, distinctive new unities, habitualities, are
> constituted -- that is, the passive and active abilities,
> abilities of perception, abilities of feeling, abilities of
> memory, intellectual abilities, etc. With these constantly
> variable abilities, we are already referred to the properly
> essential unity belonging to every psyche, the unity of an
> identical "I" as substratum for ability-characteristics
> pertaining specifically to an "I," for personal characteristics
> which are variable and, in fact, never resting, and which
> eventually, in a collapse, can change totally; among them
> are the strictly so-called character traits. The unity of
> mental individuality which persists even through character
> changes permeates all that. (PhP, 107)

As the strictly cognitive belongs to the eidetic realm, the essential structures of mind also belong to a transcendental realm, common to all beings characterized by a psycho-physical existence. The distinctly personal develops secondary to these cognitive properties of mind, and represent the locus of historical-cultural existence. His contemporaries had also assigned a role to history as it influences knowledge itself, not only personality -- the major divergence in the two programs. For Husserl, historical influences exist, but they must be stripped away in valid science. Thus, knowledge and the base of the psyche is prior to the world of appearances, and will have its own "modes of appearance" secondary to the existence of the truth of appearances (PhP, 110).

The affects are aspects of the modes of appearance of the psyche, and thus are only elements of the world of appearance which can be removed; they are not primary processes of mind:

> For here, the difficulties arise when the merely subjective moment is to be excluded [in a science] at any time; all the subjective modes of orientation, perspective variations of appearance, modes of dubiousness, nullity, correction and the like are not foreign to psychic life, and they belong necessarily to the psychic or personal domains, precisely to those domains in which they appear. [T]herefore, they can not drop out of the thematic domain so simply as out of the thematic sphere of natural science, which is in principle subject-alienated. All the subjective modes which the investigator of physical nature excludes are his appearances . . . (PhP, 111)

The subjective must, therefore, be excluded from the methodology of a science, yet included as the data of appearances for that science, along with any other appearances of nature and culture. The scientist must retain only the objective domain of the psyche, while eliminating the personal (PhP, 114).

After this, Husserl carries out an analysis of the contents of a mental act, parallel to Brentano's. The subjectivity of personal affect must be eliminated from internal representations in order that scientific objectivity be maintained in examining their correlate mental operations. If the new science of psychology is to emerge, it must reduce the subjective to physical appearance -- as experienced world. Husserl explains, "Rather, now the subjective itself is to be our theme; our question now concerns the tasks of a rigorously scientific treatment of the subjective" (PhP, 119). The psychologist thus turns his eye on *how* these appearances of subjectivity are given as part of world experience, and on how the perspectives on these appearances may be uncovered by intentional cognition (PhP, 120-1):

> [They may be uncovered] as identical spatial objects, and as multiplicity of perspective modes of appearance. . . . both the multiplicities in their continual change, and the unity which appears in them, which is presented in them, are inseparably united; they belong to perception even if the perceiver, lost in his object, does not notice the multiplicity at all, and just carries out no reflection. (PhP, 122)

The scientific observer must reflect to uncover these properties.

The perceptual field, the field of the data of appearance, may thus be "reduced" so that the *eidos* behind the subjective may emerge, just as in the methodology of phenomenology in general (PhP, 123-124). These *eide* are the stable forms which persist behind perspectivism. They break the region of data into two sectors corresponding to those elucidated by Brentano:

> In this way we have also gained a very marvelous distinction of two domains of objects: the objective data which are straightforwardly perceived in the perceiving of spatial things refer back to subjective data, the "hyletic data," the pure sense data. These are themselves something in their own specific character; they have their own being -- a being which is not objective. They themselves are not perspectives, but they become that by what we also call apprehension, precisely what gives them the subjective function of being just an appearance of what is objective. (PhP, 125)

Therefore, Husserl equates the apperceptive process with apodictic subjectivity masquerading as objective assessments of external data. The subjectivity of all apperception is grounded, Husserl asserts, on inherent tendencies of the mind. One example is perceiving in three dimensions, while the visual field itself is only two dimensions (PhP, 126).

The "hyletic data" (hyle = core or essence) "can become nuclear contents of marvelous functional characters which all have this in common: that by means of these nuclear contents and as it were endowing them with mentality, they make other objects become present to consciousness" (PhP, 127). These functional characters are the ways in which such data can be used by the mind. They are also intentional characters directed by the interest of the mind. The hyletic data are eidetic sense data, removed from individual existence. Hyletic data do have a transcendental organization. For example, there is a temporality inherent in this data, which is not that of subjective experience (PhP, 130):

> In just that way we have also defined a certain distinction which can be exhibited purely within this scope: between "external" perception as perception directed toward objective space-time and internal perception as perception of what is purely subjective.
>
> Now we can also say, internal perception is perception of what is immanent -- external perception, of what is transcendent. (PhP, 131)

This is Husserl's statement of the constitution of reality. The transcendent is the external, the objects of perception; the immanent is subjective -- all knowledge is knowledge constituted by and for the subject. Yet in the narrowest sense, knowledge is the domain of phenomenology, while psychology is to accommodate only the affects accompanying it. Phenomenological psychology is, therefore, the science of what to discard in order to reach the domain of knowledge.

Such a statement constitutes a reversal of the position of psychology with respect to knowledge, a move explicitly refuting conceptual psychology. The transcendence of which Husserl speaks is that containing the objective truth of the world for all observers, the *eidos* of the life-world as appearance, forms a "unitary intentional lived experience in which one objective thing can appear" (PhP, 133):

> The object transcends the real content of the stream of lived
> experiences; only its real moments are "immanent" to it.
>   Yet this concept of the transcendent, of the object
> present to consciousness in its imminence, still includes
> several great difficulties . . . (PhP, 137)

The worst of these difficulties is the issue of multiple significations
or appearances of the object, and the necessity to differentiate
between the meaning of an object and its various intentional
meanings (PhP, 141). This difficulty can be removed through use
of the "phenomenological reduction" -- the technical term for
Husserl's intentional reflection on objects of perception to
determine what is objectively given by them, in order to focus on
the perception of the perception -- on what constitutes the
"house-ness" of the house-as-appearance (PhP, 143-144).[15]

> [The phenomenological attitude] opens the way to a quite
> different science, to the science of *pure subjectivity*, in
> which thematic discourse concerns exclusively the lived
> experiences, the modes of consciousness and what is
> meant in their objectivity, but exclusively *as* meant. This is
> an important point which should be considered again and
> again: *that* a perception perceives something transcendent
> and that it posits its object existentially in its certainty of
> belief and posits it with a transcendent sense of such and
> such a structure. This is a type of truth which, understood
> in phenomenological purity, includes not the least opinion
> concerning the unqualifiedly transcendent world, the
> existent world. (PhP, 147)

Husserl's new term, "pure subjectivity," expresses transcendence,
the realm outside of history that is the purview of his psychology.
     At this point, with the constitution of the life-world left to be
uncovered by the phenomenological reduction as the hyletic data
behind the appearances engendered by mental acts, Husserl
interjects considerations of the body of the perceiver who is
attempting to undergo the reduction. In an explication similar to

Mach's, Husserl realizes that the reduction must be extended to accommodate the image of the body itself as appearance, as a part of the objectively perceived world, and not necessarily in a special category of consciousness (PhP, 150-53). The body, too, is part of the stream of life perceptions:

> In this way, it becomes evident that concrete perception as original consciousness (original givenness) of a temporally extended object is structured internally itself as a streaming system of momentary perceptions (so-called originary impressions). But each such momentary perception is the nuclear phase of a continuity, a continuity of momentary gradated retentions on the one side, and a horizon of what is coming on the other side: a horizon of "protention," which is disclosed to be characterized as a constantly gradated coming. (PhP, 154)

The ego thus is constituted from the position of the body in the experienced world, and is situated according to the memories and expectations of relations with the world to be encountered. Again, this is a description we have seen in Husserl's contemporaries in conceptual psychology. However, Husserl has removed it from the questions of truth as accountability to stress the normed perceptual core of a perceiving consciousness. Any shifts in truth are, for Husserl, correlates with the locus of individuality superimposed on the eidetic data of truth.

In this model, the "I" can "be awake" or not in assuming the critical position which will distinguish the subjective and the true (PhP, 159-60). Nonetheless, reality is not gone; each mental act (*actus*, in Husserl's terminology) will be affected by the ego at least to the point of a locus for that act's focal point:

> The "I" performs activities. But it is not an empty ideal polar point, merely determined as the point of intersection of the activities which flow forth from it and are then given as already there; rather, precisely thereby it is also a pole of corresponding habitualities. But they are not in it as perceptually given and exhibitable material properties in a material object; rather, they are dispositions which accrue

to it by a genesis, by the fact that it has carried out the respective *actus*, and which belong to it historically only in recourse to them. With the original decision, the "I" becomes originally the one who has thus decided. It can then immediately see itself as that and later see itself as the same, as the same one still thus decided. The "I" has its history, and on the basis of its history, it creates an "I" which persists for it habitually as the same "I." (PhP, 161)

We must recall, however, that Husserl has constituted personal history as a unity of states in perception, where his contemporaries in conceptual psychology did so as the sum of experience in the life-world and reactions thereto by mental functions.

This history, this "I" as appearance, is the locus from where convictions, decision-making processes, recollections, assent and belief stem (PhP, 161-64). And "every change of conviction is a change of the 'I'" (PhP, 164). This subjective "I" is only itself an appearance:

> What we have set forth suffices to give you an idea of pure subjectivity, self-contained and everywhere inseparably connected. Taken in its concretely complete nexus this subjectivity comprises what we call the concrete pure subjectivity or the monad; thus in this context, "monad" is not a metaphysical concept but the unity of the subjective within the phenomenological reduction, to be explored in direct intuition by painstaking analysis. (PhP, 165)

Even the science which deals with the subjective must, therefore, be phenomenological in nature, in order to distinguish uncritical subjectivity from the pure subjectivity which will be the key to uncovering the workings of the personal mind (PhP, 166-67). This will be a psychology participating in a grounding of the cultural sciences, "an eidetic essential science of the psychic, in contrast to the descriptive concrete socio-cultural sciences" (PhP, 169). Even phenomenological psychology is meant to accompany cultural sciences as "the unitarily explanatory foundation for the natural exploration of the mind and for its personal exploration in the socio-cultural sciences" (PhP, 170). This stands apart from phenomenology, which is the science of mind and knowledge as immune from historical influences.

From this proceeds Husserl's definition of the role of culture and history with respect to cognition and the personal mind:

> Culture is not a layer of properties pertaining to natural objects as psyches, rather, it is a psyche in objects of the surrounding world, objects which admittedly are natural objects whenever they are investigated from the point of view of natural truth, but which as such have only natural properties. . . . The world, considered personally, is the nature of the natural scientist and of all personalities interested in nature; the orientation of the socio-cultural sciences, nature, and correlatively the natural scientist, is a personal theme. History is an all-inclusive personal science, a science of the personal and of its facticity taken all-inclusively. Eidetics [phenomenological psychology] is the all-inclusive science of ideally possible forms of personality in the unity of a personally regarded, and thereby historical, world. (PhP, 176)

Again, truth lies only behind these appearances, dealing with the ideal forms behind the personal, and constituting the transcendental unity of personal perception of the world. History and society do not constitute valid knowledge.

Husserl summarizes his own role as a psychologist whose discipline stands in this relation to the other world sciences:

> 1) I am an inductive psychologist, but would like to know how the psyche looks "internally." I intend, of course, "parallel" and altogether inductive research. Naturally, I hit upon this: that here a great science of psyches arises which is not inductively related to internality but is immanent, a science to which induction itself belongs as internal.
>
> 2) Likewise, I can be a personal researcher and be interested in personal internality. Here I would have to consider specifically personality and personal doing; the creating of personal products enters the naturally

experiencing regard. In any case, the personal "I" has an "internal" life to be disclosed and a personal self-development. And there I come again upon the demand for a deeper exploration of pure subjectivity, and this leads to the same result as above. Therefore, I could give merely the outline, the presentation of a pure internal psychology as fundamental science of the socio-cultural sciences -- but also for a natural psychological research, the purely subjective consideration of inter-subjectivity, then the psychological reduction to the transcendental-phenomenological. (PhP, 179)

This is a summary of the program which deals with the relation of cognition to psychology only in the narrower sense of solipsism. By propounding a science of the mind predicated on the ontological existence of the human psyche, Husserl has, in fact, contributed to the renascence of a self-confirming, normative cognitive psychology which Austro-German psychology had attempted to repudiate since Kant and Herbart. Phenomenological psychology was probably Husserl's way of dealing with the empiricism he could not otherwise ignore.

6.7 Phenomenology Versus Conceptual Psychology

The brief samples of the programs of both Brentano and Husserl suggest that their phenomenology or phenomenological psychology differs significantly from the program which has been associated with conceptual psychology in this volume to this point. Each purports to be concerned with the interface of mind and world, and with the position of the individual with respect to knowledge (and in Brentano's and Husserl's cases, also to truth). Moreover, statements about the stasis of mind in world perception, and of the necessity to distinguish the individual from the perceptual seem superficially to stem from similar assumptions in all cases.

A closer view belies these similarities, however, despite the fact that phenomenological psychology and conceptual psychology start from similar premises. The fundamental differentiation between the phenomenological position and that of conceptual psychology lies in the very inclusion of phenomenology as a science of pure knowledge next to the results of psychology as a science of relative knowledge. Since they attribute an existence as *eidos* -- as pure or absolute truth -- to knowledge, Brentano and Husserl consign to the province of psychology only the science of the individual. This psychology is the science of idiosyncrasy and individuation due to the perspectives of the senses, and the science of the affects, passions, and habits. Such individuation may be studied on its own as "pure subjectivity." However, cognition in its pure form may not have anything to do with it. In doing this, they reject the historicism of the nineteenth century and the specific relativity of conceptual psychology. They also relegate culture to the level of habituation, and to an expression of a psyche, and of the individuation of a people, and not as a valid repository of its pure knowledge or of its truth -- a truth which would then have to be acknowledged to be relative to a particular time, place, and conceptual habituation. This was not a question for Kant, for empiricism was not an accessible truth. In contrast, phenomenological psychology was attempting to reverse the relativizing trend of the nineteenth century by refuting conceptual psychology.

The phenomenalism which will be associated with the work of Ernst Mach and Freud (finding truth in the system of the mind as appearance and as survival in the world rather than behind it) must thus be considered in strict isolation from phenomenology, no matter what the superficial similarities in methodology and terminology. For the proponents of conceptual psychology, truth will retain value only as survival in the world, and as communication among the members of a conceptual community. Attempts such as those of Brentano and Husserl to subjugate the validity of the knowledge of this world to knowledge of the eidetic world must necessarily be rejected by such as Mach, Herbart, or Freud. Brentano and Husserl take the dynamic model of mind evolved in the work of Kant, Herbart, and the empiricists discussed above, but they reject the cultural conclusions based on it.

CHAPTER 7

MACH'S PSYCHOLOGY OF INVESTIGATION
AND THE LIMITS OF SCIENCE

As we have seen, the conceptual psychology which is the underlying paradigm for the latter nineteenth century stems from a synthesis of Empiricism and Idealism. Another name playing a role in this synthesis is Ernst Mach, an Austrian physicist, who is remembered for his delineations of the concept of "frame of reference" and the Doppler effect -- that is, his work in scientific epistemology.[1] Mach's reputation is that of the psychologist among physicists. His program ranges through the culture and history of the sciences as well, including: the history of science and its relativity,[2] thought experiments (influencing ultimately even Einstein),[3] Monism as a joint psychological and physical perspective on scientific investigation (especially in the circles around the journal *The Monist*),[4] and the biological or economic adaptation of organisms -- all topics at the core of Mach's psychological approach to the methodologies of science.

Despite the considerable attention paid to Mach in the context of his contemporaries and of those whom he influenced,[5] none of these topics exhaust the largely overlooked core message of Mach's work. Because his oeuvre is laden with textbooks and popular-scientific lectures, it is susceptible to being undervalued as a coherent whole. An approach through the paradigm of conceptual psychology gives us a way to make sense out of his broad activities. Mach is the scientist who introduced relativity and a biological viewpoint into physics; he is the father of neutral monism, the developer of the tactics of thought experiments, and a leader in early perceptual psychology due to his work on visual thresholds and in the history of science due to his textbooks -- these roles have all been recognized but only treated as facets of his complete message in terms of his relationships to contemporaries and followers. Perhaps because of the early interruption in his productivity due to health reasons, Mach did not issue a final statement or provide a holistic self-interpretation, thereby leaving scholars with many potential implicit connections between his thought and that of others, but without an epistemology for his own work.

It is the contention of the present chapter that, despite Mach's fundamental disinterest in addressing overtly the epistemological questions associated with his work, a consistent underpinning exists throughout Mach's oeuvre. As virtually all the secondary studies on his work agree, he is indeed an epistemologist, but one who was speaking to a different audience, one which included scientists, lay people, and students of science and therefore allowed little explicit discussion of the epistemological convictions about knowledge and validation on which his work is predicated. Mach's discussions revolve around the formalizations of science: the concepts and laws which are the tools of the practicing scientist, the relationships between the notational systems in which these laws are recorded and the observed reality which they purport to describe, and the validation criteria for both notational systems in which these laws are recorded and the theories built on them. Mach's innate epistemological assumptions, however, are largely implicit, covered and obscured by his explicit discourse of the problems of the experimental physicist.

As a result, each of the roles attributed to Mach may be refuted on the grounds of its inability to account for the full range of his activities as a scientist as documented in his writings, and as the introduction to this volume shows, Mach's work cannot be exhausted by a theme or problem history. For example, Mach was not a biologist, nor was he interested in a narrow biological perspective in the sciences, despite his use of terms such as "interest," (biological) "economy," and "adaptation," which suggest an interest in evolutionary Darwinism. Instead, Mach's interest in the "survival of the fittest" was in terms of culture. He explored the roles of science and technology as they facilitate the survival of man in his environment.[6] This clearly is the origin of Mach's notions of the cultural relativity of thought patterns. Different peoples in different epochs have varying survival requirements as they deal with various environmental data. The result in each age is a culture-specific thought pattern, relative to its individual survival values. Concomitantly, Mach assumes that the knowledge each people possesses will only be informative relative to the desires and values of their culture's frame of reference. Mach does, then, rely on the principles of Darwinian biology; he is not, however, a "biologist of the mind" because he was concerned only with the biological restrictions on the formulation of physical laws for the sciences.[7] For Mach, thinking under the influence of the environment yields survival, not biology.

Similarly, Mach's work on perceptual psychology was only peripheral to his work on the pure sciences. His experiments on the Doppler effect, on visual thresholds, on the psychologies of geometry and of thought experiments all serve to delimit the applicability of physical laws. They demonstrate limits on data collection as restricted by the discrimination of the eye or ear, or when clear physical data cannot be found and therefore may be posited in the mind of the experimenter. Thus Mach's "psychology" concentrates on the limitations imposed by the organism and reinforced by the community, subsumed under more general considerations of the adequacy of scientific description. Still, his work fulfills the criteria for conceptual psychology based on a feedback loop between mind and world and an emphasis on the cultural specificity of knowledge.

Although his work was both translated and referred to by the Monists (including Paul Carus), Mach distanced himself from epistemology -- "not a philosopher, and not even wishing to be one," as the preface to *The Analysis of the Sensations* expressly states. He approached the relativity of knowledge strictly as a working physicist and therefore did not attempt to explicate totally the parameters and preconditions for knowledge in a culturally relative frame of reference. Mach chose instead to demonstrate practical genealogies of scientific concepts in the textbooks. Mach's precise focus correlates scientific experimentation and results through the agency of the mind and not the general principles behind the validity of such correlations -- that is, he explicates mind *in* the world, not *behind* it. Because of this explicit bracketing of ontology, Mach did not systematically explore the premises and preconditions for knowledge in the sciences.[8] Thus, the epistemology of Mach's work has not been adequately treated as coherent.[9] To start a reconceptualization of Mach's work, one must begin with the best description of Mach's oeuvre, treating it as coherent. We will do so by starting with his epistemological premises, as explicated in his *Analysis of the Sensations*, and then moving on to his other works.

First and foremost, Mach's reputation is that of a brilliant experimentalist interested in refining and justifying the role of observation in experimentation, even after a stroke precluded his direct presence in a laboratory.[10] His observations of human perceptions of tones and of the learning habits of animals and children were aimed at improving validation criteria for such experiments, and therefore tended to highlight the advantages and disadvantages inherent in various modes of experimentation, rather than discussing the ontological systems or cognitive systems through which experimental data were processed. As such a scientist, Mach is rightly acknowledged as a major source for Einstein's concept of special relativity,[11] and as a positivist/mechanist whose work (particulary on acoustics) closely paralleled that of Helmholtz.[12]

What were, then, the contributions of this scientist who addressed the epistemological questions of the necessity behind and consistency of theory-building in the sciences? He did not generalize the ontological claims appropriate to theoretical knowledge, no matter how often particular concepts or formulae were shown to be relative to the considerations surrounding their derivation. Mach's work lies in a realm distinctively his own, for he, like Edmund Husserl, was in the position of bracketing both absolute ontological proofs and personal subjectivity, while still concentrating on the relationship between knowledge and perception.[13] Mach's theory of knowledge, therefore, must be adduced from the underpinnings of his scientific discourse. The consistent beliefs about the constitution of knowledge are located there, not in his explicit choices of topics.

To move beyond the premises of this early work, we will identify this hidden epistemology as the conceptual psychology under discussion here. It is derived from Mach's implicit discourse about the conditions under which the formalizations of the pure sciences arise. His variant of conceptual psychology is an explication of the possible mechanisms or paths within human cognition through which ideas, words, concepts, and ultimately formalizations of the order of theories arise when the human organism attempts to adapt to or describe a field of data as a set of related scientific phenomena. Mach's psychology does not necessarily correspond to that which Mach labelled "psychology" for his audiences; it does, however, represent a contribution to epistemology which has not been acknowledged as coherent by Mach scholars.[14]

This conceptual psychology is presented in two major works: *The Analysis of the Sensations*, and *Knowledge and Error: Sketches Toward a Psychology of Investigation*.[15] The first of these two texts has received greater attention since it delimits the concept of cultural relativity with respect to the perceptual limitations on the formulation of data into concepts (known as the "doctrine of elements"). The latter text has received less attention, and is considered mainly a key to Mach's physics (particularly on the psychology of tones and of mathematics). Yet these are the texts which join the epistemologist to the experimental physicist -- the key to the program hidden in part by the public image. This public image needs a clear outline if that program is to emerge, and so we will turn to Mach's influence before we turn to his texts.

Mach is most familiar today from his fundamental contributions to science: his fundament to the theory of relativity,[16] his assertion that thought-experiments (*Gedankenexperimente*) open the door to innovation in science,[17] and his "theory of elements" as representative of the more modern concept of "frame of reference" in experiments.[18] *The Analysis of the Sensations, and the Relation of the Physical to the Mental* is the most familiar source for Mach's reputation, and to a less obvious degree, *Knowledge and Error: Sketches toward a Psychology of Investigation*. The first of these two texts presents a collection of essays explicating his theory of elements and its implications; the second is a collection of popular speeches and essays designed to demonstrate the consequences of the theory of elements within the context of the pure sciences. In the secondary literature, the most considerable number of studies is devoted to these two major texts.[19] Yet Mach's more direct impact on his contemporaries outside the sciences (on writers and thinkers such as Hermann Bahr,[20] Husserl,[21] and the populations of Prague and Vienna[22]) has only begun to be assessed -- a reputation stemming from a broader public and program than today's scholars admit.

How could a figure so prominent in the history of science also achieve a visibility so far outside his narrow sphere of specialization? The answer to this question helps tie Mach to the program of conceptual psychology.

7.1 Mach and His Public

On the most rudimentary level, Mach's influence on his age began at the heart of the population with middle-school children; yet today, his work on the history of the sciences is largely overlooked because it was published under the guise of a series of textbooks: *Physics for High School, Mechanics, Optics,* and *Physics for Medical Students.*[23] These texts were written while Mach held a relatively obscure chair of physics in Prague, away from the major center for biological and medical research in Vienna.[24] The contents of the textbooks represent the work of a man whose research laboratory had virtually no equipment and only one assistant; here, the man who while still a student demonstrated the then-disputed Doppler effect was able to determine threshold values for the optical receptivity of the human retina.[25] If Mach was tied into the major programs of his day, it was, indeed, in an almost hidden discourse. Yet his work did have impact.

That a scientist such as Mach was working under such reduced circumstances did not by any means imply that the work he produced in this period was relegated to a level "for student consumption." Instead, these textbooks are hallmarks of originality, showing the relativity inherent in the supposedly "pure" sciences, and how cherished concepts such as measurement scales and mass have been formulated under historically relative conditions according to varying requirements inphysical research.[26] Implicit in these expositions are critiques of inherited scientific nomenclature and problem-solving techniques. For Mach, they are mutable constructs which evolved in specific contexts under specific observational conditions and which therefore change as conditions and data change. In all cases, scientific nomenclature and even theories do not correspond to an ontic reality but rather only to a specified observed reality and stated purpose. Since the purposes differ for which various temperature scales (Centigrade, Fahrenheit and Kelvin) are efficient, so, too, should the operative definitions of physical concepts such as "wave," "mass," and "causality" -- they should remain flexible in the progress of scientific investigation.[27]

These textbooks and the large public attending his *Popular Scientific Lectures* both in Prague and in Vienna suggests that Mach maintained a profile well within the public view, at least after he was called to Vienna to a "Chair for the History and Theory of the Inductive Sciences" and belatedly began to sell *The Analysis of the Sensations*.[28] Such evidence would tend to confirm the greater scope assumed here for the breadth of Mach's work and activities. Mach's contemporaries saw a body of work which affected not only their sciences, but also their world view.

In 1904, Hermann Bahr, an Austrian journalist and essayist, reflects a typical perception of Mach's importance in the title of an essay, "The Unsalvageable Ego" -- a literary essay about the fact that the personal ego has only a heuristic value, which was very important in the turn-of-the-century context of cultural pessimism.[29] Here, Bahr popularizes Mach's key distinction about "things" and "ego": both concepts are "provisory fictions"[30] serving habituated thought patterns, but which lack an ontological status because they only describe a restricted field of perceived data without explicating the origins of that field. Bahr's essay is a classic feuilleton, a "quote and commentary" column written for a Viennese newspaper, and therefore it does not pretend to delimit the full scope of Mach's work.[31] Yet it does identify the two major goals of that work: first, its "anti-metaphysical stance" (the incorporation of the frame of reference of an observer into the formalization of a scientific experiment);[32] and second, its validation of the results of the sciences in terms of the history of a discipline, the data involved, and the mental processes which allow its formalization to arise.

This popularization -- a merger of work in the sciences with a psychology of perceptual and conceptual mechanisms -- is the key to Mach's innovation. For Mach, "scientific truth" is a product of mental mechanisms which are self-restricting and relative to the "interest" or field of data to be considered in the context of a particular experiment. This relativity extends to the "ego" and the "world" also, since their absolute constitution is unverifiable; the models used for the world in the sciences do not correspond to a static reality, but only to a system of perceptions constituted for a particular purpose.

Such suggestions must therefore frame a reconsideration of Mach's work, particularly of the *Analysis of the Sensations*. Mach's covert program was not only a set of investigations into the nature of the pure sciences, but an attempt to incorporate a group or conceptual psychology into the criteria for objectivity, verifiability, and recreatability for those sciences. Mach's work thus outlines its own status as a case study in conceptual psychology: it demonstrates a different definition of "science" than today's historians recognize.

7.2 Sense Data and Physics: Fundaments of Psychology

Mach's foreword to the *Analysis of the Sensations* acknowledges that his expositions were aimed at reconstructing the mental principles on which any science as a systematic discipline is built. He wished to integrate the principles of science with the restrictions of history and culture. He concedes:

> I have repeatedly been led into this field through a deep conviction that the whole of the sciences, and physics in particular, have to expect their next great enlightenments about fundamental principles from biology, and specifically from the analysis of the sensations. (AS, v)

His conviction was enhanced, as has been indicated, by an "antimetaphysical thrust" (AS, vii). Considering physics in isolation is too one-sided an enterprise for Mach. The physical sciences must stand next to biology and his new psychology, his "analysis of the sensations." Only such an integrated approach to science will bring the advances Mach seeks. To stay in the narrower realm of physics will not serve the purpose of charting the progress of knowledge because "in spite of its considerable progress, physics is only a part of the greater total knowledge, and cannot, with its one-sided intellectual means created for one-sided purposes, exhaust the materials presented by the physical world" (AS, 1). These materials are the "elements of sensation": colors, tones, and the psychological factors of our perceptual apparatus, such as moods, feelings, and volition (AS, 2).

The reduction of the field of the sciences to this pool of the elements of the sensations sets a boundary for all possible sciences: they derive from the materials which can be formalized. Such a field of data is not neutral, nor does it exist as a free-form continuum, but rather it presents itself to an organizing consciousness as a series of complexes:

> Relatively stable and persistent [entities] stand out from this network; they become imprinted in memory and expressed in language. As relatively more persistent, *complexes* of colors, tones, and pressures which are linked spatially and temporally are distinguished primarily; they therefore have received special names and are designated *bodies*. Such complexes are by no means absolutely persistent. (AS, 2)

The primary consequence of this setting of premises is made clear for both physics and psychology. A discipline is restricted not by its correspondence with a reality behind appearances, but by its chosen field of data and by the goals framing that data: "Thus, then, is constituted the great cleft between physical and psychological investigation for a habituated, stereotyped observational perspective. . . . Not the data, but the direction of observation, differs in the two fields" (AS, 11-12). This echoes Fechner because Mach, too, has dislodged the observer from a fixed position in the observed data.

With these statements, Mach places his psychology (his analysis of the sensations) in a unique setting, as a science in its own right, capable of achieving results as valid as those of the physical sciences. On the surface, this seems an attempt already made successfully by Franz Brentano[33] or Edmund Husserl.[34] Yet the empirical psychology of the former and the phenomenology of the latter differ from Mach's psychology in several key premises.

Their difference in programs is crucial to any comparison. The stated program of phenomenology is to investigate the intentional or meaning-sponsoring acts of consciousness.[35] In contrast, Mach focuses on the relationships within complexes of elements in appearance. That is, phenomenology (and its immediate predecessor, Brentano's psychology) analyzes the ways in which complexes of data are presented as appearances to a perceiving consciousness. Then it differentiates which facets of these appearances are attributed to the perceiving consciousness and which to the *eidos*, the essence, behind the appearances. In an alternate approach, Mach explicitly brackets the question of the reality behind the appearances, and instead focuses on the data or elements and the interests which form associations and combinations in them as complexes. For Mach, there is no question of an *eidos* like the phenomenologists maintained. Phenomenal sensations stem from the existence of a physical world whose absolute constitution is unknowable, but which has an existence verifiable as a set of functional dependencies of elements impinging on a perceiving consciousness. As such, this bracketed reality is at best a regional ontology of appearances which are classified according to their stability and persistence. When certain classes of sensations persist in association, they will be designated by names which signify the constellation of elements to be manipulated as units within the full field of experience (AS, 2).[36] Seen from this perspective, Mach's psychology deals with the region between a locus designated as a "perceiving consciousness" and the elements of which reality may be composed. It is neither a truly empirical nor an idealist psychology, and it allows neither for the absolute dominance of reality over the perceiving consciousness, nor for an absolutely constituted perceiving ego which conditions the appearance of reality. This psychology lies, therefore, in the interface between the spheres traditionally designated "objective" and "subjective," and when choosing between the two will not conform to the aims of phenomenology or a phenomenological psychology.[37]

The non-absolute perceiving consciousness conditions the second major differentiation between Mach's psychology and phenomenology: its methodological approach. Husserl and his followers rely on the existence of a permanent layer in the perceiving ego, a layer which grounds the results of the eidetic reduction (*Idea*, 7). Mach, in contrast, asserts that the perceiving ego itself is only a matter of habit, a construct based on the relative stability of a stream of sensations (AS, 3). The ego of personal identity changes in response to alterations in the body and in the "intellectual and moral egos" influenced by culture (AS, 3). Therefore, Mach does not give primacy to a perceiving consciousness, but rather to a system of elements in a perpetual reorientation and readaptation to the total world field of elements. Any conclusions reached about the constitution of an "ego" or a "personal existence" beyond an analysis of system stability are false conclusions. They would be based on the ungrounded projection which assumes that a stable entity behind appearances must cause them; the ego must exist as a "thing in itself." For Mach, "[t]he world does not consist of puzzling entities for us" (AS, 21); to assume such is a willful stance, a prejudice which will impede the progress of the sciences.

Mach's program -- a how-to for hands-on science --is the most pragmatic of those we have seen thus far. It will lead to a psychology which is non-phenomenological in the sense used by Husserl. Despite its lacking ontology, the pragmatism of Mach's psychology caused its greatest impact, for it pointed the way to key principles in the formation and validation of formalized disciplines. Not only the physical sciences, but any discipline which purports to be scientific in the application of its concepts and principles, must have recognizable standards for the recreatability, verifiability, and validity of its results (today's formulation of the scientific method). Mach identified the mental mechanisms of continuity, consistency, and least variation as the fundamental regularities on which a scientific formalization can be built (AS, 16). These mechanisms treat data in predictable patterns based on pragmatic unities of perceived data. Moreover, the same mental mechanisms which underlie the higher-order descriptions of a formalization in the pure sciences must also be the mechanisms describing a scientific psychology. In neither case do these mechanisms for the association of data constitute an explanation of the data involved; they only describe the field of data for the specific purposes of that discipline.[38]

Mach's inclusion of the mechanisms of the psyche in the preconditions for the sciences in general represents a redefinition of systematic, formalized knowledge. Systematic knowledge will be relative to the experience of the group it serves:

> Science always originates in a process of the adaptation of
> thoughts to a specific region of experience. The results of
> the process are the elements of thought which are capable
> of representing the entire region. The results will naturally
> differ according to the type and magnitude of the region. If
> the region of experience expands, or if a number of regions
> unite which had been separate to this point, then the
> inherited, habituated elements of thought no longer suffice
> for the expanded region. In the struggle of acquired habits
> with the attempt to adapt, *problems* originate, which
> disappear with the completed adaptation, in order to make
> room for whatever others will arise. (AS, 22)

This call for a redefinition of formalized knowledge differs from the
monism sought at the turn of the century, since Mach finds a
unified science approach inappropriate.[39] Physics,
phenomenology, and psychology must operate as distinct
disciplines with different modes of analysis reflecting their
underlying premises and interests as sciences. As sciences, each
deals with different constellations of the elements of experience,
and each has evolved independently through history in its own
adaptation to its region of data. While the mental strategies which
underlie scientific formalizations are common to all disciplines, the
explicit analytic strategies of each discipline are contingent upon its
chosen region of data or elements and its history (that is, the
varying goals which the discipline has set for itself and then
fulfilled or discarded).

With this differentiation between the formalization of a science
and the elements or data which that science describes, Mach is
setting a program similar to that of Jean Piaget in the twentieth
century which is a description of the development of a science as a
product of: 1) the set of data which that discipline chooses to
address; 2) the direction of interest taken by that discipline, the goal
or class of problems to be explained in description of data; and 3)
the manipulations of data and the emerging disciplinary-specific
patterns of analysis which become raised to the level of that
discipline's explicit methodology or problem-solving techniques.[40]

Piaget characterizes his position with respect to the development of
the sciences in a formulation commensurate with Mach's:

> [F]or the genetic epistemologist, knowledge results from
> continuous construction, since in each act of
> understanding, some degree of invention is involved; in
> development, the passage from one stage to the next is
> always characterized by the formation of new structures
> which did not exist before, either in the external world or
> in the subject's mind. The central problem of genetic
> epistemology concerns the mechanism of this construction
> of novelties which creates the need for the explanatory
> factors which we call *reflective abstraction* and
> *self-regulation.* (GE, 77-78)

Piaget describes the individual mind here, but Mach will describe
disciplines in similar fashion, stressing operations on a field of
data.[41] Piaget concludes that "a great deal of work needs to be
done" in this differentiation between the formalizations of
disciplines and their formative mechanisms. Mach, however, had
much earlier already provided a breakdown of the fundamental
processes involved in the genesis of systematic knowledge and its
formalizations: his "psychology of the senses," a discipline
systematically exploiting the premises established by the analysis of
the sensations (AS, 210).

7.3 The "Psychology of the Senses": Preconditions and Operations

Mach delimits several preconditions for a successful application
of psychological principles to an analysis of a scientific
formalization, the most important of which concerns the route to
this analysis: the elements of experience which constitute the region
for a particular science must be analyzed in terms of functional
relationships of data, in terms of interdependencies, of "basic
variables and varying dependency relationships" (AS, 26). When
the interdependencies of a region of elements are determined and a
statement of their functional relationships developed, a "complete
orientation" within that region is achieved; this orientation

constitutes Mach's highest scientific ideal (AS, 26). It can, moreover, only be useful if the locus of the observer is determinate, and if this observer remembers that the "reality" of these functional interdependencies is indifferent to the analysis.[42] Whether the interdependencies exist in nature or only in perception, their shifting relationships or functional dependencies constitute the grounds for a formalization which may at any point have to be abandoned or restructured in the face of new data, or as the observer changes location.

Mach's second precondition for any analysis concerns the perspective or frame of reference from which the elements of the sensations are considered: "No point of view has an absolutely permanent applicability; each is only important for a designated purpose" (AS, 27). When a technical thinker, for example, wishes to give a lecture to a lay audience, he or she must shift into an everyday frame of reference. Similarly, in the validation and verification of the results of the sciences, the analysis and data must be considered together with the perspective or direction of interest which the formalization itself represents. If the inherently assumed frame of reference of the formalization is not considered, the scientist's results will be clouded by preconceived notions, and even the most meager guarantees for the meaningfulness of his results will be lost.

The third precondition which Mach sets for the development of scientific formalizations is the surrender of perhaps the most pernicious preconceived notion -- solipsism, a psychologistic theory of the origins of the outside world: "The entire theory of the psychological origin of the outside world in a projection of sensations rests on a misconstrued application of physical perspectives" (AS, 29). Mach warns his readers that the opposite is true. One does not introject the world (pure psychologism or solipcism), but rather "extrojects," extracting and idealizing the concept of "ego" or "self" out of the given region of elements of the sensation comprising the world. When the elements themselves are granted primacy in a formalization, neither dualism nor solipcism results. The world is presented as a region of sensations; its forms, as appearances, are idealizations created for specific purposes and must therefore not be posited to exist in a causal relationship with an unknowable reality (AS, 42). The mind does not create the world, it registers and limits the world as perception. We are, however, habituated to idealized concepts such as "world," and thus tend to use them in ways which hinder the free progress of knowledge. However, in a successful science, the scientist must never forget that all physical concepts have their origins in a mental displacement of experiential data, falsely attributed to an unknown reality.

This series of preconditions or warnings circumscribes Mach's psychology as it relates to science. The only difference he finds between physical and psychological research is one of direction or perspective:

> . . . whether we direct our attention to one form of dependency or another. I see therefore no contrast between the mental and the physical, but rather an identity with respect to elements. In the sensible sphere of my consciousness, each object is at the same time physical and mental. (AS, 33)

More specifically, a differentiated field of either physical or mental research will emerge when one subset of elements is set as a constant in the region of dependencies under consideration, and thus is not deemed integral to the development of that field's formalized description (AS, 34). Contrary to the assumptions of a number of Mach's contemporaries (Mach identifies Richard Avenarius as a chief opponent in his extreme Darwinism [AS, 38]), psychology does not deal strictly with either the nervous system of the human organism or with the innate construction of the human brain. For Mach, psychology, as any other science, is a study of the dependencies among certain classes of elements of experience. As such, it is not removed from the pure sciences, but must be derived as an absolutely parallel formalization. The core of Mach's psychology, then, is found in the description of the mechanisms through which data becomes interrelated and presented as appearances -- in other words, a science of appearances. Of what will Mach's catalogue of mental mechanisms consist? "Preservation of memories, their connection, recall prompted by each other, memory and association are the fundamental conditions for a developed mental life" -- this is Mach's summary of the mechanisms of the psyche (AS, 151).

The actual catalogue of mechanisms or operations is much more highly differentiated within the content of memory and association, each level constituting a specific type of association facilitated by memory. The successive chapters of the *Analysis of the Sensations* explicate and exemplify these levels, which break down as follows:

1) *adaptation* (Anpassung): forces a maximum economy of thought patterns in a condensed storage of elements of sensation as acclimated habits which allow for efficient manipulation in new contexts or when new problems or data arise;

2) *constancy and continuity* (Stetigkeit und Kontinuität): condition habituated storage of elements as identifiable members of a specified region or field;

3) *sufficient distinctness or differentiation* (zureichende Bestimmtheit oder Differenzierung): represents the opposite of the constancy and continuity principle and allows sensations to appear separately within the region;

4) *perception of wholes* (eine Vollständigkeit, eine Geläufigkeit des Verhältnisses): a tendency to supplement missing elements (AS, 44);

5) *sufficiency principle*: a criterion for fixing associations into habits, allowing no habituation unless the complex of sensations is recallable or recreatable (AS, 45);

6) *similarity and partial equivalence*: the ability to produce parallel chains of associations as reflex actions to slight variances on known chains (AS, 53); and

7) *interest, the will to see* (Aufmerksamkeit): the foregrounding of subsets of information in the region under consideration with respect to the purpose of the deliberations (AS, 123).

These seven modes of association of data constitute Mach's catalogue of the first-order mechanisms of thought, the modes of data registration. They are the mechanisms which facilitate, debilitate, and motivate organization of data as appearances (at the level of apperception), not necessarily as elements of higher-order thought patterns. Moreover, it is a catalogue of the organism's limitations in perceiving which acknowledge threshold values for differentiation of data. Most importantly, however, this catalogue comprises the fundamental principles for a perceptual psychology unrestricted by an individualized perceiving consciousness. This variant of conceptual psychology focuses on the evolution of higher-order conceptual processes from lower-order ones in a prototypical situation proscribed by direction of interest, goal of the association, and the data involved. Such a psychology will develop its descriptive formalizations using this catalogue of possible strategies for the association of data and formation of concepts. Emphasized in this context is that the *concepts* which will form the basis for the systematic science (concepts such as "mass" and "temperature" in physics) must be developed out of the data and not *a priori*; only the concepts that refer to useful properties of the data within the stated goals of the systematic investigation will prove fruitful for the development of the discipline.

The descriptive tools associated with the formalizations of higher-order thought, tools such as "concepts" and attributions of "final cause," are for Mach linear developments of the basic modes of data association. In his example, the differentiation between "efficient cause" and "final cause" or "purpose" is traditionally developed in terms like "a dose of cause" equals "a dose of effect" (AS, 66). Yet in fact, the designations "cause" and "effect" result from determining similarities in regions of data, as is the case in biology, where periodic functions of organisms allow certain judgments about future effects. Similarly, "teleology" is a projection on the basis of similarity: one supplies missing data in a chain of associated sensations, a statement of goal-directedness without explicit reference to a specific purpose. Mach stresses, "[t]here seems to exist no necessity to assume a deep differentiation between a teleological and a causal investigation. The former is merely temporary" (AS, 66).[43]

Other formalizations evolve as similar abstractions. Spatial orientation summarizes comparisons and contrasts of sizes and shapes; geometry relates similarities in the properties observed. On a more abstract level, the will of an organism is "[t]he totality of conditions on a movement, partially conscious and bound up with probable success" (AS, 72). Memory itself is most clearly defined as a constellation of associated elements (AS, 156).

7.4 Operations in the Sciences

This long introduction to the *Analysis of the Sensations* demonstrates the links between Mach's scientific thought and the cultural sciences described by other conceptual psychologists, especially Hermann Paul: they all describe the systematics of the sciences as backed up by a consistent psychology based on the few principles of analogy and association. Mach's sketch of these psychological mechanisms serves as a preliminary blueprint for the development of higher-order formalizations in a descriptive science. No matter what field, the fundamental mechanism in its advancement is adaptation: "The fundamental viewpoints of humans develop naturally through an adaptation to a narrower or broader circle of experience and thoughts" (AS, 207).[44] With this communality of basic mechanisms, how can sciences develop differently?

For Mach, each science must be subject to the same initial conditions in the development of its formalization: the psychological mechanisms described above explain the premises of science possible on the basis of very few principles applied to a plurality of data (AS, 208). Yet Mach also acknowledges that, despite their shared premises, each science will itself constitute a "special area of investigation" (AS, 208). The core of the differentiation will be found in the distinction already drawn by Mach. Physicists, epistemologists, and other scientists are subject to restrictions on regions of data in their focus on the elements of the sensations: "The sciences can be differentiated in their data as well as in the treatment of that data. All science, however, seeks to represent facts as thoughts, either for practical purposes or to remove intellectual discontent" (AS, 209). Thus sciences share their goals and aim to facilitate thought through a representation of a set of data and their interdependencies (AS, 210). The formalization of a science, therefore, serves as a heuristic aid that enables the brain to account for the facets of a set of data which could not be considered without this overview.

The judgments characteristic of a particular science are operations within the region of data considered the ground of that discipline. The function of judgments within the discipline's formalization is the rearrangement of the elements of the sensation within the region:

> A judgment is therefore always a supplement of a sense representation for the purpose of a more complete representation of a sensible fact. If the judgment may be expressed in words, it will always consist of a connection of the new representations composed from the memory signs already present. (AS, 212)

Within the context of such a mutable formalization, research is a conscious application of the ordinarily unconscious procedures through which the signs of memory and preliminary judgments are formed. The method of sufficient differentiation, intentional adaptations of thoughts, or a reapplication of established habits of thought may all be modes of judgment which can be consciously applied to systematize or expand the formalized functional dependencies within a region of data (AS, 214-15).

Abstractions and concepts serve the development of the formalization of a science in similar fashion. They originate in a projection of an ideal similarity within a region of data, and then direct further work within the area (AS, 215). Contrary to popular assumptions, "[a] concept is by no means a finished representation" (AS, 216). Rather, it is the result of a number of associated thought operations which can then be verified within the terms of the formalization. The concept "heptagon," for example, is a logical extension or projection of the concepts "triangle," "octagon," and "pentagon." Thus, projected concepts are valid because they further knowledge of the formalization in terms of its available field of data and posit a stability in its results. When abstractions and concepts are applied to further a formalization, the functional dependencies within the field of data become enriched for us: "Through [mental] activity, we enrich and expand facts too poor for us" (AS, 216).[45] In this, Mach's work anticipates deconstructionism -- he reveals the limits of applicability and artificiality of concepts in use.

Mach stresses that essential elements in the formalization of the sciences derive from the consciousness which formulates that science with respect to an articulated set of goals. Mach's radical position, however, derives from his attribution of the final form of the formalization not to a fixed set of operations (as in Kant, or later in Piaget), but to a set of associative patterns (dynamic acts or functions) which emerge into fixed capacities or operations according to the constraints on the region of data chosen and the goal of the formalization. Mach therefore locates the factors innate to formalizations on a pre-logical level, a level prior to Kant's categories or Piaget's operations. As Mach states: "As in intuitive cognition, everything here is reducible to the location, highlighting, and separating out of the most central sense elements. Research reaches here only in a detour, that which intuitive cognition offers without mediation" (AS, 218). For Mach, then, the sciences begin at the level of formalization -- at the levels of abstraction and concept formation -- schematizing, as we have seen in conceptual psychology.

Mach's particular analysis of the sciences determines conscious and unconscious or chosen and automatic strategies in the schematization. Idealists posit a fixed developmental sequence in the strategies underlying all formalizations, even those of science. For Mach, however, only *strategies* for manipulating data are innate; yet, they are not present in any fixed order. The mechanisms for developing a formalization, in contrast, represent conscious decisions. "Abstraction," for example, may be conceived of as "negative attention," a conscious and potentially useful decision as to which elements to consider in a particular region of data and which to overlook (AS, 218). Such decisions will not lead to unsupported speculation, even considering their willful nature, because sense elements themselves control the retention of abstractions and concepts. The processes which form them may occasionally undergo a "detour," as Mach saw, but only the utility and concreteness ("Anschaulichkeit," literally "visibility") of concepts guarantee their use in a formalization. Over time, a successful abstract concept will in all cases be a recreation of the constant data in the chosen region of elements (AS, 220). Moreover, the use and development of a successful concept will be regulated inherently because of its constancy, continuity, and economy within a formalization representing "healthy thought."[46] The consistent series of developmental patterns which Piaget identifies (an advance on Kant's categories through an explicit addition of history) is for Mach a danger. The concepts which arise might reify and impede the free progress of knowledge:

> A truly unconditional constancy does not exist . . . what we term matter is a certain regular construct of elements [sensations]. We must remember that this regularity is posited to exist for all perceiving locuses -- but not as a constant something, rather as a constant law. (AS, 223)

Thus for Mach, science represents a conscious decision reflecting healthy thought; it is a drive to extend the continuities and constancies in the elements of the sensations as schematizations serving the purpose of orientation under specific conditions. Finally, Mach's explications of the operations underlying the sciences delimit a formalized discipline as *descriptive*, or provisory, for limited purposes. Kant, in the nineteenth century, and Piaget, in the twentieth, in contrast, use the operations of consciousness to delimit a formalization as explanatory of the mind's relation to any subject matter. Mach's sciences describe functional relationships of data for a determinate purpose; Kant's and Piaget's explain the origins of formalizations as they are activated by data, but also as they exist earlier in the mind. With his differentiation between the mechanisms of the mind and the operations leading to formalizations, Mach is able to establish psychology as a discipline standing next to the other sciences based on mental mechanisms of association common to all, yet treating varying regions of data in distinctive patterns.

In the *Analysis of the Sensations*, Mach separated several levels affecting the formal development of the sciences, which was a necessary process before commencing the discussion of any particular science. Each will constitute a limitation on the accounting a science can offer:

> It will be most purposeful to acknowledge the limits of our knowledge which show themselves everywhere, and to consider our search for univocal determinacy as an ideal which we realize in our thinking as far as is possible. (AS, 237)

The first level identified by Mach is the region of the elements of the sensation, the field of data for all the sciences. The functional relationships of these data constitute appearances to an observing consciousness. These are, however, representations of *perceived* associations and constancies within that region of data, and have no claim to represent a reality behind the appearances. The mechanisms of this association, though, are inherent in mental life: "Our mental life, to the degree that we understand representations under that rubric, appears to be independent of physical processes, so to speak, a world in itself, with freer laws, with laws of a different order" (AS, 229). Mach's mental laws ground the formalizations of all sciences, and also for higher-order mental operations such as concept development and abstractions, as well as for operations in the sense used by Piaget.

Mach's second level of restrictions on mental processing refers to the formalizations of the sciences themselves, the large-scale functional relationships and dependencies of data: not the preconditions for the science, but the science itself. Since each science deals with a particular orientation to the data of the sensations, any one science cannot exhaust the knowledge derivable from these elements. For this reason:

Psychology is a science aiding physics. The two areas support each other reciprocally and form only in their connection a complete science. The contrast of subject and object (in the conventional sense) does not exist from our perspective. (AS, 230)

For Mach, psychology is a discipline capable of the level of formalization of other sciences, yet differentiated in its chosen data and proclaimed direction of interest in description. This is not a therapeutic psychology, nor a perceptual psychology which would focus on the modes in which thoughts are contingent on the perceptual apparatus. It is, rather, a conceptual psychology in the sense used above, resembling Piaget's genetic epistemology, focusing on the generation and development of conceptual life as conditioned by an economy of thought, a drive to adaptation and orientation within a field of data, and a primacy of the association of data. Both the knowledge obtainable and the locus of the perceiving consciousness are only provisory centers for a designated region of data, and as such, do not enjoy an *a priori* status.

The third level of restrictions in science specified by Mach is only rudimentarily discussed in *The Analysis of the Sensations*: the hypothetical or theoretical level, which guides projections of associated constellations of data. Like concepts and abstractions on a more fundamental level, these projections posit probable functions within a field of data which must then be confirmed through systematic observation and research -- or rejected in favor of new theories and hypotheses -- if the data available does not correspond to the formalization posited. In his later text, *Knowledge and Error: Sketches Toward a Psychology of Investigation*, Mach concentrates on the theoretical level of a scientific formalization in greater detail by describing a psychology of higher-order thought.

Yet how is this a "science of culture"? And why was his work not received more directly by thinkers like Dilthey or Husserl who were interested in developing such a science?[47] A simple answer is that Mach was working in a common assumption for his age, and that others did not need to go outside their field to find a model for a science of culture; the conceptual psychology underlying the age automatically accommodated both science and the humanities. Further answers to these questions may lie in the multiple levels on which Mach worked under the guise of a discourse appropriate to popular science. In consequence of its diversity, Mach's work seems deconstructionist in nature when compared to current scientific practice, pointing to the *limits* of what is known instead of attending directly to what can be known. There is little room in traditional scientific discourse for a psychological perspective such as Mach's, and thus his numerous examples of the scientifically possible and impossible are dismissed as *Popular Scientific Lectures* (their publication title) not appropriate to the progress of science. Mach's work on the history of the sciences, with its clear acknowledgement of serendipity and solutions with restricted applications, betrays similar deconstructionist tendencies and is similarly inappropriate to the theoretical discourse of the pure sciences, while at the same time adding the core insight to conceptual psychology.

Perhaps because it was among the first that emphasized the role of the pure sciences as products of culture, Mach's work on the sciences was never generally received as a blueprint for a general "science of culture," a *Geisteswissenschaft* in the sense used by Dilthey.[48] Yet, he has, in the context of a discussion on the development of the sciences, located the point of connection between individual and group psychology in the mechanisms of the psyche which process data and the individual's desire to orient himself within that region. Moreover, since Mach's examples were drawn solely from the sphere of the pure sciences, the generality of his claims can be overlooked by both scientists and humanists because he is explicitly not discussing only the formalizations of the pure sciences, but rather the mechanisms of dealing with data which can apply to *any* field of data, cultural or scientific.

The readers of *The Analysis of the Sensations* saw only the results of his investigation -- the dissolution of the personal ego -- and not the applications of his principles for data, goal, and procedures which could be applied as general analytic strategies within a science of culture (a situation persisting today in the secondary literature). Many in his audience still seem to consider the formalizations of the pure sciences different from those requisite to a science of culture. Yet Mach insisted that the formalization of a science served the cause of orientation within a body of data. Bahr and his contemporaries stressed the prevailing mood around Mach's work when they focused on the individual instead of on the general strategies of culture which Mach's analyses could have revealed.

Thus, Mach's innovative synthesis created a discourse which hindered the overt acceptance of his "psychology" into either the humanistic or the scientific discourse of his day. The three levels of analysis for synthetic disciplines outlined in the *Analysis of the Sensations* were not, and are not, considered pertinent to the culture of science nor to the humanities for they violate the prevailing ideologies of the scientific method. For the pure sciences, Mach's insistence on the descriptive nature of systematic thought violated the need for univocal proofs of the explanatory adequacy of theories. While a concept like relativity was acceptable on the level of experimental constructs, it was less so when extended through a historical dimension, since it called into question the correspondence of formalizations with ontic reality. From the scientist's point of view, Mach was not adding psychology to science, he was questioning the constitution of ultimate reality, whether that reality be located in nature or in the conceptual apparatus of mankind. Neither sphere could be independent.

The program of the *Analysis of the Sensations* was also destined to be misconstrued by humanists. For the humanistic disciplines, Mach's focus on data conditioning inherited thought patterns constituted only an acknowledgement of the restricted control which an individual enjoyed over his world. The standards for verifiability and recreatability of analytic results within the confines of a formalization were not perceived by humanists as relevant.[49] The correlation between individual and group experiences which would be accounted for in a formalization of the functional dependencies of data regions in a human science was not a topic of interest for thinkers and writers like Bahr, Fritz Mauthner, Robert Musil, or the Vienna Circle, all of whom read Mach.[50] The discourse of the *fin de siècle* humanist received Mach's message only as a confirmation of the dissolution of the primacy of the individual ego and not necessarily as a blueprint to advances in the humanistic disciplines in exploiting the regularities of group consciousness.

Mach's work on the sciences and on psychology constituted a discourse which was destined not to be received by his contemporaries on its own terms as a science of culture as well as an adjunct to a pure science. Yet his differentiation between the mental mechanisms which condition the treatment in any science and the formalizations of the sciences themselves which arise as descriptions of specific regions of data considered for specific purposes constitutes a move to raise psychology to the level of the pure sciences, as well as a recognition that all sciences are in fact sciences of culture, subject to the historical limitations of their development. In this, Mach's work represents the most developed form of the paradigm of conceptual psychology, since he explains not only its inherent questions of referentiality and concepts, but also adds full explications of the historicity of descriptions.

7.5 The Position of *Knowledge and Error* with Respect to *Analysis of the Sensations*

A later and less widely considered collection of Mach's essays, *Knowledge and Error: Sketches toward a Psychology of Investigation*, is the best source with which to complete his outline of psychology as a discipline. Again, *Knowledge and Error* is not the text on which Mach's influence on his contemporaries was based, and its origins as companion to the popular-scientific lectures have led later critics to overlook its content. Yet Mach took great pains with the final shape of the collection in the ordering, supplementing, and selection of the essays included.[51] By editing meticulously, Mach created a text with two purposes. First and most obviously, it is a documentation of his researches into topics concerning the history of science, as these researches were presented to a lay public; and second, it is a text whose progression of chapter topics constitutes an outline of the possible levels on which the conceptualization and development of a formalized discipline could occur. His proclaimed "Psychology of Investigation" is in a more developed form than in *Analysis of the Sensations*. Seen in this light, *Knowledge and Error* deserves independent consideration as a statement of a distinct program.[52] Each chapter in this "psychology of investigation" seems to signal one of a set of reports on advances in the sciences. However, the underlying message of these chapters points not to an exposition of specific scientific advances, but rather to a clarification of the principles of scientific investigation leading to them. In other words, Mach's true goal with the text seems to be the placement of physics into the larger context of a discourse about the possibility of science, and hence into close proximity with his work on psychology. *Knowledge and Error* is, then, a discourse with two levels and directions: its explicit content from physics, and its implicit hierarchy of tasks of the investigator. *Knowledge and Error* adds history to the program begun in the *Analysis of the Sensations*.

The core of *Analysis of the Sensations* reconceptualized scientific data (his "theory of elements") and analyzed the effects which the direction of interest inherent in a conceptualization has on the validity of results in a particular science (the modern idea of "frame of reference"). The new text brought with it a new approach: a higher-order consideration of science in culture. When the formalization of a particular science represents a specified interest and field of data, this science becomes raised above the level of "vulgar thought," and thus serves as a conscious tool for the orientation of an organism within a world and for the science within a particular region of data (KE, 2).

Drawing the relation between every-day thought and scientific formalizations is the innovation of *Knowledge and Error*. Mach defines the different stance he takes in his populatization as essential to the program of this book: "That which a philosopher considers a possible *beginning* only appears to the natural scientist as a very distant *end* for his work" (KE, 4). That is, the scientist concerns himself with the facets and the mechanisms for the orientation of an organism within the data region of the world, while Mach's more general work must reach beyond to deal with the preconditions for sciences and not only with the practical implications. In the earlier text, Mach was dealing explicitly with the data criteria and formalizations of the sciences. In *Knowledge and Error*, he is dealing with the preconditions for formalizations within the whole potential field of conceptual life. He is not discussing those mental mechanisms on which the formalizations of the sciences are built, but rather he wishes to locate these formalizations within the field of higher-order thought. In so doing, Mach also evolves a systematic psychology on the basis of his earlier investigations of the relationships between physical data and mental mechanisms. He thus extends the formalization of psychology applicable to mental life in cultural-historical context instead of only to scientific investigation.

In developing this broad form of conceptual psychology, Mach again returns to the premises of Immanuel Kant.[53] All conceptualizations or formalizations must be located in either time or space (KE,9). Yet each such conceptualization also represents a set of the elements of the sensations and the findings (*Befund*) about that set. Within this model, then, Mach's challenge remains to explain higher-order thought processesas those thought processes above the level of Kant's apperception and above rudimentary concept formation as delimited in the *The Analysis of the Sensations.* Mach stated expressly that this challenge had not been met by his predecessors. Herbart's psychology, for instance, pointed towards a methodology for the examination of representations in themselves, which Mach felt was one of the desiderata of the field (KE, 11). Yet according to Mach, Herbart did not recognize the provisory and mutable nature of conceptualization, particularly of designations such as "things" and "ego," and so assumed a too simplified concept of the human soul which did not allow sufficient latitude for models of conceptualization (KE, 13).

Mach also explicitly rejected a second possible model for psychology: the attempt to explain conceptualization as a product of the spiritual capacities inherent in the organism. The body's sensations, perceptions, and representations of experience are held in memory as associations created under the pressure of interests in the preservation of the organism. Like Kant, Mach finds that higher-order thought patterns consist of four constellations of experience: representations, feelings, affects, and moods (KE, 21). Yet Mach does not feel that these constellations are inherent in the ego or soul of man. If, for example, in addition to identifying a complex constellation of sensations, one clarifies the goal of a certain chain of associated sensations, then one can term the entire constellation of sensations the "will." This will is not an inherent power of the soul, but a summary of a recognizable "way of acting" (KE, 21). Like the other potential powers of the soul, it is an extended reflex based on the memory of a constellation of sensation, of actions innate to the organism, and of acquired patterns of response aiding the adaptation and survival of that organism. Thus for Mach, it is impossible to develop a psychology of higher-order thought on the basis of the innate capacities of the human soul. *Knowledge and Error* traces a different course to develop its psychology, allowing for both the provisory nature of conceptualization and the biological stance of adaptation of an organism to its environment.

7.6 Memory as the Ground for Conceptualization

Mach felt that the bases for conceptualization traditionally were assumed to be reproductions or representations and their associations. Yet this assumption must be in error, because only through the activity of the memory may any constellations of experience be presented to thought processes as "reproductions" (KE, 29). In contrast, "representations" correspond only to those elements of the sensations which are immediately present to a perceiving locus; their essential nature is simultaneity (KE, 31). Thus neither representations nor reproductions are in themselves a sufficient ground for conceptualization, since they are acquired associations reinforced by individual experience, not innate knowledge (KE, 33). Moreover, when either reproductions or representations are presented to the mind simultaneously, they are further subject to association as thought becomes increasingly more complex. They are not fundamental.

Mach must therefore redefine conceptualization so that he may develop the formalization of a scientific psychology at the base of a more advanced cultural science. "Reproducibility" and "associability" of sense data do form the basis of consciousness, anchored on the ground of memory (a habituation of reactive patterns of the organism, a registration of energy). Still, this "consciousness" and its associated representations and reproductions cannot be conceived as a state or specific energy apart from its associations of data:

> Consciousness is no special [mental] *quality* or class of qualities which is differentiated from physical qualities; it is also no special quality which must be added to the physical in order to make the unconscious conscious . . . [Introspection teaches] that consciousness has its roots in reproduction and association . . . Consciousness does not consist of a special quality, but rather in a *special construct* of given qualities. (KE, 41)

Mach thus construes conceptualization as an activity, not a

structure. In his model, sense data is in a continual process of association in the interest of adapting consciousness to the requirements of the environment. Those associations which best serve the adaptation become habits or memories, and may be recalled as reproductions of the original associations when more complex associations are undertaken. They range from "unconsciousness" through "consciousness." This continuum reflects varying complexities of perceived elements of the sensations, requiring the brain to adapt through association and reproduction of sensations (KE, 41-42).

If Mach's model for the process of conceptualization is assumed, all higher-order levels of thought (consciousness, will, and the ego) are predicated on a ground of organic memory, particularly as this memory focuses on the preservation of the organism as a locus of consciousness. Memory also serves as the ground on which individual personality develops, contingent on environmental factors. Since the requirements of the environment (biological or cultural) govern the adaptation of every individual, memory also grounds the conceptual strategies of an entire culture (KE, 69-70). While animal instincts are conditioned almost uniquely by the environment, humans may choose an indirect path toward achieving a goal, or may go beyond immediate purposes in planning in an attempt to stabilize their surroundings (KE, 75). Such planning is the foundation for culture, possible only because one can recall environmental stimuli as reproductions. Language and writing, distinctive products of culture, represent extensions of the human capacity to remember, aiding and fulfilling the innate human drive to systematization and, ultimately, ornamentation -- the progression of human taste from system to elegance (KE, 79).

In designating memory as the basis for all conceptualizations in culture, Mach is thus offering an extremely reduced ground for the formalizations of a scientific psychology compared to his predecessors. In his strict scientific approach, he offers the minimal effective definition of conceptual psychology. The traditionally accepted categories of psychological explanation -- representations, affects, emotions, and moods -- have been collapsed together on the basis of their common origin as associations of the elements of the sensations. At the same time, the model focuses on the conservation of energy in the adaptation of the organism to its life environment, and it allows for a univalent discussion of conceptual life. Mach's psychology will, in consequence, focus on data as data: the data of appearances as they interact with consciousness in terms of individual intent and of the remembered requirements of that individual organism within the world and social environments.

First-order thought is, in consequence, an activity confined to the realm of apperception, to the associations of data made in the immediate present on the level of experiential data or basic conceptualizations. Thereafter, the formalizations representing higher-order thought correspond to activities of representation and reproduction of constellations of elements, evolving more complex associations of data from the habituated past and the experiential present. All other "capacities" or "functions" attributed to the conscious or unconscious mind are only names given to reactions predicated on larger associated constellations of data within the experiential field of a particular organism. Such "capacities of the mind" are, therefore, not proper objects for independent investigations as psychology, according to Mach's premises. Going much further than his predecessors in conceptual psychology, he has defined the activities of the mind on which both first-order and higher-order conceptualization are grounded: memory, representation, and reproduction. The psychology studying these fundamental activities will be formalized by investigating the *products* of the activities of the mind and determining the purposes and limits of such products as they further the organism's knowledge.

7.7 Knowledge and Error: Concepts and Validation

Mach's first advance in formalizing psychology was defining all capacities of the soul as based on memory. In moving to discuss the higher powers of conceptualization, however, Mach must turn to traces in the mind -- to representations and reproductions -- as memories constituting both knowledge and error.

The function of a representation (*Vorstellung*) is the facilitation of a perceiving consciousness in following or predicting a series of facts. If experienced elements complete that chain of facts as predicted, the representation of the chain is designated *knowledge*. If not, and lapses or inconsistencies in the chain emerge as compared to perceived reality, then the representation constitutes an *error*, an inadequate consideration of available elements or facts. The history of civilization documents many an error. Superstitions, ghosts, the fetishes of primitive peoples, as well as the poetry of civilization, are all "fantasies of experience" (KE, 97). On a broader scale, religion, philosophy, and the idea of nature represent similar unprovable generalizations which may constitute either knowledge or error about the facts of our experience (KE, 103).

On the most rudimentary level, representations (the basis for which are concepts) are differentiated from judgments (which are based on the elements of experience). A representation is a summary of a set of dependencies within a field of the elements of the sensation, as they have registered in a consciousness as significant to the survival of an organism. As such, a representation corresponds to the memory of a set of stimuli (KE, 106-7). Nonetheless, a judgment was involved in the formation of that representation. The essence of this judgment is a willed foregrounding of certain aspects of the sensations as the representation is formed: "Thus we learn to consider the more important determinants of an experience *in isolation* from each other, to separate them into components or to compose them out of parts. In considering one facet of experience *more determining* than another, and in expressing this in language, we are making a *judgment*" (KE, 110).

Because of its position in the formation of representations, then, judgment is the source of error, especially when the direction of interest for the organism represented has neglected or overlooked crucial stimuli or dependencies. Still, Mach recognizes the value of errors in judgment: "Knowledge and error flow from the same mental source; only success can differentiate the two. The clearly recognized error is, as a corrective, just as beneficial to knowledge as is positive knowledge" (KE, 114). The sole inherent danger in judgment is its ability to become hypostatized. Judgment can mislead the users of a representation to forget the difference in kind between representations which correspond to a concretely verifiable field of sensations and dependencies, and those which do not. In all cases, an error is a representation formed through an incomplete judgment of the importance of aspects of the field of data under consideration. It is, moreover, a state of confusion between veracity (*Wahrheit*) and verisimilitude (*Wahrscheinlichkeit*),[54] caused by inadequate attention to secondary factors in the field of data, or by homomorphisms with a false similarity to the data under consideration.

This is the synchronic dimension of thought. A diachronic dimension is still needed to accommodate the effects of culture and history. Mach's representations are a level of thought embedded in the present. In contrast, reproductions of various types enable judgments beyond the field of immediate experience into the past. As such, they thus constitute the focus for a psychology of higher-order conceptualizations. Reproductions correspond to the field of remembered data and dependencies, be they designated "abstract" or "concrete" in the conventional sense. All reproductions are representations of particular fields of data made for specific purposes and held in memory because of their utility in the orientation of the organism. Because of the broad application of reproductions, then, Mach must differentiate and classify them according to their scope and inherent intention in representation. In this classification, Mach develops a taxonomy of reproductions as they serve the purposes of higher-order thought.

The first and most fundamental reproduction is for Mach a *concept*: a representation of knowledge which has been granted a degree of psychological realism on the ground of its relative permanence in the field of sense data (KE, 124).[55] A set of associations becomes a reproducible concept when it has a degree of permanence which will guarantee its use. The realism of a concept is documented in its history, which may be traced and correlated with empirical data in an exegesis of its referentiality and usage (KE, 125). This history will reveal the stages in the complex dependencies in which it is enmeshed. Words adhere to concepts as names and convenient labels for the complex of sensations which they summarize. Moreover, once a typical concept has been put into general use, it may serve as the model for other concepts or names on the ground of their similarities or differences.

In Mach's eyes, the scientific or systematic use of a concept does not differ significantly from the everyday use. The scientist just adds an explicit definition to the concept in order to use it precisely and with maximum facility (KE, 127). Because of this need for explicit definition, each science will naturally tend to develop its own technical vocabulary, corresponding to the concepts representing its particular direction of interest and the region of data to which it attends. The scientist, however, has an option in his attitude toward concept use: "He is able to awaken the potential knowledge in the concept, but he is not always *necessitated* to do so" (KE, 130). The everyday thinker uses the concept without necessary reference to the constellation of the elements of the sensations which constitute it. In contrast, the scientist remembers that this body of data exists, and that he may tap it for use when his systematic approach to knowledge requires.

Abstraction or schematization thus provides Mach with a systematic approach to knowledge, which is the basis for all formalizations. When applied to a single concept or set of concepts, abstraction associates a set of characteristics which have become foregrounded or backgrounded in the process of judgment. This weighting of characteristic elements allows a concept to emerge with a distinct profile and as a correlate to the psychological reproduction which engendered it. With such a concept, the general economy of thought is facilitated, and the basis for a schematization laid (this harkens back to Kant, but on a broader basis). Each concept, then, serves a greater purpose than referentiality. Particularly when a word is attached to it, a concept serves to lend a preliminary organization or orientation to *classes* of characteristics highlighted for a specific purpose (KE, 133). With the orientation represented by the concept, the set of characteristics achieves a degree of substantiality for the thinker. Through the mediation of the concept, the isolated system of sensations which is designated the body is correlated with a distinct set of associated processes in its immediate environment. The concept highlights a distinction between the "body" and "outside objects," and explains the primary orientation for an organism in its environment: "We are *just the same* sort of objects as the objects of the *physical* environment, which we also learn *through ourselves*" (KE, 135).

The abstraction represented by a concept is a necessary part of physical investigation. When abstraction continues, "principles" will emerge, principles which summarize the essentials of categories of concepts. Principles function to isolate and make independent classes of circumstances of interest in the organism's orientation. Such circumstances deserve to be highlighted in memory for further application in the formation of concepts. Yet even when principles become consciously applied, the danger inherent in concepts remains: "Even though concepts are not empty words, but rather have their roots in facts, one must take care and not consider concepts and facts to be of equal value, to confuse them with each other" (KE, 139).

Despite the increasing complexity of associations, concepts are not to be confused with the elements of the sensations which constitute facts. Any representation, as well as the concepts based on it and the principles applied in their formation, is fabricated. Their complexity bridges between the focus of the individual and the group. A representation is concentrated around the orientation of the individual, "while concepts, influenced by the intellectual requirements of the totality of mankind, bear the stamp of the culture of their time" (KE, 139). Thus for Mach, knowledge is influenced by the milieu and by the particular cultural interests which prescribe the interest directing its uncovering. Since the concepts which constitute our knowledge are themselves relative, all logic and higher-order formalizations represent provisoria conditioned by the interests of a particular age or culture: "*Logical* deductions from concepts are *supportable* as long as we maintain these concepts; the concepts *themselves*, however, must always be accessible to correction on the basis of facts" (KE, 139-40).

With this stance, Mach is providing a formalization for thought processes which accommodates both cultural relativity in data and a criterion for validity and verifiability in mental processing. Not to separate the data of thought from its processes is "epistemological backwardness" (KE, 141). As Mach summarizes:

1) Thinking does not deal with things in themselves, but rather with our mental representations (concepts) of them. 2) Objects are only known to us through their relations to other objects. Relativity is therefore a necessary predicate of the objects of (conceptual) knowledge. 3) A specific act of thought never includes the totality of all the knowable properties of an object, but only those relations belonging

to a specific category. (KE, 140)[56]

This model for thought presents a more subtle picture of the nature of higher-order conceptualization than is generally acknowledged in Mach's work. The primary consequence of Mach's model is a new warning. Facts, representations, and concepts can become detached from each other; a higher-order formalization may sustain concepts whose referentiality to facts of the experience may be lost (KE, 143). As a meaning system gets larger, it will necessarily pull away from the intuitive obviousness of its referentiality.

Mach's model of the life of a concept, then, resembles Ferdinand de Saussure's definition of the linguistic sign, which is composed of a signifier (a word) and the signified facts of the experience[57] Mach used several analogies to delineate the roles of representations and concepts within the field of thought:

> Our actual mental workers are sense representation; concepts, though, are the orderers and overseers which put the numbers of the former into their places and show them their business. . . . The sensations are the actual *impetus* to originate, while concepts appeal to them, often only through other conceptual medial stages. (KE, 142-43)

Mach consciously designates concepts (and the formalizations based on them) as tools, subject in application to the thresholds of perception and interest of the humans who use them. Data from the environment are schematized as representations to use; the reproduced concepts, in turn, mutually reinforce a formalized representation of the organism's adaptation to its environment, and so may influence further uptake of data.

A second consequence of this model focuses around the relativity of thought. Following Oswald Wiener, Mach posits that alien beings with different sense organs would develop the technical apparatuses for their sciences on premises other than humans would use, and they would consequently explore different avenues in their search for a unified theory of scientific investigation (KE, 146-47). They would, for example, develop telescopes with hard rubber lenses if optical refraction were not their basis for vision (KE, 147). Mach here wishes to underscore the notion that physical theory building does not depend uniquely on the essential nature of our sense impressions, but rather on the functioning of our whole conceptual apparatus in a process of abstraction directed by the interest of the organism. Thus in a modified sensationalism, the world is given higher priority than is usual in this model (KE, 148-49). Both the formalizations of physical theory and the fantasies of the artist are predicated on similar associations of sense data. Their differentiation lies in the fact that the fantasies of the artist betray a greater degree of singularity than those of the scientist, since they are not as closely predicated on the requirements and limitations of the physical organism as are the products of the scientist's imagination.

Mach's model grounds the formalizations of abstract thought, as well as delineating the limitations on representations of sense data as they are raised to the level of concepts for free manipulation:

> The owner of a richly differentiated conceptual system which does justice to his interests, which he has made his own through language, education, and teaching, enjoys greater advantages than those people restricted to perceptions alone. Whoever lacks the capability of being able to convert sense representations quickly and easily into concepts and the reverse could also, on occasion, mislead through concepts; this could become for him a pure onus with prejudices. (KE, 161)

This, then, is the purpose of formalization or abstract schematization for Mach: it eases the adaptation of the organism to a given field of facts.

7.8 Symbol Manipulation and Heuristics

The process of concept-formalization and manipulation outlined by Mach as the limitations of the validity of knowledge establish not only formalized knowledge, but also the manipulation of symbols enabling conscious problem-solving or heuristics: "The Adaptation of Thoughts to Facts and to Each Other" (KE, 162 [chapter title]). Yet the symbol manipulation used in scientific research presents a catalogue of the possible manipulations of data which the mind uses in all situations. Complex analogy-building, extensions of the channels of everyday thought processes, could not consciously be accomplished without symbols summarizing the categories of data represented in the concepts (KE, 179).

The most clearly constituted form of symbol manipulation, and that most susceptible to investigation as psychology, is the "thought experiment," particularly in its fundamental form, the "method of least variation" (KE, 180 ff.).[58] The thought experiment establishes a model of categories of physical fact which extends and clarifies the implications of those categories. If the model succeeds, the categories provide a prediction of facts likely to be observed in future considerations of data. The clear advantage of a thought experiment over direct observation is that elements which superficially seem to bear little influence in a specific framework may be systematically varied in order to ascertain their specific effects which often occur in variations difficult, if not impossible, to achieve in a physical experiment. When an even greater degree of idealization or abstraction is employed in a thought experiment, elements may be varied into infinity or to a vanishing point, again uncovering boundary values and effects in situations unable to be reproduced experimentally.

For Mach, then, the thought experiment is perhaps the chief heuristic tool for the sciences. Yet it does not constitute a lesser substitute for the results of physical experiments: "The great apparent division between experimentation and deduction does not exist in reality. It always depends on a correlation between thoughts and facts and among thoughts themselves" (KE, 196). With this, Mach asserts that physical research, thought experiments, and other formalizations all have similar logical forms: all correspond to the general nature of thought in identifiable environments, and thus are teachable or interchangeable under specific conditions (KE, 197).

Each facet of a potential thought experiment can be isolated and therefore taught or consciously applied as a "Leitmotif of Investigation" (KE, 198 [chapter title]). These leitmotifs fall into determinate categories, which represent specific purposes in directing the investigation of facts:

I. determination of dependencies/independencies (development of formulae and calculation rules)

    1) qualitative dependencies
    2) quantitative dependencies (a special case of qualitative)
    3) continuity

II. limitation (inclusion/exclusion)

    1) simplification (problem reduction)
    2) parallelism (establishing analogous directions of problem reduction)

III. summation of effects (positing that a system acts as an integrated whole)

    1) duplication (producing similar results)
    2) substitution (for example: replacing a disabling element with an enabling one)
    3) compensation (in extreme form, the "zero method," where specific effects of the system are held constant in order that others be ascertained without contamination)

IV. composition (adding partial effects in order to determine results beyond those immediately available in the partial frames)

    1) overview (examining one system as two parts, and determining their interactions)
    2) blind or negative experiments (varying the elements or dependencies within a system without anticipating or even achieving specific results)
    3) collectives (focusing on groups rather than on individual results)

V. comparison/contrast (identity or difference of the new and the usual)

1) similarity (partial identity)
2) analogy (special case of identity)
3) specialization (to pinpoint a restriction arising in individualization)
4) idealization (extreme form of analogy [KE, 226-27]).

All these possibilities represent a conscious setting of either the frame of a particular investigation (the scope of facts to be considered for a particular purpose) or the field of data to be considered (the first- and second-order dependencies of elements expressed in physical laws, for example, or the primary data elements reflected in less precise judgments of similarity). The most encompassing of these leitmotifs or methods of investigation are analogy and similarity, because they point the way to the most extensive transfer of concepts and dependencies among varying contexts. Yet each of these methods constitutes manipulations of concept systems as formalizations. Moreover, it is unlikely that any of these "methods" will be strictly isolated from each other. Mach does not himself summarize these leitmotifs into a table, as presented above. However, his discussions of sample experiments taken from the history of science move systematically through the categories thus enumerated.

These categories are a catalogue of the fundamental tools of heuristics which enable an efficient, conscious manipulation of symbols. Each specifies a conscious selection or limitation of the field of data to be addressed in a problem and sets the particular goal for the extension of knowledge sought. Therefore, just as Mach's earlier discussion of concepts constituted a statement on the limits of symbol *formation*, his discussion of heuristics delimits symbol *manipulation* within the validity of a systematic discipline. Each type of symbol manipulation may be expanded into either a hypothesis to be explored or a problem to be solved; that is, he moves into speculation.

Mach defines a hypothesis as "a provisory and trial assumption for the purpose of the easier understanding of facts, which, however, has not actually been proved" (KE, 232). Such a hypothesis can fill in missing data in chains of experience, in order that larger-scale dependencies be made reproducible and accessible. Even when individual pieces of data may be missing, the conditions on the associated chain may be uncovered through the hypothesis. Because it supplements perceived reality, a hypothesis is a "psychological-logical entity" (KE, 233). It does *not* represent the results of an analytic investigation of facts, but rather an *extension* of an extant analysis: "The central function of a hypothesis consists in its leading to new observations and experiments through which our conjecture is confirmed, gainsaid, or modified -- in short, experience is expanded" (KE, 237). A hypothesis thus serves to fix a consideration of a field of facts within a specified frame for a designated purpose, and to do justice to the "properties of a fact under special restricted conditions" (KE, 239). The particular advantage of a hypothesis is its utility and its role in facilitating and overtly directing the interest which expands knowledge. This is a spur to psychology, since it studies the impediments on knowledge acquisition.

The hypothesis is an attempt to deal with partially recognized and analyzed fields of facts. When, however, an irresoluble difference or confusion appears in the field of fact, the investigator faces a problem, not a hypothesis. The existence of a problem is ascertainable in a "mental sensation of difference," or an "incongruity of thoughts and facts" (KE, 247). The special advantage of a problem is its largely psychological effect on concepts: the discomfort caused in the development of a problem inherently dislodges the concepts involved from their accustomed associations and forces their rethinking.

Three strategies are involved most directly in the rethinking of concepts while problem-solving: analysis (breaking a problem into components), reduction or subdivision (dividing a problem into component problems), and the reduction to impossibilities (reducing a problem to a set of options which are possible only under determinate conditions) [KE, 252]. After concepts are rethought, there are two strategies for problem-solving: progressive or synthetic (moving from the conditions to the *conditioned* dependency), and regressive or analytic (moving back from a conditioned dependency to the *conditioning* elements).[59] The synthetic method is not seen by Mach as useful, since it approximates the building of hypotheses. It involves a systematic development towards an answer with use of a plan, following a strict "if x and y, then z" logic in *composing* answers (KE, 266). In contrast, productive, analytic problem-solving reconceptualizes the field of data and the concepts involved in the problem; there is a complete deconstruction of the hidden facets of concepts and groups of concepts, as well as of the dependencies within the data itself in light of the difficulties of the problem.[60]

With a deconstruction of covert assumptions as the basis for problem-solving, Mach has built a coherent heuristics beginning with the elements of the sensation selected in a process of judging, through the development of representations reproducible as concepts, and finally reaching its highest level in the hypotheses and problems which extend knowledge beyond the level of the immediately reproducible. This corresponds to Kant's distinctions between intuition, understanding, and reason, but it ties individual and group psychology into mind. Concepts are in commerce, held as utilitarian by the group, and enter into scientific dialogues in textbooks.

7.9 Investigation as Psychology

In what sense does a discussion of heuristics constitute a psychology for Mach? His discussion of "Deduction and Induction in a Psychological Light" answers that the essence of psychology is the impairment or enablement of the investigation which facilitates the orientation of the organism to the environment (KE, 299 [chapter title]). Deduction is a syllogism, or logical argument, moving from the general to the specific; induction, from the specific to the general. Yet both forms of logical investigation are united as abstractions representing a specific direction of interest of the organism applied to a determinate set of properties.

There is a danger to orientation inherent in the induction: the danger of anticipation, forcing an incomplete induction which will not adequately represent the state under consideration because of an erroneous generalization (KE,305). But adaptation and anticipation are crucial to the happiness or unhappiness of the mind, both for the group and the individual. When, however, a generalization is developed which aids the survival of the organism, a "law of nature" is posited: "according to their origin, the laws of nature are restrictions which we prescribe to our expectations under the direction of our experience" (KE, 441). In positing such abstractions, we limit the scope of our orientation to the environment, restricting the possibilities seen in the dependencies among elements of the sensation, and setting a reduced scope of expectations. In this way, our physical survival is correlated to expectation values about the states available in our environment. "Natural laws are, according to our formulation, a product of our *psychological* need to orient ourselves in nature in order not to approach processes in a strange or confused fashion," thereby equating posited laws of nature with the primary expression of the higher-order psychological processes of the human organism (KE, 445-6). Mach continues: "This is clearly expressed in the motifs of these [natural] laws, which always correspond to this need [for orientation], but which also correspond to the respective *state of culture*. Mythological demonological, poetic -- such are the first crude attempts at orientation" (KE, 446).

The "laws of nature" are therefore specific to the perceptions of particular time and place, and do not *prescribe* any necessity to nature, but only *describe* a possible contingency ("Facts are not required to order themselves according to our thoughts" [KE, 447-48]). Thus natural science is, in essence, the first of the sciences of culture, of the *Geisteswissenschaften* in Dilthey's sense,[61] because it describes the interactions between an organism and its environment in a systematic accounting. Natural and cultural sciences are just systematic disciplines along side of psychology, *not* two types of science. Moreover, laws of nature form the basis for a univocal orientation for the organism, that is, for a theory: "Only a theory, which represents the facts of observation as influenced by ever more complicated and multifarious secondary circumstances than can be accounted for by observation, can correspond to the ideal of univocal determinacy" (KE, 449). Such theories, even more so than the laws of nature on which they are based, summarize the point of view and means of orientation for a particular culture. They are complex abstractions on the basis of specific interests and articulate the ideal of knowledge even in the face of the subjectivity of the individual. A theory represents a communicable view of reality, and it may point more than a single individual towards a viable orientation for life and survival. Again, this accommodates both science and the humanities.

In this description of a scientific theory as a cultural artifact, Mach realizes that he has destroyed the dualism inherent in a Kantian world view, because he has bracketed the differentiation between things in themselves and things as appearances. Such a differentiation does not serve the cause of the orientation of the organism, and so must therefore be discarded (KE, 451). Theories serve only to exhaust that which is knowable about the elements of the sensation. Solutions to problems formulated from the point of view of the individual ego and then extended into a theory may not themselves serve to exhaust or explicate the inner nature of the world, because the ego is at best a *provisory fiction*, "a mental organism which corresponds to a physical organism" (KE, 453). But physical and psychological viewpoints on the same data can minimize the dichotomy between the results achieved in the context of either discipline. They point out the relativity in each other's stances to iterate perspectives on the knowable and therefore form each other. Physical theory represents a model for the orientation of the organism to the world; introspection refers to the "inner life" of the organism. Neither alone constitutes knowledge, and neither alone could have provided the description of concept formation as provided in the *Analysis of the Sensations* and *Knowledge and Error*. Therefore, an analysis of the principles of investigation with their restrictions does indeed constitute a fundamental psychology explicating the generation of knowledge as a function of data, interest, and context or environment. The same effect should be possible in any systematic discipline.

7.10 Conclusion

In the delineation of principles on which his psychology is built, Mach's "psychology of investigation" represents a synthesis of more traditional psychological programs with a new thrust.

Very much in line with the redefinitions proposed by Kant and

Herbart, Mach has expressly rejected the theory of the capacities of the soul (*Vermögenslehre*) in his argument that words like "will" are actually summarial descriptions for bundles of associated reactions, and not terms for identifiable and separate functions within the psyche or soul. Still, Mach has simplified the system by reducing all such potential capacities to the level of representations or reproductions on the ground of memory, each expressing a different interest. With "interest" affecting the direction of conceptualization, Mach has subsumed the key aperçu in the theory of the capacities with the realization that different fields of data interact with conceptualization differently, according to varying needs of the organism. Mach's texts show that different sciences may arise.

Similarly, Mach's description of concept, law, and theory formation rests on the premises of the empiricism outlined above. Mach agrees that the conceptual life of an organism is conditioned by the sense data it receives from its environment and the resemblances, contiguities, and causal relationships in such data as it presents itself to consciousness. Yet in his "anti-Kantian stance," Mach explicitly rejects the differentiation between the world of appearances and any purported reality behind these appearances. The fact that the *data* of reality are received by a consciousness does not concomitantly imply that the *structure* of a reality is also available. A relativistic view of "perceived reality" seems to correspond more closely with the realities of scientific investigation, because there exists only realities relative to a certain frame of reference, point of view, or biological interest, expressible as theories which act as previously shared frames.

This acknowledgement of the relativity of conceptualization lies at the heart of Mach's version of conceptual psychology. Through this avenue, Mach takes the work of predecessors and transforms it into a science of culture -- a systematic discipline like Wundt's work on mythology -- dealing with cultural data and the mind. He identifies several sources for the relativity of conceptualizations: varying environmental conditions taken into consideration, varying purposes or interests directing the conceptualization, a tension between inherited and newly arising conceptualizations, and a random tendency to foreground certain data and dependencies perceived in an inadequately analyzed field of data. The question of "absolute knowledge" is therefore bracketed as effectively as questions concerning the constitution of the soul or psyche. For Mach, there is only a continuum of knowledge evolved for special purposes from perspectives which are recoverable and on the basis of limited fields of the data of the sensations. Moreover, once this knowledge serves more than an individual for orientation within the environment, it becomes a cultural-historical entity, subject to the pressures for stability and against modification which only a social structure and its institutions can exert. Experimental tradition, for example, provides the grounds for a steady advance in knowledge, in that the results achieved by one generation are passed down to the next; conversely, the establishment of such a tradition underrates or discounts paths of research which may prove more fruitful in newly-arising problems. This is a fully interactive model of the interface between mind and environment only matched in scope by Hermann Paul's, yet applied to the sciences.

Aside from the establishment of psychology as a discipline relating to conceptualization within a cultural context, Mach describes his "psychology of investigation" as a truly scientific discipline according to the requirements of modern theory-building. His model is simple, consistent in the applications of premises and principles, and hierarchically developed to show a continuum between levels of conceptualization from the most rudimentary to the most complex, from concept formation to theory-building. In the rigor of his expositions, Mach has incorporated the main supportable assumptions from the psychologies of his predecessors and from the major scientific trends of his day, including experimental physiology and Darwinian notions about the mechanisms of adaptation under pressure from the environment.[62] In so doing, he has made psychology a *science* in its rigor of explanatory modes but still kept it an equal to all other sciences, either natural or cultural. The *data* considered represents the limits to knowledge attainable within the problems addressed by any specific discipline, while the *procedures* through which a science develops are common to all systematic disciplines.

The "Psychology of Investigation" developed by Mach in *Knowledge and Error* is the statement of principles for a scientific approach to culture bridging the gap between the individual's knowledge and intentionality and the historical life of cultural institutions, whether those institutions be monuments in physical theory or the premises of art or justice. Mach's distinctions among concepts, problems, hypotheses, laws, and theories will apply to any systematic discipline. *Knowledge and Error* presents the outline of a discipline conceived to accommodate various fields of data, differing interests, and goals set for specific purposes in the general progress of knowledge. *Knowledge and Error* is most often seen as the example or blueprint for the development of a modern experimental physics. It represents more than that, however, for it delineates the points of juncture among all the sciences of culture: biology and physics, history and philosophy, and a personal psychology in a cultural context.

Mach's particular contribution to conceptual psychology is that he incorporated the supposedly pure sciences as cultural artifacts by showing that historical textbooks about the sciences are requisite material for understanding the implications of theory for humans in cultural environments, as well as for the growth of science itself. Only through his redefinition of the discourse of the sciences as historically relative -- a deconstruction of their referentiality -- was the notion of psychology joined with science. Moreover, Mach's attention to frame of reference brings a further implication of conceptual psychology into light: that changing levels of difficulty in a discourse should not change its validity, but only its scope. Thus, Mach's work necessarily placed "popular science" next to high theory, for both aid the adaptation of an individual and a culture to the requirements of their environment. Mach evolved the ultimate message of conceptual psychology without achieving the full visibility of its discourse possibilities. The totality of his works, added together, show the potential of adding psychology to a systematic science. However, these works were nonetheless misconstrued by successive generations, illustrating that once again, the discourse of conceptual psychology was overlooked, even when fully exploited.

CHAPTER 8

FREUD: THE PSYCHOLOGY OF PSYCHOANALYSIS

Both the meaning and the significance of Freud's epochal work remain at the focus of heated disputes within the psychoanalytic and the intellectual communities in general. This is perhaps due to the control of Freud's legacy by his students and colleagues. Only in a situation such as this would the control and curatorship of personal archives cause both a major court case and the report of that situation in a popular magazine such as the *New Yorker*.[1] In the late 1960's, this phenomenon was noted by Paul Roazen, himself one of the surviving members of Freud's circle in Vienna. He stresses the "contemporary psychoanalytic state of affairs":[2]

> [T]o the extent that Freud himself ranged beyond medical or therapeutic issues, laymen are peculiarly able to understand his speculations. Laymen, however, are also especially liable to take the mistaken short cut of focusing solely on Freud's social thought, exclusive of the concerns of clinical psychoanalysis (as one can best understand them). (Roazen, 21)

This statement reflects the stance taken by many of the Freudian analysts and theorists in both the United States and Europe. "Outsiders" cannot challenge facets of Freud's work unless they are also initiates. Such a challenge will immediately constitute a defilement of the image of the master which has been so reverently built.

This control of an intellectual legacy by a virtually closed society has led to the literature and discussions of Freud's work to be directed within a comparatively narrow range. In terms of the discussion in the present volume -- the development of a conceptual psychology in the nineteenth century --, the situation within the Freudian establishment has created one particularly uncomfortable lacuna in scholarship. Freud's social, cultural, and anthropological thought has often been relegated by analysts to a position secondary to or apart from his major contributions in psychoanalytic theory. These analysts downplay those aspects of Freud's work which were adapted by Margaret Mead in anthropology, Kenneth Keniston in sociology, and Albert Bandura in psychology, among many others.

Theodor Reik summarizes the devoted follower's point of view in the years immediately after Freud's death:[3]

> The last writings of Freud have caused many who call themselves his followers serious and even painful embarrassment. It was hard to assign them their proper place in scientific literature; they did not quite fit in. They had little to do with the actual theory of the neuroses. Instead, they were an unusual sort of interpretation and criticism of occidental civilization, reflections on culture undertaken from the same point of view as that of Freud's study of psychoneuroses. (Reik, 97)

Freud's followers considered Freud's cultural work "disquieting" and "subjective" (Roazen, 98), yet still "eccentric and stimulating" (Roazen, 167). These are, however, Freud's great works in social anthropology, such as *Totem and Taboo*, *Civilization and its Discontents*, and the late *Moses and Monotheism*.[4] Yet non-psychoanalysts, such as sociologists and anthropologists, also pick up aspects of Freud's work. In these circles, Freud's work is said to display a rather unconsidered reliance on the works of Frazier and other early anthropologists; today, it is admired as fascinating, but superceded. Yet within the Freudian community, a book like *Moses and Monotheism* is often still considered as sign of "a partial loss of mastery in [Freud's] work" (Roazen, 173).

The unmitigated hero-worship of Freud's person has diminished somewhat today as a new generation of analysts follow principles at variance with those which Freud developed, and as a new generation of intellectual historians have produced biographical material which tends less to whitewash the weaknesses in Freud's personal life.[5] Even in a book which purports to examine Freud's social thought as a valid body of theory in its own right, Roazen betrays an underlying ambivalence towards his subject:

> If psychoanalysis is to be considered a science, it must be verified apart from Freud's own biography. . . . Surely part of Freud's criticism of his own social works arose from his fears of damaging the standing of psychoanalysis as a science. (Roazen, 111)

The underlying tension of Freud's reception is thus whether theory should be discussed apart from biography. At the same time, this theory can take on a life of its own (particularly when its core propositions are suggestive but "banal"), especially when the theories are considered colored by Freud's personal development. Implicit in the analysts' reception is an assertion that Freud felt his own cultural anthropology was deficient and needed defense, because it lacked real experimental justification. The fact remains that analysts want to isolate Freud's work in cultural anthropology and social theory from the main body of his analytic work and theory, thereby avoiding its impact in these fields. The analysts prefer to apologize for Freud's synthesis in cultural studies, while other disciplines try to evaluate it fairly.

The approach suggested here will correct this compartmentalization by including Freud as the last, and most likely the finest, representative of conceptual psychology. This is not a willful inclusion, but rather one which is justified in Freud's own works. The Freud who wrote the *Interpretation of Dreams*[6] considered his works such as *Totem and Taboo* and *Moses and Monotheism* to be different applications of principles derived from a single underlying theoretical framework. This chapter will suggest that such a unification can be validated out of Freud's own work, and that this unification reflects the premises of the conceptual psychology explored heretofore with its underriding coherence of individual psychology and cultural relativity. We cannot exhaust all of Freud's work, but a set of texts from various periods in his career will suggest his hidden accounting for psychology.

Why is such a synthesis desirable? Most obviously, it will bring Freud's psychoanalytic theory and his social anthropology into closer proximity. More importantly, however, this synthesis can point to the origin (and resolution) of major terminological difficulties which still exist in discussions today. As an example, we may again turn to Roazen for his assessment of one of the central terminological questions in Freud's theory, which is the differentiation between id, ego, and superego, or preconscious, conscious, and unconscious thought:[7]

> While the theory of psychoanalysis is still not very well coordinated with what goes on in clinical practice, it is generally agreed that Freud looked on the self from four distinct points of view: 1) the topographical, 2) the dynamic, 3) the economic, and 4) the structural. . . . By the topographical point of view, Freud meant the concepts conscious, preconscious, and unconscious. (Roazen, 66)

The "dynamic" model deals with mental forces or energy, showing the mind in an equilibrium of energy. The "economic" model stresses normalcy as a conservation of energy within the individual psyche; it was one of Freud's earliest formulations of his mind model. The "structural" view divides the psyche into a set of repositories -- id, ego, and superego -- for experience. Freud recognizes that each of these models prescribes a very different direction of argument, because they predicate virtually distinct fields.

Roazen, along with many others, is content with designating these "four points of view" as the core perspectives which Freud applied, and rarely follows the methodological dicta established by Mach and others to find out the core sets of data which lie at the basis of all four of these systems. Some variants of these models are preserved, no matter how radical the reformulation of Freud's work seems to be (as, for example, those of Erik Erikson or Karen Horney); such innovations actually rewrite Freud from within his models. Conceptual psychology, however, stresses that all four perspectives rest, in fact, on a single set of premises. The *id, ego,* and *superego* belong more properly to the realm of psychoanalysis, since they in actuality refer to the environmental conditions and the historical environment of the individual: biological needs, personal volition, and the inherited or imposed prohibitions which can be traced to the cultural inheritance to which the individual is subjected. In contrast, the terms *unconscious, preconscious,* and *conscious* refer to the depth in which the experiences of the individual are stored as memory or affects. As such, they are energetic levels within the neuronic structure of the organism. (Freud dropped these models after the *Interpretation of Dreams,* but they remained active as underpinnings to his analytic work.)

In order to place Freud in the tradition of conceptual psychology, the first section of the present discussion will develop a consistent model for the psyche in Freud's language which will accommodate both series of terms. To do so requires that Freud's psychology be distinguished from his psychoanalysis. That is, the science of the psyche's mechanisms will be differentiated from the science of the mind's interactions with the environment, as Freud himself did in an essay entitled "The Claims of Psycho-Analysis to Scientific Interest" in 1913.

The sources for this discussion are Freud's *Interpretation of Dreams,* which outlines the ways in which the mind functions with the data it remembers (its memory-traces), and the *Project for a Scientific Psychology,*[8] which yields a detailed description of the relationships between memory-traces and energy levels in the neurones. The focus of these two texts from 1895 (the date of the earliest drafts of the *Dreams*) is a delineation of the psychology of the mind, on what Roazen would term the topical, the dynamic, and the economic models of mental function simultaneously. This approach necessarily takes the *Project* much more seriously than is customarily done, assuming that it is not merely a position to be left behind. In these expositions, Freud develops a dynamic model of the mind, one focused on the effects of memory and perception on the central nervous system and on established patterns of thought within the mind. In both texts, the ontogeny of the individual psyche is described as a question of nervous adaptation and economy, in terms of the organism's biological drive to preserve an equilibrium in its functionings and to accept or adapt new information and experiences to its life as a whole. This psychological model manifests itself in the construction of dreams and the aetiology of neuroses. The neuroses are the proper region of study of psychoanalysis, the therapeutic science dealing with the interaction of a developed psyche and its environment in the enlarged sense.

The second section of this discussion will focus on Freud's texts in cultural anthropology as the avenue through which Freud's psychology can be merged with his psychoanalysis. Here, the goal is to analogize the ontogeny of the individual psyche to phylogeny, the development of a group as a culture or society. The model for the analogy between psychological and cultural development is "The Claims of Psycho-Analysis to Scientific Interest";[9] the products are *Totem and Taboo* and *Moses and Monotheism*.

The investigation will delineate the distinction between Freud's psychoanalysis and his psychology on the basis of their differing premises as *discourses* and as *disciplines*, or, following Foucault and Derrida, as different *practices*. In this, Freud emerges as perhaps the finest representative of the nineteenth century tradition of conceptual psychology. His unique and final contribution to the paradigm is his overt accommodation not only of the adaptation and dynamic (energetic) equilibrium of the psyche, but also the historical and cultural environments of the individual psyche. Moreover, this synthesis allows his model of the mind to accommodate a factor only unsatisfactorily delimited by his predecessors. Moving further than even Mach, Freud interrelates an individual's affective and conceptual lives, as the affects specifically impede or facilitate acquisition or utilization of the knowledge of the environment which impinges on him.

First, a discussion of the *Interpretation of Dreams* will explore Freud's own synthesis of psychoanalysis and conceptual psychology; and second, redefinitions and expansions of the premises of the *Interpretation of Dreams* will be found in the *Project for a Scientific Psychology*, "The Claims of Psycho-Analysis to Scientific Interest," *Totem and Taboo*, and *Moses and Monotheism*. No matter how unconventional this association is, Freud managed to draw these disciplines together:

> Freud presented his findings in an integrated, internally consistent system. Throughout his life he tried to incorporate his fresh observations into increasingly encompassing theoretical form. . . . Freud's thought is coherent enough to comprise a system, centering as it does on the unconscious, and at certain points it is abstract enough to attract speculative minds. (Roazen, 6)

Yet if we realize that the *Project* and the *Interpretation of Dreams* both originated in 1895, we have the key with which to follow Freud's development coherently.

8.1 Phase I: The Program of *The Interpretation of Dreams*

Freud announces his program in a clear statement found at the beginning of *Dreams*:

> In the pages that follow I shall bring forward proof that there is a psychological technique which makes it possible to interpret dreams, and that, if the procedure is employed, every dream reveals itself as a psychical structure which has a meaning and which can be inserted at an assignable point in the mental activities of waking life. I shall further endeavour to elucidate the processes to which the strangeness and obscurity of dreams are due and to deduce from those processes the nature of the psychical forces by whose concurrent or mutually opposing action dreams are generated. Having gone thus far, my description will break off, for it will have reached a point at which the problem of dreams merges into more comprehensive problems, the solution of which must be approached upon the basis of material of another kind. (DR, 1)

This program is decisively stated, and deceptively simple: Freud suggests that dreams are innately connected with the function of the psyche, and thus are not random, strange or completely unpredictable. They "can be inserted at an assignable point into the mental activity of waking life," that is, dreams relate to the mechanisms generating neuroses, as well. Dreams are formed along the same mental channels in which the conscious mind interacts with its environment. This model includes the material source of dreams and the mechanisms ("processes," in Freud's usage) through which they are generated, which together, in their detachment from the everyday waking sphere, then yield the psychic "strangeness" or "obscurity" of dreams. The break in the execution of this program heralded by Freud in this opening statement is reflected in the summarial and somewhat sporadic nature of Chapter 7 of the *Interpretation of Dreams*.

The bibliography and overview of others' work on dreams presented as the first chapter of the *Dreams* summarize the scientific debate into which Freud's own work will be inserted. Yet the bibliography is organized in order to support several of Freud's theses which are keyed by the section titles: "The Relation of Dreams to Waking Life" (Freud insists there must be one); "The Material of Dreams" (drawn from memories of physical and psychical experience which often are not otherwise remembered); "The Stimuli and Sources of Dreams" (in sensory stimuli, both internal and external in origin, in organic stimuli, and possibly -- although under extreme debate, according to Freud -- in psychical stimuli); "Why Dreams are Forgotten after Waking" (only because of the lack of interest the dreamer shows); "The Distinguishing Psychological Characteristics of Dreams" (a different modality of consciousness is demonstrated in their logic, evidence of a possible withdrawal of consciousness from the normal constraints on its activity); "The Moral Sense in Dreams" (there is one for Freud); "Theories of Dreaming and its Function" (Freud states that scientists have tended to discuss dreaming somatically, as well as in relation to therapy and healing); and "The Relations between Dreams and Mental Diseases" ("There can be no doubt that alongside of the psychology of dreams physicians will some day have to turn their attention to a *psychopathology* of dreams" [DR, 89]).

The undertone of this review of the literature is a self-justification. Still, the review establishes the central tenet of Freud's new position: "the validity of a causal connection between the somatic and the mental" (DR, 41). Before considering the dreams themselves, Freud must delimit the ground rules for his investigations. One must include both the physical and the mental in a model for dreams. Freud's new systematics of investigation reveal dreams as a source of information about the human psyche and the interaction of the psyche with an individual's physical experience. Each section of the review of the literature serves to reinforce the definition of science which accommodates dreams. On these generally accepted achievements of the scientific establishment, Freud will build his new interpretation of dreams. According to these sources, the science of dream interpretation will accommodate the mental and physical data of dreams, as well as the conscious and unconscious levels of a psyche. To be sure, Freud later dropped explicit reference to this biological perspective, but it was still tacitly retained when he, like his contemporaries, spoke of "adaptation."

The second chapter of the book differentiates Freud's scientific procedures from those of his predecessors. His program must be unique for his audience. Freud establishes this difference graphically by presenting "An Analysis of a Specimen Dream" which demonstrates his procedures in contrast to older methods of dream interpretation. Traditionally, Freud states, there have existed two major trends in the interpretation of dreams material: "symbolic" dream interpretation, and the "decoding method" (DR, 97). The first of these methods (the mystic's divination) reaches through the material of the dream into the environment or history in order to discern its meaning. The other, dream books, transliterates dream material as if it were a paraphrase of meanings which could be formed as conscious sentences. Neither approach will, in Freud's view, exhaust or even successfully pinpoint the meaning encompassed in the discourse which is a dream. Traditional interpretive methods are clearly not enough.

The dream of "Irma's Injection" provides the material with which Freud is able to demonstrate his new interpretative procedures on the many levels of meaning which form the dream discourse:

> I will not pretend that I have completely uncovered the meaning of this dream or that its interpretation is without a gap. I could spend much more time over it, derive further information from it and discuss fresh problems raised by it. . . . If we adopt the method of interpreting dreams which I have indicated here, we shall find that dreams really have a meaning and are far from a fragmentary activity of the brain, as the authorities have claimed. *When the work of interpretation has been completed, we perceive that a dream is the fulfillment of a wish.* (DR, 121)

"Irma's Injection" is a complex web of Freud's personal fears, recent experiences, jealousies, and desires. Yet Freud reduces the scope of his demonstration by claiming that this dream, as all others, are "the fulfillment of a wish." He has done the so that he can treat the dream as a coherent whole meaning produced by the mind of the dreamer, conveying remembered emotions and physical sensations related to both the conscious and unconscious workings of the psyche. Each dream organizes itself around units of meaning drawn from the dreamer's life as original, situationally specified messages, and not universal meanings nor stock symbols that can be codified into dream books. This is commensurate with conceptual psychology because experience is diverted and suppressed on the basis of habit and memory.

Moreover, in the dream material, Freud has uncovered a juncture at which a scientific psychology may meet psychoanalytic treatment. As conceptual psychology showed, the shape of mental function may perhaps be explored through its product, in this case, dreams and the discourse of meanings which dreams present to the investigator.

The importance of this "discovery" is highlighted by Freud in an extended metaphor with which he begins the third chapter of *The Interpretation of Dreams*, the chapter which starts his formal exposition on dreams:

> When, after passing through a narrow defile, we suddenly emerge upon a piece of high ground, where the path divides and the finest prospects open up on every side, we may pause for a moment and consider in which direction we shall first turn our steps. Such is the case with us, now that we have surmounted the first interpretation of a dream. We find ourselves in the full daylight of a sudden discovery. Dreams are not to be likened to the unregulated sounds that rise from a musical instrument struck by the blow of some external force instead of by a player's hand; they do not imply that one portion of our store of ideas is asleep while another portion is beginning to wake. On the contrary, they are psychical phenomena of complete validity -- fulfillments of wishes; they can be inserted into the chain of intelligible waking mental acts; they are

constructed by a highly complicated activity of the mind.
(DR, 122)

The scope of Freud's program thus parallels Mach's. One may examine the pattern, potential meaningfulness, and referentiality of any mental construct with respect to the source of their material and their relation to the workings of the mind -- either in the forms of theories or dreams. Freud's exposition follows the structure of the book. His next step is a deeper investigation into the materials of which dreams are formed in Chapters 3, 4, and 5 of the *Interpretation of Dreams*. Here, he specifies the modality of the discourse of dreams -- that is, the ways in which dream material is coherent in itself and as the bearer of meaning, of a wish to be fulfilled. This also parallels Mach's statement that concepts and theories fulfill the needs, not necessarily the wishes, of a group and that a mental construct answers a need for communication.

8.1.1 *The Material of Dreams*

Freud poses a question as a check on the validity of his program: is the universal statement "A dream is the fulfillment of a wish" indeed valid for known dreams? Freud's empirical evidence consists of a series of sample dreams, all analyzed to demonstrate that a wish exists at the basis of each. This wish, though, will always be presented in distorted fashion in the dream, because the way in which a dream signifies its meaning is in a mode different from that of everyday logic. A dream presents its own form of discourse in its own pattern of relations among signified, signifiers, and truth claims.

The difficulty that most people will have in accepting his position, Freud realizes, stems from the common tendency to overlook the essentially different character of a dream discourse as an individual expression of knowledge:

> It is only necessary to take notice of the fact that my theory is not based on a consideration of the manifest content of dreams but refers to the thoughts which are shown by the work of interpretation to lie behind dreams. We must

> make a contrast between the *manifest* and the *latent* content
> of dreams. (DR, 135)

This, then, is the first characteristic of the material of dreams which must be accounted for in any discussion of their meaning. Manifest and latent content are differentiated in their distorted relationship; what is seen is not necessarily the overt purpose of the dream.

Freud finds, however, that it is possible to identify the source of dream distortion in a conflict between the agency of the mind which generates the wish, and that which attempts to ignore, deny, or defend itself against the realization of that wish:

> We may therefore suppose that dreams are given their
> shape in individual human beings by the operation of
> two psychical forces . . . ; and that one of these forces
> constructs the wish which is expressed by the dream,
> while the other exercises a censorship upon this
> dream-wish and, by the use of that censorship, forcibly
> brings about a distortion in the expression of that wish.
> (DR, 144)

The censor stems from the group; the wish originates in the individual. The dream, as a way of knowing and self-expressing, is caught between the two.

After this, Freud turns to "The Material and Sources of Dreams" (Chapter 5 title). He finds that the images and information which make up the dream content stem from reproduced impressions of experiences from the last twenty-four hours of the dreamer's life. These recent impressions serve, however, only as the trigger or instigating factors in the dream: "Dreams can select their material from any part of the dreamer's life, provided only that there is a train of thought linking the experience of the dream-day (the 'recent' impressions) with the earlier ones" (DR, 169). That is, the full field of memory stages the dreams.

Since the dream-content represents a mixture of impressions from the dreamer's lived experience, there will be not only the problem of censorship or distortion as mentioned above, but a more severe problem of *displacement*, of the weighting of the relative importance of the impressions as they emerge in the manifest content of the dream. That is, mental processing weights their relations away from the norm; therefore, the individual will use the censor's norms and the content of his or her own impressions in an idiosyncratic mixture. In the formation of the manifest content, the censor will attempt to substitute indifferent impressions for impressions which would more directly indicate the latent content of the dream. That is, the group norm will try to force itself on the individual. To counteract this normativeness, more direct impressions, more explicit references to the wishes in the dreamer's psyche become more highly charged with mental energy, which is the indicator of their importance for that individual. In a displacement of mental energy, however, this relationship is overturned, and the individual yields to the group:

> [I]deas which originally had only a *weak* charge of intensity take over the charge from ideas which were originally *intensely* cathected and at last attain enough strength to enable them to force an entry into consciousness. Displacements of this kind are no surprise to us where it is a question of dealing with quantities of *affect* or with motor activities in general. (DR, 177)

This situation reflects not only survival and economy in communication, but also an economy of personal affect.

The fact that a certain quantity of mental arousal accompanies ideas, not only biological habits -- Mach's "interest" -- , is also an explicit tie between dreams and physiology. When the idea itself cannot be directly addressed in consciousness, the energy attached to it becomes attached to a dream-image, often to an image which would seem to be inconsequential in the everyday life of the dreamer. This is the origin of the communicative distortion characteristic of dreams.

The consequences of the way in which the material of the dreamer's experience is translated into dream structure refines Freud's concept of a dream. The dream is a unit of meaning within the mind of the dreamer which is structured according to the intensity of the dreamer's personal impressions and inherited prohibitions, either conscious or unconscious in origin, assimilated through direct choice or through pressures of inheritance or environment. The dream is therefore not merely a *product* of mental activity (a static unit of meaning), but also a dynamic processing of the available material within the accepted norms of expression of the culture.

The individual's access to cultural materials is not under full control. The source of dream material does not always constitute a unity in itself from the point of view of the dreamer; many connections remain tacit. Therefore, the impressions and memories of dreams must be combined through "dream-work," to constitute the data of the dream into the whole of the dream: "If in the course of a single day we have two or more experiences suitable for provoking a dream, the dream will make a combined reference to them as a single whole; *it is under a necessity to combine them into a unity*" (DR, 178). The triggering instance for the dream must be drawn from the recent impressions of the dreamer. Nonetheless, the material is drawn from whole memory. Freud states:

> The source of a dream may be either --
> (a) a recent and psychically significant experience which is represented in the dream directly, or
> (b) several recent and significant experiences which are combined into a single unity by the dream, or
> (c) one or more recent and significant experiences which are represented in the content of the dream by a mention of a contemporary but indifferent experience, or
> (d) an internal significant experience (e.g. a memory or a train of thought), which is in that case *invariably* represented in the dream by mention of a recent but indifferent impression. (DR, 180)

Freud's presentation of these facts is somewhat oblique and overburdened with examples. His archive of personal-cultural data starts with indifferent material and then extends into wider considerations of both present and past impressions which will be part of either the latent or the manifest content of a dream. Yet Freud set a further limitation on the material of dreams as a unit of meaning: "The reader will rightly conclude from the foregoing arguments that I am asserting that there are no indifferent dream-instigators -- and consequently no 'innocent' dreams" (DR,

182). This does resemble Brentano's and Husserl's idea of intentionality, but here Freud includes both individual wishes and a cultural norm.

Thus, Freud has described the materials of dreams in terms of the units of meaning in which they will appear and the genesis of that material. The manifest and latent contents of the dream rest on all the experiences available to the dreamer through present experience, memory, and nervous energy or innervation. Censorship and displacements in the material will be caused by the patterns of mental function in the dreamer, stemming from group and individual norms respectively. The dream is innately distorted by infantile material (impressions drawn from childhood), somatic impressions (experiences of the body), as well as a melange of the dreamer's forgotten or unaccentuated present and past experiences. Because of environment and interest, all material is not processed to a depth which replicates direct experience.

Freud adds a scaling factor that was either not dealt with explicitly in earlier variants of conceptual psychology or subsumed under broad notions of "interest." The material of the dream is marked by enormous variances in the degree of explicitness in the availability or susceptibility of that material to dream-distortion. Childhood memories, for example, are often dimly registered in the mind, and corroboration of the child's experience which could sharpen the details of the impression and affect its depth of processing is often unavailable. Moreover, childhood memories may even be stored in a different mode than adult ones -- children are more likely to remember in pictures, adults in words. The degree of registration may even dampen memory, in a negative registration of especially somatic sources of dreams based on subjective sensory stimuli or desires: "All dreams are in a sense dreams of convenience: they serve the purpose of prolonging sleep instead of waking up. *Dreams are the guardians of sleep and not its disturbers*" (DR, 233). Such material -- somatic desires and childhood experiences -- will tend, in the finished dream-unit of meaning, to be referred to more obliquely by the manifest content of the dream than will that material drawn from more recent experiences. While the interest of the dream-material is charged, its expressibility is not, and the finished dream-units are not acknowledged by the communicative norm.

With these restrictions on the sources and modalities of meaningfulness available to dream material, Freud is making a strong case for the individuality of dreams within the norms of expressibility of a particular culture -- a further characteristic of latent content. The meaning of the dream is not its systematic reference to an outside world -- to the greater course of fate or the world, or to standardized human experience -- but rather in the meaning unit of the dream itself, derived from the experience of the dreamer and reorganized according to the function of the psyche itself. Its manifest level and latent level are under dual control by the censor and the distorting tendencies of that individual psyche. Due to certain communalities in human experience, Freud cannot deny that "typical" dreams do exist and that a norm of meaningfulness is stored in strong group experiences:

> It now appears, however, that, in complete contrast to this, there are a certain number of dreams which almost everyone has dreamt alike and which we are accustomed to assume must have the same meaning for everyone. . . . they presumably arise from the same sources in every case . . . (DR, 241)

These are not universally applicable, as older dream books assume. They lead back to childhood prohibitions, or to general childhood fears inherent in a particular cultural milieu; the symbols are drawn from impressions of everyday life to which virtually all Western people have access. Typical dreams, therefore, confirm Freud's account of the origin of the material in dreams and do not refute the individuality of the meanings embedded in dream-units. Here again, Freud expands the model inherited from conceptual psychology. He adds personal interest in a way his predecessors had not.

8.1.2 *The Morphology of the Dream*

The issue of typical dreams led Freud to a crucial differentiation about the meaning systems of dreams. The latent and the manifest contents of the dreams of an individual psyche are conditioned by the pool of experience and impressions open to that individual, in terms of material for the dream and the criteria for censorship. However, the *dream-work* (the work of distortion which goes into unifying the dream material into a meaningful unit) will betray typical structures, because it is not totally contingent. The structure of the finished dream will follow similar, recognizable patterns for all dreamers, a consistent morphology similar to that in any other dream for any other dreamer. Thus where Freud heretofore spoke of the latent and the manifest contents of dreams, he now refers to "dream-thoughts" (the material which constitutes the dream on either level) and "dream-contents" (the specific manifest material of the imagery in the dream, together with the logic patterns or morphology of the specific dream-work which has taken place).

With this new differentiation, Freud has changed the focus of his investigation. Instead of describing the genesis of dreams, he now investigates the relations between the inherent material and distortions in dream-contents and the constituent material of latent dream-thoughts. This set of relations between individual intentionality and personal material can trace out the morphology of the dream-work, the processes of the psyche which can change the latter into the former. This tracing also requires a model of the mind expressed differently, stressing interrelations.

Freud presents dream-thoughts and dream-contents in such a new formulation:

> [They are] like two versions of the same subject-matter in two different languages. Or, more properly, the dream-content seems like a transcript of the dream-thoughts into another mode of expression, whose character and syntactic laws it is our business to discover by comparing the original and the translation. The dream-thoughts are immediately comprehensible, as soon as we have learnt them. The dream-content, on the other hand, is expressed as it were in a pictographic script, the characters of which have to be transposed individually into the language of the dream-thoughts. (DR, 277)

Thus Freud conceived of dreams as a discourse between the dreamer and the norms of expressibility of a culture, as the vehicles through which meanings are coalesced and communicated within the mind of the dreamer, as an idiosyncratic system of language predicated on the cognitive abilities of the human being.[10] Freud criticizes his predecessors for treating this discourse as a mere rebus, that is, as a random set of pictures designed to stand for a meaning which is concealed behind it, but which in itself has few laws and virtually no significance in its own construct. Such a view is necessarily erroneous according to Freud's description, for it is the laws of the dream's construction which must reflect the mechanisms of the mind which constituted it. These laws -- the morphological units of the dream's construct -- are the units of significance of the dream within itself as a discourse. The complete system of dream discourse, its full syntax, will only be addressed later by Freud, when he will consider alternate modalities of translation between the level of dream-thoughts and that of dream-contents. Chapter 6, "The Dream-Work," will thus necessarily focus on the articulation of the units which will enter into this syntax: morphology in the narrow sense.

Freud's first morphological unit of dreams is condensation, a disparity of scope between dream-content and dream-thought:

> Dreams are brief, meagre and laconic in comparison with the range and wealth of the dream-thoughts. If a dream is written out it may perhaps fill half a page. The analysis setting out the dream-thoughts underlying it may occupy six, eight or a dozen times as much space. This relation varies with different dreams; but so far as my experience goes its direction never varies. As a rule one underestimates the amount of compression that has taken place . . . (DR, 279)

Condensation defines a unit of meaning in dream-content, characterized by its reference to a greater amount of thought-material than is retained on the surface of the dream, yet which may be recovered through a systematic analysis. An objection may be raised to this analysis, since other thoughts may be grafted onto the dream-content by the waking mind:

> I can only give limited assent to this argument. It is no

doubt true that some trains of thought arise for the first time during the analysis. But one can convince oneself in all such cases that these new connections are only set up between thoughts which were already linked in some other way in the dream-thoughts. (DR, 280)

Freud terms the new connections made between dream-thoughts "loop-lines" or "short-circuits," and reiterates that they only correspond to connections among thoughts already present in the mind of the dreamer, albeit on a deeper or more oblique level than those which emerged into the dream-content. They are thus evidenced only on this deeper level of neurological habituation of the dreaming organism.

Condensation will utilize mental paths established in the organism's everyday contact with the world, and will produce a dream-content which is an abstraction of the possible meaning options associated with the experience referred to in the dream.[11] Freud finds his justification for this assertion in an example, "The Dream of the Botanical Monograph" (DR, 282). Here, the central dream-thought -- the issue of professional competency or jealousy -- was refracted onto a multitude of images drawn from Freud's professional and personal life at various periods of time. In this case, the material dream-content was enormously redundant -- or "overdetermined," in Freud's usage -- to the dream-thought:

> Thus a dream is not constructed by each individual dream-thought, or group of dream-thoughts, finding (in abbreviated form) separate representation in the content of the dream . . . a dream is constructed, rather, by the whole mass of dream-thoughts being submitted to a sort of manipulative process in which those elements which have the most numerous and strongest supports acquire the right of entry into the dream-content . . . (DR, 284)

The "manipulation" (in this case, condensation) also will tend not to differentiate between real and imaginary material. For example, in the "Lovely Dream," a juxtaposition of fantasies and real events serves as the material of the dream (DR, 285 ff.). Moreover, the resulting collective figures resemble the common neuroses as described by Freud, often characterized by a transference of features from one object to another, even making a whole through a process of "verbal malformation" (misremembered or garbled words [DR, 303]).

Condensation is Freud's first key to the meaning of dreams, because he acknowledges the disproportion of the dream-content to the dream-thoughts and the coherency of the dream-content through overdetermination. This description of condensation, however, is not without precedent: it parallels the definition of "abstraction" used by Ernst Mach in *The Analysis of the Sensations* (an idea also traceable in nascent form back as far as Immanuel Kant). Where Freud relates the process of condensation to the translation of dream-thoughts into dream-contents, Mach describes abstraction as the process leading the human mind from the apperception of facts or "elements of sensation" towards concepts acting as summaries for composite sets of experiential data.[12]

This similarity of definition is important because of the validity ascribed to either the concept or the dream involved. Both dreams and concepts are derived from a person's lived experience, incorporating the limitations on that person's perception even to the point of delusion or imagination. Thus they both represent a summary from a particular, identifiable viewpoint, always summarizing or underweighting the particular information encapsulated. As summaries, the validity of the concepts and dreams is always restricted to the framework and immediate purpose for which they were constituted. Their meaningfulness, if any remains, is predicated on the systematicity of the process of abstraction or condensation of the data. As in the "Dream of the Biological Monograph" and other of Freud's dreams, if more material is involved in the dream-thoughts than the surface dream can control, the overdetermination of the dream becomes ever greater and the dream-content denser. The dream also becomes more abstract, predicated on concept relationships such as "professionalism," instead of more concrete linkages such as shapes, colors, or the features of associated objects or people. Mach also stressed that the further the process of abstraction goes on a body of physical data, the more detail is effaced from the implications of that concept, and the more prone it is to be used erroneously.[13] For Freud, then, "condensation" is a restriction on meaningfulness, a statement of hierarchy of the importance of the dream-thoughts involved. Mach stressed that the most important physical features within a field of data will be highlighted. With similar emphasis, Freud posited that the most important dream-thoughts emerge into the dream-content. These important thoughts are the key to the overdetermination within the field of dream-thoughts.

Freud's next category of dream-work is *displacement*, a second relationship of meaning between dream-thoughts and their corresponding dream-contents: "what is clearly the essence of the dream-thoughts need not be represented in the dream [as dream-contents] at all" (DR, 305). Again, displacement is predicated on a juxtaposition of dream-thoughts and dream-contents, which is different from condensation. Freud posits that a dream-thought has associated with it a degree of vividness, and therefore a determinate quantity of psychic energy; the weighting of elements which appear in the dream-content, however, may not reflect this inherent valuation. Intensely charged elements of dream-thoughts "may be treated as though they were of small value," and their place may be taken in the dream by "other elements, of whose small value in the dream-thoughts there can be no question" (DR, 306). The new elements become overdetermined in "a transference and displacement of psychical energies" (DR, 307).

Condensation constituted units of meaning on the basis of a scope difference between the dream-thoughts and the dream-content. In contrast, displacement is an indicator of the *quality* of the dream-thoughts involved, a measure of their mental intensity and importance within the dreamer's mental life. Intense dream-thoughts will attempt to become a highlighted element in the dream-content, or they will diffuse their intensity through a number of symbolizing elements which all refer obliquely to the single dream-thought and which are consequently overdetermined. "The censorship of endopsychic defense" may cause such an oblique reference to mental intensity (DR, 308).

After discussing the paths for the transfer of meaningfulness, Freud delimits the restrictions on the meaning-units themselves in "The Means of Representation in Dreams" and "Considerations of Representability" (DR, 310 ff. and 339 ff.). Choosing the material for the dream is part of its "synthesis." If it could be completed (which is an impossibility), this synthetic process would involve a blueprint of the entire mental function and experience of the dreamer. What can be investigated, though, is the logic of the dream, the relationship between dream-contents to allow the dream to form a coherent whole:

> What representations do dreams provide for 'if,' 'because,' 'just as,' 'although,' 'either-or,' and all the other conjunctions without which we cannot understand sentences or speeches? . . . What is reproduced by the ostensible thinking in the dream is the *subject-matter* of the dream-thoughts and not the *mutual relations between them,* . . . (DR, 312-13)

Whatever the relationships between dream-thoughts and dream-content, they expressly will *not* be the logic patterns which appear on the surface of the dream as the dream-contents. Analysis must be individual to find even those parts of the dream-thought represented conventionally in the dream-content. Freud associates a lack of such individual resolution with the main failing of the visual arts, their inability to resolve an image into concisely delineated concepts.

Freud finds the drive for totality of a dream in visual images as a kind of intentionality in a form different from Husserl's -- Freud defines meaning-units for dreams as collocations of visual images in established patterns. Thus elements in a single situation or event reproduce visually their logical connectedness in a "simultaneity in time" (DR, 314). Similarly, causality is often expressed by a two-scene dream which conveys the impression to the dreamer that the two scenes may be "equally valid" (DR, 316). Contradictories or contraries seem to be virtually irreproducible in dreams -- the dream cannot mark for positive and negative:

> The way in which dreams treat the category of contraries and contradictories is highly remarkable. It is simply disregarded. 'No' seems not to exist as far as dreams are concerned. They show a particular preference for combining contraries into a unity or for representing them

as one and the same thing. (DR, 318)

Just as contraries, other similarities, consonance, and common attributes all appear as composite structures in dreams, as unitary dream pictures.

No matter their variation, then, the meanings of dreams are concentrated around the dreamer, and, as such, are "completely egotistic":

> Whenever my own ego does not appear in the content of the dream, but only some extraneous person, I may safely assume that my own ego lies concealed, by identification, behind this other person; I can insert my ego into the context. (DR, 323)

The separate purview of the id, ego, and superego can also not be expressed univalently. They will each contribute a weighting of intensities which will confound us in unravelling the meaning of a dream, even though we know its center:

> Most prominent among these formal characteristics, which cannot fail to impress us in dreams, are the differences in sensory intensity between particular dream-images and in the distinctness of particular parts of dreams or of whole dreams as compared with one another. (DR, 329)

Clarity and intensity, vagueness and explicitness all are keys to the psychic value of the dream, and as such, constitute a clearness and distinctness criterion within the weighting of the dream's morphological units. Although indifferent material lies at the basis of the surface dream-representation, intensity or vividness points to the weighting of the various meaning-units or morphemes within the dream construct. Judgments and fantasies, for example, are colored by vague sensations of approval or disapproval about the dream material, just as intensity is a key to its information value (DR, 331).

In terms of model building, why does Freud need this section? To this point, he has described the materials of which dreams are made. The divisions in dream-content which Freud posits correspond to a set of criteria for the establishment of morphemes within the dream-content. In dealing with overdetermination, condensation, displacement, and the intensity and clarity of representations, Freud gives a general characterization of the allowable forms of the meaning-units which must be established by the investigator before a particular dream may be interpreted. This is coordinated in terms of signs. The sources of dreams are in the outside world; their morphology reflects the analyses of modern structural linguistics. This section thus describes dream-thoughts as an iteration of the needs of the individual and the communications available between mind and world. Each morpheme -- a displacement, a condensation, a clear coordination in time or space which indicates a link between dream symbols -- will identify the initial units of dream-thought within the dream-content. Thus, this is an analysis of the intentionality of the dreams plus their content -- how the mind contributes to making a whole of inner experience.

Since the dream-morphology documents mainly the mind's contribution to the finished dream, every dream-morphology must be accompanied by a statement of dream-syntax, which is a detailed description of the modalities or channels of articulation between dream-thoughts and dream-contents. These modalities represent varying ways for the unconscious dream-content to be communicated to the dreamer's preconscious or conscious psyche. The properties of dreams as wholes will be the focus of Freud's further discussions of dreams. The syntax of dreams will describe the interactions which occur as the dreams are constituted into wholes, as potential communication.

8.1.3 *The Syntax of Dreams*

Heretofore, we have seen Freud's discussions of the units of meaning within dreams, the units of representation which stem from the mind and the world within the structure of a dream. Now Freud turns to the structure of the dream as a whole, to its inherent syntax, and to "Considerations of Representability" in the compromise between the dream-thoughts and the corresponding dream-contents: "the further topic of the general nature of the modifications which the material of the dream-thoughts undergoes for the purpose of the formation of a dream" (DR, 339). As the elements of dreams are submitted to representation by collecting representations from the world, the dream system will cause another "displacement along a chain of association" (DR, 339). That is, each dream will constitute its own whole; each dream is constructed in a different *modality*.

The intended relationship of dream-thoughts and dream-contents is not enough to explain a dream. Each dream will also show a particular channel of "phraseology," a style or system of representation (DR, 341). Its condensation or displacement will tend towards ever greater concreteness, an idea which is probably tied to Freud's prejudice for a dream primarily as a visualization. Nonetheless, the substitutions effected set up dream patterns in various modes to mediate between the control of the individual and the group. A dream can, for example, be predicated on verbal substitutions, as in the case of a verbal rebus or pun; an alternative could be a transliteration of thoughts into related pictures. The dream may choose any of these patterns (pictorial, verbal, conceptual, or phonetic, for example). The morphemes of the individual dreams must then be composed according to the pattern. The mind, in providing dream-thoughts, will be constrained by the conditions of representability of the morphemes, plus the pressure of the developing syntax of the dream:

> A dream-thought is unusable so long as it is expressed in an abstract form; but when once it has been transformed into pictorial language, contrasts and identifications of the kind which the dream-work requires, and which it creates if they are not already present, can be established more easily than before between the new form of expression and the remainder of the material underlying the dream. (DR, 340)

This seeming restriction is actually the cognitive strength of the dream -- associations can be present in the material even when concepts are not, and so can be expressible outside conventional avenues.

The dream-syntax is therefore a holistic structure, an avenue

through which a dream-thought finds the most economical
dream-content in any of the various symbolic modes available to the
mind. Thus, it allows clearness and distinctness for the individual.
Nonetheless, it is also a provisory structure, linking the latent logic
patterns of the dream-thoughts to the manifest structure for the
dream-content, in a modality (a pattern of potential connectedness)
to be interpreted along with the dream-content. This is the
weakness of the dream as communication with anyone other than
the individual dreamer:

> In interpreting any dream-element it is in general doubtful
>   (a) whether it is to be taken in a positive or a negative
>   sense (as an antithetic relation),
>   (b) whether it is to be interpreted historically (as a
>   recollection),
>   (c) whether it is to be interpreted symbolically, or
>   (d) whether its interpretation is to depend on its
>   wording.
>   Yet, in spite of all this ambiguity, it is fair to say that
> the productions of the dream-work, which, it must be
> remembered, *are not made with the intention of being
> understood*, present no greater difficulties to their
> translators than do the ancient hieroglyphic scripts to those
> who seek to read them. (DR, 341)

The dream is contingent upon the present and past conflicts and
experiences of the dreamer, the external material symbols and
words contained in the psyche in which the dream-work is taking
place. It contains a logic pattern internal to the psyche, a logic
which originally evolved constrained by the requirements of
external communication. At most, the material found in the finished
dream will retain a semblance of meaning corresponding to the real
world referentiality from which it is drawn.

Yet a dream remains a region unto itself. This apparent
resemblance of a pre-established meaning for a symbol may,
however, prove false in the final formation of the
dream-interpretation, because material from the outside world is not
left intact. The claim of a dream modality also supports Freud's
assumption that all the dreams of a single night are related to the

same core of dream-thoughts; through over-determination, a single dream-thought may assume a number of dream-content forms organized through different syntactical means, as verbal dreams, symbolical dreams, or the like. Further, the dream-thought, as the mental contribution to the dream, is not left intact. This is Freud's "third factor" in dream formation:

> . . . namely, *considerations of representability in the peculiar psychical material of which dreams make use* -- for the most part, that is, representability in visual images. Of the various subsidiary thoughts attached to the essential dream-thoughts, those will be preferred which admit of visual representation; and the dream-work does not shrink from the effort of recasting unadaptable thoughts into a new verbal form -- even into a less usual one -- provided that that process facilitates representation and so relieves the psychological pressure caused by constricted thinking. This pouring of the content of a thought into another mould may at the same time serve the purposes of the activity of condensation and may create connections, which might not otherwise have been present, with some other thought; while this second thought itself may already have had its original form of expression changed, with a view to meeting the first one half-way. (DR, 343-44)

A dream-syntax thus forms in an iterative process similar to the historical development of the morphology and syntax of an existent language used for communication: as new shades of implication emerge in the dream-content, the pressures of the unconscious revealed by the dream for the conscious mind force changes in the dream-morphemes (the fundamental units of the dream-thought) or in the plot of the dream, that is, the syntax of the dream. This dream is a feed-back loop as it forms.

Freud terms this "secondary revision," the fourth characteristic mechanism of dream-formation. Internal to the psyche, this feedback leads to censorship, a reworking of the dream-content "aimed at reducing the importance of what has just been experienced and of making it possible to tolerate what is to follow" (DR, 448). Focusing on statements appearing in dreams such as "this is only a dream," secondary revision makes a dream-content harmless, so that psychic energy reflected in the dream can be properly discharged without waking the dreamer. In other words, the mind does not want to face what it has seen. The secondary revision builds a new façade for the dream, in order that the energy of those thoughts do not disturb the equilibrium of the mind in sleep.

This censorship takes place in the preconscious, where the thoughts are almost at the energy threshold of waking attention. Thus secondary revision is responsible for the idiosyncrasy of the dream-syntax, for the inability of dreams to act as communication. The mind has distorted the emerging material; the censorship involved in the transformation of dream-thoughts to dream-contents skews the inherent logic of the dream and dream-contents. When the meaning to be expressed is unacceptable to the conscious mind or the cultural framework of the dreamer, this dream-syntax will be altered in a process of revision to produce a dream-content more acceptable to the dreamer. If the dream-thought is charged with extra energy due to an individual's worry or fear, this energy is rechanneled to distort the syntax of the dream to cover its morphology, its underlying significance for the dreamer. The dreamers edit themselves.

The dream-syntax, together with the dream-work which constructs the dream independent of individual control, is thus a region unto itself. The signifying function occurring here is not under the control of pure individuality:

> Two separate functions may be distinguished in mental activity during the construction of a dream: the production of the dream-thoughts, and their transformation into the content of the dream. The dream-thoughts are entirely rational and are constructed with an expenditure of all the psychical energy of which we were capable. . . . This dream-work proper diverges further from our picture of waking thought than has been supposed even by the most determined deprecator of psychical functioning during the formation of dreams. The dream-work is not simply more careless, more irrational, more forgetful and more incomplete than waking thought; it is completely different

from it qualitatively and for that reason not immediately comparable with it. It does not think, calculate or judge in any way at all; it restricts itself to giving things a new form. It is exhaustively described by an enumeration of the conditions which it has to satisfy in producing its result [censorship, displacement, condensation, and considerations of representability]. (DR, 506-07)

The waking consciousness generates part of this censorship, but the cultural unconscious, together with the individual's wishes, do as well. Thus one must clarify the relationship between the syntax of dreams and the structure of the mind, not only the activity. Freud discusses this as the last chapter of his exposition "The Psychology of the Dream-Processes" (DR, V, 509). The structure of the psyche itself must play a decisive role here, because those activities of the psyche ordinarily assumed to be random, such as the forgetting of dreams or names, are intimately connected with the processes of the psyche. Signs of old experiences, memories, prohibitions, or personal fears remain traces which contribute to the formation of a syntax region away from the control of the things to which they refer.

In the *Dreams*, Freud uses this structural outline to justify that dreams are a valid area of investigation. One can argue that we forget dreams, and thus will report only distorted versions of dream-material. Freud agrees but adds that the modifications which the dream-material undergoes in the reporting will be conditioned by the structure of that individual's psyche and past experience. The reports will only be modified along paths of thought or association which were already more or less represented in the dream itself. Just as the original dream represents the free play of an individual mind, so too will the modifications of that dream in report reflect innate restriction on that psyche:

No conclusions upon the construction and working methods of the mental instrument can be arrived at or at least fully proved from even the most painstaking investigation of dreams or of any other mental function taken *in isolation*. To achieve this result, it will be necessary to correlate all the established implications derived from a comparative study of a whole series of such functions. (DR, 511)

Thus dreams are only one source of information on the workings of the mind -- visions and human behavior can also show the mind's mechanisms.

This model of the mind again guides the next chapter of the *Dreams*. Both the final chapter of the *Interpretation of Dreams* and the whole of the *Project for a Scientific Psychology* seem to shift the discussion focus away from the products which manifest the workings of the psyche. This is not an aberation. Freud must turn from a discussion of the syntax of dreams to the innate structure of the mind and its functions. For if the syntax of dreams is a separate region of intentionality, lying apart from world logic and individual intention, the psyche must be its medium. Now that Freud has "parsed" dreams, he may turn to this sponsoring medium.

8.1.4 *The Syntax of the Psyche*

Freud must prove that the affects which the psyche exerts on dreams or other products of its activity are not random, and that they in themselves represent a consistent pattern of relation, broader than that available to the individual's consciousness. This is the psyche's contribution to the syntax of the dream and in the present context can be called the "syntax of the psyche," meaning a system of logical tendencies or fixed strategies relating materials which consistently underlie the formation of dreams.

In this context, Freud has already noted censorship or "editorship" as an innate tendency of the psyche, allowing it to displace its intensity onto harmless or less provoking dream-contents. Forgetting dreams serves a similar function for the psyche. Such censorship effects, as well as the existence of alternate dream-contents to express identical or similar dream-thoughts, suggest to Freud that the units of meaning in a dream must stem from a psyche which is a "compound instrument" with many "agencies" or systems (DR, 536). These agencies may be in a spatial organization, but a temporal model for the organization of these systems will suffice. Freud's apparatus is not a physical one correlated with an organ or faculty. Instead, he draws on a model for the excitation or *innervation* of the nervous system.

The innervations of the nervous system leave traces (*Bahnbrechung*) of the activity of the senses in the mind. The basic model assumes that perceptions innervate the system, leave traces, and form memories in the narrow sense (DR, 538). Such memory-traces may seem to be only primitive modifications of the nervous system, but in reality, they are the basis for a fully interactive system of memories -- the mnemic system, according to Freud:

> It is a familiar fact that we retain permanently more than the mere *content* of the perceptions which impinge upon the system *Pcpt.* [perception]. Our perceptions are linked with one another in our memory -- first and foremost according to simultaneity of occurrence. We speak of this fact as "association." . . . Association would thus consist in the fact that, as a result of a diminution in resistances and of the laying down of facilitating paths, an excitation is transmitted from a given *Mnem.* element more readily to one *Mnem.* element than to another. . . . The first of these [several] *Mnem.* systems will naturally contain the record of association in respect to *simultaneity in time*; while the same perceptual material will be arranged in later systems in respect to other kinds of coincidence, so that one of these later systems, for instance, will record relations of similarity, and so on with others. (DR, 538-39)

Here Freud describes a differentiated system of association and perception, which confines perception to a present activity and opens a way to higher-order thought based on association and memory.

Memory is in large part unconscious, existing as dormant traces of past innervations of the nervous system. It is free from many of the relational constraints which characterize conscious thoughts, and therefore associates the material it contains along many paths. The work of memory is not constrained by the origin of various sensations in a specific time or place; it can also associate according to secondary characteristics of the material contained within it. Thus an unconscious memory as a storehouse of available material explains the multifarious sources and faces of dream-contents. The memory seemingly draws randomly on the past and present experiences of the psyche. Because the relationship between random memory and dream representation is not specified, the translation between dream-thoughts and dream-content in the development of the dream requires a transmission medium; conscious perception and an unconscious memory are insufficient agencies to do this alone.

Freud begins to describe the third missing system: "We will describe the last of the systems at the motor end as 'the preconscious,' to indicate that the excitatory processes occurring in it can enter consciousness" (DR, 541). The preconscious is the staging area for any activities of the psyche bridging the conscious and the unconscious. Here, voluntary movement accrues the necessary psychic energy and attention to translate a conscious or unconscious desire into movement. Similarly, dreams are initiated by energy in the unconscious, triggered by "recent and indifferent experiences," and are assembled into their final syntactical form in the preconscious. If sufficient attention is paid to them, these dreams can be recalled into consciousness.

Freud thus proposes a structural layering of the psyche. Its division into the unconscious, preconscious, and conscious levels is, at its heart, a model expressing an innate ordering of the functions and energies of the psyche. Unconscious memory-traces act as a reservoir of impressions in the psyche, but they are impressions to which little further attention is placed until voluntary memory is applied or associations arise in the unconscious due to unrelieved conflicts. Conscious thought is composed of those elements of perception to which attention is paid by the psyche (and which have enhanced energy in consequence). Preconscious thought holds an intermediate position in terms of the amount of attention which must be paid to the material in it in order to raise that material to consciousness. As in the case of the formation of dreams and neuroses, the preconscious is the area in which a transmittable form is given to the material of the unconscious. Either that material is brought to consciousness, as is possible in dreams, or it is returned to the unconscious after it has been reordered. In either case, the preconscious is the place where energy is attached to memory-traces. The preconscious is thus the instrument of regression and repression within the psyche -- the system which, like dream-work, reworks the contents of the unconscious. The preconscious remains a level out of an individual's conscious control.

In addressing the ways in which the preconscious can regress the material of the unconscious, Freud summarizes:

> . . . regression plays a no less important part in the theory of the formation of neurotic symptoms than it does in that of dreams. Three kinds of regression are thus to be distinguished: (a) *topographical* regression, in the sense of the schematic picture of the ψ-systems which we have explained above; (b) *temporal* regression, in so far as what is in question is a harking back to older psychical structures; and (c) *formal* regression, where primitive methods of expression and representation take the place of the usual ones [symbols drawn from nature in place of symbols drawn from culture, for example]. All these three kinds of regression are, however, one at bottom and occur together as a rule; for what is older in time and in psychical topography lies nearer to the perceptual end. (DR, 548)

This regression is meant to decompose the associations in the stored material of the unconscious and free the perceptions normally affected by resonances of memory-traces. Freud confirms the parallelism of the regressive activity of the preconscious and the dream-work: "In regression the fabric of the dream-thoughts is resolved into its raw material" (DR, 543). Both regressions serve to defuse the intensities of associations of memory-traces which are disturbing the psyche -- in sleep or in waking life -- to depersonalize and deculturize the information at hand.

"A dream is the fulfillment of a wish" was the dictum of the beginning of the *Interpretation of Dreams*. Now Freud adds that: "an unconscious idea is as such quite incapable of entering the preconscious and that it can only exercise any effect there by establishing a connection with an idea which already belongs to the preconscious, by transferring its intensity on to it" (DR, 562).

Here he explicitly adds the notion of energy to the model. An unconscious wish cannot emerge into the preconscious without a trigger; it enters only along a temporary bridge, such as a recent impression. This unconscious material is then modified relative to conscious impressions not yet completely abreacted in the preconscious. With this modification, the unconscious material accrues enough psychic or nerve energy to submit itself to a reconsideration or a reorganization by the psyche. With this, the material in the psyche may attain a new stable state. Moreover, the psyche itself is modified in its reaction to the world. Thus the psychic systems described by Freud in his aetiology of the neuroses and hysterical symptoms parallel the formation of dreams.[14] The formations, the syntaxes available to the final dream or symptom, depend on the associations of the psyche's material, regulated through the mind's three-tier system of energetic levels. Moreover, the *distortions* censoring relations between dream-thoughts and dream-contents parallel those inhibitions in hysterical symptoms. Both are attempts of the psyche to avoid the displeasure accompanying certain associations of material within its experience (DR, 597-98). Therefore, the free structure of dreams remains the best index to the actual structure of the psyche, apart from the normative structures of group cognition.

The syntax of dreams is therefore contingent upon this regression or decomposition at the preconscious threshold of consciousness. A dream is not "the forming of a second thought situated in a new place, like a transcription continues to exist alongside the original" (DR, 610). Instead, it acts as a dynamic system which attempts to regulate and maintain an equilibrium within the three-tiered psychic system of the organism. Yet all layers of the mind are tied together. Since this is so, there are no conscious activities of the organism which are not linked to unconscious ones:

> The unconscious is the true psychical reality; *in its innermost nature it is as much unknown to us as the reality of the external world, and it is as incompletely presented by the data of consciousness as is the external world by the communications of our sense organs.* (DR, 613)

The study of the syntax of dreams as influenced by the structure of the psyche has led Freud to a general description of the way in which the human perceptual apparatus leads to a world view: the nerve-impulses generated by perception breach paths in the nervous system, which then become registered as virtually permanent memory-traces. Each of these traces, however, cannot remain in isolation from others, and so associations of traces form temporally, spatially, or characteristically within memory. As further traces are input into consciousness, rearrangements of the prior associations must be made; these are regressions, a negative formulation of what Mach said about the dynamic equilibrium of memory. Because of conscious resistance, and because of the intensity associated with established constellations of traces, these rearrangements of psychological traces are not always accomplished without an expenditure of psychic energy, either unconsciously, in the preconscious (facilitated by dreams), or through a conscious application of attention to the area of sense data involved.

Freud's work on dreams thus makes the distinction central to a conceptual psychology: the content of thought is distinguished from the forms of thought maintained by a habituated organism. Freud's unconscious, conscious, or preconscious (later discarded) describe the interface between an organism and its environment, maintaining a mental equilibrium in the face of new impressions. However, the *Interpretation of Dreams* focuses only on the forms which the mind's products assume under the influence of mental habits. Although this system has repeatedly been described by Freud as an energetic one, *Dreams* does itself not contain the supporting research for these assertions. Rather, *Dreams* stays focused on the individual. If its companion piece from 1895, the *Project*, is considered its supplement, we have a fuller description of the dynamic equilibrium of the mind. Taken together, these models suggest that Freud was moving ever closer to the model of conceptual psychology -- a psychology as a science of culture.

8.2 Phase II. After Dreams: Freud's Science of Culture

The Interpretation of Dreams is Freud's attempt to tie one specific category of products of the psyche to both the mechanisms of the mind and to its social and cultural environment. Freud established a cultural relativity in these products by acknowledging the role of the environment in conditioning a dream and by outlining the existence of ψ-systems, the mind's functions. *The Interpretation of Dreams* thus establishes the existence of both a psychology and a psychoanalysis relating to the study of dreams, that is, a science of mind and a science of personal behavior. Moreover, the study of dreams is an exemplary science of culture adequate not only to its chosen area of data (dreams), but also to a particular model of the mind's function.

Yet questions remain about Freud's idea of a science of culture. These questions fall outside Freud's immediate concern of the establishment of psychoanalysis as an independent discipline, and stray into the domain of a cultural critique. However, since they relate directly to his mind model, Freud could not ignore these questions totally. They are answered gradually throughout the course of his writings. Starting with the *Project for a Scientific Psychology*, extending through "The Claims of Psycho-Analysis to Scientific Interest" and *Totem and Taboo*, and ending with almost his last work, *Moses and Monotheism*, Freud enlarged the groundwork laid in the *Interpretation of Dreams* in order to explore the consequences of his dynamic mind model, a model which correlates stimuli and innervation with memory, reflex, and conscious thought. Freud also had to correlate mental function with group behavior to expand the psychological program, implicit in *Dreams* and explicit in the *Project*, to sciences of culture by analogising the facilitations of stimuli and the mental structures found in individual psyches to the adaptation of the group and to its cultural inheritance.

8.2.1 *The Science of the Psyche*

In 1895, while writing the original drafts of the *Interpretation of Dreams*, Freud was also corresponding with Wilhelm Fliess. As is commonly known, a part of this correspondence is referred to as the *Project for a Scientific Psychology*. The substance of this essay draft parallels the central Chapter 7 of the *Interpretation*, but it presents the only coherent statement of Freud's neurological researches at the basis of his psychology and psychoanalysis.[15] The work, however, remained a fragment. Various explanations have been proffered for Freud's dropping the project, most deciding simply that Freud was dropping neurology.[16]

The core of Freud's expositions in the *Project* do revolve around the principles of a dynamic neurology of the mind. However, the text also delineates levels of consciousness and unconscious activity -- the dynamics of mental structure corresponding to the unconscious, preconscious, and conscious levels of processing in the *Interpretation of Dreams*. Freud introduces his own work:

> The intention of this project is to furnish us with a psychology which shall be a natural science: its aim, that is, is to represent psychical processes as quantitatively determined states of specifiable material particles and so to make them plain and void of contradictions. (OPA, 355)

To carry out this project, Freud relies on a model of the nervous system, which he termed a system of "neurones." The neurone system is never at zero-load, no matter how much the system as a whole tends towards the discharge of energy contained within it (OPA, 356). Stimulus, conversion, and discharge of energy are all characteristics of this "principle of neuronic inertia" regulating this system's dynamic interface with the external environment at an energy level it seeks to preserve.

With this model, Freud seeks to define the function of the brain quantitatively, in terms of specific levels of excitation and the neurone's ability to bear a load of energy while remaining receptive to further input (OPA, 363). He first distinguishes between permeable and impermeable neurones: those which correspond to the system of perception, and those stemming from the body's internal stimuli or memory (OPA, 360). These two sets of neurones in the body function as the ϕ-system and the ψ-system. The first is the interface of the body with the world; the second, the interface of stored stimuli with consciousness. Yet a third group of neurones exists, corresponding to the conscious activity of the brain. These "perceptual neurones" explain the origin of *qualities* within perceived sensations:

> We may ask *how* qualities originate and *where* qualities originate. . . . Not in the external world; for out there (according to the views of natural science, to which, in this discussion, psychology too must submit) there are only masses in motion and nothing else. In the φ-system perhaps [the physical perceptive system]? This would tally with the fact that qualities are connected with perception, but it is contradicted by everything that rightly speaks in favour of the seat of consciousness being in the higher levels of the neuronic system. In the ψ-system then [the recollective system]? . . . This process, however, is, speaking generally, *devoid* of quality. . . . Thus we must summon up enough courage to assume that there is a *third* system of neurones . . . whose states of excitation give rise to the different qualities -- are, that is to say, conscious sensations. (OPA, 369-70)

Freud has thus divided perceptions in a fashion similar to the division of the "elements of the sensations" posited by Ernst Mach in *The Analysis of the Sensations*. Tying sensations to nerve groups, or to what will in later research be called "synapses," Freud recognizes three types of nerve excitation: the φ-system (physical sensations from the outside world), the ψ-system (internally generated, recalled sensations), and the perceptual system ("ω" for "Wahrnehmung"). The third system is exclusively conscious; the first two may not be.

This is a radical move allowing him to account for both a general consciousness of the group and the individual: "Only by means of these complicated and far from self-evident hypotheses have I so far succeeded in introducing the phenomenon of consciousness into the structure of quantitative psychology" (OPA, 372). The first two systems of neurones correspond to the stable states of energy within the nervous system, constituting a physical equilibrium for the dynamic system of the mind. The perceptual system, however, supplements these two sources of nerve impulses as a channel of input to the system conditioned by perception itself -- a source of novelty. In this, "perception" is not defined as a passive receptivity of the nervous system. Instead, perception is associated with attention, with a conscious intake of information. This redefinition is crucial to preserving the position of the individual, as Freud knows:

> First, however, a word upon the relation of this theory of consciousness to others. According to a modern mechanistic theory, consciousness is no more than an appendage added to the physiologico-psychical processes, an appendage whose absence would make no difference to the course of psychical events. According to another theory, consciousness is the subjective side of all psychical events and is thus inseparable from physiologico-mental processes. The theory which I have here propounded lies between these two. According to it consciousness is the subjective side of a *part* of the physical processes in the neuronic system -- namely, of the *perceptual* processes (ω-processes); and its absence would *not* leave psychical events unchanged but would imply the absence of any contribution from the W(ω)-system. (OPA, 372-73)

In this model, the qualities of pleasure or unpleasure arise when a rise in the quantity of energetic excitation enters the system, to then be discharged. Sensations of extreme heat, for example, send ever increasing pain messages to the psyche; they are discharged when the heat is removed and a pleasurable, normal heat balance is restored to the body. The relation of these three systems in the mind is not unidirectional. The stimuli arising in the outside world are continuous; the qualities discharged are discontinuous, because the energy involved must be built up beyond a certain threshold level before it can be perceived in the stable state load in the neuronic system. Heat builds up slowly; it becomes unbearable only after the quantity reaches a determinable threshold value which triggers a reflex.

Thus Freud delimits the transfer of stimuli into conscious information as a serial transfer of energy. This model has a priority of experience in its simultinaeity. The φ-system is the first recipient of outside energy through the body and spinal cord. This energy is then transferred into the ψ-system, setting the habituated traces referred to in the *Interpretation of Dreams* and affecting later processing. Finally, if the energy to be transferred is great enough, it will pass into consciousness in the ω-system, attracting a sense of quality to the original quantity of excitation. The original quantity of the φ-excitation corresponds to a motor excitation; when it passes into the ψ-system, it lays down "paths of conduction" or facilitations in the brain matter, which are aimed at habituating the organism to an available threshold of excitation without stress. This conditions the system to a distinct energy level, the characteristic energy of each individual mind:

> During the passage of the quantity (Q) the resistance is suspended, but afterwards it is restored -- but only to a particular height, according to the quantity (Q) that has passed; so that next time a smaller quantity will be able to pass, and so on. When the most complete facilitation has been established, there will remain a certain resistance, equal in amount in the case of all contact-barriers [synapses]; so that quantities (Q) will have to increase above a certain threshold in order to be able to pass it. This resistance would be a constant. (OPA, 378)

Stimuli are thus in equilibrium in the psychic apparatus: paths are breached to facilitate passage of the energy associated with particular classes of stimuli, in order that the energy be efficiently conducted (cathected) through the system.

Freud adds another distinction allowing for individuality, which parallels Mach's model. Higher-order activities of the mind are associated with the quality -- not just the quantity -- of excitation. Will, moral instincts, and the like, according to Freud, correlate to the habituated paths of conduction within the brain. The system will tend to maintain a particular level of energy -- the mind's own dynamic level: "We are familiar with this force as the 'will' -- the derivative of the 'instincts'" (OPA, 379).

The sum total of all innervations of the system is commonly termed the "ego." Satisfaction of the "instincts" or the "will" correspond to the specific action which will satisfy or cathect a given stimulus energy according to the ego's characteristic responses. In the simplest cases, the resulting motor action is called reflex; in complex situations, social action results, such as nurturing children and aiding helpless. Since a particular activity will be associated with a specific release of energy, there are consequences for the group. The group will tend to find similar patterns of energy release:

At early stages the human organism is incapable of achieving this specific action. It is brought about by extraneous help, when the attention of an experienced person has been drawn to the child's condition by a discharge taking place along the path of internal change [e.g., by the child's screaming]. This path of discharge thus acquires an extremely important secondary function -- viz., of bringing about an understanding with other people; and the original helplessness of human beings is thus the primal source of all moral motives. (OPA, 379)

Human thus train each other's minds.

As in the model for conceptual psychology also followed by Wundt, Dilthey, and Mach, Freud sees that wishes, affects, memory, and the ego also tie into this stability and culture-specific action. Affects and wishful states both "involve a hardening of the quantitative tension in ψ: in the case of an affect this is brought about by sudden release, and in that of a wish by means of summation" (OPA, 383). In a wish, for example, a positive attraction for an object is formed on the basis of the memory associated with the satisfaction it will bring, or which similar objects have brought. That is, an anticipation of a cathexis (or discharge of energy) constitutes the wish. Such a wish-fulfillment becomes permanently incorporated into the path-breaking of the psyche, and is attributed to the ego as an affective response. Affects, positive or negative, tally similarly with prior experiences of pleasure or pain. The ego is thus for Freud a secondary formation, affecting the stimuli experienced directly or remembered:

With our hypothesis of "wishful attraction" and of a tendency to repression [of unpleasure] we have in fact already touched upon a state of ψ which has not been discussed. For both these processes indicate that an organization has been formed in ψ whose presence interferes with the passage [of quantities] if that passage occurred for the first time in a particular manner [i.e., if it was accompanied by satisfaction or pain]. This organization is called the "ego." . . . The ego may thus be defined as the totality of ψ-cathexes at any given time: and in these a permanent portion may be distinguished from a changing one. . . . While it must be the ego's endeavour to get rid of its cathexes by the method of satisfaction, it (the ego) must inevitably influence the repetition of experiences of pain and affects; and it must do so in the following manner, which is generally called "inhibition." (OPA, 384-85)

This is different from strict empiricism because it relies on a consensus between the individual and the world, nor is it idealism, since the reflexes of the individual depend on learned patterns. Freud's description of the ego as a summary complex of the cathexes in the neurones, since these cathexes represent facilitations or passages of energy beginning in the body, the memory, or the conscious mind, is a definition which goes far beyond pure empiricism.

Instead, Freud proposes a more comprehensive model. The *Project* connects the nervous system with memory, which functions as an interface between the objective reality of the body mechanism and the seemingly subjective reactions to stimuli which have breached paths in the neurones. With this two-time-frame system, Freud has bridged a gap between "qualitative" as a structural term (referring to types of stimuli in the neuronic organization) and "qualitative" differences among stimuli. Each qualitative difference is a pleasure/unpleasure association, a memory left from the passage of a *quantity* of nervous excitation. If that quantity is in excess of the facilitated load of the system, the new experience will be unpleasant, and will thus be judged harmful, to be avoided. Human judgment is also based on the habituation of the organism to its environment. The regulator and final determinant of any judgment will be the past experience of the individual coupled with input from the group and world. Judgments are thus linked to survival of the organism, and to the individual's coexistence with other members of the species who aid that organism in its initial facilitations or survival.

This description merges cultural relativity into a scientific/quantitative description of the interactions between the mind and world. This two-tier model allows for the possibility that the mind may work against itself in situations where the ϕ-neurones are receiving different stimuli than are coded in the habits of the perceptual or the memory neurone systems. In the *Project* and *Dreams*, this model accommodates conflicts between the individual and the group manifesting themselves as inhibitions or repressions. The conflicts also constitute the hidden material which is released in dream-analysis or in psychoanalysis. By acknowledging this link of the organism to history, Freud has merged the description of concept-formation in the individual (from the *Interpretation of Dreams*) with the model for the interface between the organism and the environment (from the *Project*).

As in has in other works of conceptual psychology, this model also accommodates the higher powers of the mind. In a typical formulation, judgment is a compromise between the facilitations or cathected experiences which have already conditioned the mind and the inhibitions exercised against the cathexis of a new experience. When enacted, a judgment is a conscious cathexis based on memory: "If the perception is not an absolutely new one, it will now recall and revive the *memory* of some perception with which it will have at least something in common. And now the process of thought [cathexis] that I have previously described will be repeated in connection with this memory image, though to some extent without the aim provided by the cathected wishful idea" (OPA, 393).

A series of such judgments establishes the individual organism's reality, based on the energetic residues of past experiences and a stable state of adaptation to the environment. This reality is the organism's dynamic "state of identity":

Cognitive or judging thought seeks for an identity with a
somatic cathexis; reproductive thought seeks for an identity
with a psychical cathexis (an experience of the subject's
own). Judging thought operates in advance of reproductive
thought, since the former furnishes the latter with
ready-made facilitations to assist further associative
travelling. If at the conclusion of the act of thought the
indication of reality also reaches perception, then a
judgment of reality, a *belief*, is achieved and the aim of the
whole activity is attained. (OPA, 394-95)

These definitions link the innervation of the human organism and
that organism's resulting concept of reality. This reality is, to be
sure, conditioned by an individual's interactions with the
environment, and as such, it is materialist. Yet the perception of
that environment is also contingent upon the judgments of that
individual, the recollections and psychic cathexes based on prior
experience, stored in the dynamic equilibrium of the mind.

As facilitated paths are established through experience, the
resulting patterns (the dynamic identity of a person) influence the
direction of interest and the associations among data which
condition that individual's developing picture of reality. This is
Freud's variation on the self-preservation of the organism. The
pain and pleasure of reality, based on memory and judgment,
function as organisms need to establish a constant level of energy
within their nervous system; this energy level is the threshhold of
an individual's conceptual realm. Memory-traces are differentiated
from perceptual-traces in their apparent level of energy. Sleep and
dreams work off the uncathected energy residues of the day, where
physical and psychical needs of the individual have not been
entirely met. These dreams do not attain the status of reality-traces;
they are the unfulfilled wishes of reality, of insufficient energy to
emerge into consciousness, and so are fulfilled at night. Memory
affects judgment, as it can dreams, when its energy traces alter
reality for an individual. Memory-traces will affect the processing
of new experiences in each judgment -- despite their lower level of
inherent energy -- because they are the deep level of habituation.

This psychology ties into psychopathology on these levels.
Compulsions, hysteria, and other atypical judgments are symptoms

of an incomplete   confrontation of the organism with its environment. The nervous energy associated with a set of stimuli has not been cathected and has not formed normal associative paths in the brain. Yet, in a neurotic compulsion, this energy has still breached paths in the brain and has thus been integrated with the material of memory. Such neuroses are thus difficult to change, since they require a total reorientation of the associative paths of experience -- physical and mental reorientation. In cases of less serious incomplete processing, displacements, transferences, and associations of the dream-work act as vents to allow more or less healthy dealings with the environment.[17] If memory-traces have been artificially enhanced and force themselves into a dominant position to blot out healthy reactions or judgments to new experiences, they can override attention, new cathexes, and independent judgments.

For Freud, then, the psychical orientation of an individual to the environment is a product of attention. Yet the specific attention is affected by the body's memories of moments when its equilibrium was disturbed:

> Attention is biologically justified; the question is merely one of how to give the ego guidance as to *which* expectant cathexis it is to establish: and this purpose is served by the indications of quality. (OPA, 417-18)

Energy and memory allow biology to be accommodated in the model without diminishing individuality.

Interest and attention correlate with the individual's psycho-physiological dynamics, conditioning both ordinary or observant thought, by which the organism judges potential action on the basis of more or less consciously anticipated cathexes and satisfaction of wishes (OPA, 420). This integration of biological interest, as identified by contemporaries such as Mach, with the explicit energetics of the nervous system constitutes Freud's overriding contribution to conceptual psychology. Freud related the nervous system and the mind to the biological capacity to perceive. This model accounts for both cognitive and affective behaviors of humans, both thought and instinct, rationality and wishes. When he links attention to physical perception (in its essence often unconscious) and to pathological thought (with repressions of both conscious and unconscious thought), Freud is able to tie together broadly the function of language, symbol systems, the paths of association of data, and the knowledge or error in which the organism stand with respect to the world in a model integrating biology and theory.

The facilitating activity sets down habituated paths in the nervous system, which allows the organism's survival. Through habituation, everyday information is processed without conscious attention. These habits of association establish everyday behavior, but also a "world view." This world view is shared and signified as the sets of data to which attention is habitually paid or not paid, and which receive designations as language in an experience community. In this, Freud's extended model has connected the habits of the individual with the episteme or world view of an age, going beyond either Foucault or Thomas Kuhn.[18]

In this sense, contradictions in the world view of the organism are associated with unpleasure and the discomfort of the psyche within its environment -- a discomfort affiliated both with neuroses and with errors in judgment. In contrast, pleasure is pragmatic in preserving an equilibrium; utilitarian summaries of data fields associate perceptual data economically, without excess energy from mind or body. This pragmatism also leads us to designate as "thing-complexes" data with relative permanency, as "properties" the data which generally shifts: "thinking with judgments instead of with single, orderless perceptual complexes is a great economy" (OPA, 441). This encompasses, as Mach pointed out, error as well as economy; faulty premises, ignorance, or insufficient information affect judgment.

In Freud's model, "attention," the "economy of thought," the associations of data, and judgments on the basis of insufficient data are all associated with the practical side of psychology, that point at which psychology integrates into a cultural science. In this, the logical and economic models drawn from Mach's science and Paul's philology are added to Freud's own accounting for the human nervous system and its contribution to the habituated thought and behavior patterns of the human in a cultural environment.

The unfinished *Project for a Scientific Psychology* thus

represents Freud's delineation of psychology as a cultural science whose theory lies outside of psychoanalysis. In his psychoanalysis, Freud accounts for the behavior of humans in terms of their prior experience, their physical and psychic desires as tempered by the society in which they live. In contrast, Freud's psychology outlines the consistent biological underpinnings which limit and condition the behaviors studied in psychoanalysis.

This differentiation of sciences in not highlighted in Freud's thought, but it is consistently upheld. His abandoned psychology is a science which amalgamates neurology with the biology of organic adaptation, and uses the principles of economy, pleasure and unpleasure which result from this amalgamation to explain behaviors conditioned by environments. Freud did not preserve this science when he gave up neurology. Instead, he stressed psychoanalysis as the discipline which seeks to render knowledge of the affects of environment and habituation on an organism's mental apparatus. Thus, in contrast to the achievements of cultural psychologists such as Jung, Freud provides a complete picture of humans in society: as organic being, as self-willed yet instinct-driven individual, and as an environmentally conditioned representative of his culture's inheritance. The psychology which underlies both the *Project* and *Dreams* relates the individual to an environment. This corresponds to the tenets of conceptual psychology by explaining the higher-order mental functions of humans, but it also is Freud's cultural psychology. Through his focus on the individual's experience, Freud states most clearly the relationships between an individual and the net of culture: the interface between individual psychology, psychopathology, and group behavior. What Freud begins describing as symptoms stemming from indivdual experience ends as the basis for a cultural psychology.[19]

8.2.2 *Psychology versus Psychoanalysis*

The differentiation between psychology and psychoanalysis stressed here was preserved through other of Freud's writings. His short 1913 essay, "The Claims of Psycho-Analysis to Scientific Interest," explains his own view of the relationship among psychoanalysis, psychology, and other cultural sciences. Here, he provides "the only at all comprehensive account that he has given of the non-medical applications of psychoanalysis" (Strachey, CP, 164). Applications are justified, since Freud stresses the position of psychoanalysis to its associated cultural sciences.

These sciences are discussions of the individual's place in the normed social and cultural community; psychoanalysis treats the differences from these norms. Moreover, psychoanalysis as such deals most effectively with neuroses and psychoses, not with the more severe mental illnesses. The realm proper to psychoanalysis lies on the border between normal and abnormal (but truly individual) behavior. Freud concludes:

> It may safely be said that the psycho-analytic study of dreams has given us our first insight into a 'depth-psychology' whose existence had not hitherto been suspected. Fundamental changes will have to be introduced into normal psychology if it is to be brought into harmony with these new findings. (CP, 171)

This depth-psychology studies the processing mechanisms of the mind, conditioned by individual and cultural experience; it is not the study of behavior, which is the purview of psychoanalysis.

Freud stresses that there is, indeed, a "general psychology" to which the results of psychoanalysis and other disciplines must conform (CP, 175): psychology is the theoretical discipline, while psychoanalysis is only an application of psychological principles to humans in a cultural setting. The mind's workings are revealed by psychoanalysis in the narrower sense, but the affects tend to be what is primarily uncovered: "an unexpected amount of affective disturbance and blinding of the intellect in normal no less than in sick people" (CP, 175). Psychoanalysis concentrates on affects; psychology focuses on the human cognitive and sense apparatus.

As psychoanalysis is an application of psychological principles to affective behavior, other applications to various regions of cultural data are possible. For example, an investigation, on the basis of psychological principles, can be carried out by "experts in speech." Unlike psychoanalysts, these experts will not be concerned with the relations of the affects to the intellect.   Instead, they explore "the expression of thought in words" (CP, 176).

Freud's description of the relation between thoughts and words parallels his investigation of dreams. As dreams use images to express their distinctive syntax (dream-content) and an inherent underlying logic (dream-thought), language uses words. Further, unlike languages using words, dream-contents will tend to be hieroglyphic, that is, a system of pictures which refer to dream-thoughts:

> If we reflect that the means of representation are principally visual images and not words, we shall see that it is even more appropriate to compare dreams with a system of writing than with a language. (CP, 177)

Here Freud considers the surface structure of language as a hieroglyphic to be diciphered. Like a dream, the system of writing is the final topical encoding of a meaning derived from a deeper level of the mind.[20]

A psychoanalyst and an expert in speech share not only a model, but also a goal. As analysts look to the personal meaning under a dream, "experts in speech" are less interested in the signs of language than in its systematics. For them, language is a phenomenon based on mental processes composing the signs of writing, much as dream-work composes the images of dreams. Each group of professionals would look to cultural data to decompose the images of the dream into the underlying meanings along typical paths of formation. These typical paths of formation are similar for dreams and verbal expressions in Freud's view: both expressions conform to human psychology and its dynamic structure and habituations.

Freud is defining psychology as a consistent approach to cultural data, a juxtaposition of the products of the mind with the information and mental processes which yield them.   It is a supplementary discipline, providing a series of corrective measures for other humanisitic disciplines such as anthropology, history, or philosophy. Freud wants to integrate a psychology of mind into the procedures and validation of various humanistic fields. Freud's first example is philosophy, a discipline chastised for overlooking the applicability of psychology to its procedures. In his critique, Freud identifies a tendency in humanistic disciplines to constitute themselves on the basis of a region of data, omitting discussion of the mental processes addressing this data. Philosophy in particular addresses the mind without allowing for the unconscious' effect on the mind's function, thus assuming one of two simple, but inaccurate, positions:

> Either their unconscious has been something mystical, something intangible and undemonstrable, whose relation to the mind has remained obscure, or they have identified the mental with the conscious and have proceeded to infer from this definition that what is unconscious cannot be mental or a subject for psychology. (CP, 178)

Freud calls these spurious assumptions. His psychology incorporates both conscious and unconscious workings; their patterns can be recovered from the mind's products, from dreams, for example.

A philosophy which ignores the psychology of the scientist has a second serious weakness, its procedures:[21]

> In no other science does the personality of the scientific worker play anything like so large a part as in philosophy. . . . psycho-analysis can indicate the subjective and individual motives behind philosophical theories which have ostensibly sprung from impartial logic work, and can draw a critic's attention to the weak spots in the system. . . . that a theory is psychologically determined does not in the least invalidate its scientific truth. (CP,179)

From Freud's perspective, psychoanalysis and psychology must both play roles in philosophy. Only the two disciplines in unison can investigate the inherent interestedness of philosophical theory. Too, they can discuss the validity of the theory-building mechanisms according to the mind's psychological habituations.

The juxtaposition of psychoanalysis and psychology leads Freud to recommend another supplement to humanistic studies. The psychoanalysis of children can clarify developmental questions associated both with the individual and with groups of people: "in the last few years psycho-analytic writers (Abraham, Spielrein and Jung) have become aware that the principle that 'ontogeny [the development of the individual] is a repetition of phylogeny [the development of the group]' must be applicable to mental life" (CP, 184).[22] Freud posits that the transmitted or inherited history and *mores* of a group affect the psychological mechanisms of the individual, as well as the formation and rationale of that group's myths and belief structures.

In similar fashion, a discussion of the myths themselves may uncover the motivations behind a culture's identity. These motivations parallel neuroses, which point to modifications in the individual's history according to self-interest, just as myths reflect cultural justifications or distortions:

> The study made by psycho-analysis of dreams and neuroses has given it the necessary experience to enable it to guess the technical procedures that have governed these distortions. But in a number of instances it can also reveal the hidden motives which have led to this modification in the original meaning of myths. (CP, 185)

For Freud, myth, religion, justice, philosophy, and other theories all serve the same purpose in the mental life of a people. Each accommodates emotional tendencies deriving from confrontations with realities, and edits out or represses those elements of reality not to be dealt with directly.

Myth and history therefore constitute culture as a direct parallel to the individual psychology of dreams. Just as individuals compromise their wishes in light of the requirements of the group, a culture with its institutions serves as a regulator for such individual wishes. Civilization, then, is a concretization of the prohibitions which all members of a group must respect if that group is to survive.

Freud does not reduce a civilization to a single pattern. The institutions and compromises of a particular civilization constitute the basic "world view" of an individual within that group. They reflect the aspects of the environment which that group can understand and/or control:

> Psycho-analysis has established an intimate connection between these psychical achievements of individuals on the one hand and societies on the other by postulating one and the same dynamic source for both of them. . . . The principle of avoiding unpleasure dominates human actions until it is replaced by the better one of adaptation to the external world. *Pari passu* with men's progressive control over the world goes a development in their *Weltanschauung*, their view of the universe as a whole. . . . Myths, religion and morality find their place in this scheme as attempts to seek a compensation for the lack of satisfaction of human wishes. (CP, 185-86)

The compromise between the individual and the world in civilization also produces art.[23] Psychology gives rise to the forms and directions of art; it alleviates group needs as dreams do for individuals. Yet where a neurosis is a sign of an unfulfilled wish, and a dream is a substitute fulfillment of one, art pays explicit attention to the prohibitions of culture representing the fulfillment of personal fantasies in the mental sphere.

Freud's distinction between psychology and psychoanalysis becomes crucial in a prevelant popular reading of Freud. Purportedly, he attributes a dual nature -- creator and neurotic -- to an artist. Freud actually posits the opposite role for the artist; he is the healthy one among his people, not suffering, but able to control affects:

> Whence it is that the artist derives his creative capacity is not a question for psychology. The artist's first aim is to set himself free and, by communicating his work to other people suffering from the same arrested desires, he offers them the same liberation. He represents his most personal wishful phantasies as fulfilled; but they only become a work of art when they have undergone a transformation which softens what is offensive in them, conceals their personal origin and, by obeying the laws of beauty, bribes other people with a bonus of pleasure. (CP, 187)

Psychoanalysis may discover the personal in an artwork, the

particular conflicts or fears which generate a work of art on the personal level. Yet psychology, the science of the mind's structure, elucidates the transformations of latent to manifest content which constitute the symbolic representation being communicated to the group as art. Psychoanalysis uncovers the individual in the artwork; psychology, the general, typical, and communicable:

> Art is a conventionally accepted reality in which, thanks to artistic illusion, symbols and substitutes are able to provoke real emotions. Thus art constitutes a region half-way between a reality which frustrates wishes and the wish-fulfilling world of the imagination . . . (CP, 188)

The psychology of art therefore analyzes its function in maintaining the dynamic equilibrium of the individual within the environment. The avenues for maintaining these equilibria resemble the analogies, transferences, repression, and the like, already familiar from the psychology of dreams and neuroses. Art, then, is particularly crucial in Freud's cultural psychology, since it mirrors the transitions which the group must make in dealing with its environment.

Art challenges cultural repressions and presents new data in a form which will circumvent habituated thoughts and the cultural self-image restricting the individual. Art also exposes the internalized limits to thought which lie at the core of a culture:

> What is to-day an act of internal restraint was once an external one, imposed, perhaps, by the necessities of the moment; and, in the same way, what is now brought to bear upon every growing individual as an external demand of civilization may some day become an internal disposition to repressions. (CP, 189)

Because of mental habituation, any of the historical sciences of civilization, be they art, religion, or philosophy, must account for the heredity of world view implied by Freud in these discussions. What we read or see and how we are educated may break paths in our neuronic make-up as directly as do first-hand experiences, and so neuroses or transferences may not only be personal in origin, but also cultural. There must, in consequence, be both a psychoanalytic (personal or ontogenetic) perspective and a psychological one (general or phylogenetic) taken in the sciences of culture. "The Claims of Psycho-Analysis to Scientific Interest" is actually espousing both perspectives under the guise of a psychoanalytic presentation.

8.2.3 Psychology and the Sciences of Culture

Freud restricts his essay on "The Claims of Psycho-Analysis" to a "psycho-analytical" perspective. He has not overtly addressed the need of scholars to consider both ontology and phylogeny, both psychology and psychoanalysis, in their studies. This may reveal a ruse in his diction. Rather than stating and attempting to justify a broad methodological model, Freud points to the work of Jung and others to attract notice to psychoanalysis' results on human behavior which could have impact in other, more established humanistic fields. This is a pragmatic decision on Freud's part. By obscuring his psychology systematically and insisting on the therapeutic utility of psychoanalysis, he maintains, in best Derridean fashion, both a text and a repressed text in his model-building. Yet, as Derrida stressed, and contrary to the assertions of many Freud readers, the psychology was not removed from the model just because it was dropped by Freud as an overt theme. He repressed the psychology in favor of the psychoanalysis. Still, the distinctive mixture of ontogenetic and phylogenetic problems represented by the combined model (the problematics of conceptual psychology) continued throughout Freud's work. Just as the psychological component of the *Interpretation of Dreams* was subordinated to a psychoanalytic and therapeutic description of the field, so, too, is the psychology serving as the underpinnings of such texts as *Totem and Taboo* (1913) and *Moses and Monotheism* (1934-38).

These texts take on a new face when read as historical investigations juxtaposing psychology and psychoanalysis. Because of his consistent appeal to the psychology underlying analysis, Freud analogized individual and group behavior as a case of ontogeny versus phylogeny. Yet, contrary to many assertions made about these anthropological texts, Freud was quite aware that to use individual psychology to explain the history or psychology of a people would be spurious, because an individual is aberrant within the norm of the group. The interpretation of a single dream does not define the meaning of the dream-material; like each myth, it can only indicate the typical meanings which such material would assume in the *particular* psyche of a dreamer. Because of its inherent juxtaposition between individual and group norms of communication, each dream contains many possible spheres of interpretation, but rarely a single meaning. In the broader sphere of culture, however, the multifarious experiences of a group would, if reduced to a univalent set of causal interpretations, be even more improbable as univocal cultural meanings. Therefore, for Freud, a *psychoanalysis* of culture or civilized groups appeared impossible. This would be untenably reductionist in positing a specific character-type resulting from a group cultural experience. Eros and Thanatos, the life and death instincts of the group, tend to create a distinct prototype -- not a normed type -- in a particular environment, allowing for cultural communication for each individual. Psychoanalysis cannot analyze an entire culture because it would reduce the available thought patterns, as in an interpretation of a single dream. General analyses are not possible, only specific ones where the data of a unique life history may be juxtaposed with larger histories of the group.[24]

Nonetheless, a *psychology* can expose the principles on which the group experience of that culture tends to habituate its members -- the basis for a true science of culture. Such a science of culture explains the interface between individuals, their environment, and heredity, including also the affective responses which will characterize their individual world views (which is the purview of psychoanalysis). This psychology does not deal with the culture as a whole, but with the memory-traces which are implicit components of individual psyches, that is, the elements of experience with a high statistical probability of affecting an individual of the group (by no means a necessary part of his/her psychopathology).

This distinguishes between a psychology as an analysis of deep cognitive structures and an analysis focusing primarily on individual affective structures. It also opens a rereading of Freud's two great texts in cultural anthropology and religion, *Totem and Taboo* and *Moses and Monotheism*. They do not provide models for the applications of *psychoanalysis* to cultural data, as is commonly assumed. Instead, they use a *psychology* to derive results appropriate to a science of culture and to a classification of the group, leading only to general conclusions about the affective problems which an individual in that group may confront. The preface to *Totem and Taboo* indicates Freud's awareness of the difference of his program:

> They represent a first attempt on my part at applying the point of view and the findings of psycho-analysis to some unsolved problems of social psychology (*Völkerpsychologie*). Thus they offer a methodological contrast to Wilhelm Wundt's extensive work, which applies to the hypotheses and working methods of *non*-analytic psychology to the same purposes, and on the other hand to the writings of the Zürich school of psycho-analysis, which endeavour, on the contrary, to solve the problems of individual psychology with the help of material derived from social psychology. . . . They seek to bridge the gap between students of such subjects as social anthropology, philology and folklore on the one hand, and psycho-analysts on the other. (TT, xiii)

Here, Freud does not mean to exhaust either psychology or psychoanalysis; he knows this is *not* cultural psychoanalysis. Hidden in this self-effacing preface is a tripartite division of disciplines: individual psychology, social or group psychology, and psychoanalysis. Moreover, this division is further complicated by Freud's assertion that there are two ways to do group psychology: Wundt's, termed "non-analytic," and (implicitly) Freud's own, which must be "analytic." This "analytic psychology" is that conceptual psychology which has been underlying all of Freud's work on dreams and normal/abnormal human behaviors and which breaks down the patterns of the group.

The thesis of *Totem and Taboo* is familiar: the totem and taboo prohibitions which exist in primitive cultures have been replaced in modern, civilized cultures by more informal prohibitions. While both types of prohibitions serve to orient the individual to the exigencies of behavior imposed by the environment, civilized taboos tend to put greater stress on the responsibility of the individual by requiring situational considerations of the restricted activities. Yet the "primitives" must not be dismissed by modern investigators. Their myths satisfy affective needs in primitive fashion; these needs exist today as well, and so their solutions may speak to us:

> If that supposition is correct, a comparison between the psychology of primitive peoples, as it is taught by social anthropology, and the psychology of neurotics, as it has been revealed by psycho-analysis, will be bound to show numerous points of agreement and will throw new light upon familiar facts in both sciences. (TT, 1)

Taboos are, therefore, controls for obsessions; totems are the forms of desires translated into an institution of society. Both externalize individual affect, rendering it less problematic for the group.

This institutionalized control of individual desires in favor of the survival of the group is fundamental to the "economy of thought" for the culture's rationale. The individual under pressure from society will develop habits which may either contradict or actively direct that individual's experience of the environment:

> The neuroses exhibit on the one hand striking and far-reaching points of agreement with those great social institutions, art, religion and philosophy. But on the other hand they seem like distortions of them. . . . The divergence resolves itself ultimately into the fact that the neuroses are asocial structures; they endeavour to achieve by private means what is effected in society by collective effort. (TT, 73)

The totem and taboo structure thus fits into the model of conceptual psychology as an alternative formulation of its cognitive and affective structure. Each institution is a set of possible experience acting as pre-given habits or a world view which supplements or even supplants a world view developed through personal experience alone.

Totems and taboos thus constitute world views for a people, and reflect the cognitive patterning familiar to a cultural group. Even when totems assume more "civilized" forms as religious or social institutions, they serve virtually identical functions for the psyche of the individuals involved. Like language and symbol systems, they provide a coherence and continuity in experience, a set of innervational habits serving individuals as habits. With them, an individual in a normal situation need not confront the premises of the environment actively: "There is an intellectual function in us which demands unity, connection and intelligibility from any material, whether of perception or thought, that comes within its grasp" (TT, 95). Normal culture functions to aid this acclimation. As normal function shades into illness through compromises, however, cultures can also fossilize non-utilitarian arrangements of data into patterns which may, but do not necessarily, cause affective strains on individuals. Nonetheless, each system "explains" something, while actively pre-structuring the environment for its participants: "Thus a system is best characterized by the fact that at least two reasons can be discovered for each of its products: a reason based on the premises of the system (a reason, then, which may be delusional) and a concealed reason, which we must judge to be the truly operative and the real one" (TT, 96). The reality of such systems lies in the psyche's tendency to the economy of thought. Each culture is a coherent pattern established on the basis of the material available to a mind. The "truth" of such mental systems, then, lies both inside and outside them simultaneously. They are built out of the material which a group needs to explain for its survival; they exclude or repress materials in order to construct a functioning world view. Again, such a world view is characteristic of a communication group, but not necessarily descriptive of its individual members.

In *Totem and Taboo*, Freud kept as his focus the tendency of individuals and groups to build belief systems to maintain their orientation in the environment. He also stressed that such systems evolve across time, without a causal explanation for change in many cases. As in other representatives of conceptual psychology, individuals can innovate within the system, leaving permanent traces which others in the tradition learn to emulate with remembering their original rationale. Traces can be passed on with the details of their formation suppressed for reasons of economy:

> If so, however, we may safely assume that no generation is able to conceal any of its more important mental processes from its successor. For psycho-analysis has shown us that everyone possesses in his unconscious mental activity an apparatus which enables him to interpret other people's reactions, that is, to undo the distortions which other people have imposed on the expression of their feelings. An unconscious understanding (such as this) of all the customs, ceremonies and dogmas left behind by the original relation to the father may have made it possible for later generations to take over their heritage of emotion. (TT, 159)

These, virtually the concluding statements of *Totem and Taboo*, summarize the results of Freud's differentiation between psychoanalysis and psychology in an anthropological context: groups, like individuals, will have to deal with affects resulting from cognition.

The underlying mechanisms of thought described by psychology allow the comprehensibility of customs and myths among various generations and peoples. The surface structure of these myths -- the "personal" aspect of the material involved which is predicated on the individual experience of a people --, however, represents an emotional or psychic reality for that group which may or may not correspond to what Freud terms factual reality. This emotional reality is delusional or illusory in the strict sense, yet it is a cultural norm allowing communication of a mental reality, a set of values or taboos not overtly contingent upon the environment. Psychoanalysis may reach this mental affective reality in individuals when it pays attention to the specific content and context of repressions and transferences. However, the mental structures which underlie it are the domain of psychology. They aid in producing affects in successive generations when they are transmitted in cultural inheritance. This differentiation anticipates the work of Claude Levi-Strauss in *The Savage Mind*.[25] So-called primitive societies are distinguished not through thought patterns which are less sophisticated or less developed than those used by modern man, but rather through those which are only constituted on different experiential premises, and so which communicate differently. Levi-Strauss' concept of "structure" differs from Freud's. Levi-Strauss disregards what for Freud are the essential and non-interchangeable surface elements of culturally revelant mental realities in order to describe the nexes of an almost culture-free psychology. Levi-Strauss thinks that this psychology describes mental structures functioning in binary oppositions; Freud retains a greater attention to the surface manifestations of cultural transmission which affect such structures through individual habituation.

As a representation of a conceptual psychology, *Totem and Taboo* is not alone in Freud's corpus. *Moses and Monotheism* also attempts to illustrate the relations between group repressions and the structures of the mind, again studying affects out of both psychology and psychoanalysis. His specific example is the biblical story of Moses, considering how its historical tradition may have been obscured through a contamination of the Jewish people by the Egyptian heresy of Aten, a nascent monotheism. Freud's text presents three essays on the topic, each written from a slightly different perspective, each also reflecting difficulties which Freud had in his emigration from Vienna to England. Freud's approach to this combination of historical and traditional materials remains consistent with *Totem and Taboo*. He again relied on psychology and psychoanalytic applications in evaluating the status of quasi-historical material as mental truth:

> Two mutually opposing treatments have left their traces on [the material]. On the one hand it has been subjected to revisions which have falsified it in the sense of their secret aims, have mutilated and amplified it and have even changed it into its reverse; on the other hand a solicitous piety has presided over it and has sought to preserve everything as it was, no matter whether it was consistent or contradicted itself. . . . in many cases of textual distortion, we may nevertheless count upon finding what has been suppressed and disavowed hidden away somewhere else, though changed and torn from its context. Only it will not

always be easy to recognize it. (MM, 43)

This is the statement about the nature of historical truth that Freud was not able to make in *Totem and Taboo*; this is his direct commentary about the distortions which occur in transmission of a culture's symbols but which preserve its affective truth. Again, however, this is only analytic psychology, not psychoanalysis, up to the point where affective strength is given credence as the distortion of a mental pattern in an individual. The study of group wellness is psychology; of illness, psychoanalysis.

In *Moses*, then, Freud was able to expand on the development of group consciousness. In the case of the Moses material, for example, he posits that the new monotheism took some time to be assimilated by the Jewish people. This time is a "latency period," about which he concludes: "What we learn from this is merely that it takes time for the reasoning activity of the ego to overcome the objections that are maintained by strong affective cathexes" (MM, 67). That is, cognitive patterns can be overridden by affects. When a culture finally accepts new information into its tradition, it enters into the consciousness of the people involved. Moreover, what real facts have been lost or suppressed in the latency period in terms of precise information will be embellished. An economy of affective thought, like that in symbol use, preserves affective truth:

> [T]his offers the artist a peculiar attraction, for in that case he is free to fill in the gaps in memory according to the desires of his imagination and to picture the period which he wished to reproduce according to his intentions. One might almost say that the vaguer a tradition has become the more serviceable it becomes for a poet. (MM, 71)

The missing material in a tradition is supplied by the poetic imagination, which recreates a psychically valid reality without the necessity of explicitly addressing the material which was repressed (or not acknowledged as valid) by the group.[26]

Freud thus demonstrates that the mechanism familiar to us from the individual psyche may be generalized into a description of historical stages of traditional symbol systems:

> Early trauma -- defence -- latency -- outbreak of neurotic
> illness -- partial return of the repressed. Such is the
> formula which we have laid down for the development of a
> neurosis. The reader is now invited to take the step of
> supposing that something occurred in the life of the human
> species similar to what occurs in the life of individuals . . .
> (MM, 80)

Thus a historical tradition, just as a personal history, contains a
portion of "forgotten truth" which may, in the need to create a
mental whole out of material that has repressed elements, represent
distortions or errors in historical fact, yet not in psychic fact (MM,
85). Like the symbol systems described in other conceptual
psychology models, this also contains both knowledge and error.

As an additional confirmation that Freud was changing
emphases, not his fundamental model, in this text, he provides a
supplementary re-translation of this mechanism into terms more
familiar to those of his readers who have encountered the *Lectures
on Psycho-Analysis*:

> We must introduce another distinction which is no longer
> qualitative but *topographical* and -- what gives it special
> value -- at the same time *genetic*. We now distinguish in
> our mental life (which we regard as an apparatus
> compounded of several agencies, districts or provinces)
> one region which we call the *ego* proper and another which
> we name the *id*. (MM, 96)

Again Freud differentiates between the group mind and individual,
yet stresses that they must function according to the genetic criteria,
or the developmental series, which differentiate the id, the ego, and
the superego in the individual. In terms of the group, the id
represents survival desires; the ego reflects conscious life and
symbols; and the superego encompasses the institutions and
prohibitions of the society which take over the role of educator or
parent. All three "agencies" function for the group as they did for
the individual, in that they are regulators trying to maintain the
economy of thought and experience, providing both integration into
the group and the environment as well as satisfaction of individual

desires within the group framework (MM, 116-17).

Because of this greater theoretical explicitness, Freud was able to entitle the last two sections of *Moses* "Historical Truth" and "Historical Development," and to address a viewpoint which was a compromise between an ontogenetic and a phylogenetic explanation of human development within a group.[27] Freud stresses that the individual and the group do not function the same -- a "collective unconscious" in a generic sense does not exist:

> The processes in the life of peoples which we are studying here are very similar to those familiar to us in psycho-pathology, but nevertheless not quite the same. We must finally make up our minds to adopt the hypothesis that the psychical precipitates of the primeval period became inherited property which, in each fresh generation, called not for acquisition but only for awakening. In this we have in mind the example of what is certainly the "innate" symbolism which derives from the period of the development of speech, which is familiar to all children without their being instructed, and which is the same among all peoples despite their different languages. What we may perhaps still lack in certainty here is made good by other products of psycho-analytic research. We find that in a number of important relations our children react, not in a manner corresponding to their own experience, but instinctively, like the animals, in a manner that is only explicable as phylogenic acquisition. (MM, 132-33)

This explanation makes the distinctions familiar from psychoanalysis, arguing more than a biological relationship between ontogeny and phylogeny. The contents of the unconscious are those commonly held elements of human experience conditioned by the environment in general. Such experience conditions the individual's nervous system, and thus also the symbolism of language or art.

Standard, but not identical, cognitive patterns exist. Children conceptualize differently than do adults; they rely on the concrete rather than the abstract, using formulaic stock phrases they learn rather than the highly individualized usages they relinquish under social pressure ("one doesn't say it that way . . . "). As in the case of the Moses tradition, this represents the group's tendency to edit the material, producing a representation of the psychological mechanisms of the individual. Even children use the mechanisms of analogy, transference, repression, and the like, which preserve the energetic economy of the individual representation in the face of sensory or intellectual input from the environment or from the cultural tradition in which they exist.

This, then, is Freud's definition of phylogeny: the tendency of the human nervous system to become habituated in predictable fashion. Each being (cognitive and organic) develops under particular inherited environmental and cognitive constraints. However, no strict causality exists to force us to assume that these habits take one single final form for all individuals within the group, no matter how intense their common culture and environment. This definition, therefore, allows for the individuality of an ontogentic view while ascribing a reality to structures within the general human mind. This compromise, allowing as it does for the affective life and desires of the individual within the established parameters for the group, represents Freud's most striking contribution to the tradition of conceptual psychology.

Others have described *typical* mind, which is represented in communication patterns, that is, environmental or cultural patterning of the individual mind as it manifests an economical interface between an individual, the group, and the world. Freud preserves this model, while adding emphasis on the relation between the cognitive and the affective life of the mind. Moreover, in his studies of neuroses, he has pointed out the negative side of conceptual psychology: the tendency for symbol systems to be removed from reality, producing negative affect, error, and stress. He describes the possibility of culturally based neuroses (*not* neurotic cultures). His work thus supplements conceptual psychology (the study of the group) with psychoanalysis (the study of the individual). Each science will apply under different circumstances, depending on the evaluation of normative behavior as good for maintaining a group and ill in the expression of individuality vis-à-vis the communicative norm.

8.3 Freud and Conceptual Psychology

Throughout his work, Freud maintains a reference to psychology as a set of fundamental premises for establishing humanistic disciplines stressing individual or group behavior in a historical or social context. Psychoanalysis is the first of these disciplines. It seeks to explain the relation of human behavior to human psychology in social context; it pays particular attention to affects which enable or disable behaviors and memory. Anthropology, in turn, stresses group behavior in history. Other disciplines, such as art history, may stress the social context for human psychology.

However, the psychology which underlies Freud's studies of human behavior, neuroses, dreams, and cultural anthropology cannot be called Freud's unique creation, for it resembles the conceptual psychology represented in the work of Ernst Mach, Hermann Paul and Wilhelm Wundt, as well as the cultural studies initiated by Wilhelm Dilthey. All these studies consider both the mechanisms of the psyche and the environment of data which impinge on it. Where, then, does the originality of Freud's contribution to conceptual psychology lie?

First and foremost, Freud has integrated descriptions of the conscious and unconscious minds into the models for concept formation and usage delineated by Mach. Mach stated that all concepts are habitual groups of perceived sensations, bundled together into associated units and named to facilitate thought processes. Husserl and Brentano extended this into a model for a common unconscious, largely value-free. Freud adds to this model more extended and explicit statements about the restrictions placed on thought processes. Habituation, repression, and transference restrict communication and processing of impressions which are too unpleasant or too alien to be dealt with in terms of more neutral analogy and association. The conscious mind does not function in terms of its attention or lack of attention alone; its experiences are stored in unconscious memory as facilitations in the brain's neural pathways to affect all future decisions. Mach implicitly used the concept of the unconscious when he posited that certain data may be slighted in terms of attention, yet still recovered on conscious demand. Freud, however, added an acknowledgment that conscious attention was not the only factor in memory; unconscious habituation may play an even greater role in conscious thought than Mach assumed. Similarly, cultural inheritance, like the inherited concept identified by Mach, may serve as a superficial orientation of the individual to the environment. However, these cultural norms may then unconsciously direct the acquisition of all further knowledge in a deeper fashion than the terms "attention/inattention" suggest. There may be more active selection and repression than Mach assumed.

Freud's second addition to conceptual psychology is a focus shift. He includes the affects when speaking of both conscious and unconscious products of human thought. Where Mach and Paul had spoken of the economy of thought and of the adaptation of the organism to his environment, Freud explicitly adds the reactive processes of the organism. Communication between members of a community within a specific environment had been the concern of Mach; Dilthey stressed the accessibility of minds to cultural products. Freud, in contrast, concentrated on affective impedances to the broader sphere of communication within a given cultural context, on the individualizing factors of personal history which necessarily hinder free communication. In this light, psychoanalysis is the science which deals with the facilitation of communication between an individual and his group, because it attends to behaviors, the environment, and the individual's unconscious. As such, it validates Freud's contention that psychoanalysis has "claims to scientific interest" across its underlying psychological assumptions which reach further than therapy.[28]

Freud's third contribution to conceptual psychology was an expansion of the definition of the discipline as a science of culture. Mach and the Neogrammarians were concerned with the systematics of sign systems as they functioned as communication among members of a group. Dilthey assumed such common stored signs were essential for the life of a culture. In a shift of emphasis, Freud assumed that such sign systems *constituted themselves* as part of mental systems in the form of history, myth, or the institutions of culture (as in *Totem and Taboo* and *Moses and Monotheism*). In "The Claims of Psycho-Analysis," Freud shows how these sign systems constitute themselves between repression and communicative requirements, thus adapting the mind model into a model for scientific investigation, examining sign systems within conscious and unconscious mind. Freud sought psychological validation for civilization, its institutions, and its traditions within the general framework of adaptation and survival for the human race. In these terms, he redefined the issue of phylogeny versus ontogeny and suggested a convincing explanation for their interface. Personal values, repressions, and transferences differentiate the individual within the group and validate personal history as a force resisting group cultural or conceptual heritage. Mach, therefore, delineated the *conditions* for progress within the group; Freud, the *limitations* on progress in light of the self-interest and desires of individual humans who cannot achieve the impartiality of a scientific investigation -- a decisive division between psychoanalysis and conceptual psychology.

Freud's contribution to conceptual psychology is, therefore, his delineation of human value within the conceptual system. His investigations into culture, traditions, normal and abnormal behavior, and dreams all serve the purpose of tying the psychology explained neurologically in the *Project for a Scientific Psychology* to the economy of thought, the adaptation, and preservation of the individual within the group and the environment.

However, Freud's adherence to conceptual psychology may not have positively enhanced his reception. In fact, it may have exacerbated the terminological difficulties often identified in psychoanalysis. Usually associated with individual psychology, terms such as "repression" can actually refer to the innate organizing mechanisms of the mind which affect all realms of sense data, both rational and affective, originating in the past or present, preserved in the memory of the observer or the group, or actually present -- "repression" is not only a personal term. In a parallel situation, two often confused triads -- "id-ego-superego" and "unconscious-preconscious-conscious" -- are easily differentiated through the premises of conceptual society. "Unconscious-preconscious-conscious" is a triad associated with the discourse of psychology. It specifies the amount of energy of sensations and memories and how much force they exert (as habits or breached thought-paths) on that psyche's orientation and receptivity to the environment. As such, this triad explains the *interface* of humans to their world, human habituation, and "world view" as conditioned by inheritance and environment. In contrast, the triad "id-ego-superego" refers to the breached thought-paths themselves within the human psyche. This formulation stresses the information which the organism and its psyche has assembled about its environment: the *structure of knowledge* which represents the individual. The first triad is thus dynamic and genetic, while the second predicates a structural model.

Freud's discourse does not usually facilitate such distinctions, for Freud highlighted psychoanalysis and its therapeutic efficacy throughout his corpus, often to the detriment of other fields. The psychology of psychoanalysis remains largely hidden in Freud's work, because he set himself a goal outside theory. He wished to establish psychoanalysis as a therapeutic discipline dealing with human affective and emotive life.

Despite its position in the background, however, Freud's psychology represents the synthesis lacking in conceptual psychology in the nineteenth century. He accommodates both the individual and the group, and elucidates the individual's role in maintaining, blocking, or altering inherited thought patterns. Despite this success, Freud's psychology necessarily places a restriction on his own psychoanalytical studies. When a term such as "superego" occurs in the context of an analysis of an individual, Freud wishes only to present a *typical* situation, a sample of the way cultural inheritance may restrict healthy behavior in the individual. His results should not be generalized outside the context of the specific analysis without full acknowledgment that they are culture-specific and statistically typical to a specified group of individuals. Thus, the science of psychology underlying Freud's psychoanalysis presents a set of *principles* about the constitution and development of the psyche. The results of one particular analysis do not constitute a psychology. Instead, an analysis provides examples of the psychological principles of adaptation and innervation as employed in all the major works of Freud, and demonstrates misfunctions within the norm of cultural communication.

Placing Freud's psychoanalysis in the tradition of conceptual psychology thus serves the end of Roazen's recommendations cited at the outset of this study.   It splits the biographical from the scientific validity of Freud's work and considers Freud's oeuvre not as psychoanalytic works with "embarrassments" or "eccentricities," but as a scientific discipline of heretofore unsuspected breath and continuity.[29]

SOME CONSEQUENCES OF CONCEPTUAL PSYCHOLOGY

In *Freud and Man's Soul*, Bruno Bettelheim introduces his work with these words: [1]

> The English translations of Freud's writings are seriously defective in important respects and have led to erroneous conclusions, not only about Freud the man but also about psychoanalysis. This applies even to the authoritative *Standard Edition of the Complete Psychological Works of Sigmund Freud*. After reading the criticisms of this translation that I present in this book, the reader may well ask why I have waited so long to publish them, and why others have not made similar criticisms long ago. Obviously, I cannot answer the second question with any certainty, but the reasons for my own reluctance may suggest why others too have hesitated to criticize the translations. . . . . The number of inadequacies and downright errors in the translations is enormous; merely to correct the more blatant ones would be a tremendous task, and the decision where to begin and what to concentrate on would be extremely difficult. But the reluctance to discuss openly the inadequacy of the available translations has been ultimately due, I believe, to much deeper psychological reservations. (Bettelheim, vii)

According to Bettelheim, these reservations involve the genesis of the translations themselves (read or authorized by Freud and/or his executors), a lack of knowledge of the cultural environment from which Freud's diction and style originated, and a desire to subtly change the direction of Freud's thought as espoused by sections of the modern Freudian establishment. Bettelheim locates the origins of today's difficulties with Freud in scholar's pervasive unwillingness to acknowledge Freud's diction, examples, and patterns of analysis as they are anchored in his own cultural milieu -- the Vienna of the end of the nineteenth century.

The discussion of conceptual psychology in the nineteenth century which this volume provides has attempted to address the issue of the cultural environment of Freudian thought from a perspective which expands the critique of Freudians suggested by Bettelheim, Peter Gay, Jeffrey Masson, and others.[2] Bettelheim stressed to today's psychoanalytic establishment that Freud anchored his thought in assumptions about the collective experience of a cultural group. The present volume goes further than Bettelheim in the direction he suggests. It insists that a paradigm for psychology existed in the nineteenth century and is crucial to the definition of collective experience which Bettelheim seeks. Two of its tenets are key in understanding Freud's work. First, peception and knowledge do not originate only in the group; they are also conditioned by the historical, cultural, and environmental data in which that group is constituted. Second, individuals will assimilate the patterns available to the group in shared tradition and experience, but their responses will not necessarily be identical to the group's, since the randomness of individual history will ultimately determine the knowledge and perception of the single human, constrained only by communicative norms. These two assumptions form the core of the paradigm for nineteenth century psychology, a psychology stressing the dynamics between the individual and the group in both synchronic and diachronic frames.

This tradition is still alive in intellectual discussions today: the priority of individual versus the group (which determines responsibility for knowledge -- is a criminal a victim of society, or responsible for his/her own choices?); the relationship of experience to truth (Freud's stress on the individual truth of each psyche as manifested in neuroses, versus the phenomenologist's contention that there is an absolute, eidetic basis for perception); and the relationship of historical-cultural conditioning to perception and truth (individual ethics versus the raison d'etat in wars). The thrust of recent critiques of Freud is thus wider than is seen at first glance, because they question the "insoluble problems" of culture and cultural analysis not as they originate in any system, but as they result directly from discrepant premises about the nature and origin of truth and knowledge. They suggest the necessity of drawing history and the cultural environment into the study of any science or system of ethics, laws, philosophy, or politics. The particular focus of Bettelheim's criticism was the translations of Freud's works done by a group whose scientific principles did not allow them to bring into focus the history and culture of the milieu of psychoanalysis as a science. Therefore, they could not frame it in a fashion commensurate with Freud's aims.

If Bettelheim and others are correct, then current scholars must reframe not only their concept of psychoanalysis as a cultural science, but also revaluate the nineteenth century tradition which allowed Freud's distinctive historical-cultural methodology to emerge, looking at not only the individual therapeutic or archetypical psyche version of his work set into commerce by the psychoanalytic community. Such criticisms are beginning to be raised today with ever-greater frequency, not only in the academy, but even within the psychoanalytic community and its general public. The roles of psychology, psychoanalysis, and psychotherapy are being questioned, particularly in America, where the emigrant Freudian influence is beginning to die out as a direct control over the intellectual legacy, leaving the documentation in the hands of a new generation of scholars educated in a different sense of social responsibility and different intellectual traditions for their disciplines. Bettelheim's critique of the Freud translations thus points to an avenue for the renewal of the position of the human sciences in general (and not only Freudianism) within modern culture and society. Each discipline's methodology must be placed within a historical context and considered as a systematic set of premises regarding the origin and nature of perception, knowledge, and truth framing that discipline's results.

The discussions of conceptual psychology as a tradition culminating in Freud's work thus point to a cause for the tensions in interpretations of Freud for which Bettelheim does not explicitly account, but which scholars such as Derrida stress. Not only the cultural milieu and the cultural politics of translation affect the reading of Freud, but also the specific history of the scientific discourse in which it emerge -- in this case, a heretofore unrecognized paradigm of psychological research preceding and surrounding Freud's work. From the point of view of a paradigm and its discourse, the communalities of language and approach uncovered between Freud and his contemporaries in conceptual psychology suggest that these other psychologists, even if they are in "different disciplines" such as philology, played equal roles in the development of Freudian thought and in the first-generation readings of his texts; contemporaneous thought will influence the pattern of a discipline as easily as the more traditionally acknowledged sources for direct inspiration, such as Charcot's psychotherapy. Charcot and his contemporaries were, to be sure, the inheritors of a tradition of "Seelensorge," focusing on the treatment of individuals mentally unable to accommodate societal demands. This therapeutic psychology, however, was representative of the discourse of psychology which constitutes only one dimension of Freud's contribution to his field -- it is a medical paradigm, not necessarily a cultural one. The medical paradigm tends to be most highlighted today, obscuring Freud's fundamental framing of this therapy in an epistemology accommodating the ethics and the cognitive structure of the society which norms the behavior of an individual. From this perspective, Freud's discussions of the origins of various neuroses and hysterical systems were more than interesting examples for his readers, in that they constitute a preliminary analysis of the particular system of knowledge and truth of his age -- an analysis pointing to a historically grounded cultural psychology.

Freud's approach to psychology as a system of epistemology parallels the paradigm of conceptual psychology as outlined here, starting with Kant and Herbart. They introduced the idea of a mental system in dynamic equilibrium between thought constellations and the data of the real world, and thus established psychology as a discipline concerned with knowledge and the individual passions as tied to human existence in this world, not to an absolute standard of truth. Fechner, Avenarius, and Wundt took over this style of analysis in their respective psychophysics, epistemology, and cultural anthropology. With it, they could accommodate the individuation of thought for individuals or groups, accounting for the relativity of thought as a product of human habituation and programming by the conditions of their historical environment. In focusing on language as the medium for cognitive habituation, Paul added to their historical-genetic studies the realization that the systems of thought established in the individuals will themselves further influence the development of historical-cultural artifacts within the group. Studies of cultural symbols stress that the mind is not only programmed by the environment, but is also in a reciprocal relationship with it, a relationship which can enable or inhibit any cognition as a condition for survival, limiting its ontic truth value to a pragmatic one. Dilthey, late in his career, attempted to integrate a psychological criterion into his human sciences to ground the truth of an epoch in the individual's cognitive stability, maintained through the group and through the cultural environment. Brentano and Husserl acknowledged the necessity of integrating individual psychology into classical epistemology, but dismissed the psychological to a realm secondary to the question of the eidetic truth of the world of appearances. As a consequence, they assumed the constancy of mental structure, while their contemporaries emphasized a dynamic stability and world view which guides the experience of individuals instead. Both Freud and Mach emphasized such stability rather than permanency in thought patterns.

In institutional terms, the style of psychology, epistemology, and ethics which was the root of the paradigm of conceptual psychology never coalesced into an institution for modern historians of psychology to trace. Kant and Herbart never developed experiments on affect as a distorter of truth, choosing rather to discuss it as a mental tool which correlated a bundle of survival truths with which the mind would operate. Fechner, Avenarius, and Wundt addressed the broader issue of the products of the mind as correlated to affect and the survival requirements of the environment and culture. Yet they did not seriously account for the historicity of truth as a product of the transmission of human thought systems (mental habituation through cultural pattern learning), and not only as a product of the environment. They asserted these conditions without pursuing their consequences. Dilthey accommodated both the "life-world" and the individual into his descriptive psychology, yet denied a true individuation to these individuals because of his overriding assumptions about the spirit of an age as the chief condition underlying an epoch's intellectual products. Brentano and Husserl also subverted the individual while acknowledging the need to start with the empirical evidence of an individual consciousness, not a group, as Dilthey had. Their phenomenological reduction is designed to bracket the individual and remove from the field of truth those facets of individual experience which obscure the eidetic nature of the world behind appearances; they stress that all individual truths and perceptions are reducible to one truth in many refractions conditioned by history and individuality. Only Mach and Freud, in their varied studies, developed consistent overall frames for a conceptual psychology, accommodating historicity and knowledge, individuation and group influence, and the effect of thought- and sign-systems on human knowledge.

From this perspective, the work of Freud, and of later twentieth-century epistemologists such as Piaget and Foucault, must be assessed in a different light. Freud himself never sought to norm a cure for his patients, but rather worked to establish their successful functioning in their environments. In a similar move towards balance, the thrust of conceptual psychology was directed towards the description of human knowledge as a product of the human organism, human culture, history, and environment, survival requirements and habituation, and the individual's need for both stability and self-expression in dealing with the cultural and biological environments. These, then, constitute the content-model for the paradigm of nineteenth-century psychology.

The first consequence of acknowledging conceptual psychology as the underlying paradigm of nineteenth-century thought is a necessary revision of the prevailing image of epistemology in the period. Kant's work did not open only a two-pronged discussion in the sciences, focussing on objectivity versus subjectivity (ontology versus relativity of knowledge) in the face of a truth or knowledge normed by an unseeable world or never to be revealed (or even to be sought). Instead, conceptual psychology introduced a third pole into this discussion: a shift towards questions of utility, validity, and consistency within determinate frames of reference, all of which throw the scientist towards a development of models, methods, and procedures instead of a search for unassailable facts of existence. From the perspective of this three-pole model for science, work such as Nietzsche's and Marx' seems less idiosyncratic and more consistent with the nineteenth century's systematic pattern of experimentation in the human sciences.

Acknowledging conceptual psychology produces a second consequence: an altered picture of the evolution of the human sciences in Germany. Long before psychology emerged as an academic discipline, psychological considerations were discussed and applied in a broad range of disciplines, spanning the natural and pure sciences. Influences may be traced from one thinker to another through a web of institutional and professional contacts in the close German academic world, and footnotes give evidence of much wider reading habits than normally assumed today for scholars in various disciplines. The complete history of psychology and the human sciences in the nineteenth century must therefore be reassessed to accommodate both institutional and circulation criteria, that is, to accommodate personal contacts and the popular books of the day, even if they were not definitive of distinct fields.

Conceptual psychology as a case study is a history of simultaneous discoveries, communalities of method and data and commensurate goals constituting a discourse without public recognition (either at its origin or today) as an independent movement, integral despite the variety of its speakers. Each thinker subordinated his conceptual psychology to what seem to modern eyes to be different disciplines. Kant stressed pure epistemology and historiography; Herbart, mathematics; Fechner, experimental physiological psychology; Avenarius, a modified pure epistemology diverging from Kant's positions by acknowledging the relativity of conceptualization to some degree; Wundt, ethnology; Brentano and Husserl, ontology and sciences of first principles; and Dilthey, *Geistesgeschichte*, the history of ideas under the auspices of the differing spirits of ages. In this diversity of adherents, conceptual psychology did not find disciples within the German university system, for the students of each of the thinkers under consideration followed the reputation of their teachers into their main disciplines, like Heidegger who followed Husserl into ontology and helped to obscure his teacher's work in psychology. The paradigm underlying all these major disciplines -- conceptual psychology as outlined here -- did not achieve recognition as an autonomous contribution within the university. It was not granted status as an independent discourse.

Ironically, the voices who were in the intellectual position to give the definitive formulation to the program and discourse of conceptual psychology were not in the institutional positions to do so. Both Mach and Freud were partial outsiders to the academies of their fields, forced to make their reputations and conduct their researches under less than optimal conditions. When they finally reached the point of professional influence, each was diverted from their individual course: Mach by a disabling stroke which forced him to lay down his university chair, and Freud by the difficulties created by the Austrian social and medical establishments. Because of this void in leadership, the discourse of conceptual psychology was gradually supplanted by other fields with institutional support -- by Wundt's students in experimental psychology and Husserl's students in ontology and pure epistemology, by the emigree psychoanalysts as therapists, by Nietzsche through his sister's publicity campaigns which echo Dilthey's efforts to ascertain (or, in this case, create) the spirit of their age. Each of these lines of intellectual descent, however, represents only one facet of the total face of conceptual psychology as formulated by Mach and Freud, which was as a discipline accommodating the effects of history and culture, the individual and the group in a reciprocal context, and the relation of epistemology and ethics or truth criteria to perception and conceptualization.

As Foucault's work suggests, however, the more visible discourse does not necessarily have to be the one central to the episteme, to the conceptual patterns of the day which Derrida stressed that the visible discourses may exclude. The outline of conceptual psychology sketched here should call into question the assumed episteme of psychology and its related disciplines, and prompt a reevaluation of the continuities between the theories of knowledge and culture in the nineteenth and twentieth centuries.

The result of such questioning should be threefold in the context of modern humanistic thought. First, the relationship of the ontology-relativity question in philosophy and related disciplines would be brought into sharper focus with an acknowledgment of its origins and of the cultural politics which obscured its emergence into the academic disciplines. Second, such a reconceptualization would aid in breaking down the isolation currently asserted between the pragmatic sector of society and the realm of purported "pure theory." The present focus on "pragmatic solutions" as answering only to immediate problems (with little eye to the long-term implications of such "objectively necessary" solutions as cultural-historical politics) will thus be placed into a clearer juxtaposition to theory in politics, society, ecology, and ethics or law. Finally, the issues raised in examining the relativity of knowledge would be of crucial importance in establishing a conceptual basis for discourse among disparate cultures. With the sense of validity as relative to the net of thought processes of a culture, questions of right and wrong which are often damaging to open discussion may be replaced by strategies for determining the validity and variables inherent in others' positions.

1. The Case for a Reorientation in the History of Psychology

[1]Edwin G. Boring, *A History of Experimental Psychology* (New York: Appleton-Century-Crofts, 1950/57), and *Sense and Perception in the History of Experimental Psychology* (New York: Appleton-Century-Crofts, 1942). Boring had a distinct program in establishing this canon, as several scholars have noted, but this program has not hindered his work from setting a standard. See, for example, John M. O'Donnell, "The Crisis of Experimentalism in the 1920s: E.G. Boring and His Uses of History," *American Psychologist* 34, No. 4 (April 1979): 289-295, on Boring's program, and Richard P. High, "In the Image of E.G. Boring" (Review of *The First Century of Experimental Psychology*), *Journal of the History of the Behavioral Sciences*, 18, No. 1 (January 1982): 88-89, on the persistence of Boring's model.

[2]This definition of a paradigm relies on the work of Michel Foucault particularly. For a definition of Foucault's épistemè, see the essay review by David E. Leary, "Michel Foucault, An Historian of the *Sciences Humaines*," *Journal of the History of the Behavioral Sciences*, 12, No. 3 (July 1976): 286-93. Leary provides an overview of Foucault's work, while disagreeing on the utility of his innovations.

[3] For a review of the types of histories available in the mid-sixties, see Robert M. Young, "Scholarship and the History of the Behavioural Sciences," *History of Science*, 5 (1966): 1-51; he includes information on Boring and the consequences of his work.

[4]See particularly Mitchell G. Ash, "The Self-Preservation of a Discipline: History of Psychology in the United States between Pedagogy and Scholarship," which discusses "textbook histories," and Ulfried Geuter, "The Uses of History for the Shaping of a Field: Observations on German Psychology," in Loren Graham, Wolf Lepenies, and Peter Weingart, eds., *Functions and Uses of*

Disciplinary Histories (Dordrecht: D. Reidel, 1983): 143-189 and 191-228.

[5]Josef Brozek, "History of Psychology: Diversity of Approaches and Uses," *Transactions of the New York Academy of Sciences*, 31, Ser. II, No. 2 (February 1969): 115-127.

[6] "Psychology: A Prescriptive Science," *American Psychologist*, 22, No. 6 (June, 167): 435-443.

[7]For a discussion of Watson's use of "paradigm" and an example of the information constituting one, see Irving Kirsch, "Psychology's First Paradigm," *Journal of the History of the Behavioral Sciences*, 13, No. 4 (October 1977): 317-25.

[8] The best overview of the field is *Historiography of Modern Psychology*, ed. Josef Brozek and Ludwig J. Pongrantz (Toronto: C.J. Hogrefe, 1980).

[9] Bernard J. Baars, *The Cognitive Revolution in Psychology* (New York/London: Guilford Press, 1986).

[10]These are only representative voices. For some further perspectives on the uses and misuses of histories of psychology, see: William R. Woodward's review of the Graham volume (op. cit.), "Disciplinary History," *Journal of the History of the Behavioral Sciences*, 22 (July 1986): 212-4, and his "Commentary on the Symposium: The Use of History in the Social Sciences Curriculum," *Journal of the History of the Behavioral Sciences*, 18 (July 1982): 286-9; and Georg Eckhardt and Lothar Sprung, eds., *Advances in Historiography of Psychology* (Berlin: VEB Deutscher Verlag der Wissenschaften, 1983), especially Heinz Metzler, "Does a Disciplinary Change of Paradigms Exist in Psychology?" (181-6), and Michael Wertheimer, "Why We Should Study the History of Psychology" (11-25).

[11]William R. Woodward and Mitchell G. Ash, eds. *The Problematic Science: Psychology in Nineteenth-Century Thought* (New York: Praeger, 1982).

[12] Much current research explores seventeenth- and eighteenth-century psychology. See for example: Kurt Danziger, "Origins of the Schema of Stimulated Motion: Toward a Pre-History of Modern Psychology," *History of Science*, 21 (June 1983): 183-210; Karl M. Figlio, "Theories of Perception and the Physiology of Mind in the Late Eighteenth Century," *History of Science*, 12 (1975): 177-212; David E. Leary, "Berkeley's Social

Theory: Context and Development," *Journal of the History of Ideas*, 38 (1977): 635-49; David E. Leary, "The Intentions and Heritage of Descartes and Locke: Toward a Recognition of the Moral Basis of Modern Psychology," *Journal of General Psychology*: 102 (1980), 283-310; David E. Leary, "Nature, Art, and Imitation: The Wild *Boy of Aveyron as a Pivotal Case in the History of Psychology*," *Studies in Eighteenth-Century Culture*, 13 (1984): 155-172; and Roger Smith, "The Background of Physiological Psychology in Natural Philosophy," *History of Science*, 11 (June 1973): 75-123. The bibliographies in these articles can lead the reader into a field outside the scope of this volume.

[13] Aside from Boring's work, the classical histories of psychology are: Max Dessoir, *Outlines of the History of Psychology*, trans. Donald Fisher (New York: MacMillan Co., 1912); and Otto Klemm, *A History of Psychology*, trans. Emil Carl Wilm and Rudolf Pintner (New York: C. Scribner's Sons, 1914). More recent histories of note that organize their data according to schools and trends include: Thomas Hardy Leahey, *A History of Psychology: Main Currents in Psychological Thought*, 2nd ed. (Englewood Cliffs, NJ: Prentice-Hall, 1987); Gardner Murphy, *Historical Introduction to Modern Psychology*, rev. ed. (New York: Harcourt, Brace and Co., 1949); William S. Sahakian, *History and Systems of Psychology* (New York: Halsted Press/John Wiley & Sons, 1975), and *History of Psychology: A Source Book in Systematic Psychology* (Itasca, IL: F.E. Peacock, 1986); Michael Wertheimer, *A Brief History of Psychology*, rev. ed. (New York: Holt, Rinehart and Winston, 1979); and (as a 15-volume series) *Die Psychologie des 20. Jahrhunderts* (Zürich: Kindler, 1976 ff.), especially *Bd. I: Die europäische Tradition: Tendenzen, Schulen, Entwicklungslinien*, ed. Heinrich Balmer, and *Bd. II & III: Freud und die Folgen: Von der klassischen Psychoanalyse bis zur allgemeinärztlichen Psychotherapie*, ed. Dieter Eicke.

[14] Notable examples of histories of pscyhology arranged specifically around themes, and only secondarily around names or schools are: Claude E. Buxton, ed., *Points of View in the Modern History of Psychology* (Orlando: Academic Press, 1985); Robert W. Lundin, *Theories and Systems of Psychology* (Lexington, MA:

D.C. Heath & Co., 1979 [1972]); John Forrester, *Language and the Origins of Psychoanalysis* (New York: Columbia University Press, 1980); and R.W. Rieber, *Body and Mind: Past, Present, and Future* (New York: Academic Press, 1980).

[15] For an example of the former, see *History of Psychology: An Overview*, by Henryk Misiak and Virginia Staudt Sexton; for the latter, *The Unconscious before Freud*, by Lancelot Law Whyte, both cited in the bilbiography.

[16] Again, the source book for virtually all histories of psychology is Boring, *A History of Experimental Psychology* (New York: Appleton-Century-Crofts, 1957/1929). See the bibliography for a further selection of other references on the history of psychology.

[17] See John D. Lawry, *Guide to the History of Psychology* (Totowa, NJ: Littlefield, Adams, and Co., 1981): 19, for a brief sketch of Wolff's impact.

[18] For the core of Fries' work on psychology, see: Jakob Friedrich Fries, *Sämtliche Schriften, I.1: Handbuch der psychischen Anthropologie oder der Lehre von der Natur des menschlichen Geistes [1837]* (Aalen: Scientia Verlag, 1982), and *Sämtliche Schriften I.4: Neue oder anthropologische Kritik der Vernunft [1828]* (Aalen: Scientia Verlag, 1967). The importance of Fries' work as an attempt to correct Kant through biology is explained by David E. Leary in "The Psychology of Jakob Friedrich Fries (1773-1843): Its Context, Nature, and Historical Significance," *Storia e Critica della Psicologia*, 3, No. 2 (December 1982): 217-48. For general introductions of the problem of Idealism and psychology, see: Nicolas Pastore, "Reevaluation of Boring on Kantian Influence, Nineteenth Century Nativism, Gestalt Psychology and Helmholtz," *Journal of the History of the Behavioral Sciences*, 10, No. 4 (October 1974): 375-90; David E. Leary, "German Idealism and the Development of Psychology in the Nineteenth Century," *Journal of the History of Philosophy*, 18, No. 3 (July 1980): 299-317; David E. Leary, "The Philosophical Development of the Conception of Psychology in Germany, 1780-1850," *Journal of the History of the Behavioral Sciences*, 14 (1978): 113-21; and David E. Leary, *The Reconstruction of Psychology in Germany, 1780-1850*, Diss. University of Chicago, 1977.

[19] See David E. Leary, "The Historical Foundation of Herbart's Mathematization of Psychology," *Journal of the History of the Behavioral Sciences*, 16 (1980): 150-63.

[20] *Microcosmus: An Essay Concerning Man and His Relation to the World*, trans. Elizabeth Hamilton and E.E. Constance Jones, 4th ed. (New York: Scribner and Welford, 1890). See also the essay by William R. Woodward, "From Association to Gestalt: The Fate of Hermann Lotze's Theory of Spatial Perception, 1846-1920," *Isis*, 69, No. 249 (December 1978): 572-82.

[21] For the definitive presentation of Gall's work, see Robert M. Young, "The Functions of the Brain: Gall to Ferrier (1808-1886)," *Isis*, 59, No. 198 (Fall 1968): 250-268, and *Brain, Mind, and Adaptation in the Nineteenth Century: Cerebral Localization and its Biological Context from Gall To Ferrier* (Oxford: Clarendon Press, 1970).

[22] For information on the organization of the German university, see: Mitchell G. Ash, "Academic Politics in the History of Science: Experimental Psychology in Germany, 1879-1941," *Central European History*, 13, No. 3 (September 1980): 255-86; and R. Steven Turner, "University Reformers and Professional Scholarship in Germany 1760-1806," in *The University in Society, Vol. II*, ed. Lawrence Stone (Princeton: Princeton University Press, 1974): 495-531.

[23] See again Mitchell and Turner, as well as Joseph Ben-David, *The Scientist's Role in Society: A Comparative Study* (Englewood Cliffs: Prentice-Hall, 1971), especially "German Scientific Hegemony and the Emergence of Organized Science," 108-131.

[24] Turner says that, because of the "research imperative" of the time, medical chairs often paid better.

[25] Of the historians cited, Boring divides his history by field, Sahakian by geographically-separated schools, Murphy by schools and fields, Wetheimer by schools, and Baars by areas. For a more complete survey of the older histories, see Robert M. Young, "Scholarship and the History of the Behavioural Sciences," op. cit.

[26] See John Theodore Merz, *A History of European Thought in the Nineteenth Century*, 4 vols. (Edinburgh and London: William Blackwood & Sons, 1904-1912), especially the work on Kant and Lotze in Chapter 11 (591 ff.) and on Wundt in Chapter 12 (Vol. 4).

[27] See also William R. Woodward, "From Association to Gestalt."

[28] Literature on Wundt is copious, and some will be discussed below. For an introduction, see William R. Woodward, "Wundt's Program for the New Psychology," in his *The Problematic Science*, op. cit.

[29] This undervalution is beginning to be remedied. See, for example, Mitchell G. Ash, *The Emergence of Gestalt Theory: Experimental Psychology in Germany, 1890-1920*, Diss. Harvard, 1982, and "Gestalt Psychology: Origins in Germany and Reception in the United States," in *Points of View in the Modern History of Psychology*, ed. Buxton, op. cit., 295-344.

[30] William James' work on psychology will not be considered here, but it is important to note that the structure of his volume on psychology strongly resembles the proponents of the conceptual psychology outlined here, particularly Wundt, Hermann Paul, and Mach, in his account of the development of higher-order thought out of lower. For information on James, see particularly William R. Woodward, "William James's Psychology of Will: Its Revolutionary Impact on American Psychology," in *Explorations in the History of Psychology in the United States*, ed. Josef Brozek (Lewisburg: Bucknell University Press, 1984): 148-195.

[31] See David Lindenfeld, *The Transformation of Positivism: Alexius Meinong and European Thought, 1880-1920* (Berkeley: University of California, 1980).

[32] See John J. Sullivan on "Franz Brentano and the Problems of Intentionality," in *Historical Roots of Contemporary Psychology*, ed. Benjamin B. Wolman (New York: Harper & Row, 1968): 248-74.

[33] For an introduction to Husserl's work, see *Phenomenology: The Philosophy of Edmund Husserl and Its Interpretation*, ed. Joseph J. Kockelmans (Garden City: Anchor/Doubleday, 1967).

[34] See the work by Mitchell G. Ash on Gestalt psychology, op. cit.

[35] Boring, *History of Experimental Psychology*, p. 379.

[36] Some alterations in this canon are beginning to arise, as indicated in earlier notes. Moreover, work on the early twentieth century is causing a reassessment: see, for example, Siegfried Jaeger and Irmingard Staeuble, *Die gesellschaftliche Genese der*

Psychologie (Frankfurt: Campus, 1978), and Goeffrey Cocks, *Psychotherapy in the Third Reich: The Göring Institute* (Oxford: Oxford University Press, 1985).

2. Counterproposition: Psychology as Discourse

[1] Two books on Wilhelm Griesinger are examples of attempts to correct such assumptions by placing their subject in his natural context. See Bettina Wahrig-Schmidt, *Der junge Wilhelm Griesinger im Spannungsfeld zwischen Philosophie und Physiologie* (Tübingen: Gunter Narr, 1985), and Gerlof Verwey, *Psychiatry in an Anthropological and Biomedical Context* (Dordrecht: D. Reidel, 1985). For Griesinger's original, see *Medical Pathology and Therapeutics* (New York: William Wood & Co., 1882 [1865]).

[2] For an overview of the post-structuralists' work, see Richard Harland, *Superstructuralism: The Philosophy of Structuralism and Post-Structuralism* (London: Methuen, 1987); for an introduction to the *Annales* historians, including Fernand Braudel, see *The Return of Grand Theory in the Human Sciences*, ed. Quentin Skinner (Cambridge: Cambridge University Press, 1985).

[3] The term "discourse" refers to the developments in linguistics of the last ten years; see Michael Stubbs, *Discourse Analysis: The Sociolinguistic Analysis of Natural Language* (Chicago: University of Chicago Press, 1983). The perspectives of discourse analysis stress the inter-sentential aspects of communication, as introduced first in the notion of the linguistic sign by Ferdinand de Saussure. For an introduction to the history of linguistics, see Arthur L. Blumenthal, *Language and Psychology: Historical Aspects of Psycholinguistics* (New York: John Wiley & Sons, 1970).

[4] For an example of discourse approaches to the sociology of knowledge, stressing the influences of groups on knowledge, see Jaeger and Staeuble, op. cit., and Pierre Bourdieu, "The Field of Cultural Production, Or: The Economic World Reversed," *Poetics*, 12 (1983): 311-356.

[5] The literature on the French post-structuralists and psychoanalysts is growing rapidly as the translations of major

works become available. See also Foucault's *The Birth of the Clinic: An Archaeology of Medical Perception*, trans. A.M. Sheridan Smith (New York: Vintage/Random House, 1975 [1963]), and *Madness and Civilization: A History of Insanity in the Age of Reason*, trans. Richard Howard (New York: Vintage/Random House, 1965 [1961]). On Foucault, see also Charles C. Lemert and Garth Gillan, *Michel Foucault: Social Theory and Transgression* (New York: Columbia University Press, 1982), which has an appendix of Foucault's terminology.

[6] Jacques Derrida, *Writing and Difference* (Chicago: University of Chicago, 1978) [=SW in text].

[7] Paul Ricoeur, *Freud and Philosophy: An Essay on Interpretation*, trans. Denis Savage (New Haven: Yale University Press, 1970) [originally in French as "the Terry Lectures" = FP in text].

[8] Most prominently, Jacques Lacan, *Écrits: A Selection* (New York: Norton, 1977).

[9] Michel Foucault, *The Archaeology of Knowledge* (New York: Harper and Row, 1972) [=AK in text].

[10] For Lacan, see also: *Speech and Language in Psychoanalysis*, trans. and commentary by Anthony Wilden (Baltimore: The Johns Hopkins University Press, 1968), and *Returning to Freud: Clinical Psychoanalysis in the School of Lacan*, trans. and ed. by Stuart Schneiderman (New Haven: Yale University Press, 1980). On Lacan as a public figure and teacher, see Stuart Schneiderman, *Jacques Lacan: The Death of an Intellectual Hero* (Cambridge, MA: Harvard University Press, 1983), and Catherine Clément, *The Lives and Legends of Jacques Lacan*, trans. Arthur Goldhammer (New York: Columbia University Press, 1983). For introductions into Lacan's work, see Ellie Ragland-Sullivan, *Jacques Lacan and the Philosophy of Psychoanalysis* (Urbana: University of Illinois Press, 1986), and Jane Gallop, *The Daughter's Seduction: Feminism and Psychoanalysis* (Ithaca: Cornell University Press, 1982) and *Reading Lacan* (Ithaca: Cornell University Press, 1985).

[11] Other than a linguistic expansion of the post-structuralist model, there is also a psychoanalytic extension. Treatments of the relationships between Lacan's work and other fields of note are

Shoshana Felman, *Jacques Lacan and the Adventure of Insight: Psychoanalysis in Contemporary Culture* (Cambridge, MA: Harvard University Press, 1987), and Joseph H. Smith and William Kerrigan, eds., *Interpreting Lacan* (New Haven: Yale University Press, 1983) [= Psychiatry and the Humanities, Vol. 6]. The work of Julia Kristeva draws on both post-structuralism and Lacan to speak of relationships between speech, power, and self-identification. See for an introduction: Toril Moi, ed. *The Kristeva Reader* (New York: Columbia University Press, 1986), and Toril Moi, *Sexual/Textual Politics: Feminist Literary Theory* (London: Methuen, 1985). See also: Julia Kristeva, *Revolution in Poetic Language*, trans. Margaret Waller (New York: Columbia University Press, 1984), and *Powers of Horror: An Essay on Abjection*, trans. Leon S. Roudiez (New York: Columbia University Press, 1982).

[12] John Forrester, *Language and the Origins of Psychoanalysis*, op. cit.

[13] It is true that the *Project* was not published, and so had no influence. This is, however, not the issue in the determination of a discourse paradigm, which argues typicality instead of overt influence. As another example, the biological paradigm presented in Sulloway's *Freud: Biologist of the Mind* (to be discussed below) was not a position for Freud, the neurologist, to overcome, but rather served as an avenue for Freud to accommodate a historical-genetic aspect of the paradigm in which he was working. The *Project* was not isolated; it was accompanied by a set of papers in metapsychology which were presumed lost until a draft for one was rediscovered and published as: Sigmund Freud, *Übersicht der Übertragungsneurosen: Ein bisher unbekanntes Manuskript*, ed. Ilse Grubrich-Simitis (Frankfurt/M: S. Fischer, 1985); and *A Phylogenetic Fantasy: Overview of the Transference Neuroses*, trans. Axel Hoffer and Peter T. Hoffer (Cambridge, MA: Belknap/Harvard University Press, 1987).

[14] This aspect of Freud's work had been noted by Mach, the early behaviorists, and perhaps Piaget. See William R. Woodward, "The 'Discovery' of Social Behaviorism and Social Learning Theory, 1870-1980," *American Psychologist*, 37, No. 4 (April 1982): 396-410.

[15] Sigmund, Freud, *The Interpretation of Dreams*, Vols. 4 and

5 in *The Standard Edition of the Complete Psychological Works of Sigmund Freud* (London: Hogarth Press, 1953); "Project for a Scientific Psychology" in *The Origins of Psycho-Analysis: Letters to Wilhelm Fliess, Drafts and Notes: 1887-1902* (New York: Basic Books, 1954): 347-446 [=OPA in text].

[16] It is possible that Freud turned further to ego psychology and social psychology in his late works under the influence of his students and colleagues, such as *The Ego and the Id* (1923). Representative for early ego psychology is Anna Freud, *The Ego and the Mechanisms of Defense* (New York: International Universities Press, 1966 [1936 in German]); for a more socially-oriented ego psychology, Erik H. Erikson, *Identity and the Life Cycle* (New York: International Universities Press, 1959). A second trend of the time that may have influenced Freud is the ever-widening split between psychology, psychoanalysis, and psychophysiology. Representive of the latter would be Lotze, William James, James Ward (c.f. *Psychological Principles* [Cambridge: Cambridge University Press, 1918], especially for Ward's critique of Kant on the grounds of immediate experience), and Theodule Ribot in France (c.f. *The Diseases of Personality* [Chicago: Open Court, 1910; 1884/91 in French]; *The Psychology of Attention* [Chicago: Open Court, 1903 {1890}]; and *La Psychologie Allemande contemporaraine [École expérimentale]* [Paris: Germer Bailliére, 1885]; and an essay introducing his work by Daniel N. Robinson in *The Mind Unfolded: Essays on Psychology's Historic Texts* [Washington, D.C.: University Publications of America, 1978]: 275-292), and F.E. Beneke in Germany (*Die neue Psychologie* [Berlin: Mittler, 1845]). These psychologists were interested in a more physiological approach to mind, especially in constructing higher-order thought out of sense impressions.

[17] Jacques Derrida, *Of Grammatology* (Baltimore: The Johns Hopkins University Press, 1976) [=GR in text].

[18] See J.T. Merz, *A History of European Thought in the Nineteenth Century* (op. cit.) or Alfred Kelly, *The Descent of Darwin: The Polularization of Darwinism in Germany, 1860-1914* (Chapel Hill: University of North Carolina Press, 1981), for suggestions that biological and cultural metaphors arose in proximity in the nineteenth century.

[19] For specific bibliography on each of these authors, see below in the chapters dedicated to them.

[20] Michel Foucault, "History of Systems of Thought" in *Language, Counter-Memory, Practice: Selected Essays and Interviews* (Ithaca: Cornell University Press, 1977) [=HST in text].

[21] For an overview of the most modern canon of nineteenth-century psychology, adding Dilthey and Spranger to more familiar names, see *Die Psychologie des 20. Jahrhunderts, Bd.I: Die europäische Tradition*, ed. Balmer (op. cit.).

[22] Frank J. Sulloway, *Freud: Biologist of the Mind* (New York: Basic Books, 1979): 87 [=BM in text].

[23] Ernst Mach may have achieved the role of psychologist-practicioner in his *Popular-Scientific Lectures*, discussed below. The closest Freud came was in his analysis of Leonardo.

[24] Included on the reprinted frontispiece of *The Interpretation of Dreams* in the *Standard Edition*; discussed by Freud in a letter to Fliess of 4 Dec. 1896 (OPA, 172).

[25] This cover-up did not go unnoticed. See Philip Rieff's *Freud: The Mind of the Moralist* (Chicago: University of Chicago Press, 1979 [1959, 1961]), in which he stresses that Freud did not abandon physiology. Moreover, Freud used the idea of cultural conflicts as a basis to seek the genetic causes of mental illness -- a historical approach that was underplayed in the descriptions of neuroses, at least. See also Rieff's student Edwin R. Wallace IV, *Historiography and Causation in Psychoanalysis: An Essay on Psychoanalytic and Historical Epistemology* (Hillsdale, NJ: Analytic Press/Lawrence Erlbaum, 1985).

[26] Most are cited above; see also Adolf Trendelenburg, *Geschichte der Kategorienlehre* (Hildesheim: Georg Olms, 1963 [1846]), who redoes Kant's table of categories to accommodate biological categories such as feelings and apperception.

[27] See particularly Kristeva, cited above, Luce Irigaray, *This Sex Which Is Not One*, trans. Catherine Porter (Ithaca: Cornell University Press, 1985 [1977]), and Gilles Deleuze and Félix Guattari, *Anti-Oedipus: Capitalism and Schizophrenia*, trans. Robert Hurley, Mark Seem, and Helen R. Lane (Minneapolis: University of Minnesota Press, 1983 [*L'Anti-Oedipe*, 1972]).

[28]See Martin Jay, *The Dialectical Imagination: A History of the Frankfurt School and the Institute of Social Research, 1923-1950* (Boston: Little, Brown, & Co., 1973); Alexander Mitscherlich, *Society without the Father: A Contribution to Social Psychology*, trans. Eric Mosbacher (New York: Harcourt, Brace & World, 1969 [1963], and *Massenpsychologie ohne Ressentiment: Soziologische Betrachtungen* (Frankfurt/M: Suhrkamp, 1972); *The Essential Frankfurt School Reader*, eds. Andrew Arato and Eike Gebhardt (New York: Continuum, 1982); and Wolf Lepenies and Helmut Nolte, *Kritik der Anthropologie* (München: Carl Hanser Verlag, 1971).

3. Kant and Herbart: The Initiation of Conceptual Psychology

[1]The literature on Kant's *Critiques* is voluminous, if not oceanic. Perhaps the classic overview is that by Ernst Cassirer, *Kant's Life and Thought* (New Haven: Yale University Press, 1981 [1918]); a more modern treatment, particularly significant in light of its acknowledgment of both a formal and a material logic running through the *Critiques*, is that by Thomas Kaehao Swing, *Kant's Transcendental Logic* (New Haven and London: Yale University Press, 1969).

[2] For older evaluations of the position of Kant as a psychologist, see Max Dessoir, *Geschichte der neueren deutschen Psychologie*, 2nd ed. (Berlin: Carl Duncker, 1902), and *Outlines of the History of Psychology*, trans. Donald Fisher (New York: MacMillan, 1912). A more modern overview of Kant's position is offered in the work of David E. Leary, *The Reconstruction of Psychology in Germany, 1780-1850* (Diss. University of Chicago, 1977), and follow-up articles, "The Psychological Development of the Conception of Psychology in Germany, 1780-1850," *Journal of the History of the Behavioral Sciences*, 14 (1978): 113-121, and "Immanuel Kant and the Development of Modern Psychology," in Woodward and Ash, eds., *The Problematic Science* (op. cit.). The position of psychology in the face of Idealism is presented by Leary in a further article, "German Idealism and the Development of Psychology in the Nineteenth Century," *Journal of the History of Philosophy*, 18, No. 3 (July 1980): 299-317. A discussion of one

representative late-nineteenth-century reception of Transcendental Idealism in psychology is Winich de Schmidt, *Psychologie und Transzendentalphilosophie: Zur Psychologie-Rezeption bei Hermann Cohen und Paul Natorp* (Bonn: Bouvier, 1976). A readable popularization of main figures in nineteenth-century psychology, including chapters on Kant/Helmholtz, Wundt, and Freud is Raymond E. Francher, *Pioneers of Psychology* (New York: Norton, 1979).

[3] Psychological considerations also enter into the *Critiques*, but the *Anthropology* is the text which systematically approaches the field as a pragmatic science. The *Anthropology* will serve as the key to Kant's psychology here, even though it is a lesser text in Kant's corpus. From the point of view of a paradigm, such a choice is valid: Kant was between paradigms with his "Copernican Revolution," and so various of his works are more or less representative for either the old or new paradigms and discourses. We maintain here that the *Anthropology* is the text which most clearly represents not only the new paradigm initiated by Kant, but also the new discourse which it forms.

[4] J.G. Herder was probably the stimulus who turned Kant towards a consideration of history. See the history of terms like "Bürger" in Otto Brunner, Werner Conze, and Reinhart Koselleck, eds., *Geschichtliche Grundbegriffe: Historisches Lexikon zur politisch-sozialen Sprache in Deutschland* (Stuttgart: Ernst Klett, 1972 ff. [not yet complete]).

[5] Herbart, who enjoyed a renaissance in American educational psychology around the turn of the century (with a concomitant flood of book-length discussions of his work and its applications), remains a little-discussed figure today. Of general use as background is the biography and work-discussion by Harold B. Dunkel, *Herbart and Education* (New York: Random House, 1969), and a discussion of his effects in Germany: Bernhard Schwenk, *Das Herbartverständnis der Herbartianer* (Weinheim/ Bergstr.: Julius Beltz, 1963). The *Text-Book in Psychology* was translated as part of this renaissance by Margaret K. Smith (New York: Appleton, 1891).

[6] These statements stress the paradigm rather than traditional scholarship on "Idealist psychology," which tends to stress the teleological aspects of the model which Kant inherited rather than

his particular novelty. On descriptions of this teleology from an eighteenth-century perspective, see James Ward, *A Study of Kant* (Cambridge: University Press, 1922), John D. McFarland, *Kant's Concept of Teleology* (Edinburgh: University Press, 1970), and Reinhard Löw, *Philosophie des Lebendigen: Der Begriff des Organischen bei Kant, sein Grund und seine Aktualität* (Frankfurt: n.p., 1980). Together with Leary on Kant (op. cit.), all three assert almost a scholastic version of teleology and human history, ignoring the dimension of social intercourse which Kant's ethics stressed. In so doing, they portray Kant's model of the mind as more formalistic than it need be. Two recent books have done much to correct this formalism by stressing the degree to which Kant adopted a biological metaphor: Eve-Marie Engels, *Die Teleologie des Lebendigen* (Berlin: Duncker & Humblot, 1982), and Timothy Lenoir, *The Strategy of Life: Teleology and Mechanics in Nineteenth Century German Biology* (Dordrecht: D. Reidel, 1982). Both texts add proximate causation to the teleological model Kant used -- Engels, as an organic causation, and Lenoir with a "teleo-mechanist" approach to life sciences in the period. The effect of these additions is to add an empirical (mechanist) dimension to the traditionally assumed teleological model for the Enlightenment, arguing that Kant knew biologists of his time. The effect of these additions is to make a psychology possible which still cannot use mathematics on the soul, but which can relate the biology of the body to the individual soul. We will assert here that this is the joint Empiricist-Idealist model that Kant actually was working with in the *Anthropology*, and that is at the basis of the nineteenth-century paradigm for conceptual psychology.

[7] Citations in the presents discussion have been modified from the English translation by M.J. Gregor of Immanuel Kant, *Anthropology from a Pragmatic Point of View* (The Hague: Nijhoff, 1974), on the basis of the German edition by Karl Vorländer of Immanuel Kant, *Anthropologie in pragmatischer Hinsicht* 7th ed., Philosophische Bibliothek, Bd. 44 (Hamburg: Felix Meiner, 1980). References in the text are cited as (KA) plus the page number from the English edition. For recent secondary literature, see the introduction by Joachim Kopper in the Vorländer edition.

[8] Cited in Vorländer edition, p. 336.

[9] Cited in Vorländer edition, p. 340.

[10] Cited in Vorländer edition, p. 347.

[11] Particularly Mach, an acknowledged Kantian, will adopt this stance for the starting point of his investigations.

[12] This is, however, the model which Gerlof Verwey stresses as the background for Wilhelm Griesinger's work (op. cit.).

[13] Wilhelm Griesinger discusses mental illness in these terms, as deficient processing affecting an individual's interface with the environment.

[14] This anticipates the communication model which Karl-Otto Apel attributes to Kant in "Von Kant zu Peirce: Die semiotische Transformation der transzendentalen Logik," in *Transformation der Philosophie* (Frankfurt/M.: Suhrkamp, 1973): 157-177, and in other essays.

[15] It is well-known that Kant rejected the possibility that psychology is a science, since mathematics could not be applied to the soul (see Leary, op. cit.). However, this is not what we are speaking of here. Psychology in the new paradigm becomes a cultural science: a synthesis of history and systematics. Herbart will add mathematics not to the investigation of the soul, but rather to a study of the senses and their receptivity to data.

[16] In a model positing a telos for mental development, the analysis of data is no longer neutral, due to presetting the direction in which data is associated. A telos presets any sorting strategies and many of the activities of mind used on the data. This remained an obstacle to the purely scientific orientation of Kant's theory. For further discussions of teleology, see Lenoir, *The Strategy of Life*, cited above.

[17] Johann Friedrich Herbart, *Lehrbuch zur Psychologie* in: *Sämtliche Werke*, Karl Kehrbach and Otto Flügel, eds., Bd. 4 (Aalen: Scientia Verlag, 1964) [= L in text]; *Psychologie als Wissenschaft neu gegründet auf Erfahrung: Erster synthetischer Theil*, in: *Sämtliche Werke*, Bd. 5; *Zweiter analytischer Theil*, in: *Sämtliche Werke*, Bd. 6 [=PaW in text]. For an overview of Herbart's work in English, see also: Harold B. Dunkel, *Herbart and Herbartianism: An Educational Ghost Story* (Chicago: University of Chicago Press, 1970).

[18] Older treatments of Herbart (e.g., Flügel, Dessoir, Klemm) deal with Herbart as a metaphysician. David Leary, in "The Historical Foundation of Herbart's Mathematization of Psychology," *Journal of the History of the Behavioral Sciences*, 16 (1980): 150-63, agrees with the present discussion that Herbart's program derives from Kant's, while still placing Herbart in the Idealist tradition, following Leibniz and Wolff. This tradition will explain Herbart's turn to mathematics, but it will not explain the affinity of his psychology with educational psychology. That educational psychology has a pronounced social dimension, commensurate with the post-Idealist paradigm we are positing here.

[19] The term "series" is often used in speaking of psychophysics, but I will keep to the usage "series-form" because of its Gestalt connotations.

[20] Usually "Kraft" is rendered as "force" before Helmholtz. I am using "energy" instead for the visual impact of the metaphors involved.

[21] Freud's contributions will be discussed below in a separate chapter.

[22] This use of survival is pre-evolutionary, resembling more closely Piaget's sense of necessary operations for mental operations.

[23] J. Ben-David argues for a hybrid between physiology and philosophy. However, this switch toward a process model is also crucial for the new paradigm.

[24] The term comes from Lenoir, op. cit.

[25] See William R. Woodward on "From Association to Gestalt" and on Fechner (discussed below) for examples of combining physiology and psychology to overcome these problems.

[26] This is a full relativizing of the mental processes, anticipating Nietzsche and the solipcism in Max Stirner's *Der Einzige und sein Eigentum*. See also Brunner, Conze and Koselleck, eds., *Geschichtliche Grundbegriffe*, op. cit.

4. Empiricism and Conceptual Psychology: Psychophysics and Philology

[1] Gustav Theodor Fechner, *Elemente der Psychophysik*, 3. Auf. (Leipzig: Breitkopf und Hartel, 1907 [1859/60, 1888]) [= ElP in text].

[2] Richard Avenarius, *Kritik der reinen Erfahrung*, 3rd Ed., Vol I (Leipzig: O.R. Reisland, 1921 [1908]) [= KrE in text].

[3] Wilhelm Wundt, *Völkerpsychologie: Eine Untersuchung der Entwicklungsgesetze von Sprache, Mythus und Sitte*, Bd. I & II, *Die Sprache*, 3rd ed. (Aalen: Scientia, 1975 [1911/12, 1900]) [= V in text]. An older translation exists, which was not used due to limited availability: *Elements of Folk Psychology: Outline of a Psychological History of the Development of Mankind*, trans. Edward Leroy Schaub (London: George Allen and Unwin; New York: MacMillan, 1916).

[4] Hermann Paul, *Prinzipien der Sprachgeschichte*, 6th ed. (Tübingen: Max Niemeyer, 1960 [2nd ed., 1886]) [= PS in text].

[5] Wilhelm Wundt, *Grundriß der Psychologie*, 15th ed. (Leipzig: Alfred Kröner, 1922 [1896]) [= GrP in text]. For a translation of the *Outlines of Psychology*, see C.H. Judd, trans. (Leipzig: Wilhelm Engelman, 1897; New York: Steckert, 1897). This is but one of a series of textbooks that Wundt published in his career.

[6] For a general overview of Fechner's work and influence, see J.C. Flügel, *A Hundred Years of Psychology*, 2nd ed. (London: Duckworth, 1951), esp. II.3 and III.6.

[7] For a biography and overview of the work of Fechner, see Max Wentscher, *Fechner und Lotze*, Geschichte der Philosophie in Einzeldarstellungen, Bd. 36 (München: Ernst Reinhardt, 1925). See also "Gustav Theodor Fechner: Rede zur Feier seines 100-jährigen Geburtstages," given by Wilhelm Wundt (Leipzig: Wilhelm Engelmann, 1901), and G. Stanley Hall, *Founders of Modern Psychology* (New York: D. Appleton, 1912), who has chapters on both Fechner and Wundt. A feuilleton reaction to Fechner's work, particularly his vitalism or world mysticism is

provided by Wilhelm Bölsche, *Hinter der Weltstadt: Friedrichs-hagener Gedanken zur ästhetischen Kultur* (Jena, Leipzig: Eugen Diederichs, 1912). Harold [actually "Harald"] Höffding includes Fechner in his *Brief History of Modern Philosophy*, trans. Charles Finley Sanders (New York: MacMillan, 1931 [1912]), although not in his *Modern Philosophers*, trans. Alfred C. Mason (London: MacMillan & Co., 1915 [1902]), which stresses Wundt instead. For more modern treatments of Fechner, see Richard Lowry, *The Evolution of Psychological Theory: 1650 to the Present* (Chicago/New York: Aldine/Atherton, 1971), especially   pp. 90-109, "Psychophysics and the 'New Psychology;'" William R. Woodward, "Fechner's Panpsychism: A Scientific Solution to the Mind-Body Problem," *Journal of the History of the Behavioral Sciences*, 8, No. 4 (October 1972): 367-86, particularly on the early Fechner; M.E. Marshall, "G.T. Fechner: Premises Toward a General Theory of Organisms [1823]," *Journal of the History of the Behavioral Sciences*, 10, No. 4 (October 1974): 438-47, and "William James, Gustav Fechner, and the Question of Dogs and Cats in the Library," *Journal of the History of the Behavioral Sciences*, 10, No. 3 (July 1974): 304-12.

[8] Literature on Avenarius' work is rare, yet one readable overview exists: Wendell T. Bush, *Avenarius and the Standpoint of Pure Experience* (diss. Columbia; New York: The Science Press, 1905). Kurt Danziger, in "The Positivist Repudiation of Wundt," *Journal of the History of the Behavioral Sciences*, 15, No. 3 (July 1979): 205-230, mentions Avenarius briefly, along with Dilthey.

[9] This is not Darwinism, because survival values include group decisions. The term as used today was nowhere near as well-defined in the nineteenth century. See Peter J. Bowler, *The Eclipse of Darwin: Anti-Darwinian Evolution Theories in the Decades around 1900* (Baltimore: The Johns Hopkins University Press, 1983), for an outline of variants available.

[10] For an overview of Wundt's career, see Raymond E. Fancher, *Pioneers of Psychology* (New York: Norton, 1979), Chapter 4, "Psychology in the University: Wilhelm Wundt and William James." For a focus on Wundt's pupils and influence, see J.C. Flügel, *A Hundred Years of Psychology*, esp. III.8 and III.11. For an introduction into Wundt, see Wolfgang G.

Bringmann, William D.G. Balance, and Rand B. Evens, "Wilhelm Wundt 1832-1920: A Brief Biographical Sketch," *Journal of the History of the Behavioral Sciences*, 11, No. 3 (July 1975): 287-97.

[11] Mitchell G. Ash, in "Wilhelm Wundt and Oswald Külpe on the Institutional Status of Psychology: An Academic Controversy in Historical Context," *Wundt Studies*, eds. W.G. Bringmann and Ryan D. Tweney, (Toronto: Hogrefe, 1980): 396-421, explains some of the institutional problems that have arisen in considering Wundt's contribution. Arthur L. Blumenthal attributes Titchener with turning Wundt into an introspectionist ("Wilhelm Wundt -- Problems of Interpretation," *Wundt Studies*: 435-45); he also asserts that Wundt was much more the cultural psychologist than is normally asserted, in part due to the mistranslations of central Wundtian terms ("Wilhelm Wundt: Psychology as the Propaedeutic Science," 19-50 in Bruxton, op. cit.), and stresses the *Grundriß* as the core of cultural psychology, as will be done here. Richard J. Anderson echoes the attribution of Titchener as the one who altered Wundt's image: "The Untranslated Content of Wundt's *Grundzüge der physiologischen Psychologie*," *Journal of the History of the Behavioral Sciences*, 11, No. 4 (Oct. 1975): 381-86.

[12] Kurt Danziger has led in placing Wundt in a broader historical context, including Kant, Herbart, Leibniz, Fechner, and historical linguists such as Herder and Steinthal. See: "The History of Introspection Reconsidered," *Journal of the History of the Behavioral Sciences*, 16, No. 3 (July 1980): 241-262; "Origins and Basic Principles of Wundt's Völkerpsychologie," *British Journal of Social Psychiatry*, 22 (1983): 303-313; "The Positivist Repudiation of Wundt," *Journal of the History of the Behavioral Sciences*, 15, No. 3 (July 1979): 205-230; "Wilhelm Wundt and the Emergence of Experimental Psychology," *Companion to the History of Modern Science*, eds. G.N. Carter, J.R.R. Christie, M.J.S. Hodge, and R.C. Olby (Chicago: University of Chicago, 1987); "Wundt as Methodologist," *Advances in Historiography of Psychology*, eds. G. Eckardt and L. Sprung (op. cit): 33-42; and two essays, "Wundt and the Two Traditions in Psychology," and "Wundt's Theory of Behavior and Volition," in *Wilhelm Wundt and the Making of a Scientific Psychology*, ed. Robert W. Rieber (New York: Plenum Press, 1980): 73-88; 89-116.

[13] In this context, see also David E. Leary, "Wundt and After: Psychology's Shifting Relations with the Natural Sciences, Social Sciences, and Philosophy," *Journal of the History of the Behavioral Sciences*, 15 (1979): 231-41, who argues for Wundt's work as a hybrid of natural and social sciences. For a description of one of Wundt's chief innovations, see Thomas H. Leahey, "Something Old, Something New: Attention in Wundt and Modern Cognitive Psychology," *Journal of the History of the Behavioral Sciences*, 15, No. 3 (July 1979): 242-52.

[14] For "A Bibliography of the Scientific Writings of Wilhelm Wundt" up to 1905, see E.B. Titchener and L.R. Geissler, *American Journal of Psychology*, 19 (October 1908): 541-556. For essays and bibliographies on not only Wundt, but also Kant, Herbart, and Brentano, see Benjamin B. Wolman, ed., *Historical Roots of Contemporary Psychology* (New York: Harper and Row, 1968). Early overviews of Wundt's work are: Edmund König, *Wilhelm Wundt als Psycholog und als Philosoph* (Stuttgart: Fr. Fromanns Verlag (E. Hauff), 1902); Willi Nef, *Die Philosophie Wilhelm Wundts* (Leipzig: Felix Meiner, 1923); and Arthur Hoffmann-Erfurt, ed., *Wilhelm Wundt: Eine Würdigung* (Erfurt: Kurt Stenger, 1924). For the centennial of the founding of his laboratory, a series of publications about Wundt were published: R.W. Rieber, ed., *Wilhelm Wundt and the Making of a Scientific Psychology* (New York and London: Plenum Press, 1980); Alfred Arnold, *Wilhelm Wundt: Sein philosophisches System* (Berlin: Akademie, 1980); and Daniel N. Robinson, *Toward a Science of Human Nature: Essays on the Psychologies of Mill, Hegel, Wundt, and James* (New York: Columbia University Press, 1982).

[15] As Wundt defines these terms:

> Because each psychic construct is composed of a multiplicity of elementary processes which neither all begin nor stop exactly in the same moment, the constellation which binds the elements into a whole thus in general also extends beyond it, so that various simultaneous and successive constructs will again be bound to each other, even if loosely. We call this broader constellation of psychic processes *consciousness*.

The concept consciousness accordingly designates nothing which would be present aside from mental processes. . . . its meaning is that it expresses that general relation of spiritual experiences, from which the individual constructs are distinguished as more focused relations. (GrP, 246)

[16] Wundt's definitions are:

The state characterized by idiosyncratic feelings, which accompanies a clearer conceptualization of mental content, we will term *attention*; the singular process, through which any mental content is brought to clearer conceptualization, *apperception*. We oppose the other conceptualizations of contents (without the accompanying state of attention) by *perception*. (GrP, 252)

[17] Wundt defines these as:

The constellation of mental processes which constitute the essence of consciousness has its final source in the *relational processes* which continually take place among the elements of single contents of consciousness. (GrP, 270)

In order to have brief expressions for these differences at our disposal, we will designate the relations which form in a passive state of consciousness as *associations*; those which presuppose an active state, *apperceptive relations*. (GrP, 271)

. . . therefore the *apperceptive* relations are conceived as coming to being *directly through the participation of attention*. (GrP, 307)

[18] Again, following Wundt:

[*Amalgamations*] are followed on the next level by those simultaneous associations which consist in the change of given mental constructs through the effects of elements in other constructs: we call these *assimilations*, after the elementary processes taking place in them. In addition, one adds then the generally similarly *simultaneous associations of mental constructs from disparate regions of the senses* -- already named by Herbart "*complexes*." On these follow finally the associations of mental constructs in a *temporal series*: we designate these as *successive associations*, the easiest to observe and, therefore, originally the only forms taken into account. (GrP, 274-75)

[The concept of causality] originates from the need of our thought to order all experiences given to us according to reasons and consequences, and, wherever the construction of a constellation without contradiction in this meets with resistances, to remove these through secondary explanatory concepts, occasionally of a hypothetical nature. (GrP, 386)

[19] As Wundt defines it:

The *principle of mental resultants* finds expression in the fact that each mental construct manifests characteristics, which, to be sure, after they are give, can be comprehended out of the characteristics of its elements, but which can equally not by any means be considered as the mere sum of the characteristics of its elements. (GrP, 398)

[20] Defined by Wundt as follows:

The *principle of mental relations* forms a supplement to that of the resultants, in that it connects not to the relation of the components of a mental constellation to the content-values expressed in these, but to the relation of the single components to each other. Just as the principle of resultants applies to synthetic relations of consciousness, so, therefore, does that of relations for the analytical processes of consciousness. Each dissection of a content of consciousness into single members, such as already takes place during the successive conceptualization of the parts of a whole (first represented only generally) in sense perception and associations, and then in clear and conscious form in the articulation of the total

representations, is an act of relational analysis. (GrP, 401)
[21] Wundt's definitions are:

The *principle of mental constants* is again a supplement to
that of the relations. For, like it, it relates to the relations of
mental constants to each other. It itself, though, is based
on the fundamental differentiation stemming from the
conditions of mental development -- a differentiation of
immediate contents of experience into objective and
subjective, in which the latter encompass all those elements
and connections of elements which (like feelings and
affects) appear as essential components of the *processes of
will*. Because these subjective contents of experience all
order themselves according to contrasts, these contrasts
follow at the same time in their alternation the general *law
of the intensification of contrasts*. (GrP, 402)

[22] Alternate translations of "Völkerpsychologie" are "folk
psychology" and "the psychology of culture." The objections to
the first of these are obvious; the second alternative sounds too
much like empiricism, and so we will retain the coinage
"psychology of peoples." This will avoid associations of Wundt's
work with strict physiology or empiricism, such as it is represented
in "Scientific and Philosophical Psychology: A Historical
Introduction," by Theodore Mischel, in *Human Action: Conceptual
and Empirical Issues*, ed. Mischel (New York: Academic Press,
1969): 1-40; this essay tends to ignore the reciprocal effects
between the environment and the group that my coinage is intended
to suggest.

[23] See again Danziger, especially "Origins and Basic
Principles of Wundt's Völkerpsychologie," op. cit., and the article
by James in R.W. Rieber, op. cit.

[24] Secondary literature on Paul outside of the realm of
philology is rare. One early evidence of his influence is H. A.
Strong, W. S. Logeman, and B. I. Wheeler, *Introduction to the
Study of the History of Language* (London: Longmans, Green, and
Co., 1891). The best introduction to the Neogrammarians is
Winfred P. Lehmann, ed., *A Reader in Nineteenth-Century*

Historical Indo-European Linguistics (Bloomington: Indiana University Press, 1967), which includes introductions and translations of important texts. Hans Arens, *Sprachwissenschaft* (op. cit.), does the same thing (with alternate selections) in German. The selections included in Arthur L. Blumenthal, *Language and Psychology: Historical Aspects of Psycholinguistics* (op. cit.), introduce Paul as a disciple of Wundt, which unfortunately does not correspond to the chains of influence in philology in the second half of the nineteenth century. For a discussion of the interrelations of philology and psychology in the latter nineteenth century, see Elizabeth Knoll, "The Science of Language and the Evolution of Mind: Max Müller's Quarrel with Darwinism," *Journal of the History of the Behavioral Sciences*, 22 (January 1986): 3-22.

[25] This parallels the definition of language as a means for social communication found in George H. Mead, *Mind, Self, and Society from the Standpoint of a Social Behaviorist* (Chicago: University of Chicago Press, 1934), esp. pp. 14 ff. In *Movements of Thought in the Nineteenth Century* (Chicago: University of Chicago Press, 1936), Mead draws in this definition of society as a set of individuals in communication, relying indirectly on the Neogrammarians. In both cases, however, Mead is not interested in the feedback between individuals and culture, but only in the link of individual minds the group.

[26] Comparative grammars were established in the early nineteenth century on the basis of analogies with Greek and Latin forms, which violate the principle of not dealing with grammatical forms as if they were realities in themselves.

[27] In the opposite situation, the verb forms for common verbs such as "to be" retain the most irregular forms in Western languages, probably because they are used with such great frequency so that their forms never become regularized.

[28] Wundt's work still had academic recognition, in the organismic school at Leipzig, well into the twentieth century. The vector was Felix Krüger; see Ulfried Geuter, *D i e Professionalisierung der deutschen Psychologie im National-sozialismus* (Frankfurt: Suhrkamp, 1984). This school, however, did not pursue Wundt's cultural work in a way which significantly

effected the humanities.

[29] See, particularly, the article by William R. Woodward in *The Problematic Science*, op. cit.

[30] For an account of de Saussure's position in the development of nineteenth-century philology, see E.F.K. Koerner, *Ferdinand de Saussure: Origin and Development of his Linguistic Theory in Western Studies of Language* (diss. Vancouver, B.C.: Simon Fraser University, 1971).

5. Dilthey and Descriptive Psychology

[1] For a discussion of the therapeutic psychology of the nineteenth century, see Henri F. Ellenberger, *The Discovery of the Unconscious: The History and Evolution of Dynamic Psychiatry* (New York: Basic Books, 1970).

[2] Richard Avenarius, *Kritik der reinen Erfahrung*, op. cit.; Johann Gottfried Herbart, *Werke*, eds. Kehrbach and Flügel (Aalen: Scientia Verlag, 1964), esp. vols. 1 and 2; Wilhelm von Humboldt, "Über die innere und äußere Organisation der höheren wissenschaftlichen Anstalten in Berlin," *Gesammelte Schriften*, vol. 10 (Berlin: 1903-36); Hermann Paul, *Principien der Sprachgeschichte*, op. cit.; Ernst Mach, *Erkenntnis und Irrtum: Skizzen zu einer Psychologie der Forschung* (Leipzig: J.A. Barth, 1905); Hermann von Helmholtz, *Schriften zur Erkenntnistheorie*, eds. Paul Hertz and Moritz Schlick (Berlin: Julius Springer, 1921).

[3] For the most famous example, see Ernst Mach, *Die Analyse der Empfindungen, und das Verhältnis des Physischen zum Psychischen*, 2nd ed. (Jena: Gustav Fischer, 1900).

[4] August Boeckh, *Encyklopädie und Methodologie der philologischen Wissenschaften*, 2nd ed. (Leipzig: Teubner, 1886).

[5] Boeckh: 77: "Wenn wir der Hermeneutik die Aufgabe zugewiesen haben, die Gegenstände an sich zu verstehen . . . in seiner eigenen Natur zu verstehen . . . "

[6] Boeckh: 77: "Die Aufgabe der Kritik ist also nicht, einen Gegenstand an sich, sondern das Verhältnis zwischen mehreren Gegenständen zu verstehen."

[7] For an overview of hermeneutics as a discipline, see Peter

Szondi, *Einführung in die literarische Hermeneutik* (Frankfurt/M.: Suhrkamp, 1975), and Otto Pöggler, ed., *Hermeneutische Philosophie* (München: Nymphenburger, 1972). For an introduction in English, see the introduction to *The Hermeneutics Reader*, ed. Kurt Mueller-Vollmer (New York: Continuum, 1985).

[8] For an overview and bibliography on the work of Wilhelm Dilthey, see Kurt Mueller-Vollmer, *Towards a Phenomenological Theory of Literature: A Study of Wilhelm Dilthey's 'Poetik'* (The Hague: Mouton, 1963), and Ilse Bulhof, *Wilhelm Dilthey: A Hermeneutic Approach to the Study of History and Culture* (The Hague: Martinus Nijhoff, 1980). For comments on the relationship between Dilthey and the psychologists of his age, see Mitchell G. Ash, "Academic Politics in the History of Science: Experimental Psychology in Germany, 1879-1941," op. cit.

[9] Mitchell G. Ash, especially p. 269 ff., calls this essay "Descriptive and Analytic" psychology. Original German title: *Ideen über eine beschreibende und zergliedernde Psychologie* [=IP in text], in *Gesammelte Schriften*, V. Bd. (Leipzig: Teubner, 1924 [1894]); the translations in this essay are by the present author.

[10] For an overview of the tenets of associationism as Dilthey would probably have known it, see Max Dessoir, *Geschichte der neueren deutschen Psychologie* (Berlin: Carl Duncker, 1902): I, 393; for a discussion of Empiricism, see Dessoir, *Outline of the History of Psychology* (New York: Macmillan, 1912).

[11] In each of these contexts, the structure of the mind has been the focus of explications, and not specifically the interaction of mind and world; in consequence, the conceptualization of 'world' operative in each system grants a precedent to the existence of mind structure.

[12] *Geistesgeschichte* is "history of ideas" as practiced by Dilthey and his students, focused around the leading idea of an epoch under consideration.

[13] In *Gesammelte Schriften*, Bd. V (Leipzig: Teubner, 1924 [1895/65]).

[14] Jakob Burckhardt, *Die Kultur der Renaissance in Italien* 15th ed. (Leipzig: A. Kröner, 1926).

6. Phenomenology and Conceptual Psychology

[1] For a biography and overview of the work of Franz Brentano, along with an assessment of his influence on his time (especially as compared to Wundt), see Antos C. Rancurello, *A Study of Franz Brentano: His Psychological Standpoint and His Significance in the History of Psychology* (New York: Academic Press, 1968), which includes an extensive annotated bibliography. For an overview of the history of interpretations of Brentano's work up to quite recently, see the selection and bibliography compiled by Linda L. McAlister, ed., *The Philosophy of Brentano* (Atlantic Highlands, NJ: Humanities Press, 1977). For a study comparing major terminology in the work of Brentano and Freud, see James Ralph Barclay, *Franz Brentano and Sigmund Freud: A Comparative Study in the Evolution of Psychological Thought* (diss., U. of Michigan, 1959). For two more recent studies, see Raymond E. Francher, "Brentano's *Psychology from an Empirical Standpoint* and Freud's Early Metapsychology," *Journal of the History of the Behavioral Sciences*, 13, No. 3 (July 1977): 207-227, and David E. Leary, "From Act Psychology to Probabilistic Functionalism: The Place of Egon Brunswik in the History of Psychology," in *Psychology in Twentieth-Century Thought and Society*, eds. Mitchell G. Ash and William R. Woodward (New York: Cambridge University Press, 1987), who traces the influence of Brentano as a functionalist and logical positivist.

[2] For an overview of older scholarship of Husserl, including discussions of Husserl's psychology by Jean-Paul Sartre and Maurice Merleau-Ponty, see Joseph J. Kockelmans, ed., *Phenomenology: The Philosophy of Edmund Husserl and Its Interpretation* (Garden City: Doubleday/Anchor, 1967). For an overview of the interpretations of Husserl's *Logical Investigations* see J.N. Mohanty, ed., *Readings on Edmund Husserl's "Logical Investigations"* (The Hague: Martinus Nijhoff, 1977). A discussion of Brentano's and Husserl's work as it pertains to the social sciences is by Maurice Roche, *Phenomenology, Language and the Social Sciences* (London and Boston: Routledge and Kegan Paul, 1973). For an overview of the literature on the central problem in Husserl research, see Harrison Hall, "The Philosophical

Significance of Husserl's Theory of Intentionality," *Journal of the British Society for Phenomenology*, Vol. 13, No. 1 (January 1982): 79-84.

[3] See Edmund Husserl, *Vorlesungen zur Phänomenologie des inneren Zeitbewußtseins*, ed. Martin Heidegger, 2nd ed. (Tübingen: M. Niemeyer, 1980); and Franz Brentano, *Philosophische Untersuchungen zu Zeit, Raum und Kontinuum*, eds. A. Kastil, S. Körner, and R. Christholm (Hamburg: Meiner, 1976).

[4] Franz Brentano, *Psychology from an Empirical Standpoint*, ed. Linda L. McAlister, (London: Routledge and Kegan Paul, 1973; New York: Humanities Press, 1973), translated from the fullest extant edition, *Psychologie vom empirischen Standpunkte*, ed. Oskar Kraus, (Hamburg: Felix Meiner, 1924/1955) [=PES in text]; Edmund Husserl, *Phenomenological Psychology: Lectures, Summer Semester, 1925*, trans. John Scanlon (The Hague: Martinus Nijhoff, 1977) from the *Phänomenologische Psychologie: Vorlesungen Sommersemester 1925* [=Husserliana, Bd. IX], ed. Walter Biemel (Den Haag: Martinus Nijhoff, 1962) [=PhP in text]. Husserl's most extensive statement of the *position of psychology with respect to phenomenology is found in The Crisis of European Sciences and Transcendental Phenomenology*, trans. David Carr (Evanston: Northwestern University Press, 1970 [1954]), a work in progress from 1934 to Husserl's death in 1938. Details vary from the presentation in the *Phenomenological Psychology*, but not the fundamental positions of the two disciplines.

[5] For general discussions of Brentano's work by his students, see Oskar Kraus mit Carl Stumpf und Edmund Husserl, *Franz Brentano: Zur Kenntnis seines Lebens und seiner Lehre* (München: C.H. Beck, 1919), and Alfred Kastil, *Die Philosophie Franz Brentanos: Eine Einführung in seine Lehre* (München; Leo Lehnen, 1951). For discussions of his later influence, see Howard O. Eaton, *The Austrian Philosophy of Values* (Norman: University of Oklahoma Press, 1930); Gustav Bergman, *Realism: A Critique of Brentano and Meinong* (Madison: University of Wisconsin, 1967); Jan Srzednicki, *Franz Brentano's Analysis of Truth*, (The Hague: Martinus Nijhoff, 1965); and Linda L. McAlister, *The Development of Franz Brentano's Ethics* (Amsterdam: Editions Rodope, 1982 [1968]). For an overview of work on Husserl, see:

Hermann Noack, ed., *Husserl, Wege der Forschung*, XL (Darmstadt: Wissenschaftliche Buchgesellschaft, 1973), for research up to the mid-50's; Jan M. Broekman, *Phänomenologie und Egologie: Faktisches und transcendentales Ego bei Edmund Husserl* (Den Haag: Martinus Nijhoff, 1963), for a comparison with Kant; Gaston Berger, *The 'Cogito' in Husserl's Philosophy* (Evanston: Northwestern University Press, 1972), esp. Chapter 6 on "Husserl, Kant, and Descartes" and the annotated bibliography; Joseph J. Kockelmans, *Edmund Husserl's Phenomenological Psychology: A Historico-Critical Study* (Atlantic Highlands, NJ: Humanities Press, 1978 [1967]), including a brief history of psychology with Herbart, Wundt, Dilthey and Brentano; Herman Drüe, *Edmund Husserl's System der phänomenologischen Psychologie* (Berlin: W. de Gruyter, 1963); Georg Misch, *Lebensphilosophie und Phänomenologie: Eine Auseinandersetzung der Dilthey'schen Richtung mit Heidegger und Husserl*, 2. Aufl. (Leipzig: B.G. Teubner, 1931).

[6] This is the stance represented in Martin Heidegger, *Being and Time*, trans. John Macquarrie and Edward Robinson (New York: Harper & Row, 1962 [1927]).

[7] See Ludwig Wittgenstein, *The Blue and Brown Books: Preliminary Studies for the "Philosophical Investigations"* (New York: Harper & Row, 1958).

[8] This again parallels the differentiation Heidegger will make between ontological statuses of objects, such as "Vorhandenheit" and "Zuhandenheit."

[9] See William R. Woodward on "Fechner's Panpsychism," op. cit.

[10] Husserl and Heidegger also left this out. Individual mind is not interesting to them.

[11] Again, his contemporaries in conceptual psychology tie these together under the rubric of utility.

[12] This also constitutes a reduction in the description of language as described by Paul, making it derivative and individual, ignoring communication with the group.

[13] This is an alternative notion of objectivity, locating it behind thought, instead of tying it into environment through an intensity of presentation. For developments in this vein, see Lotze's *Logik*

and *Mikrokosmos*, op. cit., and Hans Sluga's explication of logical objects in his book, *Gottlob Frege* (London: Routledge and Kegen Paul, 1980).

[14] For other studies on Husserl's extensive program, see: Marvin Farber, ed., *Philosophical Essays in Memory of Edmund Husserl* (Cambridge, MA: Harvard, 1940; rpt. New York: Greenwood Press, 1968); Aron Gurwitsch, *Phenomenology and the Theory of Science* (Evanston: Northwestern University Press, 1974); Theodor de Boer, *The Development of Husserl's Thought* (The Hague: Martinus Nijhoff, 1978 [1966]), especially on Husserl's derivations from Brentano; Iso Kern, *Husserl und Kant: Eine Untersuchung über Husserls Verhältnis zu Kant und zum Neukantismus* (Den Haag: Martinus Nijhoff, 1964), especially on Paul Natorp; Guido de Almeida, *Sinn und Inhalt in der genetischen Phänomenologie E. Husserls* (Den Haag: Martinus Nijhoff, 1972), especially on hyletics; Paul Ricoeur, *Husserl: An Analysis of his Phenomenology* (Evanston: Northwestern University Press, 1967); Alwin Diemer, *Edmund Husserl: Versuch einer systematischen Darstellung seiner Phänomenologie* (Meisenheim am Glan: Anton Hain, 1956); Jacques Derrida, *Edmund Husserl's Origin of Geometry": An Introduction* (Stony Brook, NY: Nicolas Hays, 1978); Anna-Teresa Tymieniecka, ed., *Soul and Body in Husserlian Phenomenology: Man and Nature* (Dordrecht, Holland: D. Reidel, 1983); Donn Welton, *The Origins of Meaning: A Critical Study of the Thresholds of Husserlian Phenomenology* (The Hague: Martinus Nijhoff, 1983); William R. McKenna, *Husserl's "Introductions to Phenomenology": Interpretation and Critique* (The Hague: Martinus Nijhoff, 1982); and David Woodruff Smith and Ronald McIntyre, *Husserl and Intentionality: A Study of Mind, Meaning, and Language* (Dordrecht, Holland: D. Reidel, 1982).

[15] For the clearest definition of the phenomenological reduction, see Husserl's *The Idea of Phenomenology*, trans. William P. Alston and George Nakhnikian (The Hague: Martinus Nijhoff, 1973).

7. Mach's Psychology of Investigation and the Limits of Science

[1] For overviews of the work of Mach, see: Erwin Hiebert, "An

Appraisal of the Work of Ernst Mach: Scientist-Historian-Philosopher," in *Motion and Time, Space and Matter: Interrelations in the History of Philosophy and Science*, Peter K. Machamer and Robert G. Turnbull, eds. (Columbus: Ohio State University Press, 1976): 360-89; John T. Blackmore, *Ernst Mach: His Work, Life, and Influence* (Berkeley: University of California Press, 1972); Jürgen Blühdorn and Joachim Ritter, eds., *Positivismus im 19. Jahrhundert: Beiträge zu seiner geschichtlichen und systematischen Bedeutung*, Studien zur Philosophie und Literatur des 19. Jahrhunderts, Bd. 16 (Frankfurt/Main: V. Klostermann, 1971); J. Hintikka, ed., "A Symposium on Ernst Mach," *Synthese*, 18 (1968): 132-301. The basic bibliography, supplemented by Blackmore's work, is that by Joachim Thiele, "Ernst-Mach-Bibliographie," *Centaurus*, 8 (1963): 189-237.

[2] For Mach's use of history see: Erwin Hiebert, "Mach's Philosophical Use of the History of Science," In: *Historical and Philosophical Perspectives of Science*, Roger H. Stuewer, ed., Minnesota Studies in the Philosophy of Science, V (Minneapolis: University of Minnesota Press, 1970): 184-203.

[3] For accounts of Mach's position as a scientist see especially: Albert Einstein, "Zur Enthüllung von Ernst Mach's Denkmal," *Neue Freie Presse* (Wien), 12 June 1926, Morgenblatt, p. 11; J. Bradley, *Mach's Philosophy of Science*, (London: Athlone Press of the University of London, 1971); P.W. Bridgman, "Significance of the Mach Principle," *American Journal of Physics*, 29, No. 1 (January 1961): 32-36; Erwin Hiebert, *The Concept of Thermodynamics in the Scientific Thought of Mach and Planck*, Wissenschaftlicher Bericht, 5/68 (Freiburg/Br.: Ernst-Mach-Institut, 1968); Gerald Holton, "Mach, Einstein, and the Search for Reality," *Daedalus*, 97, No. 2 (Spring 1968): 636-73; Richard von Mises, *Ernst Mach und die empiristische Wissenschaftsauffassung: Zu E. Machs 100. Geburtstag am 18. Feb. 1938*, *Einheitswissenschaft*, Heft 7 (s'Gravenhage: Verlag W.P. van Stockum & Zoon, 1938); Laurens Lauden, "The Methodological Foundations of Mach's Anti-Atomism and their Historical Roots," in *Motion and Time, Space and Matter*, Peter K. Machamer and Robert G. Turnbull, eds. (Columbus: Ohio State University Press, 1976); and Floyd Ratliff, *Mach Bands: Quantitative Studies on Neural Networks in the Retina* (San Francisco: Holden-Day,

1965), which also contains a useful biographical sketch.

[4] From its inception, "The Monist" was a vehicle for Mach's thought. Aside from publishing translations of parts of his works, "The Monist" printed a steady series of articles on Mach, some notable ones being: Paul Carus, "The Origin of Mind," *Monist*, 1 No. 1 (Oct, 1890): 69-86; Hans Kleinpeter, "On the Monism of Professor Mach," *Monist*, 16, No. 2 (Apr. 1906): 161-68; Philip E.B. Jourdain, "The Economy of Thought," *Monist*, 24, No. 1 (Jan. 1914): 134-45; Bertrand Russell, "On the Nature of Acquaintance," *Monist*, 24, No. 1 (Jan. 1914): 1-16, "On the Nature of Acquaintance, II: Neutral Monism," *Monist*, 24, No. 2 (April 1914): 161-87, and "On the Nature of Acquaintance, III: Analysis of Experience," *Monist*, 24, No. 3 (July 1914): 435-53.

[5] For an idea of the influence Mach had on his contemporaries, see: Joachim Thiele, "Zur Wirkungsgeschichte der Schriften Ernst Machs," *Zeitschrift für philosophische Forschung*, 20 (1966); Joachim Thiele, *Wissenschaftliche Kommunikation: Die Korrespondenz Ernst Machs* (Kastellaum: A. Henn Verlag, 1978); and Katherine Arens, *Fundamentalism and Fin de siècle: Fritz Mauthner's Critique of Language*, op. cit.

[6] See particularly Mach's late work, *Kultur und Mechanik* (Stuttgart: W. Spemann, 1915), for his concept of the interactions between technology and civilization.

[7] See "Einige vergleichende tier- und menschenpsychologische Skizzen," *Naturwissenschaftliche Wochenschrift* (Jena), 31 (N.F. 15), No. 17 (23 April 1916): 241-47, for an example of his biological thought; also *Populär-wissenschaftliche Vorlesungen*, 4. Aufl. (Leipzig: J.A. Barth, 1910). The term "biologist of the mind" refers to the title of a book on Freud to be discussed in the next chapter.

[8] Such practical demonstrations constitute the core of the *Populär-wissenschaftliche Vorlesungen.*

[9] The majority of Mach studies do treat him as an epistemologist, however, on different grounds than the present discussion uses; see, for example: Max Adler, "Mach and Marx: Ein Beitrag zur Kritik des modernen Positivismus," *Archiv für Sozialwissenschaft und Sozialpolitik*, 33 (1911): 348-400; Peter Alexander, "Ernst Mach," in *Encyclopedia of Philosophy*, V (New

York: MacMillan, 1967): 115-19; Herbert Buzello, *Kritische Untersuchung von Ernst Machs Erkenntnistheorie, Kantstudien,* Ergänzungheft 23 (1911); Robert S. Cohen and Raymond J. Seeger, eds., *Ernst Mach, Physicist and Philosopher,* Boston Studies in the Philosophy of Science, Vol. 6 (Dordrecht, Holland: D. Reidel, 1970); Alfonsina D'Elia, *Ernst Mach,* Pubblicazioni della Facolta di lettere e filosofia dell'Universita di Milano, 59 (Firenza: La nuova Italia, 1971); Karl Gerhards, *Machs Erkenntnistheorie und der Realismus* (Stuttgart: W. Spemann, 1914); Edmund Husserl, *Logische Untersuchungen, 1. Band: Prolegomena zur reinen Logik,* Husserliana, Bd. XVIII, ed. E. Holenstein (Den Haag: Martinus Nijhoff, 1975): esp.196-213; Hermann Lübbe, "Positivismus und Phänomenologie (Mach und Husserl)," in *Beiträge zur Philosophie und Wissenschaft: Wilhelm Szilasi zum 70. Geburtstag* (München: n.p., 1960): 161-84.

[10] See the biographical sketch in Floyd Ratliff, *Mach Bands* (op. cit.), and Friedrich Herneck, "Ernst Mach: Eine bisher unveröffentlichte Autobiographie," *Physikalische Blätter,* 14, Heft 9 (1958): 385-90; the later editions of the *Populär-wissenschaftliche Vorlesungen* contain papers on these topics.

[11] See particularly Einstein's own eulogy for Mach (op. cit.).

[12] See particularly the acoustical essays in the *Populär-Wissenschaftliche Vorlesungen.* For information on Helmholtz, see Erna Lesky, *The Vienna Medical School of the Nineteenth Century* (Baltimore: The Johns Hopkins University Press, 1976).

[13] It is instructive to note that Husserl felt he had to distance his own program from Mach's; see Joachim Thiele, "Ein Brief Edmund Husserls an Ernst Mach," *Zeitschrift für philosophische Forschung,* 19 (1965): 134-39.

[14] The clearest proof of this omission is the virtually total silence about the *Popular Scientific Lectures* in the seconary literature on Mach. Occasionally they are drawn on for supporting material, but the volume is never given credence as part of Mach's central program.

[15] On this text, see particularly: Erwin Hiebert, trans., "Introduction," *Ernst Mach: Knowledge and Error -- Sketches on the Psychology of Enquiry* (Dordrecht, Holland, and Boston: D.

Reidel Publishing Co., 1976); and W. Grosse, "Die psychologischen Grundlagen der Erkenntnis (Über Machs "Erkenntnis und Irrtum")," *Deutsche Literaturzeitung*, 27, No. 47 (24 Nov. 1906): 2925-32, and 27, No. 48 (1 Dec. 1906): 2989-96. The title *The Analysis of the Sensations and the Relation of the Physical to the Psychic* refers to the original *Die Analyse der Empfindungen, und das Verhältnis des Physischen zum Psychischen*; citations in the present chapter are from the "2., verm. Auflage" (Jena: Gustav Fischer, 1900), and are my translations [=AS in text]. The original German title of *Knowledge and Error* is *Erkenntnis und Irrtum: Skizzen zu einer Psychologie der Forschung* (Leipzig: J.A. Barth, 1905); citations used in the present discussion are translated for this situation and are taken from the 1906 second edition of that work [= KE in text].

[16] See the eulogy written by Albert Einstein about Mach, which acknowledges the influence of Mach's work.

[17] Mach discussed thought-experiments in a chapter of *Erkenntnis und Irrtum*, "Über Gedankenexperimente" (pp. 180-97).

[18] The "theory of elements" (*Elementenlehre*) comprises the body of *Die Analyse der Empfindungen*. The core delineation made by Mach is that among three distinct sets of data, or "elements of the sensation," on which our knowledge is based: α, β, γ, ... (moods, desires, and the like); A, B, C, ... (the elements designated as "the outside world"); and K, L, M, ... (the subset of the elements of the outside world designated as our personal body). All sets are, however, provisory, and subject to shift; they do not reflect the absolute constitution of the world, they are contingent on the point of view of observer and the direction or goal of interest (cf. particularly pp. 6-8).

[19] See the entries in Thiele's bibliography. Most notable thereafter are: "Ernst-Mach-Symposium" and *Positivismus im 19. Jahrhundert*, both cited above, and Manfred Diersch, *Empiriokritizismus und Impressionismus* (Berlin: Rütten und Loening, 1973).

[20] See Hermann Bahr, "Das unrettbare Ich" and "Die Philosophie des Impressionismus," in *Dialog vom Tragischen* (Berlin: S. Fischer, 1904): 79-101 and 102-114.

[21] For a statement of the influence of Mach on Edmund Husserl, see: *Logische Untersuchungen, Erster Band: Prolegomena zur reinen Logik,* Husserliana, Bd. XVIII, ed. E. Holenstein (Den Haag: M. Nijhoff, 1975): 196-213; Joachim Thiele, "Zur Wirkungsgeschichte der Schriften Ernst Machs," *Zeitschrift für philosophische Forschung* (Munich), 20 (1966): 118-130; and "Ein Brief Edmund Husserls an Ernst Mach," ed. Joachim Thiele, *Zeitschrift für philosophische Forschung,* 19 (1965): 134-38.

[22] Mach gave series of lectures in both cities, which were collected as an ever-expanding volume called *Populär-Wissenschaftliche Vorlesungen,* which ran into 5 editions (5th ed., Leipzig, J.A. Barth, 1923).

[23] A selection of his textbooks are: *Compendium der Physik für Mediciner* (Wien: W. Braumüller, 1863); *Leitfaden der Physik für Studierende,* with Gustav Jaumann (Prague and Vienna: Tempsky, 1891); *Grundriß der Naturlehre für die unteren Classen der Mittelschulen,* with Joh. Odstrcil (Prague: Tempsky, 1887); *Grundriß der Physik für die höheren Schulen des Deutschen Reiches* (Leipzig: G. Freytag, 1893); and *Lehrbuch der Physik für das Gymnasium* (Leipzig: G. Freytag, 1894).

[24] For a useful biographical sketch on Mach, see "Ernst Mach: Eine bisher unveröfentlichte Autobiographie," ed. Fr. Herneck, *Physikalische Blätter* 14.9 (1958): 385-90; and a short sketch in Floyd Ratliff, *Mach Bands: Quantitative Studies on Neural Networks in the Retina* (San Francisco: Holden-Day, 1965): 14 [for Prague era].

[25] For a sketch of Mach's work on the Doppler effect, see Ratliff, p. 11; on optics, Ratliff, p. 13.

[26] This discussion is in the initial chapters of *Die Principien der Wärmelehre: Historisch-kritisch entwickelt* (Leipzig: 1896).

[27] These correspond to chapter titles in the history volumes. Cf. *Die Mechanik in ihrer Entwicklung historisch-kritisch dargestellt* (Leipzig: J.A. Barth, 1896); *Die Geschichte und die Wurzel des Satzes von der Erhaltung der Arbeit* (Prag: Calve, 1872); *Die Prinzipien der physikalischen Optik: Historisch und erkenntnispsychologisch entwickelt* (Leipzig: J.A. Barth, 1921).

[28] The first edition of the *Analysis of the Sensations* was published in 1886; the second, 1900; the third, 1902; the fourth,

1903; the fifth, 1906; the sixth, 1911; the seventh, 1918; the eighth, 1919. All editions through the sixth were designated "expanded." This publishing history indicates an upswing in popularity for Mach's work after the turn of the century.

[29] See Bahr, "Das unrettbare Ich." Bahr is chosen as a representative of a very popular cause at the turn of the cnetury. For other presentations about the relativity of the ego, see also Robert S. Cohen, and Erwin Hiebert, op. cit., and *Erkenntnis oder Dogmatismus: Kritik des psychologischen "Dogmatismus"-Konzepts*, eds. Peter Keiler and Michael Stadler (Köln: Pahl-Rugenstein, 1978).

[30] In the *Analysis*, Mach states: "Das Ich ist unrettbar" (p. 17); in the 4th edition, he adds: "Ein isoliertes Ich gibt es ebensowenig, als ein isoliertes Ding. *Ding* and *Ich* sind provisorische Fiktionen gleicher Art" (p. 15). ["There is no more an isolated "I" than there is an isolated thing. *Thing* and *I* are provisory fictions of the same type."]

[31] The "feuilleton" in European newspapers is akin to satirical editorials in American papers, aimed at stirring the sentiments of readers while marginally informing them.

[32] "Preliminary Anti-Metaphysical Remarks" is the title of the initial chapter of the *Analysis of the Sensations*.

[33] See Franz Brentano, *Psychologie vom empirischen Standpunkt*, vol. 1 [no vol. 2 appeared] (Leipzig: Duncker and Humblot, 1874).

[34] For a concise exposition of the program of phenomenology in its classic formulation, see Edmund Husserl, *The Idea of Phenomenology* (The Hague: Martinus Nijhoff, 1973).

[35] Husserl, in *Idea*, outlines his program of "the sciences of cognition" on page 1.

[36] For a more detailed discussion of the "theory of elements," see again Katherine M. Arens, *Functionalism and Fin de siècle*.

[37] This is also not identical with what has been come to be known as "neutral monism," since Mach explicitly allows for the historical relativity of cognition in a way that the monists deny.

[38] In this, Mach shows he is an avowed Kantian, like Fries and Lotze of earlier generations.

[39] For a more complete definition of the original program of

monism, see particularly the work of Paul Carus, esp. "The Origin of Mind," *Monist*, 1, No. 1 (Oct. 1890): 69-86, which defines the desiderata for a unified scientific methodology to apply to descriptions in any systematic discipline.

[40] Jean Piaget, *Genetic Epistemology* (New York: Norton, 1971).

[41] See Piaget, *Genetic Epistemology*, Chapter 2, for a discussion of "operative thought" and "operations" related to systematic knowledge.

[42] Again, this is similar to Fechner's work, but expanded because the observer remains in Mach's focus.

[43] This parallels Kant's differentiations between the realms of understanding and reason: one is analytic, and the other essentially speculative. This is the essence of a scientific pragmatism, picked up by many of the nineteenth-century Kantians, among them Fries and Lotze.

[44] Robert Cohen stresses that advancement is equivalent to adaptation; see his essay in the volume he edited, op. cit.

[45] This is a stance also adopted by Hans Vaihinger, in his *Philosophie des Als-Ob*.

[46] "Healthy thought" is Mach's term for the economic and stable thought patterns which aid the orientation of an organism to the world.

[47] See Wilhelm Dilthey, *The Crisis of European Sciences and Transcendental Phenomenology* (Evanston: Northwestern University Press, 1970) for a definition of a human science as a systematic discipline of principles, with recreatability and verifiability.

[48] For an overview of Dilthey's program, especially with reference to poetics/aesthetics, see Kurt Mueller-Vollmer, *Towards a Phenomenological Theory of Literature* (The Hague: Mouton, 1963). Otto Neurath and the Vienna School attempt to enact Mach's program to a limited degree, see Viktor Kraft, *The Vienna Circle*, trans. Arthur Pap (New York: n.p., 1953). For Mach's influence in psychology, see also Kurt Danziger, "The Positivist Repudiation of Wundt," op. cit.

[49] The Vienna Circle seemed to be a typical reaction. They tried to remove cultural influence from notation.

[50] For this situation, see Arens, *Functionalism and fin de siècle*, as it outlines the prevailing tendencies of the time.

[51] Mach states in the foreword that his aims were "erkenntnis-psychologisch" ("dealing with the psychology of perception"), and concludes: "Maybe even philosophers will at some time recognize in my undertaking a philosophical explication of the methodology of the natural sciences, and will meet me a step further from their side" (p.ix).

[52] From one perspective, his pervasive assumptions about the relation of physical data and the structure of the psyche resemble the tenets of psychophysics as described by Gustav Fechner (see first Max Dessoir, *Outlines of the History of Psychology* [New York: Macmillan, 1912]: 251, and the section on Fechner above), focusing on the study of nerve excitation as it relates to sensations and to physical stimuli. However, Fechner's work was not concentrated on higher-order thought as it influenced individual mind, but only as products of mind.

[53] Mach acknowledged that his thought was profoundly influenced by a reading of Kant's *Prolegomena*; see "Ernst Mach: Eine bisher unveröffentlichte Autobiographie," by Fr. Herneck, *Physikalische Blätter*, 14, No. 9 (1958): 387.

[54] "Wahrscheinlichkeit" is normally translated as "probability" (see Hiebert's translation of *Knowledge and Error*). Here, however, that translation is inadequate to Mach's purpose of differentiating what might be ontologically real (and hence subject to probability of existence) from what is utilitarian in a particular frame (and hence what *seems* real in accounting for a determinate frame of reference). See also the essay by Lorraine Daston on "The Theory of Will versus the Science of Mind," in Woodward and Ash, eds., *The Problematic Science*, for a description of associationism, which also uses this term.

[55] This is Mach's residual Kantianism and not "realism" in any technical sense.

[56] This summary is drawn up with reference to J.B. Stallo, *The Concepts and Theories of Modern Physics* (1882), for which Mach wrote the foreword to the German edition in 1901.

[57] This definition is provided in *Course in General Linguistics* (New York: McGraw-Hill, 1966): Part One, I.

[58] On thought experiments, see Laurens Laudens, "The Methodological Foundations of Mach's Anti-Atomism and Their Historical Roots," in *Motion and Time, Space and Matter: Interrelations in the History of Philosophy and Science,* Peter K. Machamer and Robert G. Turnbull, eds. (Columbus: Ohio State University Press, 1976): 390-417.

[59] These, then, correspond loosely to induction and deduction in general logic.

[60] The *Logics* of Wundt (1880) and Lotze (1874) did this as well.

[61] The term is used first in relation to the work of Wilhelm Dilthey and his followers; the more modern "science of culture" is represented in the work of the French, particularly Jacques Derrida, *Of Grammatology* (Baltimore: The Johns Hopkins University Press, 1976), and Michel Foucault, *The Archaeology of Knowledge* (New York: Harper, 1972).

[62]For a model of Darwinism appropriate to psychology, see Robert J. Richards, "Natural Selection and Other Models in the Historiography of Science," in *Scientific Inquiry and the Social Sciences,* Marilynn B. Brewer and Barry E. Collins, eds. (San Francisco: Jossey-Bass, 1981): 37-76, and "A Defense of Evolutionary Ethics," *Biology and Philosophy,* 1 (1986): 265-293.

8. Freud: The Psychology of Psychoanalysis

[1] This alludes to the case of Jeffrey Masson versus K.R. Eissler and the Freud Archives, as reported under the title "Annals of Scholarship: Trouble in the Archives, I and II," *The New Yorker,* 5 Dec. 1983, pp. 59 ff., and 12 Dec. 1983, pp. 60 ff. This is, to be sure, a popularized account which nonetheless is archetypical for the strident tones occurring in Freudian debates. The literature on these debates is voluminous and no effort at completeness is made in the present study, but a valuable overview is provided by Eckart Wiesenhütter, *Freud und seine Kritiker* (Darmstadt: Wissenschaftliche Buchgesellschaft, 1974); see also K.R. Eissler, *Talent and Genius: A Psychoanalytic Reply to a Defamation of Freud* (New York: Grove Press, 1971). The debate

between Masson and the Archive continues into the *New York Times* of 25 January 1984, and from there into *The Atlantic* of February 1984. For background on the development of the discipline of psychology, see also: Heinrich Balmer, ed., *Geschichte der Psychologie* (Weinheim: Beltz, 1983), and Hans-Martin Lohmann, ed., *Das Unbehagen in der Psychoanalyse* (Frankfurt/M.: Qumran Verlag, 1983).

[2] Again, Roazen's positions are chosen here to be representative of a very typical position vis-à-vis Freud's work on social anthropology; Paul Roazen, *Freud: Political and Social Thought* (New York: Alfred A. Knopf, 1968).

[3] Reik, *From Thirty Years with Freud* (New York: Farrar and Rinehart, 1940).

[4] Sigmund Freud, *Moses and Monotheism: Three Essays (1939 [1934-38]), Standard Edition*, Vol. 23, ed. James Strachey (London: Hogarth, 1964) [= MM in text]; *Totem and Taboo (1913 [1912-13]), Standard Edition*, Vol. 13, ed. James Strachey (London: Hogarth, 1953), ix-162 [= TT in text]; *Civilization and Its Discontents (1930 [1929]), Standard Edition*, Vol. 21, ed. James Strachey (London: Hogarth, 1961).

[5] Perhaps the most notable attempt at a total revaluation of Freud's work is Frank J. Sulloway, *Freud, Biologist of the Mind: Beyond the Psychoanalytic Legend* (New York: Basic Books, 1979) [=BM in text]. The standard texts tracing Freud's influence remain the studies by Rieff, Forrester, Masson, Burnham, Hale, Shakow, and K. Levin cited in the bibliography. Even a recent volume edited by Stepansky still argues in terms of the legend and its refutations, not as an independent scientific approach.

[6] Sigmund Freud, *The Interpretation of Dreams [1900], Standard Edition*, Vol. IV (to p. 338) and Vol. V. (339-627), ed. James Strachey (London: Hogarth, 1953) [=DR in text]; the editor's introduction indicates that the text originated 1895 and

actually appeared in late 1899 with a post-dated title page.

[7] For definitions of these terms, see Sigmund Freud, *An Outline of Psycho-Analysis (1940 [1938]), Standard Edition*, Vol. 23, ed. James Strachey (London: Hogarth, 1964): 139-207.

[8] The *Project for a Scientific Psychology* is among the fragments and drafts included in *The Origins of Psycho-Analysis: Letters to Wilhelm Fliess, Drafts and Notes: 1887-1902*, eds. Marie Bonaparte, Anna Freud, Ernst Kris (New York: Basic Books, 1954) [=OPA in text].

[9] Sigmund Freud, "The Claims of Psycho-Analysis to Scientific Interest" (1913), *Standard Edition*, Vol. 13, ed. James Strachey (London: Hogarth, 1953): 163-190 [=CL in text].

[10] This is the Freud that appealed to Derrida in his essay "Freud and the Scene of Writing," from *Writing and Difference*.

[11] This places Freud's work in the context of biology, but not in the way that Frank Sulloway did in *The Biologist of the Mind*. Instead, I agree with Thomas Parisi that Freud's sense of evolution was not Darwinian, but virtually a Lamarckian position, stressing biological and cultural adaptation. See Parisi, "Why Freud Failed: Some Implications for Neurophysiology and Sociobiology," *American Psychologist*, 42, No. 3 (March 1987): 235-245; and Arens, "Characterology: From Empire to Third Reich," *Literature and Medicine*, 8 (September 1989).

[12] See Ernst Mach, *Die Analyse der Empfindungen, und das Verhältnis des Physischen zum Psychischen*, 2. Aufl. (Jena: Gustav Fischer, 1900).

[13] See Ernst Mach, *Erkenntnis und Irrtum: Skizzen zu einer Psychologie der Forschung* (Leipzig: J.A. Barth, 1905).

[14] See Freud, *The Outline of Psycho-Analysis* for this parallelism of explication. The aetiology of neuroses parallels the formation of dreams.

[15] The secondary literature unanimously calls the neurological model of the *Project* dated. However, we are not arguing here for its adequacy as biology. No matter how in error the technical descriptions of nerves may be, this model still provides a metaphor for adaptation which applies today under the notion of "learning."

[16] The clearest account is the editors' report on its English publication: "At the period in which Freud drew up his "Project" his interests were mainly focused on its connections with

neuro-physiology. When his hypotheses on that subject broke down, he simultaneously dropped for the time being others of the topics dealt with. And this may have been true in particular of his hypotheses about the ego, which, in the "project," were attached to a specially designated group of neurones" (OPA, 351).

[17]The behavior of the normal individual accommodates biological desires, conscious ego desires, and the restrictions imposed by society. In psychopathic behavior, disproportionate interest is paid to an element of one of these spheres. (Thus Brecht was able to describe healthy humans: 'Erst kommt das Fressen and dann die Moral.')

[18]Thomas S. Kuhn, *The Structure of Scientific Revolutions*, uses the term "paradigm" to refer to a scientific world view; Michel Foucault, in *The Archaeology of Knowledge*, uses "épistemè" to refer to the entire conceptual pattern which an age assumes for its arts and sciences.

[19]For a sense of this cultural psychology, see Davis Rapaport, "The Structure of Psychoanalytic Theory: A Systematizing Attempt," pp. 55-183, and Solomon E. Asch, "A Perspective on Social Psychology," pp. 363-83, in *Psychology: A Study of A Science*, ed. Sigmund Koch (New York: McGraw-Hill, 1959 ff.), Vol. 3. For approaches to group cultural adaptation, see Stephen Jay Gould, *Ontogeny and Phylogeny* (Cambridge, MA: Belknap/Harvard, 1977), and John Michael O'Donnell, *The Origins of Behaviorism: American Psychology, 1870-1920* (Diss. U. of Pennsylvania, 1979).

[20]For a discussion of Freud on language, see also John Forrester, *Language and the Origins of Psychoanalysis* (New York: Columbia University Press, 1980).

[21] For models of a philosophical critique of psychoanalysis, see Adolf Grünbaum, *The Foundations of Psychoanalysis: A Philosophical Critique* (Berkeley: University of California Press, 1984), and Daniel N. Robinson, *Philosophy of Psychology* (New York: Columbia University Press, 1985). Both books present arguments for and epistemological critiques of Freud's work as a science/philosophy. As such, their work diverges from the aims of the present discussion: they evaluate psychoanalysis according to various sets of criteria normed from other disciplines. Here, I am attempting to make the case that Freud's model cannot be

accommodated by models drawn from other disciplines, such as philosophy or natural science. They argue disciplinary paradigms where I stress an emerging discourse crossing disciplinary lines.

[22] See particularly Stephen Jay Gould, *Ontogeny and Phylogeny*, for a discussion of this issue, which was not as clear-cut in the nineteenth century as we assume today.

[23] Freud is not reducing individual mind here. Rather, he seems to be arguing almost in the sense of a paradigm, as Michel Foucault does in *The Order of Things: An Archaeology of the Human Sciences* (New York: Vintage/Random House, 1971).

[24] The phenomenon of transference is indirectly related to these concerns. The analyst/patient relationship is possible because they share cultural patterns, the affects tied to the cognitive strategies of a particular epoch. Cross-cultural analyses do not work well. For the present discussion, however, I stay in the realm of cultural communication, leaving the narrower sphere of social comunication aside.

[25] Claude Levi-Strauss, *The Savage Mind* (Chicago: University of Chicago Press, 1966).

[26] Note that this is the fundamental premise of much East German literature (including the plays of Bertolt Brecht and the prose of Stefan Heym): its educational model requires that the common "German Past" of both the East and the West be used without being explicitly dealt with as the background for the contemporary East German mind. Thus Prussia can be mythologized and Martin Luther readapted into a social reformer -- treatments which are adequate to the spirit desired in contemporary East Germany, yet less than adequate to many of the facts of these realities.

[27] See again Gould's *Ontogeny and Phylogeny*. Freud's formulation goes beyond a mere biological application.

[28] For an exemplary application of Freud's work to a more modern theory of cognition, see Jean-Marie Dolle, *De Freud à Piaget: Éléments pour une approche integrative de l'affectivité et de l'intelligence* (Toulouse: Bibliotheque de Psychologie Clinique, 1977). The use of Freud's work in French theory, both social and cognitive, is widespread. Examples of various historical and literary approaches of note are: Jacques Lacan, *Speech and*

Language in Psychoanalysis (Baltimore: The Johns Hopkins University Press, 1981); Francesco Orlando, *Toward a Freudian Theory of Literature* (Baltimore: The Johns Hopkins University Press, 1978); Jean Laplanche, *Life and Death in Psychoanalysis* (Baltimore: The Johns Hopkins University Press, 1976); and Sebastiano Timpanaro, *The Freudian Slip: Psychoanalysis and Textual Criticism* (London: NLB, 1976). A popularized account of Freud as a healer (the familiar therapeutic image) is provided by Stefan Zweig, *Mental Healers: Franz Anton Mesmer, Mary Baker Eddy, Sigmund Freud* (Garden City, NY: Garden City Publishing Co., 1932).

[29] For an explication of the core of the discussion of the "Project, see: Karl H. Pribam and Merton M. Gill, *Freud's "Project" Re-Assessed: Preface to Contemporary Cognitive Theory and Neuropsychology* (New York: Basic Books, 1976). For the scientific reception of Freud's work, see, for example, Seymour Fisher and Roger P. Greenberg, eds., *The Scientific Evaluation of Freud's Theory and Therapy: A Book of Readings* (New York: Basic Books, 1978), and its companion volume, *The Scientific Credibility of Freud's Theory and Therapy* (New York: Basic Books, 1977). For overviews of Freud's work and influence, see Richard Wollheim, *Sigmund Freud* (Cambridge: Cambridge University Press, 1981); John E. Gedo and George H. Pollock, eds., *Freud: The Fusion of Science and Humanism, Psychological Issues*, Vol. IX, Nos. 2/3 (New York: International Universities Press, 1976); Dieter Wyss, *Psychoanalytic Schools form the Beginning to the Present* (New York: Jason Aronson, 1973); Raymond E. Francher, *Psychoanalytic Psychology: The Development of Freud's Thought* (New York: Norton, 1973) [particularly for a discussion of Freud's neurological work]; and Hannah S. Decker, *Freud in Germany: Revolution and Reaction in Science, 1893-1907, Psychological Issues*, Monograph 41 (New York: International Universities Press, 1977). For a survey of areas in which Freud has had influence, see Richard Wollheim and James Hopkins, eds., *Philosophical Essays on Freud* (Cambridge: Cambridge University Press, 1982). On the quesion of psychoanalysis, its development and its applications, see Reuben Fine, *A History of Psychoanalysis* (New York: Columbia University Press, 1979), and Edith Kurzweil and William Phillips,

eds., *Literature and Psychoanalysis* (New York: Columbia University Press, 1983).

AFTERWORD: Some Consequences

[1] Bruno Bettelheim, *Freud and Man's Soul* (New York: Random House, 1984 [1982]).

[2] See Peter Gay, *A Godless Jew: Freud, Atheism, and the Making of Psychoanalysis* (New Haven: Yale University Press, 1987).

Anonymous. "Angriff auf das Reich des König Ödipus." *Der Spiegel*, No. 52 (1984): 116-131.

Adler, Max. "Mach und Marx: Ein Beitrag zur Kritik des modernen Positivismus." *Archiv für Sozialwissenschaft und Sozialpolitik*, No. 33 (1911): 348-400.

Alexander, Peter. "Ernst Mach." *Encyclopedia of Philosophy*. New York: MacMillan & Co., 1967. Vol. V, 115-119.

Anderson, Richard J. "The Untranslated Content of Wundt's *Grundzüge der physiologischen Psychologie.*" *Journal of the History of the Behavioral Sciences*, 11, No. 4 (October 1975): 381-386.

Apel, Karl-Otto. *Towards a Transformation of Philosophy*. Trans. Glyn Adey and David Frisby. London/Boston: Routledge & Kegan Paul, 1980.

Apel, Karl-Otto. "Von Kant zu Peirce: Die semiotische Transformation der transzendentalen Logik." *Transformation der Philosophie, II.* Frankfurt/M.: Suhrkamp, 1973, pp. 157-177.

Arato, Andrew, and Eike Gebhardt, eds. *The Essential Frankfurt School Reader.* New York: Continuum, 1982.

Arens, Katherine. "Characterology: From Empire to Third Reich." *Literature and Medicine*, 8 (September 1989).

Arens, Katherine. *Functionalism and Fin de siècle: Fritz Mauthner's Critique of Language.* Bern: Peter Lang, 1984.

Arnold, Alfred. *Wilhelm Wundt: Sein philosophisches System.*
Berlin: Akademie, 1980.

Ash, Mitchell G. "Academic Politics in the History of Science:
Experimental Psychology in Germany, 1879-1941." *Central
European History,* 13, No. 3 (September 1980): 255-286.

Ash, Mitchell, G. *The Emergence of Gestalt Theory: Experimental
Psychology in Germany, 1890-1920.* Dissertation Harvard,
1982.

Ash, Mitchell G. "Gestalt Psychology: Origins in Germany and
Reception in the United States." In: Claude E. Buxton, ed.
Points of View in the Modern History of Psychology.
Orlando: Academic Press, 1985, pp. 295-344.

Avenarius, Richard. *Kritik der reinen Erfahrung.* Leipzig: O.R.
Reisland, 1921 [1908].

Baars, Bernard J. *The Cognitive Revolution in Psychology.* New
York/London: Guilford Press, 1986.

Bahr, Hermann. "Das unrettbare Ich." In: *Dialog vom Tragischen.*
Berlin: S. Fischer, 1904, pp. 79-101.

Bahr, Hermann. "Die Philosophie des Impressionismus." In:
Dialog vom Tragischen. Berlin: S. Fischer, 1904, pp.
102-114.

Balmer, Heinrich, ed. *Geschichte der Psychologie.* Weinheim:
Beltz, 1983.

Balmer, Heinrich, ed. *Die Psychologie des 20. Jahrhunderts, Bd. I
-- Die europäische Tradition: Tendenzen, Schulen,
Entwicklungslinien.* Zürich: Kindler, 1976.

Barclay, James Ralph. *Franz Brentano and Sigmund Freud: A
Comparative Study in the Evolution of Psychological*

Thought. Dissertation University of Michigan, 1959.

Ben-David, Joseph. *The Scientist's Role in Society: A Comparative Study.* Englewood Cliffs, NJ: Prentice-Hall, 1971.

Beneke, F.E. *Die neue Psychologie.* Berlin: Mittler, 1845.

Berger, Gaston. *The 'Cogito' in Husserl's Philosophy.* Evanston: Northwestern University Press, 1972.

Bergman, Gustav. *Realism: A Critique of Brentano and Meinong.* Madison: University of Wisconsin Press, 1967.

Bettelheim, Bruno. *Freud and Man's Soul.* New York: Random House, 1984 [1982].

Blackmore, John T. *Ernst Mach: His Work, Life, and Influence.* Berkeley: University of California Press, 1972.

Blühdorn, Jürgen, and Joachim Ritter, eds. *Positivismus im 19. Jahrhundert: Beiträge zu seiner geschichtlichen und systematischen Bedeutung.* Studien zur Philosophie und Literatur des 19. Jahrhunderts, Bd. 16. Frankfurt/M: V. Klostermann, 1971.

Blumenthal, Arthur L. *Language and Psychology: Historical Aspects of Psycholinguistics.* New York: John Wiley and Sons, 1970.

Blumenthal, Arthur L. "Wilhelm Wundt: Psychology as the Propadeutic Science." In: Claude E. Buxton, ed. *Points of View in the Modern History of Psychology.* Orlando: Academic Press, 1985, pp. 19-50.

Boeckh, August. *Encyklopädie und Methodologie der philologischen Wissenschaften.* Leipzig: Teubner, 1886; Darmstadt: Wissenschaftliche Buchgesellschaft, 1966.

Bölsche, Wilhelm. *Hinter der Weltstadt: Friedrichshagener Gedanken zur ästhetischen Kultur.* Jena/Leipzig: Eugen Diederichs, 1912.

Boring, Edwin G. *A History of Experimental Psychology.* New York: Appleton-Century-Crofts, 1957 [1950].

Boring, Edwin G. *Psychologist at Large: An Autobiography and Selected Essays.* New York: Basic Books, 1961.

Boring, Edwin G. *Sensation and Perception in the History of Experimental Psychology.* New York: Appleton-Century-Crofts, 1942.

Bourdieu, Pierre. "The Field of Cultural Productivity, Or: The Economic World Revisited." *Poetics,* 12 (1983): 311-356.

Bowler, Peter J. *The Eclipse of Darwinism: Anti-Darwinian Evolution Theories in the Decades around 1900.* Baltimore: The Johns Hopkins University Press, 1983.

Bradley, J. *Mach's Philosophy of Science.* London: Athlone Press of the University of London, 1971.

Brentano, Franz. *Philosophical Investigations on Space, Time and the Continuum.* Trans. Barry Smith. London: Croom Helm, 1988.

Brentano, Franz. *Philosophische Untersuchungen zu Zeit, Raum und Kontinuum.* Eds. A Kastil, S. Körner, and R. Christholm. Hamburg: Meiner, 1976.

Brentano, Franz. *Psychologie vom empirischen Standpunkte.* Ed. Oskar Kraus. Hamburg: Meiner, 1955 [1924].

Brentano, Franz. *Psychology from an Empirical Standpoint.* Ed. Linda McAlister. London/New York: Routledge and Kegan Paul, 1973.

Bridgman, P.W. "Significance of the Mach Principle." *American Journal of Physics*, 29, No. 1 (January 1961): 32-36.

Bringmann, Wolfgang G., William D.G. Balance, and Rand B. Evans. "Wilhelm Wundt 1832-1920: A Brief Biographical Sketch." *Journal of the History of the Behavioral Sciences*, 11, No. 3 (July 1975): 287-297.

Bringmann, Wolfgang G., and Ryan D. Tweney, eds. *Wundt Studies*. Toronto: Hogrefe, 1980.

Broekman, Jan M. *Phänomenologie und Egologie: Faktisches und transcendentales Ego bei Edmund Husserl*. Den Haag: Martinus Nijhoff, 1963.

Brozek, Josef, ed. *Explorations in the History of Psychology in the United States*. Lewisburg: Bucknell University Press, 1984.

Brozek, Josef, and Ludwig J. Pongrantz, eds. *Historiography of Modern Psychology*. Toronto: Hogrefe, 1980.

Brozek, Josef. "History of Psychology: Diversity of Approaches and Uses." *Transactions of the New York Academy of Sciences*, 31, Series II, No. 2 (February 1969): 115-127.

Brozek, Josef, and Rand B. Evans, eds. *R.I. Watson's Selected Papers on the History of Psychology*. Hanover, NH: University of New Hampshire, 1977.

Brunner, Otto, Werner Conze, and Reinhart Koselleck, eds. *Geschichtliche Grundbegriffe: Historisches Lexikon zur politisch-sozialen Sprache in Deutschland*. Stuttgart: Ernst Klett, 1972-84.

Bulhof, Ilse. *Wilhelm Dilthey: A Hermeneutic Approach to the Study of History and Culture*. The Hague: Martinus Nijhoff, 1980.

Burckhardt, Jakob. *Die Kultur der Renaissance in Italian.* 15th ed. Leipzig: A. Kröner, 1926.

Burnham, John Chynoweth. *Psychoanalysis in American Civilization before 1918.* Dissertation Stanford, 1958.

Bush, Wendell T. *Avenarius and the Standpoint of Pure Experience.* New York: The Science Press, 1905. [Originally Dissertation, Columbia University.]

Buxton, Claude, E., ed. *Points of View in the Modern History of Psychology.* Orlando: Academic Press, 1985.

Buzello, Herbert. "Kritische Untersuchung von Kants Erkenntnistheorie." *Kantstudien,* 23 (Ergänzungsheft 1911).

Carotenuto, Aldo. *A Secret Symmetry: Sabina Spielrein Between Freud and Jung.* Trans. A. Pomerans, J. Shapley, and K. Winston. New York: Pantheon, 1982.

Carus, Paul. "The Origin of Mind." *Monist,* 1, No. 1 (October 1890): 69-86.

Cassirer, Ernst. *Kant's Life and Thought.* New Haven: Yale University Press, 1981 [1918].

Clément, Catherine. *The Lives and Legends of Jacques Lacan.* Trans. Arthur Goldhammer. New York: Columbia University Press, 1983 [1981].

Cocks, Geoffrey. *Psychotherapy in the Third Reich: The Göring Institute.* Oxford: Oxford University Press, 1985.

Cohen, Robert S. and Raymond J. Seeger, eds. *Ernst Mach, Physicist and Philosopher.* Boston Studies in the Philosophy of Science, Vol. 6. Dordrecht: D. Reidel, 1970.

Danziger, Kurt. "The History of Introspection Reconsidered." *Journal of the History of the Behavioral Sciences,* 16, No. 3

(July 1980): 241-262.

Danziger, Kurt. "Origins and Basic Principles of Wundt's *Völkerpsychologie.*" *British Journal of Social Psychology,* 22 (1983): 303-313.

Danziger, Kurt. "Origins of the Schema of Stimulated Motion: Towards a Pre-History of Modern Psychology." *History of Science,* 21 (June 1983): 183-210.

Danziger, Kurt. "The Positivist Repudiation of Wundt." *Journal of the History of the Behavioral Sciences,* 15, No. 3 (July 1979): 205-230.

Danziger, Kurt. "Wilhelm Wundt and the Emergence of Experimental Psychology." In: G.N. Carla, J.R.R. Christie, M.J.S. Hodge, and R.C. Olby, eds. *Companion to the History of Modern Science.* Chicago: University of Chicago Press, 1987.

Danziger, Kurt. "Wundt and the Two Traditions in Psychology." In: Robert W. Rieber, ed. *Wilhelm Wundt and the Making of a Scientific Psychology.* New York: Plenum Press, 1980, pp. 73-88.

Danziger, Kurt. "Wundt as Methodologist." In: Georg Eckhardt and Lothar Sprung, eds. *Advances in Historiography of Psychology.* Berlin: VEB Deutscher Verlag der Wissenschaften, 1983, pp. 33-42.

Danziger, Kurt. "Wundt's Theory of Behavior and Volition." In: Robert W. Rieber, ed. *Wilhelm Wundt and the Making of a Scientific Psychology.* New York: Plenum Press, 1980, pp. 89-116.

de Almeida, Guido. *Sinn und Inhalt in der genetischen Phänomenologie E. Husserls.* Den Haag: Martinus Nijhoff, 1972.

de Boer, Theodor. *The Development of Husserl's Thought*. The Hague: Martinus Nijhoff, 1978 [1966].

Decker, Hannah S. *Freud in Germany: Revolution and Reaction in Science, 1893-1907*. Psychological Issues, Vol. 41. New York: International Universities Press, 1977.

Deleuze, Gilles, and Félix Guattari. *Anti-Oedipus: Capitalism and Schizophrenia*. Trans. Robert Hurley, Mark Seen, and Helen R. Lane. Minneapolis: University of Minnesota Press, 1983.

D'Elia, Alfonsina. *Ernst Mach*. Pubblicazioni della Focolta di lettere e filosofia dell'Universita di Milano. Firenza: La nuova Italia, 1971.

Derrida, Jacques. *Edmund Husserl's 'Origin of Geometry': An Introduction*. Stony Brook, NY: Nicolas Hays, 1978.

Derrida, Jacques. *Of Grammatology*. Trans. G.C. Spivak. Baltimore: The Johns Hopkins University Press, 1976.

Derrida, Jacques. *Writing and Difference*. Chicago: University of Chicago Press, 1978.

de Saussure, Ferdinand. *Course in General Linguistics*. Eds. Charles Bally, Albert Sechehaye, and Albert Riedlinger. Trans. Wade Baskin. New York: McGraw-Hill, 1966.

de Schmidt, Winich. *Psychologie und Transzendentalphilosophie: Zur Psychologie-Rezeption bei Hermann Cohen und Paul Natorp*. Bonn: Bouvier, 1976.

Dessoir, Max. *Geschichte der neueren deutschen Psychologie*. Berlin: Carl Duncker, 1902.

Dessoir, Max. *Outlines of the History of Psychology*. New York: MacMillan & Co., 1912.

Diemer, Alwin. *Edmund Husserl: Versuch einer systematischen Darstellung seiner Phänomenologie.* Meisenheim am Glan: Anton Hain, 1956.

Diersch, Manfred. *Empiriokritizismus und Impressionismus.* Berlin: Rütten und Loening, 1973.

Dilthey, Wilhelm. "Ideen über eine beschreibende und zergliedernde Psychologie." *Gesammelte Schriften*, Vol. 5. Leipzig: Teubner, 1924.

Dolle, Jean-Marie. *De Freud à Piaget: Éléments pour une approache integrative de l'affectivité et de l'intelligence.* Toulouse: Bibliotheque de Psychologie Clinique, 1977.

Drüe, Herman. *Edmund Husserls System der phänomenologischen Psychologie.* Berlin: W. de Gruyter, 1963.

Dunkel, Harold B. *Herbart and Education.* New York: Random House, 1969.

Dunkel, Harold B. *Herbart and Herbartianism: An Educational Ghost Story.* Chicago: University of Chicago Press, 1970.

Eaton, Howard O. *The Austrian Philosophy of Values.* Norman: University of Oklahoma Press, 1930.

Eckhardt, Georg, and Lothar Sprung, eds. *Advances in Historiography of Psychology.* Berlin: VEB Deutscher Verlag der Wissenschaften, 1983.

Einstein, Albert. "Zur Enthüllung von Ernst Machs Denkmal." *Neue Freie Presse* (Wien), 12 June 1926, p. 11.

Eissler, K.R. *Talent and Genius: A Psychoanalytic Reply to a Defamation of Freud.* New York: Grove Press, 1971.

Ellenberger, Henri F. *The Discovery of the Unconscious: The*

History and Evolution of Dynamic Psychiatry. New York: Basic Books, 1970.

Engels, Eve-Marie.   *Die Teleologie des Lebendigen.* Berlin: Duncker & Humblot, 1982.

Erikson, Erik H. *Identity and the Life Cycle.* New York: W.W. Norton, 1980 [1959].

Farber, Martin, ed. *Philosophical Issues in Memory of Edmund Husserl.* Cambridge, MA: Greenwood Press, 1968 [1940].

Fechner, Gustav Theodor. *Elemente der Psychophysik.* Leipzig: Breitkopf & Härtel, 1907 [1859/60, 1888].

Felman, Shoshana. *Jacques Lacan and the Adventure of Insight: Psychoanalysis in Contemporary Culture.* Cambridge, MA: Harvard University Press, 1987.

Figlio, Karl M. "Theories of Perception and the Physiology of Mind in the Late Eighteenth Century." *History of Science,* 12 (1975): 177-212.

Fine, Reuben. *A History of Psychoanalysis.* New York: Columbia University Press, 1979.

Fisher, Seymour, and Roger P. Greenberg, eds. *The Scientific Evaluation of Freud's Theory and Therapy: A Book of Readings.* New York: Basic Books, 1977.

Flugel, John C. *A Hundred Years of Psychology.* London: Duckworth, 1951.

Flugel, John C., and Donald J. West. *A Hundred Years of Psychology.* New York: International Universities Press, 1970.

Forrester, John. *Language and the Origins of Psychoanalysis.* New York: Columbia University Press, 1980.

Foucault, Michel. *The Archaeology of Knowledge.* Trans. A.M. Sheridan Smith. New York: Pantheon, 1972.

Foucault, Michel. *The Birth of the Clinic: An Archaeology of Medical Perception..* Trans. A.M. Sheridan Smith. New York: Vintage/Random House, 1973 [1963].

Foucault, Michel. "History of Systems of Thought." *Language, Counter-Memory, Practice: Selected Essays and Interviews.* Ed. Donald F. Bouchard. Trans. Donald F. Bouchard and Sherry Simon. Ithaca, NY: Cornell University Press, 1977, pp. 199-204.

Foucault, Michel. *Madness and Civilization: A History of Insanity in the Age of Reason.* Trans. Richard Howard. New York: Vintage/Random House, 1965 [1961].

Foucault, Michel. *The Order of Things: An Archaeology of the Human Sciences.* New York: Vintage/Random House, 1970.

Francher, Raymond E. "Brentano's *Psychology from an Empirical Standpoint* and Freud's Early Metapsychology." *Journal of the History of the Behavioral Sciences,* 13, No. 3 (July 1977): 207-227.

Francher, Raymond E. *Psychoanalytic Psychology: The Development of Freud's Thought.* New York: Norton, 1973.

Francher, Raymond E. *Pioneers of Psychology.* New York: Norton, 1979.

Freud, Anna. *The Ego and the Mechanisms of Defense.* New York: International Universities Press, 1966 [1936].

Freud, Sigmund. *Civilization and Its Discontents (1930 [1929]).* Ed. James Strachey. Standard Edition, Vol. 21. London: Hogarth, 1961.

Freud, Sigmund. "The Claims of Psychoanalysis to Scientific Interest." Ed. James Strachey. Standard Edition, Vol. 13. London: Hogarth, 1953.

Freud, Sigmund. *The Interpretation of Dreams (1900)*. Ed. James Strachey. Standard Edition, Vols. 4 and 5. London: Hogarth, 1953.

Freud, Sigmund. *Moses and Monotheism (1939 [1934-38])*. Ed. James Strachey. Standard Edition, Vol 23. London: Hogarth, 1964.

Freud, Sigmund. *An Outline of Psychoanalysis (1940 [1938])*. Ed. James Strachey. Standard Edition, Vol. 23. London: Hogarth, 1964.

Freud, Sigmund. *A Phylogenetic Fantasy: Overview of the Transference Neuroses*. Ed. Ilse Grubrich-Simitis. Trans. Axel Hoffer and Peter T. Hoffer. Cambridge, MA: Belknap/Harvard, 1987 [1985].

Freud, Sigmund. "Project for a Scientific Psychology." In: *The Origins of Psychoanalysis: Letters to Wilhelm Fliess, Drafts and Notes: 1887-1902*. New York: Basic Books, 1954, pp. 347-446.

Freud, Sigmund. *Totem and Taboo (1913 [1912-13])*. Ed. James Strachey. Standard Edition, Vol. 13. London: Hogarth, 1953.

Fries, Jakob Friedrich. *Handbuch der psychischen Anthropologie, oder der Lehre von der Natur des menschlichen Geistes (1837)*. Sämtliche Schriften, I.1. Aalen: Scientia Verlag, 1982.

Fries, Jakob Friedrich. *Neue oder anthropologische Kritik der Vernunft (1828)*. Sämtliche Schriften, I.4. Aalen: Scientia Verlag, 1967.

Gallop, Jane. *The Daughter's Seduction: Feminism and Psychoanalysis.* Ithaca, NY: Cornell University Press, 1982.

Gallop, Jane. *Reading Lacan.* Ithaca, NY: Cornell University Press, 1985.

Gay, Peter. *A Godless Jew: Freud, Atheism, and the Making of Psychoanalysis.* New Haven: Yale University Press, 1987.

Gedo, John E., and George H. Pollock, eds. *Freud: The Fusion of Science and Humanism.* Psychological Issues, Vol. IX. New York: International Universities Press, 1976.

Gerhards, Karl. *Machs Erkenntnistheorie und der Realismus.* Stuttgart: W. Spemann, 1914.

Geuter, Ulfried. *Die Professionalisierung der deutschen Psychologie im Nationalsozialismus.* Frankfurt/M: Suhrkamp, 1984.

Geuter, Ulfried. "The Uses of History for the Shaping of a Field: Observations on German Psychology." In: Loren Graham, Wolf Lepenies, and Peter Weingart, eds. *Functions and Uses of Disciplinary Histories.* Dordrecht: D. Reidel, 1983, pp. 191-228.

Gould, Stephen Jay. *Ontogeny and Phylogeny.* Cambridge, MA: Belknap/Harvard, 1977.

Graham, Loren, Wolf Lepenies, and Peter Weingart, eds. *Functions and Uses of Disciplinary Histories.* Dordrecht: D. Reidel, 1983.

Griesinger, Wilhelm. *Mental Pathology and Therapeutics.* Trans. C. Lockhart Robertson and James Rutherford. New York: William Wood & Co., 1882 [1865].

Grosse, W. "Die psychologischen Grundlagen der Erkenntnis

(Über Machs *Erkenntnis und Irrtum*)." *Deutsche Literaturzeitung*, 27, No. 47 (24 November 1906): 2925-2932.

Grosse, W. "Die psychologischen Grundlagen der Erkenntnis, II." *Deutsche Literaturzeitung*, 27, No. 48 (1 December 1906): 2989-2996.

Grünbaum, Adolf. *The Foundations of Psychoanalysis: A Philosophical Critique*. Berkeley: University of California Press, 1984.

Gurwitsch, Aron. *Phenomenology and the Theory of Science*. Evanston: Northwestern University Press, 1974.

Hale, Nathan George. *The Origins and Foundation of the Psychoanalytic Movement in America*. Dissertation University of California (Berkeley), 1965.

Hall, G. Stanley. *Founders of Modern Psychology*. New York: D. Appleton, 1912.

Hall, Harrison. "The Philosophical Significance of Husserl's Theory of Intentionality." *Journal of the British Society for Phenomenology*, 13, No. 1 (January 1982): 79-84.

Harland, Richard. *Superstructuralism: The Philosophy of Structuralism and Post-Structuralism*. London: Methuen, 1987.

Heidbreder, Edna. *Seven Psychologies*. Englewood Cliffs, NJ: Prentice-Hall, 1933.

Heidegger, Martin. *Being and Time*. Trans. John Macquarrie and Edward Robinson. New York: Harper & Row, 1962 [1927].

Helmholtz, Hermann von. *Epistemological Writings*. The Paul Hertz/Moritz Schlick centenary edition of 1921 with notes and commentary by the editors. Newly trans. Malcolm F. Lowe. Ed. and intro. by Robert S. Cohen and Yehuda Elkana. Boston Studies in the Philosophy of Science, vol. 37. Dordrecht, Holland/Boston: Reidel, 1977.

Helmholtz, Hermann von. *Schriften zur Erkenntnistheorie.* Eds. Paul Hertz and Mortiz Schlick. Berlin: Julius Springer, 1921.

Herbart, Johann Friedrich. *Lehrbuch zur Psychologie.* Eds. Karl Kehrbach and Otto Flügel. Sämtliche Werke, Vol. 4. Aalen: Scientia Verlag, 1964.

Herbart, Johann Friedrich. *Psychologie als Wissenschaft, neu gegründet auf Erfahrung.* Eds. Karl Kehrbach and Otto Flügel. Sämtliche Werke, Vols. 5 and 6. Aalen: Scientia Verlag, 1964.

Herbart, Johann Friedrich. *Text-Book in Psychology.* Trans. Margaret K. Smith. New York: Appleton, 1891; Washington: University Publications of America, 1977.

Herneck, Friedrich. "Ernst Mach: Eine bisher unveröffentlichte Autobiographie." *Physikalische Blätter,* 14 No. 9 (1958): 385-390.

Hiebert, Erwin. "An Appraisal of the Work of Ernst Mach: Scientist, Historian, Philosopher." In: Peter K. Machamer and Robert G. Turnbull, eds. *Motion and Time, Space and Matter: Interrelations in the History of Philosophy and Science.* Columbus: Ohio State University Press, 1976, pp. 360-389.

Hiebert, Erwin. *The Concept of Thermodynamics in the Scientific Thought of Mach and Planck.* Technical Report. Freiburg/Br.: Ernst-Mach-Institut, 1968.

Hiebert, Erwin, ed. and trans. *Ernst Mach, Knowledge and Error: Sketches on the Psychology of Enquiry.* Dordrecht: D.

Reidel, 1976.

Hiebert, Erwin. "Mach's Philosophical Use of the History of Science." In: Roger H. Struewer, ed. *Historical and Philosophical Perspectives of Science*. Minnesota Series in the Philosophy of Science, Vol. V. Minneapolis: University of Minnesota Press, 1970, pp. 184-203.

High, Richard P. "In the Image of E.G. Boring: Review of Eliot Hearst, ed., *The First Century of Experimental Psychology*." *Journal of the History of the Behavioral Sciences*, 18, No. 1 (January 1982): 88-89.

Hintikka, J., et al. "A Symposium on Ernst Mach." *Synthese*, 18 (1968): 132-301.

Höffding, Harald. *A Brief History of Modern Philosophy*. Trans. Charles Finley Sanders. New York: MacMillan, 1931 [1912].

Höffding, Harald. *Modern Philosophers*. Trans. Alfred C. Mason. London: MacMillan & Co., 1915 [1902].

Holton, Gerald. "Mach, Einstein, and the Search for Reality." *Daedalus*, 97, No. 2 (Spring 1968): 636-673.

Hoffmann-Erfurt, Arthur, ed. *Wilhelm Wundt: Eine Würdigung*. Erfurt: Kurt Stenger, 1924.

Humboldt, Wilhelm von. "Über die innere und äußere Organisation der höheren wissenschaftlichen Anstalten in Berlin." In: *Gesammelte Schriften*, Vol. 10. Berlin: n.p., 1903-36.

Husserl, Edmund. *The Crisis of European Sciences and Transcendental Phenomenology*. Trans. David Carr. Evanston: Northwestern University Press, 1970 [1954].

Husserl, Edmund. *The Idea of Phenomenology*. Trans. William

P. Alston and George Nakhnikian. The Hague: Martinus Nijhoff, 1973.

Husserl, Edmund. *Phänomenologische Psychologie: Vorlesungen Sommersemester 1925.* Ed. Walter Biemel. Husserliana, Vol. IX. Den Haag: Martinus Nijhoff, 1962.

Husserl, Edmund. *Phenomenological Psychology: Lectures, Summer Semester, 1925.* Trans. John Scanlon. The Hague: Martinus Nijhoff, 1977.

Husserl, Edmund. *The Phenomenology of Internal Time-Consciousness.* Ed. Martin Heidegger. Trans. James S. Churchill. Bloomington: Indiana University Press, 1964; The Hague: Nijhoff, 1964.

Husserl, Edmund. *Vorlesungen zur Phänomenologie des inneren Zeitbewußtseins.* Ed. Martin Heidegger. Tübingen: Max Niemeyer, 1980.

Irigaray, Luce. *This Sex Which Is Not One.* Trans. Catherine Porter with Carolyn Burke. Ithaca, NY: Cornell University Press, 1985 [1977].

Jaeger, Siegfried, and Irmingard Staeuble. *Die gesellschaftliche Genese der Psychologie.* Frankfurt/M: Campus, 1978.

Jay, Martin. *The Dialectical Imagination: A History of the Frankfurt School and the Institute of Social Research, 1923-1950.* Boston: Little, Brown & Co., 1973.

Jourdain, Philip E.B. "The Economy of Thought." *Monist,* 24, No. 1 (January 1914): 134-45.

Kant, Immanuel. *Anthropologie in pragmatischer Hinsicht.* Ed. Karl Vorländer. Philosophische Bibliothek, Vol. 44. Hamburg: Felix Meiner, 1980.

Kant, Immanuel. *Anthropology from a Pragmatic Point of View.*

Trans. M.J. Gregor. The Hague: Martinus Nijhoff, 1974.

Kastil, Alfred. *Die Philosophie Franz Brentanos: Eine Einführung in seine Lehre*. München: Leo Lehnen, 1951.

Keiler, Peter, and Michael Stadler, eds. *Erkenntnis oder Dogmatismus: Kritik des psychologischen "Dogmatismus"-Konzepts*. Köln: Pahl-Rugenstein, 1978.

Kelly, Alfred. *The Descent of Darwin: The Popularization of Darwinism in Germany, 1860-1914*. Chapel Hill: University of North Carolina Press, 1981.

Kern, Iso. *Husserl und Kant: Eine Untersuchung über Husserls Verhältnis zu Kant und zum Neukantismus*. Den Haag: Martinus Nijhoff, 1964.

Kihlstrom, John F. "The Cognitive Unconscious." *Science*, 237 (18 September 1987): 1445-1452.

Kirsch, Irving. "Psychology's First Paradigm." *Journal of the History of the Behavioral Sciences*, 13, No. 4 (October 1977): 317-325.

Kleinpeter, Hans. "On the Monism of Professor Mach." *Monist*, 16, No. 2 (April 1906): 161-168.

Klemm, Otto. *A History of Psychology*. Trans. Emil Carl Wilm and Rudolf Pintner. New York: C. Scribner's Sons, 1914.

Knobloch, Clemens. *Sprachpsychologie: Ein Beitrag zur Problemgeschichte und Theorienbildung*. Tübingen: Max Niemeyer, 1984.

Knoll, Elizabeth. "The Science of Language and the Evolution of Mind: Max Müller's Quarrel with Darwinism." *Journal of the History of the Behavioral Sciences*, 22 (January 1986): 3-22.

Koch, Edmund, ed. *Psychology: A Study of a Science.* New York: McGraw-Hill, 1959 ff.

Kockelmans, Joseph J. *Edmund Husserl's Phenomenological Psychology: A Historico-Critical Study.* Atlantic Highlands, NJ: Humanities Press, 1978 [1967].

Kockelmans, Joseph J. *Phenomenology: The Philosophy of Edmund Husserl and Its Interpretation.* Garden City, NJ: Anchor/Doubleday, 1967.

König, Edmund. *Wilhelm Wundt als Psycholog und als Philosoph.* Stuttgart: Fr. Fromanns (E. Hauff), 1902.

Koerner, E.F.K. *Ferdinand de Saussure: Origin and Development of his Linguistic Theory in Western Studies of Language.* Tübingen: Max Niemeyer, 1973.

Kraft, Viktor. *The Vienna Circle.* Trans Arthur Rap. New York: n.p., 1953.

Kraus, Oskar, with Carl Stumpf and Edmund Husserl. *Franz Brentano: Zur Kenntnis seines Lebens und seiner Lehre.* München: C.H. Beck, 1919.

Kristeva, Julia. *The Kristeva Reader.* Ed. Toril Moi. New York: Columbia University Press, 1986.

Kristeva, Julia. *Powers of Horror: An Essay on Abjection.* New York: Columbia University Press, 1982 [1980].

Kristeva, Julia. *Revolution in Poetic Language.* Trans. Margaret Waller. New York: Columbia University Press, 1984.

Kuhn, Thomas S. *The Structure of Scientific Revolutions.* \Chicago: University of Chicago Press, 1970.

Kurzweil, Edith, and William Phillips, eds. *Literature and Psychoanalysis.* New York: Columbia University Press,

1983.

Lacan, Jacques. *Écrits: A Selection.* Trans. Alan Sheridan. New York: Norton, 1977.

Lacan, Jacques. *Speech and Language in Psychoanalysis.* Trans. and commentary by Anthony Wilden. Baltimore: The Johns Hopkins University Press, 1968.

Laplanche, Jean. *Life and Death in Psychoanalysis.* Trans. Jeffrey Mehlman. Baltimore: The Johns Hopkins University Press, 1976.

Lauden, Laurens. "The Methodological Foundations of Mach's Anti-Atomism and their Historical Roots." Peter K. Machamer and Robert G. Turnbull, eds. *Motion and Time, Space and Matter.* Columbus: Ohio State University Press, 1976, pp. 390-417.

Lawry, John D. *Guide to the History of Psychology.* Totowa, NJ: Littlefield, Adams, and Co., 1981.

Leahy, Thomas Hardy. *A History of Psychology: Main Currents in Psychological Thought.* 2nd ed. Englewood Cliffs, NJ: Prentice-Hall, 1987.

Leahy, Thomas Hardy. "Something Old, Something New: Attention in Wundt and Modern Cognitive Psychology." *Journal of the History of the Behavioral Sciences,* 15, No. 3 (July 1979): 242-252.

Leary, David E. "Berkeley's Social Theory: Context and Development." *Journal of the History of Ideas,* 38 (1977): 635-649.

Leary, David E. "Essay Review: Michel Foucault, An Historian of the *Sciences Humaines.*" *Journal of the History of the Behavioral Sciences,* 12, No. 3 (July 1976): 286-293.

Leary, David E. "From Act Psychology to Probabilistic Functionalism: The Place of Egon Brunswik in the History of Psychology." Mitchell G. Ash and William R. Woodward, eds. *Psychology in Twentieth-Century Thought and Society.* Cambridge: Cambridge University Press, 1987.

Leary, David E. "German Idealism and the Development of Psychology in the Nineteenth Century." *Journal of the History of Philosophy,* 18, No. 3 (July 1980): 299-317.

Leary, David E. "The Historical Foundation of Herbart's Mathematization of Psychology." *Journal of the History of the Behavioral Sciences,* 16 (1980): 150-163.

Leary, David E. "Immanuel Kant and the Development of Modern Psychology." William R. Woodward and Mitchell G. Ash, eds. *The Problematic Science: Psychology in Nineteenth-Century Thought.* New York: Praeger, 1982, pp. 17-42.

Leary, David E. "The Intentions and Heritage of Descartes and Locke: Toward a Recognition of the Moral Basis of Modern Psychology." *Journal of General Psychology,* 102 (1980): 283-310.

Leary, David E. "Nature, Art, and Imitation: The Wild Boy of Aveyron as a Pivotal Case in the History of Psychology." *Studies in Eighteenth-Century Culture,* 13 (1984): 155-172.

Leary, David E. "The Philosophical Development of the Conception of Psychology in Germany, 1780-1850." *Journal of the History of the Behavioral Sciences,* 14 (1978): 113-121.

Leary, David E. "The Psychology of Jakob Friedrich Fries (1773-1843): Its Context, Nature, and Historical Significance." *Storia e Critica della Psicologia,* 3, No.2 (December 1982): 217-248.

Leary, David E. *The Reconstruction of Psychology in Germany, 1780-1850.* Dissertation University of Chicago, 1977.

Leary, David E. "Wundt and After: Psychology's Shifting Relations with the Natural Sciences, Social Sciences, and Philosophy." *Journal of the History of the Behavioral Sciences,* 15 (1979): 231-241.

Lehmann, Winfred P., ed. *A Reader in Nineteenth-Century Historical Indo-European Linguistics.* Bloomington: Indiana University Press, 1967.

Lemert, Charles C., and Garth Gillan. *Michel Foucault: Social Theory and Transgression.* New York: Columbia University Press, 1982.

Lenoir, Timothy. *The Strategy of Life: Teleology and Mechanics in Nineteenth-Century German Biology.* Dordrecht: D. Reidel, 1982.

Lepenies, Wolf, and Helmut Nolte. *Kritik der Anthropologie (Marx und Freud, Gehlen und Habermas, Über Aggression).* München: Carl Hanser Verlag, 1971.

Le Rider, Jacques. *Der Fall Otto Weininger: Wurzeln des Antifeminismus und Antisemitismus.* Vienna: Löcker, 1985 [smaller French edition, 1982].

Lesky, Erna. *The Vienna Medical School of the Nineteenth Century.* Trans. L. Williams and I.S. Levij, M.D. Baltimore: The Johns Hopkins University Press, 1976.

Levin, Kenneth. *Freud's Early Psychology of the Neuroses: A Historical Perspective.* Pittsburgh: University of Pittsburgh Press, 1978.

Levi-Strauss, Claude. *The Savage Mind.* Chicago: University of Chicago Press, 1966.

Lindenfeld, David. *The Transformation of Positivism: Alexius Meinong and European Thought, 1880-1920.* Berkeley: University of California Press, 1980.

Löw, Reinhard. *Philosophie des Lebendigen: Der Begriff des Organischen bei Kant, sein Grund und seine Aktualität.* Frankfurt: 1980.

Lohmann, Hans-Martin, ed. *Das Unbehagen in der Psychoanalyse.* Frankfurt/M: Qumran Verlag, 1983.

Lotze, Hermann. *Logik: Drei Bücher vom Denken, vom Untersuchen und vom Erkennen.* Ed. Georg Misch. Leipzig: Felix Meiner, 1912 [1843].

Lotze, Hermann. *Microcosmus: An Essay Concerning Man and his Relation to the World.* Trans. Elizabeth Hamilton and E.E. Constance Jones. 4th ed. New York: Scribner & Welford, 1890.

Lowry, Richard. *The Evolution of Psychological Theory: 1650 to the Present.* Chicago/New York: Aldine/Atherton, 1971.

Lübbe, Hermann. "Positivismus und Phänomenologie (Mach und Husserl)." In: *Beiträge zur Philosophie und Wissenschaft: Wilhelm Szilasi zum 70. Geburtstag.* München: n.p., 1960, pp. 161-184.

Lundin, Robert W. *Theories and Systems of Psychology.* Lexington, MA: D.C. Heath & Co., 1979 [1972].

Mach, Ernst. *Die Analyse der Empfindungen, und das Verhältnis des physischen zum Psychischen.* 2., verm. Aufl. Jena: Gustav Fischer, 1900.

Mach, Ernst. *The Analysis of Sensations, and the Relation of the Physical to the Psychical.* Trans. C.M. Williams; rev. by Sydney Waterlow. New introduction by Thomas S. Szasz. New York: Dover, [1959].

Mach, Ernst. *Compendium der Physik für Mediciner.* Wien: W. Braumüller, 1863.

Mach, Ernst. "Einige vergleichende tier- und menschen-psychologische Skizzen." *Naturwissenschaftliche Wochenschrift* (Jena): 31 (N.F. 15): No. 17 (23 April 1916): 241-247.

Mach, Ernst. *Erkenntnis und Irrtum: Skizzen zu einer Psychologie der Forschung.* Leipzig: J.A. Barth, 1905.

Mach, Ernst. *Die Geschichte und die Wurzel des Satzes von der Erhaltung der Arbeit.* Prague: Calve, 1872.

Mach, Ernst. *Grundriß der Naturlehre für die unteren Classen der Mittelschulen.* Prague: Tempsky, 1887.

Mach, Ernst. *Grundriß der Physik für die höheren Schulen des Deutschen Reiches.* Leipzig: G. Freytag, 1893.

Mach, Ernst. *Kultur und Mechanik.* Stuttgart: W. Spemann, 1915.

Mach, Ernst. *Lehrbuch der Physik für das Gymnasium.* Leipzig: G. Freytag, 1894.

Mach, Ernst. *Leitfaden der Physik für Studierende.* Prague and Vienna: Tempsky, 1891.

Mach, Ernst. *Die Mechanik in ihrer Entwicklung historisch-kritisch dargestellt.* Leipzig: J.A. Barth, 1896.

Mach, Ernst. *Die Principien der Wärmelehre: Historisch-kritisch entwickelt.* Leipzig: J.A. Barth, 1896.

Mach, Ernst. *Die Prinzipien der physikalischen Optik: Historisch und erkenntnispsychologisch entwickelt.* Leipzig: J.A. Barth, 1921.

Mach, Ernst. *Populär-wissenschaftliche Vorlesungen.* 4. Aufl. Leipzig: J.A. Barth, 1910.

Marshall, M.E. "G.T. Fechner: Premises Toward a General Theory of Organisms (1823)." *Journal of the History of the Behavioral Sciences,* 10, No. 4 (October 1974): 438-447.

Marshall, M.E. "William James, Gustav Fechner, and the Question of Dogs and Cats in the Library." *Journal of the History of the Behavioral Sciences,* 10, No. 3 (July 1974): 304-312.

McAlister, Linda. *The Development of Franz Brentano's Ethics.* Amsterdam: Editions Rodope, 1982 [1968].

McAlister, Linda, ed. *The Philosophy of Brentano.* Atlantic Highlands, NJ: Humanities Press, 1977.

McFarland, John D. *Kant's Concept of Teleology.* Edinburgh: University Press, 1970.

McGrath, William J. *Freud's Discovery of Psychoanalysis: The Politics of Hysteria.* Ithaca, NY: Cornell University Press, 1986.

McKenna, William. *Husserl's "Introductions to Phenomenology": Interpretation and Critique.* The Hague: Martinus Nijhoff, 1982.

Mead, George H. *Mind, Self and Society: From the Standpoint of a Social Behaviorist.* Chicago: University of Chicago Press, 1934.

Mead, George H. *Movements of Thought in the Nineteenth Century.* Chicago: University of Chicago Press, 1936.

Merz, John Theodore. *A History of European Thought in the Nineteenth Century.* Edinburgh and London: William Blackwood & Sons, 1914 [1904-1912].

Metzler, Hans. "Does a Disciplinary Change of Paradigms Exist in Psychology?" Georg Eckhardt and Lothar Sprung, eds. *Advances in Historiography of Psychology.* Berlin: VEB Deutscher Verlag der Wissenschaften, 1983, pp. 181-186.

Misch, Georg. *Lebensphilosophie und Phänomenologie: Eine Auseinandersetzung der Dilthey'schen Richtung mit Heidegger und Husserl.* Leipzig: Teubner, 1931.

Mischel, Theodore, ed. *Human Action: Conceptual and Empirical Issues.* New York: Academic Press, 1969.

Mises, Richard von. *Einheitswissenschaft: Ernst Mach und die empiristische Wissenschaftsauffassung -- Zu Ernst Machs 100. Geburtstag am 18. Feb. 1938.* s'Gravenhage: W.P. van Stockum & Zoon, 1938.

Misiak, Henryk, and Virginia Staudt Sexton. *History of Psychology: An Overview.* New York: Grune and Stratton, 1966.

Mitscherlich, Alexander. *Massenpsychologie ohne Ressentiment: Sozialpsychologische Betrachtungen.* Frankfurt/M: Suhrkamp, 1972.

Mitscherlich, Alexander. *Society Without the Father: A Contribution to Social Psychology.* Trans. Eric Mosbacher. New York: Harcourt Brace & World, 1969 [1963].

Mohanty, J.N., ed. *Readings on Edmund Husserl's Logical Investigations".* The Hague: Martinus Nijhoff, 1977.

Moi, Toril. *Sexual/Textual Politics: Feminist Literary Theory.* London: Methuen, 1985.

Mueller-Vollmer, Kurt. *The Hermeneutics Reader.* New York: Continuum, 1985.

Mueller-Vollmer, Kurt. *Towards a Phenomenological Theory of Litrature: A Study of Wilhelm Dilthey's "Poetik"*. The Hague: Mouton, 1963.

Murphy, Gardner, and Joseph K. Kovach. *Historical Introduction to Modern Psychology*. 3rd ed. New York: Harcourt, Brace, Jovanovich, 1972 [1949].

Nef, Willi. *Die Philosophie Wilhelm Wundts*. Leipzig: Felix Meiner, 1923.

Noack, Hermann, ed. *Husserl*. Wege der Forschung, Vol. XL. Darmstadt: Wissenschaftliche Buchgesellschaft, 1973.

O'Donnell, John M. "The Crisis of Experimentalism in the 1920s: E.G. Boring and His Uses of History." *American Psychologist*, 34, No. 4 (April 1979): 289-295.

O'Donnell, John M. *The Origins of Behaviorism: American Psychology, 1870-1920*. Dissertation University of Pennsylvania, 1979.

O'Neil, W.M. *The Beginnings of Modern Psychology*. Atlantic Highlands, NJ: Humanities Press, 1982.

Orlando, Francesco. *Toward a Freudian Theory of Literature*. Trans. Charmaine Lee. Baltimore: The Johns Hopkins University Press, 1978.

Parisi, Thomas. "Why Freud Failed: Some Implications for Neurophysiology and Sociobiology." *American Psychologist*, 42, No. 3 (March 1987): 235-245.

Pastore, Nicolas. "Reevaluation of Boring on Kantian Influence, Nineteenth Century Nativism, Gestalt Psychology and Helmholtz." *Journal of the History of the Behavioral Sciences*, 10, No. 4 (October 1974): 375-390.

Paul, Hermann. *Prinzipien der Sprachgeschichte*. Tübingen: Max

Niemeyer, 1960 [1886].

Piaget, Jean. *Genetic Epistemology.* New York: Norton, 1971.

Pöggler, Otto, ed. *Hermeneutische Philosophie.* München: Nymphenburger, 1972.

Pribam, Karl H., and Merton M. Gill. *Freud's "Project" Re-Assessed: Preface to Contemporary Cognitive Theory and Neuropsychology.* New York: Basic Books, 1976.

Ragland-Sullivan, Ellie. *Jacques Lacan and the Philosophy of Psychoanalysis.* Urbana: University of Illinois Press, 1986.

Rancurello, Antos C. *A Study of Franz Brentano: His Psychological Standpoint and His Significance in the History of Psychology.* New York: Academic Press, 1968.

Ratliff, Floyd. *Mach Bands: Quantitative Studies on Neural Networks in the Retina.* San Francisco: Holden-Day, 1965.

Reik, Theodor. *From Thirty Years with Freud.* New York: Farrar and Rinehart, 1940.

Ribot, Theodule. *The Diseases of Personality.* 5th ed. Chicago: Open Court, 1910 [1841/84 in French].

Ribot, Theodule. *La Psychologie Allemande contemporaine (École expérimentale).* 2nd ed. Paris: Ancienne Librairie Germer Bailliére et Cie., 1885.

Ribot, Theodule. *The Psychology of Attention.* 5th, revised ed. Chicago: Open Court, 1903 [1890].

Richards, Robert J. "A Defense of Evolutionary Ethics." *Biology and Philosophy,* 1 (1986), 265-293.

Richards, Robert J. "Natural Selection and Other Models in the Historiography of Science." In: *Scientific Inquiry and the*

Social Sciences. Ed. Marilynn B. Brewer and Barry E. Collins. San Francisco: Jossey-Bass, 1981, pp. 37-76.

Richards, Robert J. "Wundt's Early Theories of Unconscious Influence and Cognitive Evolution in their Relation to Darwinian Biopsychology." Wolfgang G. Bringmann and Ryan D. Tweney, eds. *Wundt Studies.* Toronto: Hogrefe, 1980, pp. 42-70.

Ricoeur, Paul. *Freud and Philolophy: An Essay on Interpretation.* New Haven: Yale University Press, 1970.

Ricoeur, Paul. *Husserl: An Analysis of his Phenomenology.* Evanston: Northwestern University Press, 1967.

Rieber, R.W. *Body and Mind: Past, Present, and Future.* New York: Academic Press, 1980.

Rieber, R.W., and Kurt Salzinger. *Psychology: Theoretical-Historical Perspectives.* New York: Academic Press, 1980.

Rieber, R.W., ed. *Wilhelm Wundt and the Making of a Scientific Psychology.* New York: Plenum Press, 1980.

Rieff, Philip. *Freud: The Mind of the Moralist.* Chicago: University of Chicago Press, 1979 [1959, 1961].

Roazen, Paul. *Freud: Political and Social Thought.* New York: Alfred A. Knopf, 1968.

Robinson, Daniel N. *The Mind Unfolded: Essays on Psychology's Historic Texts.* Washington, D.C.: University Publications of America, 1978.

Robinson, Daniel N. *Philosophy of Psychology.* New York: Columbia University Press, 1985.

Robinson, Daniel N. *Toward a Science of Human Nature: Essays on the Psychologies of Mill, Hegel, Wundt, and James.*

New York: Columbia University Press, 1982.

Roche, Maurice. *Phenomenology, Language, and the Social Sciences.* London/Boston: Routledge and Kegan Paul, 1973.

Russell, Bertrand. "On the Nature of Acquaintance." *Monist*, 24, No. 1 (January 1914): 1-16.

Russell, Bertrand. "On the Nature of Acquaintance, II: Neutral Monism." *Monist*, 24, No. 2 (April 1914): 161-187.

Russell, Bertrand. "On the Nature of Acquaintance, III: Analysis of Experience." *Monist*, 24, No. 3 (July 1914): 435-453.

Sahakian, William S. *History of Psychology: A Source Book in Systematic Psychology.* Itasca, IL: F.E. Peacock, 1968.

Sahakian, William S. *History and Systems of Psychology.* New York: Halsted Press/John Wiley & Sons, 1975.

Schneiderman, Stuart. *Jacques Lacan: The Death of an Intellectual Hero.* Cambridge, MA: Harvard University Press, 1983.

Schneiderman, Stuart, ed. and trans. *Returning to Freud: Clinical Psychoanalysis in the School of Lacan.* New Haven, CT: Yale University Press, 1980.

Schultz, Duane P. *A History of Modern Psychology.* New York: Academic Press, 1969.

Schwenk, Bernhard. *Das Herbartverständnis der Herbartianer.* Weinheim/Bergstr.: Julius Beltz, 1963.

Shakow, David, and David Rapaport. *The Influence of Freud on American Psychology.* Cleveland: Meridan Books/World Publishing Co., 1968 [1964].

Skinner, Quentin, ed. *The Return of Grand Theory in the Human*

Sciences. Cambridge: Cambridge University Press, 1985.

Sluga, Hans D. *Gottlob Frege.* London: Routledge and Kegan Paul, 1980.

Smith, David Woodruff, and Ronald McIntyre. *Husserl and Intentionality: A Study of Mind, Meaning, and Language.* Dordrecht: D. Reidel, 1982.

Smith, Joseph H., and William Kerrigan, eds. *Interpreting Lacan.* New Haven, CT: Yale University Press, 1986.

Smith, Roger. "The Background of Physiological Psychology in Natural Philosophy." *History of Science,* 11 (June 1973): 75-123.

Smith, Samuel. *Ideas of the Great Psychologists.* Cambridge/Philadelphia: Barnes and Noble, 1983.

Spiegelberg, Herbert. *The Phenomenological Movement: An Historical Introduction.* The Hague: Martinus Nijhoff, 1965 [1960].

Spiegelberg, Herbert. *Phenomenology in Psychology and Psychiatry.* Evanston: Northwestern University Press, 1972.

Srzednicki, Jan. *Franz Brentano's Analysis of Truth.* The Hague: Martinus Nijhoff, 1965.

Stallo, J.B. *The Concepts and Theories of Modern Physics.* N.p: n.p., 1882.

Stepansky, Paul E., ed. *Freud, Appraisals and Reappraisals: Contributions to Freud Studies,* Vol. 1. New York: Analytic Press, 1986.

Strong, H.A., W.S. Logeman, and B.I. Wheeler. *Introduction to the Study of the History of Language.* London: Langmans,

Green, and Co., 1891.

Stubbs, Michael. *Discourse Analysis: The Sociolinguistic Analysis of Natural Language.* Chicago: University of Chicago, 1983.

Sulloway, Frank J. *Freud, Biologist of the Mind: Beyond the Psychoanalytic Legend.* New York: Basic Books, 1979.

Swing, Thomas Kaehao. *Kant's Transcendental Logic.* New Haven: Yale University Press, 1969.

Szondi, Peter. *Einführung in die literarische Hermeneutik.* Frankfurt/M: Suhrkamp, 1975.

Thiele, Joachim. "Ernst-Mach-Bibliographie." *Centaurus,* 8 (1963): 189-237.

Thiele, Joachim. *Wissenschaftliche Kommunikation: Die Korrespondenz Ernst Machs.* Kastellaum: A. Henn Verlag, 1978.

Thiele, Joachim. "Zur Wirkungsgeschichte der Schriften Ernst Machs." *Zeitschrift für philosophische Forschung,* 20 (1966).

Thompson, Robert. *The Pelican History of Psychology.* Baltimore, MD: Penguin Books, 1968.

Thornton, E.M. *The Freudian Fallacy: An Alternative View of Freudian Theory.* Garden City, NY: Dial Press, 1984.

Titchener, E.B., and L.R. Geissler. "A Bibliography of the Scientific Writings of Wilhelm Wundt." *American Journal of Psychology,* 19 (October 1908): 541-556.

Timpanaro, Sebastian. *The Freudian Slip: Psychoanalysis and Textual Criticism.* London: NLB, 1976.

Trendelenburg, Adolf. *Geschichte der Kategorienlehre.* Hildesheim: Georg Olms, 1963 [1846].

Turner, R. Steven. "University Reformers and Professional Scholarship in Germany 1760-1806." Lawrence Stone, ed. *The University in Society.* Princeton: Princeton University Press, 1974, Vol. 2: 495-531.

Tymieniecka, Anna-Teresa, ed. *Soul and Body in Husserlian Phenomenology: Man and Nature.* Dordrecht: D. Reidel, 1983.

Verwey, Gerlof. *Psychiatry in an Anthropological and Biomedical Context.* Dordrecht: D. Reidel, 1985.

Wahrig-Schmidt, Bettina. *Der junge Wilhelm Griesinger im Spannungsfeld zwischen Philosophie und Physiologie: Anmerkungen zu den philosophischen Wurzeln seiner frühen Psychiatrie.* Tübingen: Gunter Narr, 1985.

Wallace, Edwin R., IV. *Historiography and Causation in Psychoanalysis: An Essay on Psychoanalytic and Historical Epistemology.* Hillsdale, NJ: Analytic Press/Lawrence Erlbaum, 1985.

Ward, James. *A Study of Kant.* Cambridge: Cambridge University Press, 1922.

Ward, James. *Psychological Principles.* Cambridge: Cambridge University Press, 1918.

Watson, Robert I. *The Great Psychologists.* 4th ed. Philadelphia: J.B. Linnincott Co., 1978.

Watson, Robert I. *The History of Psychology and the Behavioral Sciences: A Bibliographic Guide.* New York: Springer, 1978.

Watson, Robert I. "Psychology: A Prescriptive Science." *American*

Psychologist, 22, No.6 (June 1967): 435-43.

Welton, Donn. *The Origins of Meaning: A Critical Study of the Thresolds of Husserlian Phenomenology.* The Hague: Martinus Nijhoff, 1983.

Wentscher, Max. *Fechner und Lotze.* Geschichte der Philosophie in Einzeldarstellungen, Vol. 36. München: Ernst Reinhardt, 1925.

Wertheimer, Michael. *A Brief History of Psychology.* New York: Holt, Rinehart and Winston, 1979.

Wertheimer, Michael. "Why We Should Study the History of Psychology." Georg Eckhardt and Lothar Sprung, eds. *Advances in Historiography of Psychology.* Berlin: VEB Deutscher Verlag der Wissenschaften, 1983, pp. 11-25.

Whyte, Lancelot Law. *The Unconscious before Freud.* New York: Basic Books, 1960.

Wiesenhütter, Eckhart. *Freud und seine Kritiker.* Darmstadt: Wissenschaftliche Buchgesellschaft, 1974.

Wittgenstein, Ludwig. *The Blue and Brown Books: Preliminary Studies for the 'Philosophical Investigations'.* New York: Harper & Row, 1958.

Wollheim, Richard, and James Hopkins, eds. *Philosophical Essays on Freud.* Cambridge: Cambridge University Press, 1982.

Wollheim, Richard. *Sigmund Freud.* Cambridge: Cambridge University Press, 1981.

Wolman, Benjamin B., ed. *Historical Roots of Contemporary Psychology.* New York: Harper & Row, 1968.

Woodward, William R. "A Commentary on the Symposium: The Use of History in the Social Sciences Curriculum." *Journal of the History of the Behavioral Sciences*, 18 (July 1982): 286-289.

Woodward, William R. "Committed History and Philosophy of the Social Sciences in the Two Germanies." *History of Science*, 23 (1985): 25-72.

Woodward, William R. "Disciplinary History (Review)." *Journal of the History of the Behavioral Sciences*, 22 (July 1986): 212-214.

Woodward, William R. "The 'Discovery' of Social Behaviorism and Social Learning Theory, 1870-1980." *American Psychologist*, 37, No. 4 (April 1982): 396-410.

Woodward, William R. "Fechner's Panpsychism: A Scientific Solution to the Mind-Body Problem." *Journal of the History of the Behavioral Sciences*, 18, No. 4 (October 1972): 367-386.

Woodward, William R. "From Association to Gestalt: The Fate of Hermann Lotze's Theory of Spatial Perception, 1846-1920." *Isis*, 69, No. 249 (December 1978): 572-582.

Woodward, William R., and Mitchell G. Ash, eds. The Problematic Science: *Psychology in Nineteenth-Century Thought*. New York: Praeger, 1982.

Woodward, William R. "'Visible Colleges' and Archives in Europe: First Impressions." *Journal of the History of the Behavioral Sciences*, 17 (1981): 387-398.

Wundt, Wilhelm. *Elements of Folk Psychology: Outline of a Psychological History of the Development of Mankind.* Trans. E.L. Schaub. London/New York: George Allen and Unwin, Macmillan, 1916.

Wundt, Wilhelm. *Grundriß der Psychologie.* Leipzig: Alfred Kröner, 1922 [1896].

Wundt, Wilhelm. *Gustav Theodor Fechner: Rede zur Feier seines 100-jährigen Geburtstages.* Leipzig: Wilhelm Engelmann, 1901.

Wundt, Wilhelm. *Outlines of Psychology.* Trans C.H. Judd. Leipzig/New York: Wilhelm Engelmann/G.E. Steckert, 1897, 1902.

Wundt, Wilhelm. *Völkerpsychologie: Eine Untersuchung der Entwicklungsgesetze von Sprache, Mythus und Sitte -- Bd. I & II: Die Sprache.* Aalen: Scientia Verlag, 1975 [1900, 1911/12].

Wyss, Dieter. *Psychoanalytic Schools from the Beginning to the Present.* New York: Jason Aronson, 1973.

Young, Robert M. "The Functions of the Brain: Gall to Ferrier (1808-1886)." *Isis*, 59, No. 198 (Fall 1968): 250-268.

Young, Robert M. *Mind, Brain, and Adaptation: Cerebral Localization and its Biological Context from Gall to Ferrier.* Oxford: Clarendon Press, 1970.

Young, Robert M. "Scholarship and the History of the Behavioural Sciences." *History of Science*, 5 (1966): 1-51.

Zweig, Stefan. *Mental Healers: Franz Anton Mesmer, Mary Baker Eddy, Sigmund Freud.* Garden City, NY: Garden City Publishing Co., 1932.

INDEX OF NAMES